Microfoundations and Macroeconomics

In the past, Austrian economics has been seen as almost exclusively focused on microeconomics, and defined by its subjectivist methodology and understanding of the market as a competitive discovery process, favoring a focus on phenomena such as price coordination and entrepreneurship over macroeconomic concepts. There are, however, three distinct macroeconomic issues that have been pursued by Austrian economists in the post-revival years: the extensions of the Mises–Hayek theory of the trade cycle; the idea of 'free banking' or a completely market-driven monetary system; and the pre-Keynesian monetary disequilibrium theories.

Steven Horwitz weaves these three strands to construct a systematic presentation of what Austrian macroeconomics would look like, demonstrating that traditional Austrian cycle theory is strongly compatible with the Yeagerian monetary disequilibrium perspective.

Microfoundations and Macroeconomics consists of three parts:

- Part I includes an explication of an Austrian view of the market process, with a strong emphasis on the role of capital, arguing that the 'macroeconomy' is operating correctly when it does not upset this microeconomic ordering process.
- Part II develops a market process macroeconomics, exploring monetary equilibrium as presented by Selgin, and comparing and contrasting three possible cases of monetary disequilibrium.
- Part III explores how this view of macroeconomics affects the way we understand fiscal policy, monetary regimes and banking reform, and labor market flexibility.

This original and highly accessible work provides the reader with an introduction to Austrian economics and a systematic understanding of macroeconomics. It will be of great value and interest to professional economists and students alike.

Steven Horwitz is Associate Professor of Economics at St Lawrence University, New York.

Foundations of the Market Economy
Edited by Mario J. Rizzo, *New York University* and
Lawrence H. White, *University of Georgia*

A central theme in this series is the importance of understanding and assessing the market economy from a perspective broader than the static economics of perfect competition and Pareto optimality. Such a perspective sees markets as causal processes generated by the preferences, expectations and beliefs of economic agents. The creative acts of entrepreneurship that uncover new information about preferences, prices and technology are central to these processes with respect to their ability to promote the discovery and use of knowledge in society.

The market economy consists of a set of institutions that facilitate voluntary cooperation and exchange among individuals. These institutions include the legal and ethical framework as well as more narrowly 'economic' patterns of social interaction. Thus the law, legal institutions and cultural and ethical norms, as well as ordinary business practices and monetary phenomena, fall within the analytical domain of the economist.

Other titles in the series

The Meaning of Market Process
Essays in the development of modern Austrian Economics
Israel M. Kirzner

Prices and Knowledge
A market-process perspective
Esteban F. Thomas

Keynes' General Theory of Interest
A reconsideration
Fiona C. Maclachlan

Laissez-Faire Banking
Kevin Dowd

Expectations and the Meaning of Institutions
Essays in economics by Ludwig Lachmann
Edited by Don Lavoie

Perfect Competition and the Transformation of Economics
Frank M. Machovec

Entrepreneurship and the Market Process
An enquiry into the growth of knowledge
David Harper

Economics of Time and Ignorance
Gerald O'Driscoll and Mario J. Rizzo

Dynamics of the Mixed Economy
Towards a theory of interventionism
Sanford Ikeda

Neoclassical Microeconomic Theory
The founding of Austrian vision
A. M. Endres

The Cultural Foundations of Economic Development
Urban female entrepreneurship in Ghana
Emily Chamlee-Wright

Risk and Business Cycles
New and old Austrian perspectives
Tyler Cowen

Capital in Disequilibrium
The role of capital in a changing world
Peter Lewin

The Driving Force of the Market
Essays in Austrian economics
Israel Kirzner

An Entrepreneurial Theory of the Firm
Frédéric Sautet

Time and Money
The macroeconomics of capital structure
Roger Garrison

Microfoundations and Macroeconomics

An Austrian perspective

Steven Horwitz

LONDON AND NEW YORK

First published 2000
by Routledge
2 Park Square, Milton Park, Abingdon, Oxon, OX14 4RN

Simultaneously published in the USA and Canada
by Routledge
270 Madison Ave, New York NY 10016

Routledge is an imprint of the Taylor & Francis Group

Transferred to Digital Printing 2009

Typeset in Garamond by
M Rules

British Library Cataloguing in Publication Data
A catalogue record for this book is available from the British Library

Library of Congress Cataloging in Publication Data
Horwitz, Steven.
  Microfoundations and macroeconomics: an Austrian perspective/Steven
  Horwitz.
      p. cm.—(Foundations of the market economy series)
  Includes bibliographical references and index.
    1. Austrian school of economics.   2. Microeconomics.
  3. Macroeconomics.   I. Title.   II. Series
  HB98.H67 2000
  330.157′7—dc21

                                                        00-036890

This book has been sponsored in part by the Austrian Economics Program
at New York University

ISBN10: 0–415–19762–7 (hbk)
ISBN10: 0–415–56957–5 (pbk)

ISBN13: 978–0–415–19762–5 (hbk)
ISBN13: 978–0–415–56957–6 (pbk)

Publisher's Note
The publisher has gone to great lengths to ensure the quality of this
reprint but points out that some imperfections in the original
may be apparent.

To Jody
Without you, there is nothing else

Contents

Figures

Acknowledgments

Recognizing those who have made contributions to one's work is always one of the most pleasurable parts of any research project. This book is the culmination of a process that took longer than expected and involved more people than I can possibly remember. So, let me begin with the standard apology to those whose insights and advice have been overlooked.

At a general level, I would like to acknowledge the inspiration of the work of three people. In one combination or another, they have been my imagined audience for various parts of this work as I hope to create some sort of synthesis from their contributions. Without the recent advances in Austrian macroeconomics and monetary theory put forth by Roger Garrison and George Selgin, this work would not have been possible. Roger, in particular, has toiled for years in a lonely vineyard, waiting for the fruit to ripen. I hope this is a step in that direction. George's work and his personal encouragement have meant a great deal to me and I thank him. In addition, I would like to acknowledge the work of Leland Yeager. Leland might well be the most underappreciated monetary theorist of the twentieth century. His work is central to understanding the nature of money and how it functions in the market process. Although he has long been a sympathetic critic of Austrian economics, it is my personal mission in this book to convince him that Austrian macroeconomics is more than its business cycle theory, and that it can be rendered consistent with his own work.

I would also like to extend a very big thank you to the Earhart Foundation who supported this work very generously with two summer fellowship grants. Their continued support for scholarly activity is a model for foundations everywhere. In addition, several different groups at St Lawrence deserve recognition. A good bit of the original draft of this book was done during a year-long sabbatical in 1995–96. I would like to thank the Board of Trustees for its continued commitment to granting faculty time for serious scholarly work and resources for professional travel. I would also like to thank the Dean's office at SLU for additional material support. Finally, I once again would like to thank my colleagues in the economics department at SLU for providing me with a wonderful home for the last eleven years. The atmosphere of support and tolerance, and the commitment to scholarly activity in this department, have far exceeded my expectations when I walked in the door. There is no question that they have made my job both easier and more enjoyable.

A number of individuals have provided me with feedback on this project in a number of different forms. In no particular order I thank Peter Lewin, Pete Boettke, Karen Vaughn, Dave Prychitko, George Selgin, Kevin Dowd, Dick Wagner, Bill Butos, Joe Salerno, Roger Koppl, Roger Garrison, Israel Kirzner, Karen Palasek, Bob Blewett, Jeff Young, and Catherine Beckett for their comments on various portions. In addition, I thank colloquium participants at New York University and George Mason University for their hospitality and critical reflections. Mario Rizzo and an anonymous reader at Routledge provided encouragement and suggestions. I save a special thanks for Larry White, whose detailed comments on parts of this book have improved it considerably. Finally, I single out my two friends Pete Boettke and Dave Prychitko: thanks for sharing the vision and remembering priorities.

The editorial and production staff at Routledge were not only efficient and pleasant, they also remained unperturbed by my recurring bouts of persnicketiness.

Thanks also to my other friends (especially Nicole and everyone at TNMS, AFV, and AMR) and colleagues at St Lawrence for helping to keep me sane during the bulk of the work on this book, and a tip of the musical hat to 'Burning for Buddy' for keeping the beat.

Finally, I thank my family, Jody, Andrew, and Rachel, for understanding this obsession called economics. You've let me do the things I've needed to do with a minimum of complaint and have always been there with a smile. There is nothing more that I can ask than that.

Introduction

Is there an Austrian macroeconomics?

> There are macroeconomic questions, but only microeconomic answers.
>
> (Roger Garrison)

A book that purports to explore 'Austrian macroeconomics' has a bit more than the usual burden of self-justification. In the eyes of many economists, Austrians are seen as rejecting the whole concept of macroeconomics in favor of a focus on microeconomic phenomena such as price coordination and entrepreneurship. There is some truth to this perception. In a great deal of the post-revival (i.e., since 1974) literature in Austrian economics, Austrians have tried to define themselves in terms of their methodology (subjectivism) and their understanding of the market as a competitive discovery process rather than as tending toward, or mimicking, general equilibrium. Austrians' self-described 'uniqueness' has almost exclusively been focused on microeconomics.[1] Even Hayek, in his last book, referred to macroeconomics in sneer quotes (1988: 98–99), suggesting that a rejection of the subdiscipline was still alive and well in some Austrian quarters. It comes then as little surprise that much of the microeconomic and methodological work in the post-revival literature in Austrian economics finds its roots in Hayek.

Bruce Caldwell (1988), among others, has pointed to Hayek's seminal paper 'Economics and Knowledge' as the turning point in Hayek's self-understanding of his own views on economics and as defining the approach that the post-revival Austrians would follow. Caldwell argues that it was Hayek's participation in the socialist calculation debate in the 1930s that led him to rethink the relationship between knowledge and equilibrium in order to criticize the equilibrium-oriented neoclassical mainstream. To the extent that Hayek's work on knowledge and equilibrium has defined the development of contemporary Austrian economics since, it also explains why recent, consciously Austrian, scholarship seems so centered on microeconomics and methodology.

However, there is a second side to this story that needs to be told. As Caldwell and others such as Foss (1995) have also noted, Hayek's participation in the macroeconomic debates of the 1930s was also important to how he saw himself and the tradition he was working in. Foss argues that Hayek's concerns with knowledge and equilibrium can be seen as early as his 1933 paper

'Price Expectations, Monetary Disturbances, and Malinvestments', which attempted to clarify his position in his controversies with Keynes, Sraffa, and others in the LSE–Cambridge debates of that period. One could plausibly argue that Hayek's difficulties in convincing his opponents in *both* the debate with Keynes and the debate over socialist calculation derived from differences over the role of equilibrium theory, their understandings of market adjustment processes, and the role and nature of knowledge in economic interaction. The question of what implications these latter issues have for a more completely developed Austrian macroeconomics have yet to be fully explored.

Hayek's 'pre-Keynesian' macroeconomics was not left to die on the vine. Although not much discussed in self-consciously Austrian books, there *is* an Austrian macroeconomics that is alive and well. There are three distinct issues that Austrian macroeconomists have been pursuing in the post-revival years. First are the extensions of the Mises–Hayek theory of the trade cycle (e.g., Garrison 1993; Butos 1993; and Cowen 1997). Second is the recent interest in the idea of 'free banking', or a completely market-driven monetary system. Not all of the contributors to the free banking literature would consider themselves Austrian, but many of their ideas and arguments have a distinct Austrian flavor. For example, George Selgin (1988a: chs 3–6) has examined the relationship between the institutions of a free banking system and macroeconomic theory and policy, particularly in the context of the 1930s debates about neutral money and price level stabilization. Third, and arguably even less explicitly Austrian, is the work of Leland Yeager, Axel Leijonhufvud, and Robert Greenfield that has tried to revive interest in the pre-Keynesian monetary disequilibrium theorists, or what Yeager sometimes calls the 'early American monetarists'.[2] Some contemporary Austrians have taken an interest in these ideas and attempted to show how they too have something of an Austrian pedigree. In addition, elements of the Austrian cycle theory and monetary disequilibrium theory can be found in the closely related work of W. H. Hutt (1975, 1977 [1939], 1979). Hutt pays explicit attention to the relationship between macroeconomic disturbances and price coordination, which will be central to this book's theoretical perspective.

My major goal is to tie together these three strands into a more systematic presentation of what an Austrian macroeconomics might look like. In the broadest sense, I hope to show that traditional Austrian cycle theory work is strongly compatible with the Yeagerian monetary disequilibrium perspective. Each is describing one possible scenario where monetary *equilibrium* does not hold: the Austrians focus on inflationary disequilibria, while the monetary disequilibrium theorists focus on deflation. These two theories are largely mirror images of each other, and their commonalities can better be seen by linking them both with explicitly Austrian microfoundations and the monetary equilibrium theory tradition.

Rather than simply work around the aforementioned Austrian emphasis on the market as a discovery process, I intend to incorporate these insights into my discussion as my 'Austrian microfoundations'. I wish to reconnect the most recent work in Austrian microeconomics, (discussions of disequilibrium, coordination, entrepreneurship, monetary calculation, the role of institutions and the epistemic function of prices) with the ongoing developments in Austrian macroeconomics (the three strands mentioned above). Karen Vaughn (1994) rightly, in my view, points to these microeconomic issues as outlining the path Austrian economics should take in the next century. If so, the relationship between those microfoundations and modern Austrian macroeconomics needs to be explored.

The fundamentals of an Austrian macroeconomics

Roger Garrison (1984) has argued that *time* and *money* are the 'universals of macroeconomic theorizing'. In that paper, he defines the Austrian approach to macroeconomics by its willingness to take both time and money seriously.[3] His critique of mainstream macroeconomics is that the various schools of thought (Keynesianism, monetarism, New Classicism, and, by extension, New Keynesianism) treat time and money far too superficially in comparison to the central roles that they play in real-world economies. Garrison (1984: 200) summarizes this point: 'Time is the medium of action; money is the medium of exchange . . . And it is precisely the "intersection" of the "market for time" and the "market for money" that constitutes macroeconomics' unique subject matter.' The problem with mainstream macroeconomics is that its notions of time and money are so abstract and unrealistic as to prevent serious consideration of how the markets for each actually behave.

An Austrian macroeconomics is one in which time and money, and the institutions that surround them, are taken seriously. For money, that means recognizing its role as a medium of exchange. It is not merely one good among many (e.g., the numeraire good in a general equilibrium system), but a good whose (near) perfect liquidity gives it an influence over economic activity qualitatively different from any other good.[4] It is the medium through which almost all exchanges take place. Rather than general equilibrium's picture of what are essentially barter exchanges occurring only after equilibrium prices are found by the hypothetical auctioneer, the Austrian perspective argues that real market exchanges using money are the process through which existing (disequilibrium) prices are formed. Thus money is not merely tacked on as an extra good, but is fundamental to the ongoing discovery process of the market.

Money both has no unique market of its own and is exchanged in every single goods market.[5] All purchases of goods are sales of money and all sales of goods are purchases of money.[6] As a result, money 'touches' every goods market. Unlike other goods, where excesses in either supply and demand can be removed by the appropriate change in the price of the good in question with few effects on other goods, the effects of excess supplies or demands for money cannot be isolated to one specific 'money market'.[7] Instead, such excesses affect actors' money balances and thus the whole pattern of market exchanges and, importantly for the purposes of this book, the money prices that emerge as the unintended consequences of those exchanges. Because those money prices are central to microeconomic coordination, excess supplies or demands for money undermine the coordinative ability of the market process.

Austrians have long recognized that any analysis of excesses or deficiencies in the money supply must involve the institutions that are responsible for supplying money. Because central banks can directly create and destroy both reserve media and hand-to-hand money, their activities are relevant to the effects money has on economy-wide activity. In addition, the banking system, which translates central bank-initiated changes in reserves into bank money, plays a crucial role in an Austrian macroeconomics. It is central banking institutions that are responsible for the supply of money in real-world economies, and they are the likely bearers of blame for the problems caused by persistent disequilibria on the money side of exchanges. The following chapters will attempt to flesh out this conception of a money-using economy, and explore the systematic undesirable effects of monetary disequilibria.

Garrison's other 'universal' of macroeconomics is time. Much of what differentiates the process-orientation of Austrian economics from the equilibrium-orientation of neoclassicism lies in the way each treats time. O'Driscoll and Rizzo (1996: 52–70) distinguish between 'Newtonian' time and 'real' time. The time embodied in general equilibrium models is Newtonian in the sense that 'time is fully analogized to space' (ibid., p. 53). Just as one can move in all directions through space, so can one move back and forth through Newtonian time freely and without significant consequence simply by altering the time subscript on the variable in question. In Newtonian time, there is no fundamental difference between past, present, and future.

In 'real' time, however, the analogy to space makes no sense, because in real time, only the past is known. The future, by contrast, is uncertain, and the present is that infinitesimal slice between the known past and the unknowable, but not unimaginable, future. The Austrian conception of time is related to its concern with radical uncertainty and dispersed and tacit knowledge. We are aware of the passage of time because our knowledge changes. As time passes, more of the world passes into the known past. Theories that incorporate real time must also be able to take account of changes in knowledge. Taking time seriously therefore implies that assumptions of perfect knowledge, including rational expectations, are inappropriate for discussing real-world market processes. As Lachmann (1977c [1959]: 93) argues, 'the fact that time cannot pass without modifying knowledge . . . appears to destroy the possibility of treating expectations as data of a dynamic equilibrium system'. One consequence of this view of time is that all action is inherently speculative, which is what Garrison means by saying that 'time is the medium of action'.[8] All human action, especially acts of production, take place through time and therefore are speculative to one degree or another.

Markets attempt to cope with time and ignorance through the institutions associated with the 'market for time'. The savings–investment nexus, and the interest rates that result, are institutional responses to the 'dark forces of time and ignorance' identified by Keynes. For Austrians, the existence of interest derives from the fact of time-preference. Given that human beings are neither immortal nor indestructible, we prefer the present to the future, *ceteris paribus*. To convince us to wait for a good, we must be compensated for the passage of time and its concomitant uncertainty, hence the phenomenon of interest.[9] For the saver, interest is necessary to sacrifice current consumption possibilities for future ones. For the investor (i.e., the borrower who will turn savings into capital), there must exist at least the possibility of final good whose price is greater than the sum of the prices of the inputs in order to justify the passage of time between the combining of the inputs and the sale of the output.[10] In equilibrium, that difference between the final good's price and the sum of the input prices is interest.[11]

An Austrian macroeconomics will therefore also pay a great deal of attention to the market for time and the 'price of time', the interest rate.[12] Because all productive activities involve time, all producers must pay attention to the interest rate. When the interest rate accurately reflects the time preferences of both savers and investors, actors can rely on it as a signal about those preferences and the actions that are taken based on that rate will be as informed as possible about time preferences. By contrast, if the interest rate signal is not reliable, then it creates problems for all productive activities. Producers' perception of the public's time preferences will not be synchronized with their actual time preferences, leading to intertemporal discoordination. Much as monetary disequilibria affect all money-using markets (i.e, all markets), intertemporal disequilibria affect all time-laden actions (i.e., all actions).

In addition, the Austrian theory of capital is central to its macroeconomics, and one goal of this study is to re-emphasize capital and try to wed the microeconomics of Austrian capital theory to the monetary disequilibrium approach of Yeager and others. In a macroeconomics that takes time seriously, the capital structure should come to the fore. Because all production takes time, all production makes use of one form of capital or another. The particular array of production processes that entrepreneurs will choose at any point in time (the capital structure) will therefore depend on both the structure of interest rates and the money prices of the various inputs and outputs. It is in the capital structure that the markets for time and money intersect. The capital structure is the concrete representation of entrepreneurs' best guesses about the future, based to a large degree on the (intertemporal) prices facing them in the present. Capital reflects, in Kirzner's (1996) words, the 'unfinished plans' of entrepreneurs. Because monetary disequilibria play themselves out as unwarranted changes in interest rates and money prices, we can expect many of the effects of such disequilibria to appear in the way in which capital is used and/or wasted. I will have much more to say about Austrian capital theory and its role in Chapter 2.

The Garrison quote that heads this chapter can now be explored in more detail. Changes in the supply of money and the market for time both have system-wide consequences for economic coordination. In that sense, there are indeed macroeconomic 'questions'. When there is an excess supply of money, or when savers' time-preferences shift, the phenomenon is macroeconomic because the consequences of those changes simply cannot be isolated to individual markets for money and time. Their consequences will spill over to all markets that use money and all actions that involve time. However, the effects of those spillover processes can only be understood in *microeconomic* terms. The reason why macroeconomic problems matter is because *they undermine the microeconomic coordination process by disrupting the ability of individual money prices, including the interest rate, to signal actors and facilitate market discovery processes.* This last point is the central and distinguishing characteristic of an Austrian macroeconomics: the effects of macroeconomic disturbances (changes in money and interest rates) are always microeconomic in character (they are revealed through price discoordination).

The Mises–Hayek theory of the trade cycle as developed in the 1920s and 1930s contained all of these essentially Austrian elements. The primary focus was on the oversupply of money in triggering the cycle,[13] leading to a false interest rate signal, causing producers to lengthen the structure of production in ways ultimately incompatible with consumer preferences. Hence, seeing the effects of the boom and bust phases of the cycle required an examination of the patterns of relative prices of capital and consumer goods. The causes of the cycle were macroeconomic (money and interest rates), but the effects were systematic discoordination on the microeconomic level.

Hayek recognized this point in his Nobel lecture in 1974. In explaining his own view of the causes of unemployment in order to distinguish it from Keynesian-style insufficient aggregate demand explanations, Hayek (1978b: 25) said:

> We have indeed good reason to believe that unemployment indicates that the structure of relative prices and wages has been distorted . . . and that in order to restore equality between the demand and supply of labor in all sectors changes of relative prices and some transfers of labor will be necessary.

In this particular context, Hayek was thinking predominantly of prices fixed by monopolies or government policy, but he later adds that trying to reduce this unemployment through the use of inflatión will be unsuccessful and will only further distort the array of relative prices:

> The very measures which the dominant 'macro-economic' theory has recommended as a remedy for unemployment, namely the increase of aggregate demand, have become a cause of a very extensive misallocation of resources which is likely to make later large-scale unemployment inevitable. The continuous injection of additional amounts of money at points of the economic system where it creates a temporary demand which

must cease when the increase of the quantity of money stops or slows down, together with the expectation of a continuing rise of prices, draws labor and other resources into employments which can last only so long as the increase of the quantity of money continues at the same rate – or perhaps even only so long as it continues to accelerate at a given rate. What this policy has produced is not so much a *level* of employment that could not have been brought about in other ways, as a *distribution* of employment which cannot be indefinitely maintained and which after some time can be maintained only by a rate of inflation which would rapidly lead to a disorganization of all economic activity.

> (Hayek 1978b: 29, my emphasis)

Inflation creates artificial increases in aggregate demand in particular sectors of the economy, which in turn raise prices there and attract capital and labor resources into those lines of production. The artificially high prices will last only as long as the inflation keeps ahead of expectations, and, if it does not, the demand for those goods and their prices will fall, creating unemployed capital and labor. The effects of macroeconomic disturbances are revealed as microeconomic discoordination. As my added emphasis in the second quote indicates, the Austrian concern is not the aggregate employment level, but its distribution, which is a microeconomic phenomenon dependent on the array of relative prices.

I also hope to show that the excess demand for money story of Wicksell, the early American monetarists, Leijonhufvud, and Yeager also incorporate most of these insights. These theorists argue that excess demands for money make themselves felt by preventing potential exchanges from taking place due to the lack of a medium of exchange with which to make them. These exchanges are forgone because individual prices do not adjust smoothly downward in the face of a fall in the money supply or an unmatched increase in money demand. For the monetary disequilibrium theorists it is also the case that the effects of macroeconomic problems are largely microeconomic. The missing element in their story is the insufficient attention they pay to the effects of deflation on the capital structure. This is a deficiency I hope to begin to remedy.

A brief comparison with mainstream macroeconomics

The primary purpose of this study is not to criticize mainstream macroeconomics, but to articulate an alternative theoretical framework for macroeconomics. Nonetheless, in carrying out this task, I will try to illustrate how an Austrian perspective can shed some critical light on most schools of macroeconomic thought.[14] Given that, a brief but critical assessment of mainstream macroeconomics is appropriate before proceeding with elaborating my own framework.

From an Austrian perspective, the various schools of thought in macroeconomics have many more similarities than differences. The similarities include:

a focus on statistically measurable and manipulatable aggregates such as GDP, the price level, consumption, investment and the unemployment rate; a lack of attention paid to the institutional processes of monetary and fiscal policy; a neglect of capital theory; a failure to distinguish between the natural and market rates of interest; and, finally, little discussion of microfoundations prior to the rational expectations revolution, and a link to various equilibrium-bound microeconomic foundations since that revolution.[15] More complex discussion of Keynes will come later, but for now, we can see how the similarities between modern schools of macroeconomic thought are revealed in the debates that surrounded the IS–LM model. To the extent that Keynesians and monetarists saw themselves as disagreeing over the shapes of the IS and LM curves, both groups were still accepting that flawed framework as the appropriate one for macroeconomic thought. The construction of the IS and LM curves commits two crucial errors. Let me here briefly describe those two errors and save a more complete discussion, and suggested alternative, for the chapters that follow.

The IS curve is defined by the assumption that investment and savings are equal. By postulating some relationship between investment and the interest rate (the shape of which will depend upon various assumptions about interest-elasticity), and then assuming that savings is a function of income, one can draw the curve in r, Y space. As interest rates fluctuate, investment will move in the opposite direction, and in order to maintain the savings–investment equilibrium, income will have to move in the same direction as investment. For example, a fall in interest rates will cause investment to rise, which necessitates an increase in income, which leads to the increase in savings necessary to maintain the I=S condition that defines the curve.[16] Axel Leijonhufvud (1981b: 135) gets at the problem with both curves, and how they are interrelated:

> Keynes' obfuscation of interest theory inheres in his LP [liquidity preference] hypothesis but stems from his insistence on the savings–investment equality as an identity. If saving and investment are always equal, they cannot govern the rate of interest, nor can the interest rate possibly serve to coordinate saving and investment decisions. Hence the LP theory: money demand and money supply govern the interest rate.

The fundamental problem with the IS curve is that the equilibrium condition that defines the curve ignores the crucial difference between *ex ante* and *ex post* savings and investment. *Ex post* investment always equals savings, i.e., if investment is taking place, the savings must have come from somewhere. However, investment and savings need not be equal *ex ante*, and this is the point that IS–LM analysis is unable to handle. If the market rate of interest is inconsistent with the underlying preferences of savers and investors, then *ex ante* savings and investment may not be equal, triggering system-wide changes in prices and resource allocation, including labor. The whole

Wicksellian/monetary equilibrium tradition we shall explore is centered around the way that market forces attempt to correct *ex ante* disequilibria, and the patterns of discoordination that such attempts can engender. For Wicksellians, it is *ex ante* disequilibria in the loanable funds market that explain movements in the price level and the resulting economic discoordination. However, by not addressing the possibility of *ex ante* disequilibrium, the IS–LM mechanism, and Keynes of *The General Theory*, overlook the entire set of problems that interest a post-Wicksellian, and to that extent Austrian, macroeconomist.

As Leijonhufvud also notes, the assumption of a savings–investment identity removes the interest rate as the coordinator of the loanable funds/time market. This forced Keynes, and thus the IS–LM model, into an alternative explanation for the interest rate, namely the supply and demand for money.[17] Keynesian liquidity preference theory, which assumes that the only choice facing wealth holders is money or bonds, and the identity of $M^s = M^d$ that defines the LM curve, enable the macroeconomist to also translate the money market into r,Y space. With the demand for money negatively sloped against the interest rate, and an exogenous money supply, any increase in Y will lead to an upward shift in the money demand curve. In order to maintain the money market equilibrium, the interest rate must rise to choke off the increase in the quantity of money demanded at the previous (now disequilibrium) interest rate. It is the intersection of the money demand and supply curves that determine the interest rate in the IS–LM model. Even as this model has evolved through the monetarist counter-revolution, the core idea of the interest rate being determined by the money market has remained constant, despite empirical disagreement on just how strong the interest-elasticity of money demand might be.

From an Austrian perspective, Keynesian money demand theory, the assumption that the supply of money is exogenous regardless of the surrounding monetary institutions, and the conclusion that the money market determines 'the' interest rate, are all problematic. An Austrian view of the demand for money emphasizes money's role as a medium of exchange and views the decision to hold money as one way among many that individuals might allocate their wealth. Holding money balances is a way of purchasing the availability services that money provides. Money holding is therefore an alternative to purchasing goods and services for current consumption, consumer durables, and financial instruments like bonds.[18] Viewing money as a medium of exchange recovers the pre-Keynesian insight that the interaction between the supply and demand for money determines the *price level* not the interest rate. Of course, monetary disequilibria will affect nominal rates, but the real interest rate, for Austrians, is determined by the market for loanable funds. Austrians generally conclude that the IS–LM apparatus is fundamentally flawed as a tool for macroeconomic analysis.

The Monetarist counter-revolution took some steps to correct the numerous flaws in the Keynesian version of IS–LM, mostly by re-emphasizing money and monetary policy. The IS–LM apparatus as traditionally presented has no role for the price level. Either by ignoring it, or by treating the economy as if it were producing a composite commodity, price level effects were absent from Keynes and the neoclassical synthesis. Friedman's work in the 1950s and 1960s attempted to establish both theoretically and empirically (1953, 1963 [with A. Schwartz], and 1969) the stability of the demand for money function and the relationship between the money supply and the price level. His resurrection of the quantity theory and the development of expectations-augmented Phillips curve analysis (which at least introduced some discussion of microfoundations) were both steps in the direction away from some of the mistakes of Keynes and the IS–LM model.

However, as is frequently the case in economics and other social sciences, theorists are trapped by the questions and language of those to whom they are responding. For example, the demand for money function central to Friedman's modern quantity theory begins where Keynes' left off and simply tries to broaden slightly the alternatives to holding money without ever fundamentally questioning the whole apparatus. In addition, Friedman's quantity theory framework is still focused on the price *level* rather than the effects of money on individual relative prices.[19] The emphasis on the price level has also guided much of monetarist policy thinking. Where Keynesians had focused on full employment, monetarists were guided by price level stabilization, best explicated in Friedman's various proposals for a monetary growth rule. Like Keynesianism before it, monetarism had no explicit discussion of effects of monetary policy on the capital structure.[20] By having to work largely on the terms defined by the Keynesian revolution, Friedman and the monetarists could never break free of a number of the flaws of the framework to which they were reacting.

New Classical economics took Friedman's work the next step, by providing two important advances over the Keynesian model. The first was the so-called Lucas critique. To the extent that previous models assumed that agents' expectations were policy-invariant, they were likely to generate bad results. Lucas' argument that models should assume that agents incorporate information about existing policies into their expectations brought a needed dose of reality to macroeconomic thinking. The notion that people learn as the economic process unfolds was already being incorporated through Friedman's adaptive expectations mechanism, and is in the broadest sense congenial to Austrian insights.

New Classicism also seriously addressed the issue of microfoundations by asking whether Keynesian and monetarist macroeconomic theories rested on behavioral assumptions (especially in labor markets) that were inconsistent with modern microeconomics. By substituting Muth's rational expectations hypothesis for the assumption of perfect knowledge, Lucas provided a way to render labor markets, and macroeconomics more generally, consistent with general equilibrium theory. Just as agents were assumed to maximize utility in micro theory by using all of the available relevant information, so we could transfer that model to labor markets and substitute accurate probability distributions of future events (e.g., the rate of inflation) for the more static assumption of perfect knowledge. The brilliance of Lucas' contribution was to reconnect macroeconomics with the profession's accepted microeconomic framework.

From an Austrian perspective, however, Lucas chose the wrong microfoundations. Where Lucas turned to Walrasian general equilibrium theory, Austrians would turn to Mengerian market process theory.[21] The attempts by New Classical economics to couch all apparent macroeconomic problems as equilibrium outcomes ring false to Austrians. For Austrians, existing prices and quantities are virtually always disequilibrium values and the market is seen as the process by which producers and consumers are attempting to better coordinate their behavior by using, and in turn affecting, that price and quantity information. Macroeconomic disturbances hamper the ability of the market process to produce *any* type of dynamic order. Conversely, sound macroeconomic policy will not lead to equilibrium in the microeconomy, rather it will simply not add any additional barriers to the degree of coordination that the market is capable of producing.

One additional problem shared by both monetarism and New Classicism is their understanding of the 'neutrality' of money. Both schools believe that a neutral money is one whose existence does not cause prices to deviate from the general equilibrium values they would reach under barter. This is the source of the mainstream notion that money is a 'veil' for real activity. Adding money to the model does not affect the general equilibrium solution. In a more dynamic context, *additions* to the money supply are neutral if they only scale up nominal values, leaving equilibrium relative prices unchanged. Both schools of thought conclude that money is neutral in both senses, and that at least in the long run (for monetarism) and both runs (for New Classicism) systematic changes in the money supply only increase nominal values (the Classical dichotomy) with no effect on relative prices, employment, and output. The conclusion drawn by New Classicists is that systematic monetary (and fiscal) policy can have no effects on real variables, rendering them impotent to affect economic activity.

The Austrian perspective, by contrast, denies that money is neutral in this sense and proposes an alternative conception of neutrality. As we shall see in more detail in Chapter 3, Austrian neutrality occurs when changes on the money side of the market simply facilitate changes in the demand to hold money balances and exert no independent influence on aggregate demand. Neutral money becomes a policy norm, rather than a characteristic of a particular economic model. Neutrality need not be linked to general equilibrium theory, and it takes seriously the possibility that inappropriate changes in the money supply *will* affect the array of relative prices and therefore cause reductions in economic coordination and growth. Austrians also recognize that a primary transmission process of the non-neutral effects of money is through the capital structure. In this way, Keynesianism, monetarism, and New

Classicism all share a common vice: ignoring the capital structure and ignoring or denying the effects of monetary disequilibria on the structure of production. Instead, the effects of changes in aggregate demand are largely analyzed in terms of the labor market. As a result, both monetarism and New Classicism remain fixated on price-level stabilization as the appropriate macroeconomic policy goal.[22] The approach adopted below will try to remedy these problems.

New Keynesian macroeconomics also suffers from many of the problems that plague the schools of thought to which it responds. New Keynesianism adopts a broadly equilibrium-bound perspective and retains the focus on aggregates that has defined macroeconomics since Keynes. The major difference between New Keynesians and New Classicists is whether the latter's assumptions about the quantity and quality of information available to agents, and the 'perfectness' of labor markets they imply, are sufficiently realistic to describe the world in which macroeconomic activity unfolds. By adding informational constraints, and other real-world institutions such as multi-period contracts, into an otherwise equilibrium-oriented model, the New Keynesians are able carve out scope for real effects from both monetary and fiscal policy. Even fully rational agents may choose not to search for potentially important information, or commit themselves to multi-period contracts, which leaves open the possibility that better-informed policy-makers might be able to generate real effects. As microeconomic models began to move away from full information, zero-transaction costs, institutionless descriptions of market equilibrium, it should come as no surprise that a different macroeconomics might be built on these changing microfoundations.

An important point of tangency between the approach outlined in this book and New Keynesianism is the issue of the stickiness of prices. Much of New Keynesianism is focused on providing the microfoundations for a macroeconomics of sticky prices. The objection it has against New Classicism is not so much the assumption of rational expectations, but the assumption of perfectly flexible prices built into the general equilibrium modeling strategy. What makes New Keynesianism 'Keynesian' is its insistence that real-world prices and wages are not fully flexible, and what makes it 'New' is that this stickiness can be understood as a rational, utility-maximizing strategy by market agents. Both the Austrian theory of the business cycle and the monetary disequilibrium theory of deflation also involve prices that are less than perfectly flexible. However, for Austrians and the monetary disequilibrium theorists, the stickiness of prices is a positive proposition about the way a dynamic market process unfolds, whereas for New Keynesians, the stickiness of prices represents not only a positive proposition but a normative concern. Both New Keynesians and New Classicals seem to agree that perfectly flexible prices are the policy ideal, but they differ over how closely markets approach that ideal and whether government policy can make prices more flexible. From a Mengerian perspective, this normative concern is misplaced – prices are *inherently* less than perfectly flexible and damning them in comparison to the unachievable vision of general equilibrium theory will only lead to serious errors in theory and policy.[23]

Outline of the book

The book is divided into three parts. Part I (Chapters 1 and 2) discusses Austrian microfoundations, Part II (Chapters 3 through 6) lays out an Austrian view of macroeconomics, and Part III (Chapter 7 and the Conclusion) offers a brief look at macroeconomic policy from the perspectives of the first two parts. One reason for this division is that I wish to argue that the theoretical arguments of the first and second parts are not driven by the policy analyses in the third. Austrian economics can put forth positive propositions about how economic systems operate that are open to legitimate debate and empirical verification, and that imply differing policy conclusions depending on the values and beliefs of those who make use of them.[24] Therefore it is important to try to establish the validity of the theoretical perspective first, before any applications to policy. The section on microfoundations, comprising Chapters 1 and 2, will explore the market process approach to microeconomics. Chapter 1 examines the Mengerian tradition and its uneasy relationship with neoclassical equilibrium theory. Of particular importance will be Hayek's pioneering work on the role of market competition in creating, discovering, and making possible the use of knowledge. The role of entrepreneurs in pushing forward market discovery processes by making use of the knowledge generated by disequilibrium market prices is the core of Austrian microeconomics. We will explore this process of monetary calculation in some detail. The second chapter will dig more deeply into Austrian capital theory and the role capital plays in market coordination processes. As much of the macroeconomic discussion to follow will elucidate the effects of macroeconomic disorder on the capital structure, some understanding of capital's coordinative role should come first.

Part II is the heart of the book. Chapter 3 presents monetary equilibrium theory as the analytical starting point for an Austrian macroeconomics. The historical lineage of the concept as well as a comparison to quantity theory and Keynesian approaches will occupy much of that chapter. Particular attention will be paid to the two situations of monetary *dis*equilibrium: inflation and deflation. Chapter 4 takes up the case of inflationary monetary disequilibrium by exploring its effects on the microeconomic coordination process and social order more broadly. The Mises–Hayek theory of the trade cycle will be examined from this perspective, as will neoclassical theories of the costs and consequences of inflation. The fifth chapter looks more closely at deflationary monetary disequilibria, focusing on the work of Yeager, Leijonhufvud and others. The goals there are to argue both that deflationary monetary disequilibria are mirror images of inflationary disequilibria, and that our understanding of deflation can be enhanced when it is tied more closely to Austrian capital theory, which previous writers have not done. Chapter 6 discusses the related work of William H. Hutt. Yeager (1973) has pointed to

Hutt as having a framework fairly close to his own, and various Austrian macroeconomists have also seen Hutt's work as related to their own.[25] Hutt's focus on price coordination is consistent with the Austrian perspective, as are his arguments against using inflation to reduce real wages that are stuck too high and his emphasis on market processes rather than equilibria.

The final part attempts to apply the insights of the rest of the book to policy issues. Chapter 7 explores alternative proposals for monetary reform from an Austrian perspective. After criticizing standard rules versus discretion discussions, the chapter moves to the level of monetary regimes and critically assesses various alternatives to central banking in light of the previous chapters' analysis. A brief conclusion completes the third part.

Perceiving that my readers likely fall into one of two groups, those already interested in Austrian economics and non-Austrian macroeconomists, I have two hopes for this book. For those already interested in, or contributing to, the Austrian paradigm, I hope that this book both advances Austrian macroeconomics and connects it to the emerging post-revival market process microeconomics. For mainstream macroeconomists, my hope is that this study offers a coherent alternative perspective on macroeconomic questions, even if it offers only microeconomic answers. Surely no one book can be expected to undo a generation or two of what Yeager (1973) has aptly termed 'The Keynesian Diversion', but it is not too much to hope for that we can start to shake loose some intellectual cobwebs and begin the task of reconceiving the economics of time and money.

Part I
Market process microeconomics

1 Prices, knowledge, and economic order

As briefly surveyed earlier, neoclassical approaches to the issue of microfoundations of macroeconomics usually begin by constructing some sort of utility maximization/equilibrium model (incorporating rational expectations) and then proceed to show how various macroeconomic phenomena can be derived from that microeconomic model. Because of the wide acceptance of general equilibrium theory, most mainstream discussions of microfoundations spend relatively little time exploring exactly what should constitute those foundations; it is assumed that an equilibrium model is the way to do it. By contrast, one of the defining features of late twentieth-century Austrian economics is its rejection of Walrasian equilibrium theory as the proper theoretical framework for understanding the market process. Rather than Walras, modern Austrian economics begins with another of the marginalist revolutionaries, Carl Menger. An Austrian approach to the microfoundations of macroeconomics will be essentially Mengerian in its emphasis on knowledge, process, and subjectivism.[1] This chapter's task is to lay out these Austrian microfoundations and highlight some of the aspects of the Austrian approach that will be central to providing the microeconomic answers to the macroeconomic questions discussed in the later chapters.

Austrians are not the only group in contemporary economics that questions the microfoundations of mainstream macroeconomics. David Colander (1996: 2), in his introduction to *Beyond Microfoundations: Post Walrasian Macroeconomics*, has rightly characterized much of modern macroeconomics as 'Walrasian' in the sense that it uses a 'comparative static model that assumes the existence of a unique aggregate equilibrium which is unaffected by dynamic adjustment processes'. This approach reached its apex in New Classical economics with its explicit connection to general equilibrium microfoundations. The papers in the aforementioned collection all attempt to outline a vision of macroeconomics that is not wedded to what the authors believe to be traditional Walrasian foundations.

It is worth noting, however, that Colander chose the name '*Post* Walrasian'. In many ways the contributors are still asking Walrasian questions, but simply answering them in more complex and subtle ways. For example, one of the 'distinguishing characteristics' of Post Walrasian economics is conjecturing 'that the solution to a system of simultaneous equations as complex as is necessary to describe our economy has multiple equilibria and complex dynamics' (1996: 2). This is in contrast to the single equilibrium and simple or non-existent dynamics of Walrasian approaches. The Walrasian vision of an economic system described by the concept of equilibrium and simultaneous equations is retained, but Post Walrasians believe that 'the mathematics used in Walrasian macroeconomics is too simple to correspond to the complex reality' (1996: 4).[2] The economist is still asking Walrasian questions, but the answers reflect a more sophisticated understanding of economic systems than that suggested by general equilibrium theory.

By contrast, an Austrian approach to microfoundations might most accurately be described as 'non-Walrasian' or, more in line with Colander's terminology, 'Post Mengerian'. A Mengerian understanding of the market process rejects the claim that an economy can be fruitfully understood through the use of simultaneous equations and equilibrium constructs. The market is a dynamic process of learning and discovery that cannot be spelled out *ex ante* and evolves and changes as the human actors who populate it learn, grow, and change. The Austrian approach rejects equilibrium theory as a description of actual economic events (although some Austrians would retain it as the never-achieved endpoint of economic activity) in favor of other theoretical and metaphorical devices. Austrians are asking different questions than (Post) Walrasians. To understand this alternative perspective, a recapitulation of the development and main ideas of an Austrian vision of the microeconomic process is necessary.

A Mengerian view of the market process

The relationship between Austrian economics and the neoclassical mainstream has always been a tricky one. Neoclassicism finds its origins in the marginalist revolution of the early 1870s, which included the work of Menger and the earliest Austrians, implying that Austrian and neoclassical economics share a common heritage. However, both in the pre-World War I period and in the recent post-1974 revival, Austrians have been at pains to try to delineate their distinct research program from other mainstream approaches. One can categorize the various sub-divisions with Austrian economics by the degree to which they see themselves as distinct from the neoclassical mainstream. The position to be outlined below lies toward the 'clearly distinct' end of that continuum.

The tension between Austrians and neoclassicism surely derives from Menger's work, which both founded the Austrian school and contributed to the beginnings of neoclassicism more generally. The subjectivist line of inquiry that Menger began in 1871 was highly suggestive but also incomplete and ambiguous in places. That incompleteness and ambiguity opened the door for alternative interpretations of Menger's contribution that began the tension noted above. As Israel Kirzner (1994a: xii) has argued:

Menger (already in 1871) glimpsed a radically subjectivist way of understanding the determination of economic phenomena in market economies . . . It was a vision, however, which really did differ sharply, in its radical subjectivism . . . from the broad understandings of the economic process which came to be encapsulated in Marshallian and in Walrasian economics. Menger, however, was not able to articulate the full implications of what he had glimpsed. Nor did his immediate associates fully grasp the complete perspective which their master had, at least in outline, perceived.

As a result, the lines between Austrian economics and other strands of neoclassicism became blurred, with this overlap arguably climaxing in Lionel Robbins' *The Nature and Significance of Economic Science* (1932), which fused together aspects of Austrian subjectivism with the growing formalization of utility theory in the Marshallian and Walrasian traditions. Shortly after the publication of Robbins' book came the Hayek–Keynes debate and the debate over socialist calculation, both of which would define Austrian economics for the rest of the century. Hayek's work during these two debates began to recapture a number of Mengerian themes (Vaughn 1990: 391ff.). The process of rediscovering what Vaughn calls 'the Mengerian roots of the Austrian revival' has continued in the past few decades. Kirzner (1994a: xii) makes this point as well:

> It is in the contemporary post-Misesian revival of Austrian Economics that the distinctiveness of the Austrian tradition has emerged as a natural extension of – or perhaps more accurately, the explicit unpacking of the ideas implicit in – the theoretical contributions pioneered by Menger in his 1871 *Grundsätze*.

What precisely are these Mengerian themes and how do they form the core concepts of modern Austrian microeconomics?

The central themes of both of Menger's books (the *Principles* and the *Investigations*) are spontaneous order and subjectivism. Expanding on the central idea of the discipline of economics since at least Adam Smith, Menger was concerned with explaining how desirable and orderly patterns of outcomes could emerge without direct human design intending them.[3] Some economists have argued that general equilibrium theory is also attempting to provide an elucidation of Smith's 'invisible hand'.[4] However, the differences between Mengerian and Walrasian approaches are significant and center on the way in which Menger understood the problem situation of the individual actor (i.e., subjectivism) and his understanding of how various social and economic institutions emerged to enable individuals to transcend their own ignorance and uncertainty (i.e, spontaneous order).

The first chapter of Menger's *Principles* contains a section on 'Time and Error', where he discusses their influence on economic cause and effect. Time plays a central role because all productive processes involve 'becoming' and change, and are thus taking place in time. Error enters when we consider that capital goods (goods of a 'higher order' in Menger's terms) are capital only because the owners of such goods *believe* that they can successfully produce consumer goods that will be valued by economic actors. Those beliefs may be incorrect and such errors will be revealed by market discovery processes. This emphasis on time and error is part and parcel of Menger's broader subjectivism.

The emphasis on time and error is also linked with the Austrian skepticism about general equilibrium models and the equilibrium orientation of neoclassical economics more broadly. If human actors are accurately described as having less than perfect knowledge and facing the sort of Kirznerian 'sheer ignorance' we shall discuss later, then equilibrium approaches premised on assumptions of perfect knowledge will be problematic. In the Mengerian vision, market actors use their fragmentary and often inchoate knowledge to form their divergent expectations of the future and thereby appraise the value of existing goods of various orders in terms of their ability to produce goods that they perceive will be valuable in the future. Market prices are a key element of this process. Because they are also the product of a process that emerges from the divergent expectations, existing market prices are embedded with the erroneous expectations and judgments of the previous set of suppliers and demanders. The same will be true of the prices that emerge from the current round of market activities. As long as people have imperfect and/or different knowledge, the prices that emerge from human choice processes will not be equilibrium prices and therefore cannot be error-free. The modern Austrian emphasis on the disequilibrium nature of market prices finds its roots in Menger's work on time, error, and knowledge.

What interested Menger was explaining how individual acts of subjective evaluation, which, as he notes, might be the result of previous errors by the valuers (1981 [1871]: 145ff.), might lead to market-level phenomena such as prices. Menger's book builds *toward* an explanation of prices, rather than beginning with prices and explaining how humans make use of them to maximize utility, suggesting both that prices actually formed in the market will be disequilibrium prices and that the decisions made based on those prices cannot necessarily be characterized as equilibrating because those prices will have the past period's errors embedded in them. Menger saw prices as the phenomena to be explained, rather than as an independent variable in explaining human choice, as in a more contemporary understanding. Seeing prices as emerging from subjective acts of human choice (rather than solely as parametric to those choices) will be crucial in the discussions to follow because monetary disequilibria affect price formation by disrupting the link between the subjective evaluations of actors on both sides of the market and the emergent market prices. For Austrians, understanding economic behavior means understanding both how economic institutions and phenomena (like prices) emerge as spontaneous orders from subjective human choices, and how they, in turn, serve to guide (albeit imperfectly) future actions.

In addition to the subjectivist thrust of Menger's contribution, he also began an Austrian focus on the institutional environment in which price formation takes place.[5] Unlike the perfectly competitive model, which assumes away the existence of institutions, Menger's theory of price formation describes the nature of the prices that emerge from varying market structures. His discussion begins with what today we would call 'bilateral monopoly' or what he calls 'isolated exchange' (1981 [1871]: 194ff.). From there he begins to increase the participants on each side of the market until he reaches a discussion of 'bilateral competition'. Part of his argument is that the more competitive the market is, the more narrow the range of possible prices that will emerge. Under bilateral monopoly, there is a larger range of possible prices that the market might produce, whereas with bilateral competition, the competitive process will winnow that range down very substantially. Menger argues that, over time, monopolistic markets tend to evolve into more competitive ones. Monopoly, in the sense of a single seller with no entry barriers, can be seen as an early stage in economic evolution, with bilateral competition being a more advanced stage.[6] From early on, Austrian economics has been concerned with the particulars of the process by which prices emerge and how learning takes place in disequilibrium rather than the properties of a vector of equilibrium prices.

Which way forward? Austrian microeconomics between the wars

As noted briefly above, the period between World Wars I and II marks a time when the distinctiveness of Austrian economics as a school of thought most likely reached its nadir.[7] Not surprisingly, it was also a time when the influence on economics generally of ideas with an Austrian lineage may well have been at its zenith. Deep discussion of this period would be a research project by itself, but what I hope to draw out in this section are the two conflicting tendencies that pervaded Austrian economics between the wars. Those two tendencies might best be characterized as (1) the development of a Mengerian research program distinct from the emerging Walrasian-Marshallian equilibrium research program; and (2) the attempt to bring Austrian insights into the mainstream equilibrium project. Obviously these two ongoing aspects of interwar Austrian economics were in tension with each other. Perhaps nowhere are these differing projects and the tensions between them better captured than in two contributions both published in 1932: Lionel Robbins' *Nature and Significance* and Hans Mayer's essay 'The Cognitive Value of Functional Theories of Price'.

As Kirzner (1994b) argues, it is fruitful to see Robbins' book as attempting to show how the emerging post-Marshallian equilibrium economics was qualitatively different from classical economics. In Marshall's own understanding of his project, he was simply refining what his classical predecessors had done. Robbins saw in the Austrian strand of the marginalist revolution the ideas that, when wedded to Marshall's framework, could define neoclassical

economics as a distinct research program. Kirzner (1994b: xi–xii) observes that
the Marshallian framework of the time was still more concerned with issues of
the generation of material wealth than with the study of human choice. It was
in that sense that Marshall could see his own work as but an extension of classicism. What Robbins saw in the Austrians was the centrality of choice,
particularly in the subjectivism of Menger and Bohm-Bawerk. Robbins' book
brought to British economics the methodological individualism, the subjectivism of tastes and preferences, and the ordinal utility approach of the
Austrians.

All of these insights were easily combined with the ongoing developments
of the Marshallian tradition. The first section of Hicks' (1939) *Value and
Capital* (which laid the foundation for much of the neoclassical microeconomics that would follow) is entitled 'The Theory of Subjective Value' and is
clearly the fruit of the Robbins-inspired marriage of Austrian insights with
Marshallian demand and supply analysis. The preface to the first edition notes
that most of Hicks' ideas were developed at the London School of Economics
during the period 1930–35 and indicates his indebtedness to Robbins (and
Hayek) for his leadership of the 'social process' that helped produce these
ideas. The claim made by some that neoclassical economics has incorporated
what was important in the Austrian contribution can only make sense if 'the
Austrian contribution' is seen only as the impact of Robbins on Hicks. If all
there was to Austrian economics was what Robbins incorporated into his
book, then Hicks' work could arguably have claimed to have incorporated *that*
into the neoclassical mainstream. If so, then the development of Austrian economics between the wars looks very much like a process of intellectual
assimilation. Clearly I wish to argue that the Austrian contribution goes well
beyond the set of ideas that Robbins imported, and, therefore, the claim of
assimilation is a dubious one.

The Mayer paper, by contrast, shows the ways in which his understanding
of the Austrian tradition differentiated it from the growing neoclassical program. Mayer (1994 [1932]: 57) contrasts:

> Genetic-causal theories which, by precisely explaining the formation of
> prices, aim to provide an understanding of price correlations through
> knowledge of the laws of their genesis [and] functional theories which, by
> precisely determining the conditions of equilibrium, aim to describe the
> relation of correspondence between already existing prices in the equilib-
> rium situation.

The main distinction he wishes to draw is that functional theories (which are
essentially equivalent to equilibrium theories) of price offer no explanation of
the process by which prices are formed, which for Menger was the central question. Mayer makes the following very Mengerian (and very modern Austrian)
critique of equilibrium price theories:

In essence, there is an immanent, more or less disguised, fiction at the heart of mathematical equilibrium theories, that is, *they bind together, in simultaneous equations, non-simultaneous magnitudes operative in genetic-causal sequence as if these existed together at the same time.* A state of affairs is *synchronized* in the 'static' approach, whereas in reality we are dealing with a *process.* But one simply cannot consider a *generative process* 'statically' as a *state of rest*, without eliminating precisely that which makes it what it is.

(ibid.: 92, emphasis in original)

In Mayer's view, the Austrian tradition's distinct contribution was its emphasis on explaining processes rather than equilibrium outcomes.

Compare Mayer's arguments with the supposed Robbins–Hicks assimilation noted earlier. Hicks' book lays out the foundations of general equilibrium analysis, and he begins the book with a discussion of what he calls the 'subjective theory of value', which is based on Robbins' importation of Austrian ideas. There are clearly two distinct understandings of what the core of Austrian subjectivism was, and those two understandings diverged like two paths in a wood during the 1930s. Down the Robbins path lay modern equilibrium theory built on a foundation that included the Austrian insights of methodological individualism and subjective tastes and preferences. Down the Mayer path was an alternative conception of the explanatory task of economics. While many other Austrians of the period drifted toward the Robbins path, Mises and Hayek most notably held to the Mayer path. In Mises' case, he had developed, independently of Mayer, his own critiques of the direction of mainstream economics that explored more deeply the emphasis on process found in Mayer's paper.[8] As for Hayek, we shall discuss his contribution on this issue more fully below.

Hayek on prices and knowledge

The major contributions to the modern Austrian approach to the microeconomic process are Hayek's papers on knowledge of the 1930s and 1940s and Mises' discussion of monetary calculation, which originally appeared in the 1940 German language predecessor of *Human Action.*[9] In this section, we will explore the contributions of Hayek and link them back to Mises' discussion of monetary calculation in a later section. The central theme of Hayek's papers in the 1930s and 1940s was the claim that the competitive market process had to be understood in terms of its ability to create, discover, and communicate knowledge. The two key papers in this line of argument are his 1937 paper 'Economics and Knowledge', and 1945's 'The Use of Knowledge in Society'. I will also briefly mention 'The Meaning of Competition' from 1946 and his much later 1978 paper 'Competition as a Discovery Procedure'.

The 1937 paper was one of Hayek's earliest attempts to distinguish his own understanding of the explanation of microeconomic order from the emerging equilibrium-oriented consensus. His purpose there was to show that:

the tautologies, of which formal equilibrium analysis in economics essentially consists, can be turned into propositions which tell us anything about causation in the real world only in so far as we are able to fill those formal propositions with definite statements about how knowledge *is* acquired and communicated.

(1937: 33)

For Hayek, the notion of equilibrium could only be accurately understood if it was framed in terms of the knowledge held by the actors presumed to be in equilibrium. When equilibrium is applied to an individual, it refers to a set of actions that are seen as 'part of one plan' (ibid.: 36). For an individual's actions to be in equilibrium requires that the actions were all decided on at the same point in time and, therefore, with a particular set of knowledge held by the individual. It is actors' subjective beliefs about the world (rather than some set of scientifically or objectively correct set of facts) that guide their plan formation process. Even in the case of the individual, any usable notion of equilibrium must be described in terms of the knowledge of the actor, suggesting that if the actor's knowledge changes (e.g. discovering that an expectation about the future was incorrect), those actions can no longer be said to be 'in equilibrium' with each other. The change in knowledge requires a change in plans.[10]

Hayek then moves to the relevance of equilibrium for society as a whole:

Equilibrium here only makes sense if it is true that the actions of all members of the society over a period are all executions of their respective individual plans on which each decided at the beginning of the period . . . [I]n order that these plans can be carried out, it is necessary for them to be based on the expectation of the same set of external events . . .[I]t is essential for the compatibility of the different plans that the plans of the one contain exactly those actions which form the data for the plans of the other.

(ibid.: 37–8)

Analogous to his understanding of individual equilibrium, Hayek defines social equilibrium as a state of affairs where each individual's plan could be successfully executed because each one's plan contains the plans of others as data. Social equilibrium is thus a perfect dovetailing of plans: 'Correct foresight is, then, not, as it has been sometimes understood, a precondition [of] equilibrium. It is rather the defining characteristic of a state of equilibrium' (ibid.: 42).

Hayek also points out that much of the confusion over understanding equilibrium is rooted in the ambiguities contained in the assumption that we are dealing with 'given data'. For Hayek, the 'givenness' of data is simply a restatement of Mengerian subjectivism, i.e., the data relevant for understanding individual plans and social-level equilibrium are the subjective expectations and beliefs of the actors in question. The confusion comes in when the observing economist assumes that the data he or she possesses is 'given' to the actors in the model, for example, assuming that, because the economist can draw a particular cost curve, the curve is known to everyone whose behavior is being examined.[11]

The question that faces this definition of equilibrium is then an empirical one, in that understanding equilibrium requires that we explain how it might ever be possible that the individual actors would acquire the knowledge necessary for equilibrium to exist. If economic theory postulates some empirical tendency toward equilibrium, it must be understood as a process of knowledge acquisition and communication that tends toward the perfect plan compatibility that defines Hayekian equilibrium. It is here that we see Hayek picking up the themes of the Mayer article discussed above. Notice that one crucial contribution of the 1937 paper was its emphasis on empirical processes of change. In fact, as Kirzner (1994c: xvi) notes, in the original published version of that paper (but not the reprint in 1948), Hayek included a footnote to the Mayer paper. There appears to be a clear passing of the distinctly Austrian torch from Menger to Mayer and Mises and then onto Hayek.

For Hayek the status of economics as a science was tied to explanations of process. He (1937: 44) argues that to the extent that economics is an empirical science it is because of the 'assertion that such a tendency [toward equilibrium] exists'. Such an empirical tendency toward equilibrium, however, must be understood as claiming that 'the expectations of the people and particularly of the entrepreneurs will become more and more correct' (ibid.: 45). The empirical content of economics revolves around these epistemological issues and the degree to which unhampered market processes lead to increasing levels of expectational accuracy. The 1937 paper nicely lays out this research agenda, but does little to fill it in.

In the 1945 and 1946 papers mentioned earlier, Hayek takes the first steps toward explaining this process of knowledge generation and communication. In 'The Use of Knowledge in Society', he once again puts the problem as one of 'how to secure the best use of resources known to any of the members of society, for ends whose relative importance only these individuals know' (1945: 78). He emphasizes that the knowledge in question is of the 'particular circumstances of time and place' (ibid.: 80) and is 'of the kind which by its nature cannot enter into statistics and therefore cannot be conveyed to any central authority in statistical form' (ibid.: 83). Hayek is beginning to fill in the missing empirical pieces of the learning process of the market. In particular, he claims that 'prices can act to co-ordinate the separate actions of different people in the same way as subjective values help the individual to co-ordinate the parts of his plan' (ibid.: 85). He then proceeds to his famous example involving a shortage of tin, where he illustrates how individuals will be led to behave in the economically appropriate way by simply observing movements in the price of tin without needing to know explicitly the underlying reasons for the shortage.

At this point in the argument is is useful to introduce some terminology deployed by Israel Kirzner (1992a: 42ff.), who distinguishes between what he terms the 'induced' and 'underlying' variables of the market process:

> the underlying variables [are] identified conventionally as preferences, resource availabilities and technological possibilities, [while] the induced variables [are] the prices, methods of production and quantities and qualities of outputs which the market at any given time generates under the impact of the [underlying variables].

One can read Hayek's argument in 1945 as claiming that the induced variable of price leads market participants to act as if they had a good deal of knowledge of the underlying variables. The first market actions that led to movements in the price of tin were surely the result of some explicit knowledge of the underlying variables, but the subsequent activities that economize on the use of tin result from the induced variable of price fairly accurately tracking the hypothesized change in the underlying variable, and its interaction with the expectations of those whose actions cause (and are changed by) the movement in the price. Going back to Hayek's argument in 'Economics and Knowledge', we can see that prices are one central way that the knowledge needed for more accurate expectations (and thus a closer approach to equilibrium) is communicated. The problem, he argues, with standard equilibrium theory is that by starting:

> from the assumption that people's *knowledge* corresponds with the objective *facts* of the situation, it systematically leaves out what is our main task to explain . . . [Equilibrium theory] does not deal with the social process at all and . . . it is no more than a useful preliminary to the study of the main problem.
>
> (1945: 91).

To the extent that work by Austrians between the wars had blurred the lines between a distinct Austrian approach and the emerging general equilibrium-oriented mainstream, Hayek's work between 1937 and 1945 began to untangle the two traditions.

One important observation that Hayek makes in 'The Use of Knowledge in Society' is of direct concern for the issue of the microfoundations of macroeconomics. At one point he argues that: 'We must look at the price system as such a mechanism for communicating information if we want to understand its real function – a function which, of course, it fulfills less perfectly as prices grow more rigid' (ibid.: 86). Presumably Hayek is thinking here of price ceilings and floors (which would make sense writing during World War II) and the ways in which such rigidities would prevent prices from adjusting in the face of changes in the underlying conditions of supply and demand.[12] Price controls would short-circuit the knowledge transmission process necessary to enhance the expectational accuracy of entrepreneurs, and would therefore inhibit any tendency toward equilibrium. There are two points of macroeconomic importance here. First, as we will see in our discussion of deflation in Chapter 5, downward price rigidities, whether derived from state intervention, institutional conditions or social conventions in the market, do have important and adverse microeconomic consequences. If prices are unable to fall with significant speed in the face of an excess demand for money, resource misallocation and general economic decline will ensue. This is one example of the way in which a macroeconomic problem (an excess demand for money) reveals itself in the microeconomic process.

More interesting, however, is what Hayek left out of that quote. Prices will also fail to perform their communicative function as well as is possible if *they are overly flexible*. Price controls might well prevent prices from moving quickly enough in response to changes in the underlying variables, but it is also possible that prices might move too quickly, in that they are unhinged from any relationship to the underlying variables, such as during inflation. To the extent excess supplies of money cause prices to move in ways more responsive to the particular paths by which such excesses make their way into the market rather than in ways more linked to the underlying variables, the communicative ability of prices and the expectational accuracy of entrepreneurs will be hampered. The details of this process will be explored in more detail in later chapters.

The argument that market prices lose their effectiveness when they are either too rigid or too flexible is a specific instance of a more general point about all social and economic institutions. For entrepreneurial action to be successful, and thus order-enhancing, entrepreneurs need to believe that existing prices have been sufficiently flexible to reflect the underlying variables with some accuracy. They also need to believe that prices have some continuity to them, so that the prices of the immediate past that they are relying upon in formulating their plans are not reflecting *only* momentary influences. Here too we can begin to glimpse in more detail the ways in which macroeconomically-generated excessive rigidity and/or flexibility can undermine the microeconomic entrepreneurial discovery process.

The two other contributions noted at the outset of this section (Hayek 1946 and 1978a) developed these themes in various ways. What both papers share is a sustained critique of the model of perfect competition as it developed in twentieth-century economics, claiming that it has mis-stated the explanatory task of economic theory.[13] Specifically, that model *assumes* what it should be attempting to explain (1946: 94; 1978a: 181) when it assumes that all agents in the model have perfect relevant knowledge. For Hayek, the competitive market process is precisely how we learn what sorts of goods and services people want, how to produce them most efficiently, and what price people are willing to pay for them. By assuming that consumers know enough to maximize utility and that producers know enough to maximize profit, the perfect competition model assumes away the whole problem that both groups face in real world market processes.[14] This argument is simply an extension of the claim that prices serve a communicative function.

Kirzner's theory of entrepreneurship

It is frequently argued that the period 1973–75 marks the start of the revival of Austrian economics. That period is usually chosen for two reasons. The most obvious is the awarding of the Nobel Prize to Hayek in 1974. The publicity that accompanied that event surely stimulated increased interest in Hayek's ideas. Among Austrians, 1974 is also relevant because it was the date of the Austrian economics conference held in South Royalton, Vermont, the papers from which were eventually published in Dolan (1976). That conference brought together the three main living contributors to Austrian economics (aside from Hayek) – Israel Kirzner, Ludwig Lachmann, and Murray Rothbard – as well as group of younger scholars eager to learn more about the Austrian tradition.[15] However, there is a third reason for choosing those dates. In 1973, Kirzner published his *Competition and Entrepreneurship*, the book that has arguably had the most influence on the central ideas of the Austrian revival.

In this section I want to both place Kirzner's book within the historical sketch of Austrian economics I am undertaking and elucidate the ideas within it that will be relevant for the chapters to follow. The easiest way to see Kirzner's contribution in the context of Austrian economics is that he was attempting to specify more precisely how the knowledge transmission process that Hayek identified in the 1930s and 1940s actually took place in the market process. Who or what was responsible for generating and spreading the knowledge of time and place, and the profit opportunities implied by it, throughout the market process? How, exactly, did the empirical learning process Hayek pointed to in 1937 take place? Kirzner's answer was to go back to Mises' emphasis on the entrepreneur. It is the active choices of the entrepreneur that drive the discovery process of market competition (Kirzner 1979). In this way, Kirzner was following up on the Mayer strand noted earlier, through his emphasis on the entrepreneur as the active agent in a market process characterized by disequilibrium prices. Evidence for this claim can be found in the first two chapters of the book, where Kirzner first distinguishes between competition as a process and as an equilibrium state and then distinguishes the Misesian entrepreneur from the Robbinsian maximizer. In doing so, Kirzner clearly argues that the neoclassical tradition that emerged from Robbins' work missed something essential in the Austrian tradition, namely the importance of uncertainty and disequilibrium. By bringing the Misesian entrepreneur explicitly into Hayek's work on the epistemological properties of the competitive process, Kirzner gave Austrian economics a much more complete, and more clearly distinct, research agenda in microeconomics.[16]

Kirznerian entrepreneurship is the process by which existing disequilbria are noticed and (if acted on appropriately) corrected. The problem Kirzner wanted to address was how an economy populated by what he called 'Robbinsian maximizers' could ever remove existing disequilibria. If each agent takes his prices and ends as given, how could one explain a movement from disequilibrium to equilibrium? In the perfectly competitive model, an exogenous auctioneer is invoked to change prices during the tatonnement process. Recognizing the fictional nature of the auctioneer, how could a model where all take everything as given, ever explain change? What Kirzner argued is that the entrepreneurial aspect of human action is that part

> that is responsible for our understanding of human action as active, creative, and human rather than as passive, automatic, and mechanical. Once the entrepreneurial element in human action is perceived, one can no longer interpret the decision merely as calculative – capable in principle of being yielded by mechanical manipulation of the 'data' or already *completely implied* in these data.
>
> (1973: 35, emphasis is in original)

The entrepreneur sees possibilities that have hitherto gone unnoticed and thus are not part of a Robbinsian maximization process.

The classic example of Kirznerian entrepreneurship is pure arbitrage between two identical goods with different prices. Kirzner argues that the arbitrage story can be generalized to all cases of market disequilibria, in particular those involving production through time. For example, suppose it were possible to purchase a set of complementary inputs and produce a new product for sale in the future such that the price of the output would more than cover the cost of the inputs and the implicit cost of the time. Kirzner argues that this constitutes an existing disequilibrium that is waiting to be noticed by an alert entrepreneur who can profit by his discovery. One might view this as intertemporal arbitrage. However it is viewed, the entrepreneurship involved is what spreads the knowledge of those previously unknown opportunities through the market and drives forward the learning process that Hayek identified in 1937.

Implicit in this argument is Kirzner's concept of 'sheer ignorance'. The knowledge imperfections that are most important in understanding markets are not those that could be remedied by a more thorough search for information. That sort of ignorance is only partial: we know what it is we don't know and we just need to search for the necessary information, and such a search can be conceptualized unproblematically within the framework of Robbinsian maximization. By contrast, the actor who does not notice that a number of current inputs could be combined to form a future output at a profit is not even aware of missing this opportunity. The very fact that the opportunity is 'staring people in the face', yet they are not reacting to it suggests that they are completely unaware of the possibility. This complete unawareness is Kirznerian 'sheer' ignorance, which refers to situations where we don't know what it is we don't know, and intentional search is of no use.[17] In situations of sheer ignorance (which Kirzner believes characterize much of the market process), entrepreneurial alertness is necessary to recognize opportunities for removing that ignorance. No Robbinsian maximizing process can remove sheer ignorance because we are utterly unaware of what we do not know and thus we cannot even set up the maximization problem.

The essential feature of the entrepreneurial market process in Kirzner's view is that it discovers knowledge that would otherwise be unknown. Entrepreneurs, guided by price signals in the marketplace and their own alertness to current and future opportunities, attempt to remedy existing disequilibria by discovering such profit opportunities and reallocating resources in such a way as to exploit them. Kirzner recognizes that entrepreneurs will not always correctly perceive and act upon these possibilities, but he does argue that

> There can never be a guarantee that anyone will notice that of which he is utterly ignorant . . . Yet we submit that few will maintain that initial ignorance concerning desirable opportunities costlessly available can be expected to endure indefinitely. We recognize, surely, that human beings are motivated to notice that which it is to their benefit to notice. We identify this general motivation with the alertness which every human being possesses, to greater or lesser degree.
>
> (1992a: 48)

Entrepreneurship, guided by market price signals, is sufficiently reliable to enable us to explain the degree of order that is present in most markets.

Prices in equilibrium and disequilibrium

The contention that prices are informational signals is not a controversial one in much of economics today. Many economists believe that they have absorbed the lesson that Hayek was trying to get across in 1945 and that those ideas have been incorporated into modern mainstream microeconomics. However, Austrians have begun to look more closely at these neoclassical interpretations of Hayek to determine whether what the mainstream is saying is really what Austrians have understood as Hayek's contribution (Kirzner 1992b and Thomsen 1992). Many Austrians conclude that most neoclassical references to prices as informational signals are describing the role played by prices in *equilibrium*, whereas the Austrian reading of Hayek stresses the informational content of prices in *disequilibrium*. This is a difference that makes a difference, not only in some general theoretical sense, but for the purpose of our analysis that follows.[18]

The standard neoclassical interpretation of the Hayek argument is to claim that prices can be understood as 'informationally efficient' or as 'sufficient statistics'. Hayek is viewed as claiming that prices have embedded in them all of the information necessary to make it possible for agents and firms to utility- and profit-maximize. On this view, neoclassical assumptions about information are justified because in equilibrium the necessary information is available to agents and firms in the summary form of prices. This interpretation of Hayek, usually associated with Sanford Grossman and Joseph Stiglitz, sees prices as *containing* information, or in Thomsen's (1992: 40) words: 'They analyse situations in which individuals infer information from market prices.' This literature attempts to assess what they see as Hayek's claim that the price system is optimal (or at least better than alternative systems) because it performs this informational task so well. Grossman and Stiglitz's criticism of Hayek's supposed claim is that various features of real-world markets (e.g., costly information, externalities, etc.) prevent prices from having all the necessary information embedded in them, leading to Pareto sub-optimal outcomes. This result opens the possibility that institutional arrangements other than the market might be informationally superior, undermining the fundamental normative conclusion in Hayek's 1945 paper.

Thomsen offers two lines of response to the Grossman and Stiglitz argument, based on his belief that their interpretation of Hayek's claim is a result of reading his argument through the lens of equilibrium theory. His first response is to ask whether their interpretation is the only one consistent with a description of the informational properties of equilibrium prices. Thomsen's answer to that is a clear 'no'. He rightly points out that while the 'information inference' reading of Hayek's argument is not incorrect, it ignores his more fundamental point: prices do not just provide information to economic agents, but they make it possible for actors to not need to know as much as they would otherwise. As Thomsen (1992: 41) effectively summarizes it: 'Prices in Hayek's argument are more appropriately described as knowledge *surrogates*, while in the approach exemplified by Grossman and Stiglitz they are sources for the inference of knowledge.' In Thomsen's view, equilibrium prices can be understood as performing both of these roles, and Hayek's emphasis was more on the former than the latter.

The bigger problem with the Grossman and Stiglitz interpretation and critique of Hayek is that it completely ignores the information role that prices might play in disequilibrium. For Grossman and Stiglitz, disequilibrium prices are informationally problematic because, by definition, the fact that they are disequilibrium prices implies that they have faulty information embedded in them. If agents were to treat such prices as if they were equilibrium prices and infer information from them, those agents would be led to compound the existing disequilibrium due to the faulty information. Grossman and Stiglitz conclude that disequilibrium prices are therefore informationally inefficient.

From an Austrian point of view, that claim is surely true to an extent; existing disequilibrium market prices do not reflect the choices of fully-informed agents, and they embody the ignorance and error that is part and parcel of real-world market processes. However, that does not mean that disequilibrium prices have no informational role to play. As Kirzner (1992b) and Thomsen (1992) point out, disequilibrium prices provide the information and incentive for alert entrepreneurs to discover the profit opportunities that accompany the existing disequilibrium. Prices, even when they are imperfect knowledge surrogates, nonetheless do provide information that can spur the entrepreneurial aspect of human action and lead entrepreneurs 'to find out about better available courses of action' (Thomsen 1992: 44). Kirzner's argument is that disequilibrium market prices both bring with them the possibility of profit (which creates an incentive to be alert to such opportunities) and embody enough information to facilitate that alertness. Returning to Hayek's original conception of the problem, disequilibrium prices spur the acts of entrepreneurship that drive the learning process that Hayek saw as necessary for explaining how markets might harbor any equilibrating tendencies.

In addition, the way in which Grossman and Stiglitz link the supposed informational inefficiency of prices to the claim that unhampered markets are suspect, is itself suspect. The fact that prices are imperfect information reflectors is only a problem if one's normative view is that market prices ought to be, and have to be, perfectly informative for the market to be socially justified. In other words, the market and market prices appear to stand condemned for failing to be perfect in the way in which general equilibrium theory describes them. Hayek and other Austrians have not argued that market prices are important because they lead to a Pareto-optimal general equilibrium, but that market prices provide information that could not be made socially accessible through any other conceivable process. Grossman and Stiglitz implicitly make the wrong comparison. It is not real-world markets versus general equilibrium that should be compared, but real-world markets versus real-world political intervention. The knowledge made available by market prices, imperfect though it may be, is sufficient to generate a degree of economic order superior to that produced by alternative coordination processes.[19]

Peter Boettke (1990: 130–1) argues that disequilibrium market prices play three distinct informational roles in facilitating economic coordination. The first is what he calls their *ex ante* function. As individuals decide upon a course of action, they make use of existing prices in order to calculate the desirability of their various options. Analogous to Buchanan's (1969: 44–5) distinction between 'choice-influencing' and 'choice-influenced' costs, the *ex ante* role of prices might be called 'choice-influencing'. Prices provide information that facilitates decision-making among known alternative courses of action. Boettke's second informational role of prices is what he calls their *ex post* role (or, to continue the analogy to Buchanan, 'choice-influenced' prices). After a course of action is decided upon (with the help of existing prices), a new constellation of prices will emerge from the choices of both the actor in question and others in the economic system. One crucial role of the new constellation of prices is that they inform actors as to the success or failure of their prior courses of action. *Ex post* prices tell us whether we have done the right things. It is this function of prices that also creates the incentive to efficiently exploit known opportunities: efficient resource use will pay off in terms of positive price differentials and the corresponding profits.

Boettke's third function of prices is what he terms their 'discovery' role. This is essentially identical to the points raised in the earlier discussion of Thomsen's work. Price differentials motivate entrepreneurial alertness: 'The very discrepancy between the current array and the anticipated future array of prices provides the incentive for entrepreneurs to discover *previously unknown opportunities* for economic profit' (Boettke 1990: 130–1, my emphasis). The emphasis on unknown opportunities in that quote suggests that the *ex ante* and *ex post* functions of prices apply to situations where opportunities are already known. That is why the discovery function is so important – if Kirznerian sheer ignorance is a fact of life in the market, then the discovery role of price is equally central. This tripartite conception of the various informational roles of prices captures the essence of the Hayekian argument, and its distinctiveness from the Grossman and Stiglitz-inspired literature, and will be deployed in the discussion of the effects of macroeconomic disorder in the chapters to follow.

One further point raised in distinguishing the neoclassical understanding of the core of Hayek's 1945 paper from that of modern Austrians is a difference over the kind of knowledge that each is talking about. In most neoclassical discussions, knowledge is understood as objective pieces of information that are 'out there' and potentially discoverable with the expenditure of some quantity of resources. The Austrian view, as this section suggests, has a different conception of knowledge. The relevant knowledge is not already 'out there' waiting to be searched for, but is instead waiting to be created and discovered through acts of entrepreneurship. The normative question for Austrians is what sort of institutional arrangements will best encourage the alertness necessary for the entrepreneurial discovery process that attempts to dispel the fog of our Kirznerian sheer ignorance. The issue is not how to best redistribute existing knowledge, but how best to encourage the discovery of knowledge whose absence we are not currently even aware of.

Additionally, the work of Don Lavoie and others has stressed that even the existing knowledge relevant for efficient resource use may not be of a kind that can be communicated through means other than the market.[20] Building on Michael Polanyi's work on tacit knowledge, Lavoie has argued that a good deal of the knowledge in the market process is inarticulate and would therefore not be communicable through natural language, mathematics, or statistics. Many of the things we know are in the form of skills or dispositions or inarticulate 'hunches' that we cannot put into words. This point is an extension of more embryonic ideas found in Hayek's 1945 paper, but is more fully fleshed out by Lavoie and linked to recent work in the philosophy of knowledge.

One way to characterize this argument is that the process of monetary exchange that takes place in the market is a way of communicating tacit information outside of natural languages. Monetary exchange is therefore an extension of linguistic communication. The communication made possible by monetary exchange is essential of course, because without it much of the knowledge necessary for economic coordination would go uncommunicated.

Even if we were to ignore the extremely important dynamic, discovery-oriented informational role of prices, it is hard to see how any language-based alternative to the price system could match the market's ability to marshal and make usable the existing knowledge.

Why have neoclassicists and Austrians mostly talked past each other on this issue? One explanation takes us back to the difference between the Mengerian and Walrasian understanding of 'price'. In the Walrasian view, prices are parametric to the decision-making processes of individuals and firms. In Boettke's terms, they serve *only* an *ex ante* function as 'inputs' into various maximization exercises. By contrast, the Austrian view sees prices not just as *ex ante* inputs, but more importantly as the endogenous results of an ongoing disequilibrium process, as in Menger's emphasis on the *formation* of prices, rather than their determination. These different conceptions of price derive from each group's view of the centrality of equilibrium analysis. In an equilibrium-oriented economics, the *ex ante*, parametric role of prices will be paramount, and would lead fairly logically to the reading of Hayek associated with the Walrasian mainstream. In fact, since nothing happens in general equilibrium models until the market clearing price is found, there can be no use for prices other than the *ex ante* function described by Boettke.

By contrast, in a process-oriented economics, prices would be seen as disequilibrium phenomena in that (1) they are the endogenous outcome of previous human choices that were embued with ignorance and error; (2) they have a role in serving as *ex ante* signals in the monetary calculation needed for (possibly mistaken) entrepreneurial plans that arise in response to pre-existing disequilibrium outcomes; and (3) they serve to spur the entrepreneurial discovery process by providing information to which alert entrepreneurs might react and, in so doing, find new uses for resources that (potentially) remove existing disequilibria. The epistemic properties associated with these contrasting understandings of prices are central to the differences between Austrian and neoclassical microeconomics.

A note on tendencies toward equilibrium

The previous discussion carefully avoided taking sides in the ongoing debate among Austrians as to whether it is appropriate to describe market processes as tending toward equilibrium.[21] I have articulated a position on that debate in previous work (Horwitz 1992b: Chapter 2 and Boettke *et al.* 1986), and any significant exploration of those complex and subtle issues would be too far from my main points to pursue here. More important, the major contributions of this book are valid whether or not one believes that the market process that most Austrians claim to be exploring is best described as 'equilibrating'. My own view is that equilibrium terminology and concepts are not very well suited to describing the order that markets produce. Esteban Thomsen (1992: 58) captures what I think is the important issue without using equilibrium language:

[F]rom a market-process perspective . . . [prices] are . . . sophisticated informational devices, with a feedback mechanism (profits) that induces their correction by entrepreneurial agents. This correction is never fully achieved in reality, but the degree of order observed in markets is, in the market-process view, to a large extent due to the degree of success of entrepreneurs in responding to this feedback.

Having suggested that equilibrium concepts are not ideal, I would contend that the essential insights of my argument are in no way dependent on that claim. The key claim of this study is that monetary disequilibria manifest themselves by disrupting the informational properties of prices. Whether one sees an unhampered price system as leading to a more narrow conception of equilibrium or as simply producing some broader and weaker notion of order, does not matter because both views recognize an important role for prices as knowledge surrogates and discovery prompters. The specific degree of effectiveness one believes prices have in this regard (and how one might choose to theoretically characterize that effectiveness) seems to me to be a separate issue from the effects of monetary disequilibria on prices.

Monetary calculation and the market process

With the Hayekian understanding of the interplay between prices and knowledge, and the Kirznerian conception of the link between uncertainty and entrepreneurship, we can turn to Mises' discussion of the role of monetary calculation. Much of the literature on prices, knowledge, and economic calculation (including the Austrian contributions) neglects to emphasize that market prices are constituted in terms of money.[22] The discussion of prices and knowledge usually refers to 'market' prices or 'disequilibrium' prices, but rarely to 'money' prices. Although Austrian contributors to these discussions would likely say 'of course we mean prices in terms of money', it is worth emphasizing that point here because the starting point for our discussion of macroeconomics will be *monetary* disequilibria. If the prices of the microeconomic market process are formed out of acts of exchanges of goods against money, then the scope for monetarily-generated disorder is quite broad.

For neoclassical economics and its emphasis on equilibrium prices, this is not an issue. When prices are determined by a hypothetical auctioneer and the exchange process is 'essentially one of barter' (Hahn 1970: 3), what possible influence could money have? Indeed, as Keynes (1937: 115–16) asked, 'why should anyone outside of a lunatic asylum want to use money' in that world? General equilibrium models recognize all of this by explicitly rejecting a role for money as a generally accepted medium of exchange. To the extent that such models try to incorporate something called money, it is only as a numeraire or the nth good that will serve as the point of comparison for figuring relative prices. This mere placeholding role for money is a far cry from a medium of exchange view that sees money as half of virtually every market exchange and therefore being crucial to the process of price formation that has long interested Austrians.[23]

As Mises recognized as early as 1912, there is a link between the use of money and the possibility of economic calculation. In both *The Theory of Money and Credit* and his later work on economic calculation under socialism, as well as in his general treatise *Human Action*, Mises was very careful to spell out that rational economic calculation could only take place in a money-using economy where prices are constituted in terms of money.[24] By virtue of its role as a medium of exchange, money serves as a common point of contact for all other goods. The money prices that emerge serve as a common denominator among goods, facilitating the process of calculation. In a barter economy, calculation is very difficult because no such common reckoning point exists and the comparison of value across goods is correspondingly difficult. There is almost no way to appraise which alternative use of a good is to be preferred in the absence of money prices. Where human beings have to make choices among alternative uses, money prices are indispensable. This is particularly true in the case of capital goods. If all capital goods are completely specific, or if they are all perfectly substitutable, the issue of calculation would not arise. In the first case, calculation would not be necessary as each capital good could only have one use, so there would be no choice to make. In the latter case, calculation is unnecessary because every good could be used in any production process, so there would be no need to choose in any economic sense.

Mises also clearly understood that money prices are irrelevant under conditions of equilibrium precisely because the whole issue of economic calculation was moot: 'under stationary conditions there no longer exists a problem for economic calculation to solve. The essential function of economic calculation has *by hypothesis* already been performed' (1981 [1922]: 120). In the world of equilibrium there is no need for money and money prices (and, as we will see below, entrepreneurship) because the problems they are needed to solve simply do not exist. The relationship between money prices and economic calculation is essentially a disequilibrium phenomenon.

Recognizing that money prices matter because we are never in equilibrium allows us to bring together these Misesian insights with Kirzner's work on the entrepreneur. Entrepreneurs who perceive an opportunity to turn a set of inputs into a future output for a profit are relying on their estimates of the prices of the inputs when they actually buy them, the price they can command for the output in the future, and the relevant interest rate to compensate for the time involved. Unexpected undesirable movements in any of those three factors can turn a perceived profit into a realized loss. All acts of entrepreneurship have to face this uncertainty: 'The term entrepreneur as used by catallactic theory means: acting man exclusively seen from the aspect of the uncertainty inherent in every action' (Mises 1966 [1949]: 253). The challenge for entrepreneurs is overcoming this uncertainty and guessing accurately about what the future evaluation of their product will be in comparison to the costs of the inputs. This is the process of economic calculation.

Mises (1966 [1949]: 357) argues that in attempting to see into an unknown future, people have 'only two aids: experience of past events and [the] faculty of understanding'. In the case of entrepreneurs 'knowledge about past prices is part of this experience and at the same time the starting point of understanding the future'. This captures both the *ex ante* and discovery functions of price. Entrepreneurs use past prices as part of the process of anticipating future prices, and the potential of a difference between those prices is what entrepreneurs are alert to. The success of their actions is determined by the *actual* prices in the future (the *ex post* function). Competing entrepreneurs size up the existing set of prices, compare those prices to what each imagines future prices (and consumer wants) might be and undertake those actions they see as appropriate given their appraisal of the situation.

Mises also argues that economic calculation is limited to those 'things which are . . . bought and sold against money' (1966 [1949]: 214).[25] This derives from money's role as the 'universally used medium of exchange . . . because most goods and services can be sold and bought on the market against money, and only so far as this is the case, can men use money prices in reckoning' (ibid.: 208–9). For Mises, the importance of monetary calculation is that it 'is the guiding star of action under the social system of the division of labor' (ibid.: 229). Whenever we act in the market, we make use of monetary calculation to determine which actions to take (*ex ante*) and to reckon (*ex post*) the results of those actions: 'The premeditation of planned action becomes commercial precalculation of expected costs and expected proceeds. The retrospective establishment of the outcome of past action becomes accounting of profit and loss' (ibid.: 229).[26]

Monetary calculation is intricately linked with Mises' conception of the entrepreneur. Salerno (1990b) has rightly called attention to Mises' very important discussion of valuation and 'appraisement'. For Mises, entrepreneurship is formulating expectations of the future constellation of prices and attempting to see opportunities within that vision that others are not currently alert to. One primary factor in entrepreneurial appraisement of future prices is the constellation of current prices. Entrepreneurial action begins with past prices and brings them together with what Mises refers to as the 'faculty of understanding' to form concrete expectations of future prices. Based on those expectations, the entrepreneurial aspect of human action leads us to select the perceived appropriate course of action. Entrepreneurial action on the market is crucially dependent on the existence of money prices that can inform these acts of appraisement. Without such prices, there would be no basis on which such entrepreneurs could formulate their plans nor reckon their results.

How the market process unfolds in the currently uncertain future will reveal how appropriate their actions were, with profits and losses providing that information after the fact. Because each person's faculty of understanding will be at least slightly different, people will have divergent expectations about the future. Those expectations take concrete form in the actions people choose to take in the wake of the process of economic calculation. The results of the market process, which take the form of profits and losses, inform entrepreneurs as to the accuracy of their expectations and the calculations they made based on them. Profit rewards those with more accurate pictures of the future and losses penalize those whose vision is lacking. In this way disequilibrium money prices, in all three of their roles, are essential for generating economic order. To the extent money prices become any more divorced than necessary from the underlying variables, they will perform less well in this process of economic calculation and the degree of economic order will suffer accordingly.[27]

In our discussions of inflation and deflation that follow, these insights about the role of money prices in facilitating economic calculation will return. As Mises (1920: 109, emphasis added) put it in his original contribution to the socialist calculation debate: 'Admittedly, monetary calculation has its inconveniences and serious defects, but we have certainly nothing better to put in its place, and for the practical purposes of life monetary calculation *as it exists under a sound monetary system* always suffices.' Given our earlier discussion of the informational role of prices, and given that the order produced by the market process (however characterized) is crucially dependent on calculation in terms of those money prices, Mises' claim about monetary calculation brings out the point that is central to the argument of this book: If the monetary system is *not* sound, monetary calculation will be less reliable, due to the 'noisy' influence of monetary disequilibria on prices. As prices become less reliable, entrepreneurs will find their task to be that much more difficult and we would expect that market order would suffer as a result. Even with entrepreneurs having a degree of alertness equal to what they would in an environment of monetary equilibrium, monetary disequilibria will undermine the operation of one of the central tools necessary to turn alertness into productive action: the constellation of money prices in the market. The important characteristic of the market process for my purposes here is not whether it tends toward equilibrium, but that whatever type of order it does produce is a direct result of the reliability of monetary calculation. To the extent macroeconomic disturbances disrupt money, they disrupt monetary calculation and entrepreneurship and, therefore, undermine the order produced by the market process.

Conclusion

This chapter's discussion has centered on the claim that freely evolving market prices are necessary for the production of economic order. In particular, we stressed the informational role that prices play in disequilibrium situations. Changes in the underlying variables of the market get translated into changes in the induced variables such as prices. Although that translation process does not produce a direct correspondence between the two sets of variables (as in equilibrium theory), we argued that markets provide a feedback process that allows for some relationship between the two (or at least a better relationship than would be produced by alternative institutional arrangements), which explains the degree of market order we empirically observe. One set of induced variables that we did not discuss, and that has an important role in understanding the microeconomic effects of monetary disequilibria, is the capital structure. The uniqueness of the Austrian theory of capital and the importance of capital to the subject at hand warrants separate treatment in the next chapter.

2 The missing link

Capital theory as microfoundations

We have argued that two of the distinguishing aspects of Austrian economics are its subjectivism and its description of the market as a process of discovery coordinated by money prices and entrepreneurial calculation. An Austrian conception of the macroeconomy sees the effects of macroeconomic disorder as disruptions in this microeconomic ordering process, specifically in the undermining of knowledge signals produced by market prices. However, there is one more distinct aspect of Austrian economics that needs to be brought into this discussion and that is its theory of capital.

The way in which capital goods figure in the plans of entrepreneurs, the way the uses of those goods change when entrepreneurial plans change, and how this Austrian conception differs from neoclassical capital theory are all relevant to the main themes of this study. It is fruitful to conceive of capital as the 'missing link' between microfoundations and macroeconomics.[1] As pointed out earlier, mainstream macroeconomic models since Keynes have normally portrayed labor markets as this link. Although it is important to understand the role of labor markets in transmitting and manifesting the effects of macroeconomic disorder (as we will have reason to do in the discussion of W. H. Hutt's work in Chapter 6), mainstream discussions are weakened by the absence of an explicit discussion of the role of capital in transmitting and manifesting those effects. From an Austrian perspective, the market process is generated by entrepreneurs who are combining capital and labor in various combinations to produce what they believe consumers will want. If that entrepreneurial discovery process is affected by monetary disequilibria, then we should expect to find repercussions on both labor *and capital*.

Despite the rise of human capital theory in the past several decades, there are still some reasons for treating capital and labor distinctly. The main reason is that in generally market-driven economies, labor services are the (alienable) property of the physical entity that generates the services, that is, workers are free to sell their labor services to whom they wish (within the limits of the law and any other possible contractual obligations). Capital services, by contrast, are owned not by the physical entity providing the services, e.g., a forklift, but by human beings. In this way, capital goods can be exchanged or reorganized with a great deal more freedom than can labor. A forklift is not able to quit when it is 'asked' to move to a lesser-valued use, or 'asked' to transfer to a different factory in a new city. This is not a trivial point as it creates some important differences between capital and labor.

Nonetheless, there is surely more than just a grain of truth in the essential insight of human capital theory that labor does share some important features with capital goods. Some Austrians (Lewin 1999) have suggested that one can formulate an Austrian theory of human capital by applying Austrian capital theory to labor. This is a promising avenue of research and one that will be touched upon as it is relevant to the argument below. However, I do not plan to give an exhaustive treatment of the ways in which labor is affected by macroeconomic disorder here. Some of the more Austrian insights on this question can be gleaned either by analogy to this chapter's discussion of capital, or by the discussion of Hutt's work.[2] This chapter will briefly review the standard treatments of capital, explore the Austrian alternative, especially Lachmann's contribution, and then suggest ways in which capital links up with macroeconomics and the market process.

Before proceeding with this chapter's task, a brief defense of the excursion into capital theory is in order. Putting capital theory not only in our *Hamlet*, but arguably putting it in the role of the Prince, requires a couple of comments. First, to the extent this study purports to offer a distinct Austrian perspective, then a central component of that perspective is the Austrian theory of capital. A lack of understanding of that theory can help explain the confusion that surrounded the Hayek–Keynes and socialist calculation debates of the 1930s.[3] Although its capital theory does not define Austrian economics, understanding that theory and its implications will give one a good grasp on precisely what is distinct about the Austrian approach. As we will see later, one of the pioneering contributions of Menger's work that founded the Austrian school was his perspective on the role of capital. As a result, it is not just necessary but crucial to have some, if only too brief, discussion of capital.

A second point is that aggregate measures of economic well-being often do not indicate the full effects of monetary disequilibria. As our discussion of inflation will reveal, simply looking at real GDP will understate the true costs of inflation. Many of those costs reflect the *misallocation* of resources, rather than their *lack* of allocation. In other words, we might well be using our resources fully, and GDP may reflect that, but we might be producing the wrong things with them.[4] The Austrian emphasis on malinvestment during the business cycle can be seen as one example of this misallocation point. Inflation and deflation in general may have systematic effects on the capital structure that lead to resource wastage that would not occur under monetary equilibrium. If our task is to explore the effects of monetary disequilibria on the microeconomic market process, we cannot ignore their effects on the capital structure.

An overview of classical and neoclassical approaches to capital

Capital has long been at the center of economics. Prior to the marginalist revolution, when plutological concerns about the origins and distribution of wealth were dominant, discussions of capital were centered on the phenomenon of interest. With the tripartite division of the sources of wealth into land, labor, and capital, so was income divided into rent, wages, and interest. Much of classical economics was devoted to explaining the conditions under which each of the three groups (landowners, laborers, and capitalists) would get smaller or larger shares of total income. The discussion was centered on the labor theory of value, or other cost of production explanations of the income generated by factors of production. In addition, classical economics was concerned with the relationship between the division of this wealth and the overall level of wealth in a given society. Starting with Smith, solidified in Ricardo, and extended by J. S. Mill, the causes and effects of changes in national wealth provided much of the classical research agenda.

Economists' conception of capital changed with the marginalist revolution. Neoclassicists such as John Bates Clark wedded the theory of capital to the new theory of distribution. Clark (along with others) had developed the marginal productivity theory of distribution, which allowed economics to explain the income of any factor of production by applying marginalist analysis to its productivity. The income of a factor was equal to the value of its marginal contribution to total product. Now land, labor, and capital were united under one theoretical umbrella. By jettisoning the cost of production approaches of the classicals, neoclassical economics also put the consumer front and center not only in the determination of the value of consumer goods, but via derived demand, of the factors of production as well.

The neoclassical approach was also able to offer an explanation for the relationship between capital and growth. Given that wages were a function of the marginal productivity of labor, and that the productivity of labor was affected by the capital it was applied to, one could conclude that increases in capital would raise labor's real wages by raising the productivity of the labor. It was very easy to draw the conclusion from this that one could increase national wealth by simply increasing the amount of capital that labor had to work with. The most obvious way to increase capital was through saving, and the standard 'pre-Keynesian' belief in the virtue of saving fell naturally into place. More recent neoclassical treatments of the role of capital have tended to be rather straightforward (if mathematically more complex) extensions of these basic insights.

The unifying theme in both classical and neoclassical approaches to capital is the sometimes explicit, sometimes implicit, view that capital can be treated as a homogeneous entity that semi-automatically generates value. For the classical economists this was linked to the various cost of production approaches that seemed to imply that if capital was just embodied labor, the value of that labor would ensure that the capital produced value. Given their plutological orientation, there was not much need to think otherwise about capital. If one's central concern is explaining how a category of goods generates a flow of income, it would be natural, perhaps, to treat it as a homogeneous fund. By focusing on the distribution of income across the three classes, classical economics could safely ignore questions about the *internal* organization of the capital structure.

Marginal productivity theories have fared no better. Here too the implicit, or explicit, assumption is that capital is homogeneous. In the Clark-type formulations, we speak of the marginal productivity of capital, as if the multitudinous specific capital goods could be added together to get an aggregative sum. They can, but if, and only if, the theorist assumes the market is in equilibrium. Recalling the definition of equilibrium as perfectly dovetailing plans, and viewing capital goods as elements of those plans, if equilibrium holds, then each capital good is being used in the inarguably best way it can. In such a world, there are no disputes over whose expectations (as embodied in the particular capital combinations employed) are correct, as all plans are mutually consistent. Therefore, the prices of all capital goods reflect those correct expectations, allowing for them to be summed to find the value of the total capital stock.

It is worth repeating that this procedure is valid only in equilibrium. As an explanation for the varying rates of return earned by capital in existing market processes, or as an explanation for why the structure of capital is what it is, this approach is not helpful. Where expectations and plans are not perfectly dovetailed, the current prices of capital goods (and all other assets) will reflect some degree of entrepreneurial error due to divergences of expectations. Some entrepreneurs' expectations, as embodied in capital goods, will be more accurate than others, therefore some prices are more accurate reflections of the 'real' value of the capital than others. Unfortunately, we have no *a priori* way of knowing which goods are which. In fact, the whole point of the discovery process of the market is to provide us with exactly such knowledge. The same sorts of criticisms raised in the previous chapter with respect to equilibrium approaches to the market process more broadly can be raised about such approaches to capital more narrowly.

For many classical and neoclassical economists, the main tasks of capital theory have been to construct an aggregate measure of capital (particularly so as to be able to compare capital stocks across economies) and to explain the nature of capital's contribution to the value of the final product. These two goals have tended to lead theorists to treat capital as a homogeneous entity, particularly in the form of a 'subsistence fund' or, in Knight's work, a 'Crusonia plant'. Such treatments of capital would lead one to look for the effects of macroeconomic disorder on the size of such a fund or plant and the corresponding effects on the amount of value the capital is able to create. What one would likely not look for are what we might call 'structural' or 'compositional' changes within the capital structure. Such changes can only be seen if one adopts a different conception of capital.

Plans, subjectivism, and the concept of capital

In exploring Hayek's definition of equilibrium, we focused on the plans of individual choosing entities and the degree to which those plans were, or could be, dovetailed by the market process. In our discussion of Kirznerian entrepreneurship, we located the entrepreneurial aspect of human action in our ability to imagine a future (partially of our creation) in which a combination of inputs will yield an output whose price (we believe) will be in excess of the sum of the costs of all of the inputs (with the appropriate time discounts). To the extent that all human action takes time, surely indisputable for acts of production, then such action can fruitfully be understood as an intertemporal plan.

In order to execute such a plan, two time-laden issues are important. First, executing the plan will require time to obtain the necessary inputs as well as time for the inputs to combine to form the output. Second, during this time, the planner must be able to subsist while waiting for the eventual output. As is well known since Bohm-Bawerk's pioneering contributions, individuals will be willing to engage in time-consuming ('roundabout') processes of production if they believe the value of the ensuing output will be greater than the value of the inputs used and the waiting time. Constructing a fishing rod is generally preferred to fishing with one's bare hands because, although it means forgoing fish for the period of construction, we anticipate catching enough additional fish through the use of the rod so as to justify both the waiting time and the sacrifice of the alternative uses of the inputs (wood and string, for example) used to construct the rod. Here too we can see the link between capital and saving, as anyone who constructs such a rod must have sufficient provisions to survive the period of rod construction. In a simple economy, we might imagine individuals storing up consumption goods to tide them over. The creation of capital goods requires some prior act of saving.

The Austrian emphasis on the relationship of capital to the plans of entrepreneurs is an extension of Austrian subjectivism.[5] If the value of consumer goods derives from subjective acts of appraisal by individuals, then, by extension, the value of capital goods will derive from their *perceived* ability to create those consumer goods. This argument finds its roots in Menger's (1981 [1871]) distinction between goods of different 'orders', with consumer goods being goods of the first order and capital goods being of 'higher' orders. Menger (ibid.: 58) also saw that the place of an individual good in this 'order of capital' depended on the plan of its use:

> To designate the order of a particular good is to indicate only that this good, in some particular employment, has a closer or more distant causal relationship with the satisfaction of a human need. Hence the order of a good is nothing inherent in the good itself and still less a property of it.

It is the entrepreneur who attempts to anticipate the future demand for various consumer goods ('the causal relationship with the satisfaction of a human need'). By constructing an intertemporal plan to meet that consumer demand, the entrepreneur makes use of, and thus gives value to, capital goods. Note the forward-looking aspect of value in this case. In the same way that consumers value a consumer good because of the utility they *expect* from it, so do entrepreneurs value capital goods because of the *expected* value of the consumer goods they will produce. Capital goods have value precisely because of the role they play as elements of plans that are intended to produce valuable consumer goods.

This also connects up with our observations about the relationship between disequilibrium and capital made earlier. Value flows from lower order goods to higher order goods via derived demand because expectations flow in the opposite direction. Because entrepreneurs subjectively expect that particular higher order goods will be useful in producing certain consumer goods, those higher order goods have economic value. The imperfection of entrepreneurial expectations implies that some of those capital goods are being used incorrectly (*ex ante*) and thus their current market prices will have those errors built into them. As the market process unfolds, such errors will be revealed (*ex post*) and entrepreneurs will be forced to reshuffle higher order goods, if necessary, or rethink their expectations about the demand for the consumer good. This process precisely parallels the way in which the prices of consumer goods are derived from the *ex ante* subjective perceptions of consumers, who often find out, *ex post*, that what they purchased was not what they 'really' wanted. The same discovery, feedback, and adjustment processes take place in capital markets and consumer goods markets. That parallel is first glimpsed in Menger's work and comes to fruition, in the Austrian tradition, with the later work of Mises, Hayek, and Lachmann.

Viewing capital goods as elements of entrepreneurial plans allows us to assess various definitions of capital, particularly those within the Austrian tradition. In Bohm-Bawerk's (1922: 6) original contribution to Austrian capital theory, he defined capital as 'a complex of produced means of production'. This definition enabled him to distinguish capital from labor and from natural resources such as land. The plutological heritage of classical economics is clearly at work here. In addition, the objectivism of classical value theory seems reflected in viewing capital in terms of the way in which it was produced (i.e., a backward-looking conception) rather than the way or ways it might be used (i.e., a forward-looking conception that sees it as part of a entrepreneurial plan). Hayek (1941: 54) tried to avoid some of these problems by defining capital as 'the aggregate of those non-permanent resources which can be used only in this indirect manner to contribute to the permanent maintenance of the income at a particular level'. Although this definition avoids using the way in which the object was produced as a criterion for calling it capital, it can still be argued that Hayek was not being subjectivist enough. Lachmann (1978: 12) says of Hayek's definition that it ignores 'the uses to which permanent resources are put'. In other words, the permanence or non-permanence of a resource is not the issue, its role in an entrepreneur's plan is. Lachmann's critique is particularly useful if one is concerned, as he is, with 'the series of short periods during which resources are shifted from one use to another, and the repercussions of such shifts' (Ibid.). For the purposes of understanding the capital structure effects of monetary disequilibria, it is these short periods that will interest us as well.

In contrast to Bohm-Bawerk and Hayek, Mises and Kirzner offer conceptions of capital that seem more in line with traditional Austrian subjectivism. For example, Mises (1966 [1949]: 515) says, 'Capital . . . is a mode of looking at the problems of acting, a method of appraising them from the point of view of a definite plan.' The concept of capital refers to the place of particular physical objects within the plan of the actor in question. Thus capital cannot be defined in terms of the physical qualities of the object, but rather its purpose or role in the plans of its possessor. A hammer that I buy at the hardware store for use in hanging pictures in my home is best understood as a consumer good, while the hammer that a construction company buys to hammer in roofing nails on construction sites is best understood as a capital good. It may well be the same hammer in all of its physical qualities, however, its place within the structure of production (a function of the subjectively constructed plans of entrepreneurs) determines its capital goods status.

Kirzner's (1966: 36) view is that the existing stock of capital can only be understood as a picture of the as-yet-unfinished intertemporal plans of entrepreneurs. Capital therefore refers to the 'intermediate objects' that are the representation of these unfinished, and subjectively formulated, entrepreneurial plans. This conception of capital seems a more consistently subjectivist one in that neither the process by which goods are produced nor their permanence are defining characteristics of capital. All that is relevant for viewing a good as capital is to see its place within the subjectively constructed plan of an actor.[6] It should be noted also that, although it was not stressed by most of the authors discussed above, the Austrian conception of capital clearly includes non-material assets such as a brand-name, goodwill, or information. These all figure as inputs in the plans of producers (and consumers) and are just as much capital as physical machinery.

This discussion of the centrality of 'the plan' and its relationship to Austrian subjectivism allows us to revisit a point raised earlier. It was argued that it was impossible to reduce capital down to one homogeneous, measurable quantity unless we assumed that the market was in equilibrium. That point should now be clearer. What marks a good as capital is its place in human plans. Since, in a market economy, each of those plans is drawn up more or less independently of the plans of others, and because each of those plans depends on the constructer's subjective expectations of the future, it would be only by the sheerest chance that at any one moment in time these plans would be perfectly consistent with each other. To the extent they are less than perfectly consistent, we are not in equilibrium. If these plans conflict, then we cannot simply add up the market values of individual capital goods because those prices are the result of entrepreneurial expectations, some of which will, outside of equilibrium, be incorrect, and others of which will conflict. Therefore, the market price based on those erroneous expectations will be under- or over-stating the 'real' value of those capital goods, which will be revealed in the market process yet to unfold.

Again, the Austrian view of the epistemic role of prices comes to the fore. When we start by assuming that the market is in equilibrium, we can reasonably treat prices as containing all of the information necessary to produce that equilibrium. Thus the prices of capital goods could be said to reflect their 'true' values, as all of the plans of which they are a part can be consistently executed. However, if we are speaking of an unfolding disequilibrium market process, then the informational role of capital goods prices is quite different. Rather than seeing prices as perfect reflectors of accurate information, prices simply embody the (possibly wrong) expectations of the entrepreneurs who are using them in their plans. This is also illustrative of the relationship between capital and monetary calculation. As those plans are executed, their success or failure will in turn affect the prices of capital goods. Goods that are part of successful plans will likely see their prices rise, while those that are part of failed plans will tend to be sold off at lower prices, reflecting that failure. Ongoing differences between the prices of (possibly complementary) capital goods will spur entrepreneurial discovery and the creation of new plans based on different expectations. In addition, as plans fail and capital needs to be reappraised, it is the existence of money prices in the market that enables entrepreneurs to recalculate capital values and to form reasonable, if imperfect, new expectations of the possible profitability of potential production plans. To attempt to find an aggregate measure of capital based on disequilibrium prices is to ascribe to those prices informational properties relevant only in equilibrium. In disequilibrium, we cannot aggregate capital into a homogeneous measure. The Austrian critique of aggregate conceptions of capital derives from its subjectivism and its rejection of equilibrium theorizing.

Heterogeneity and the capital structure

Starting from his strong subjectivism, Ludwig Lachmann has extended Austrian capital theory in a number of important directions, emphasizing entrepreneurial plans and the heterogeneity of capital. In his famous formulation of the issue, Lachmann (1978: 2, emphasis in original) argued that:

> The root of the trouble is well known: *capital resources are heterogeneous.* Capital, as distinct from labor and land, lacks a 'natural' unit of measure. While we may add head to head (even woman's head to man's head) and acre to acre (possibly weighted by an index of fertility) we cannot add beer barrels to blast furnaces nor trucks to yards of telephone wire.

As he was careful to point out, this heterogeneity is not a matter of physical differences but 'differences in use'. Even if every capital good were constructed out of the same material, the fact that each good is put to a different intended use means that, outside of equilibrium, there is no way to reduce capital to some homogeneous, measurable quantity. In Lachmann's view, this heterogeneity has several important implications for the theory of capital.

The three aspects of capital theory that are central to Lachmann's work are: (1) viewing capital as an integrated *structure*; (2) understanding the role played by *complementarity* and *substitutability* in that process of integration; and (3) exploring how entrepreneurs will react to the success or failure of their plans given the first and second aspects. The third aspect is where capital theory meets the other subdisciplines of economics. For our purposes, we wish to explain how monetary disequilibria affect capital-using entrepreneurial plans and what the costs of the adjustments in the capital structure that follow might be. To do so, we need to explore Lachmann's capital theory in more depth.

The history of capital theory is littered with metaphors for understanding capital. Lachmann's metaphor of choice is the concept of a 'structure', particularly in contrast to metaphors which work from the assumption of capital as a homogeneous aggregate. The structure metaphor is derived from Lachmann's very Austrian starting point of 'the plan'. Structure is at work on two different levels. At the level of the individual, each actor formulates a plan that involves 'structuring' inputs in such a way as to execute the plan. Lachmann (1978: 8) says, 'Capital uses must "fit into each other." Each capital good has a function which forms part of a plan.' From the perspective of the plan's creator, the arrangement of his capital goods embodies his plan. At the economy-wide level, the structure metaphor refers to the degree to which these various individual plans mesh together with any consistency, as revealed in the current stock of capital. Here, the structure metaphor allows us to talk of degrees of 'integration' or 'coherence' in the stock of capital. We can also use the concept of structure to talk about the changes that take place when this structure is affected by exogenous shocks or changes in expectations. Lachmann (1978: 4) sums up his project this way, 'we must regard the "stock of capital" not as a homogeneous aggregate but as a structural pattern. The Theory of Capital is, in the last resort, the morphology of the forms which this pattern assumes in a changing world.'[7]

As with any structure, understanding possible changes in the capital structure requires that we understand the current structure and its evolution. For example, if we are interested in explaining how and where new investment will take place, we have to understand it in light of the opportunities made available by the existing structure of capital. Investment is not just a matter of adding more units of a homogeneous glob to the existing glob, as might be the case with a farmer who adds additional acreage adjacent to what he already owns. Rather, investment is a matter of 'fitting in' to the historically given stock of capital. Lachmann (1978: 10) refers to 'investment opportunities' as 'holes in the pattern'. Viewing capital this way points to several issues of importance to Austrians.

First, the structure conception of capital explains why Austrians have long insisted on the difference between *over*-investment and *mal*-investment. The problem during the Austrian business cycle is not just that too much investment is taking place (a concept more consistent with a homogeneous conception of capital) but that the *wrong kinds* of investment are occurring. In Lachmann's terms, the apparent 'investment opportunities' do not reflect the underlying 'holes in the pattern', because of the distorting effects of inflation on the interest rate. Many investments made in such a situation would later be discovered not to be well integrated into the capital structure.

The second aspect of Lachmann's theory of capital is his concern with issues of complementarity and substitution. When we recognize that capital goods are heterogeneous in their uses, we also see that such goods are relatively (although not perfectly) specific to particular uses, what Lachmann calls 'multiple specificity'. Any given capital good will have a limited range of possible uses to which it can be put, some more valuable than others. Since this is true of almost all capital goods, any production process that requires more than one capital good will have to be concerned with whether the various specific capital goods being used will 'fit into' each other. This notion of 'fitting in' is what Austrians mean when talking about the 'complementarity' of capital goods. Complementarity is not a matter of physical attributes, but economic ones: can these goods be used *cooperatively* to produce the desired output? The existing structure of capital can be understood in terms of the complementarity of the various capital goods. By being useful together, they can legitimately be referred to as comprising a 'structure'. By contrast, treating capital as a homogeneous aggregate would lead one to treat each individual capital good as a perfect substitute for any other, since all comprise a homogeneous entity.[8]

The multiple specificity of capital also points toward the issue of substitution. Not only do individual goods have multiple uses, but most outputs can be produced in a (finite) number of ways. If the goal is to produce running shoes, we might envision several alternative production methods (each involving a different set of complementary inputs) capable of doing so. The question facing the producer is the decision as to which method to employ. A snapshot of the capital structure at any given time will indicate that each capital good then in existence represents 'what in the circumstances appears to its owner to be its "best," i.e. its most profitable use. The word "best" indicates a position on a scale of alternative possibilities' (Lachmann 1978: 3). In this way, one can understand each firm's capital combination as reflecting *perceived* perfect complementarity in the eyes of the firm's managers. Again, in Kirzner's terms, they are the embodiment of unfinished plans, and complementarity makes conceptual sense only within the context of a given plan of action. In some sense of the term, it is a static concept.

Substitution, by contrast, 'is a phenomenon of change the need for which arises whenever something has gone wrong with a prior plan' (Lachmann

1977a [1947]: 200). Change is necessary because what is perceived as perfectly complementary by managers will not be so in the aggregate unless everyone's expectations are perfect, i.e. we are in equilibrium. If profit and loss signals (or, perhaps more appropriately, capital gains and losses) indicate to the owner that the existing plan has not been successful, the owner is faced with the need to rethink it. In particular, it may well be necessary to reshuffle the combination of inputs comprising the plan. If so, our entrepreneur must now consider issues of substitution: what other ways can the output be produced? What other capital goods (including labor) can be substituted for those in the existing plan in order to produce the output more profitably? Would the resources be better spent producing some output other than this one?

These are questions of change and the activity of business people forced to reconsider their production plans, and doing so by thinking in terms of substitutes, cannot easily be captured by static models. As Lachmann (1978: 14, emphasis in original) argues, this process of plan reformulation is highly dependent upon the expectations of the formulator, which cannot be understood mechanistically: 'there is a *subjective* element in the *interpretation* of experience to ignore which would be a retrograde step'. The interpretive element of plan reformulation is not amenable to treatment by maximization models precisely because it is a matter of the individual attempting to discover the very means–ends framework that maximization models take as given. As such, it leads very naturally into a discussion of Kirznerian entrepreneurship.

Lachmann (1978: 13) recognized the role of the entrepreneur in this process: 'We are living in a world of unexpected change; hence capital combinations, and with them the capital structure, will be ever changing, will be dissolved and reformed. In this activity we find the real function of the entrepreneur.' One might not accept this as the 'real' function of the entrepreneur, but it is surely an aspect of entrepreneurship in the Kirznerian sense. In the face of the market discoordination manifested by the capital losses associated with unsuccessful production plans, it is the entrepreneur who must see the opportunities that have yet-to-be-plumbed by recombining inputs, or by using existing combinations to produce different outputs, in order to better serve the wants of consumers. For the entrepreneur's capital-relevant decisions, issues of complementarity and substitution will be at the forefront.

An important component of these entrepreneurial decisions will be the prices of various inputs and the expected prices of various outputs. The very fact that there has been plan failure necessitating entrepreneurial action is evidence that the prices of the capital goods in existence at the moment such failures were noticed were not equilibrium prices. For example, entrepreneurs cannot assume that the existing market prices of two capital goods accurately reflect the monetary trade-off involved in assessing them as possible substitutes. Part of the entrepreneurial task is to assess whether the entrepreneur's own vision of the substitutability of different capital goods is superior to the historical judgment manifested in their current prices. This is where monetary calculation and appraisement appear. If entrepreneurs see a substitute capital good that they think is underpriced in comparison to the value they perceive it could contribute to a production plan, they are alerted to such a possibility by the discrepancies existing among current disequilibrium prices.[9] Successful entrepreneurs will be those who are alert to genuine cases of such discrepancies, appraise future prices correctly, act on them by appropriately reshuffling their production plans, and profit by the process. Of course, successful entrepreneurship also means increased coordination with the desires of consumers. The understanding of the relationship between entrepreneurship and the capital structure is an extension of both the Austrian focus on disequilibrium market processes and the Austrian conception of capital as a heterogeneous structure.

Money, capital, and the banking system

The relationship between capital and money has been a source of confusion throughout much of the history of economics. This confusion probably results from the importance of double-entry bookkeeping in the construction and revision of production plans. In order for entrepreneurs to make decisions, they have to be able to appraise in terms of money prices, including the money prices of capital goods. The accountant's balance sheet shows the value of capital in terms of a homogeneous money aggregate, even though the entrepreneur can only act on that aggregate by adjusting specific, heterogeneous capital goods. The next chapter will give a more full-blown treatment of the role of the banking system in a monetary economy, but it is worth clarifying here some of the issues relevant to the theory of capital.

One of the first of those issues is the role of money. Understanding the origin and function of money has been a concern of Austrian economics since Menger, whose theory of the origin of money (1892) is frequently cited as the exemplary spontaneous order story. The particulars of that story have been discussed in detail elsewhere.[10] For the purposes at hand we need to recall the fundamental result of the Austrian theory is that money is best seen as a 'generally accepted medium of exchange'. This implies that money is the most 'saleable' or 'exchangeable' of all goods. In more contemporary terminology, money is (nearly) perfectly liquid.

The downside of the perfect liquidity of true moneys is that they normally pay no interest. In the neoclassical tradition, this is explained as either (1) the result of the transactions costs of paying the interest or converting less liquid assets to money (Hicks 1935) or (2) the result of various 'legal restrictions' (Wallace 1983) that limit such payments or stifle the development of alternative instruments that could provide interest. What both perspectives have in common is a shared view of the 'barrenness' of non-interest-bearing money. The trade-off facing a money-user is one between money, which provides *no* return to the holder, and bond-like assets, which provide a monetary interest payment. From an Austrian perspective, this way of characterizing the choice is mistaken.[11]

Money's general acceptability implies that it does provide a return. That return is not measurable as a monetary payment, but is subjective in the form of the 'availability services' that result from money's liquidity. The fact that money can be used to purchase virtually anything at virtually any time means it can be viewed as 'standing by' and being available when needed. Compare that quality of money to a specific capital good. Obviously particular capital goods have a fairly specific range of possible uses and an owner would face some level of transaction costs in attempting to either barter them for another specific good or turning them into money. Money, by contrast, is doing its job when it is being *held*, waiting for some use. This is why the demand for money is conceived as a demand to hold (real) money balances. The truth behind the description of money as 'liquid capital' is that it can easily be turned into more specific capital. However, its disadvantage in comparison to specific capital goods is precisely that it cannot *directly* produce output – money must be turned into capital before production can begin. Lachmann (1978: 88) argues:

> Money is largely, so to speak, a capital good 'by proxy'. It symbolizes, at the initiation of the plan, those current services we shall need later on but which, owing to their 'current' character, we cannot store until we need them. We store the money instead.

If we wish to refer to money as 'liquid capital', it has to be with this last point kept firmly in mind.[12]

Rather than seeing the trade-off as between barren money and interest-bearing bonds, we could portray all financial assets as offering some return equal to the sum of a subjectively assessed availability service and an objectively assessed interest payment. In equilibrium, the total rate of return would be equal across all assets. We can imagine different financial assets occupying different places along a continuum of interest–availability trade-offs. For example, cash would represent one extreme position where the whole return was subjective and interest was zero. By contrast, a relatively illiquid financial asset, like a corporate bond, would yield a high interest return and almost no availability services (i.e., it is effectively useless for exchange purposes). Other financial assets might represent more of a mix. A money market mutual fund account that both pays interest and offers limited checking services would be one example. In this case, we would expect a lower interest rate (and higher availability services) than the corporate bond, risk and other non-liquidity factors being equal. This seems a more fruitful way of looking at the portfolio choices among financial assets than beginning with the assumption of money's barrenness.

Lachmann (1978: 43) distinguishes between money that is earmarked for specific later uses and money holdings that are used to guard against unforeseen future circumstances. Both of these uses can be subsumed under his phrase 'those current services we shall need later on', if we recognize that not all that we *shall* need is known at present. On this basis, Lachmann (ibid.: 90) also distinguishes among first-line, second-line, and reserve assets. The former are capital goods that provide services from the inception of the production plan. Second-line assets are those that are planned to be used later in the production process. Two of his examples are spare parts and money for wage payments. Reserve assets are those 'which it is hoped that if all goes well they will not have to be thrown in at all' (ibid.). The primary reserve asset is the cash reserve. The second-line and reserve assets are differentiated by whether their use is expected or 'possible, but unpredictable'. Money, as a generally accepted medium of exchange, can fit in either category depending on the way in which the entrepreneur chooses to view money on hand. Some will be earmarked for specific future uses, some will guard against unforeseen changes.[13] What is central here is that money's uses derive from its general acceptability.

It is also clear that money is not capital in the sense that we are using the word here. This is important when examining the role of banks in the process of capital formation. After all, we talk of banks making funds available 'for investment' or see them as lending 'capital' to those who need it. What confuses this issue is forgetting that what banks really intermediate is the market for *time* not money. Because time is not a tangible good, it cannot be borrowed and lent directly, rather such exchanges take place *in the form of money*. What a saver does is to say to a bank 'I don't need these resources now, but I might need them in the future.' In return for their willingness to part with resources for some period of time, savers are compensated with interest. As above, that interest represents compensation for parting with the ability to have money available at an instant, which is another way of saying we are giving up time when we save. A borrower, by contrast, is looking to acquire time. A borrower can be seen as saying to the bank 'Look, I would really like to have some resources now, but I don't. I could wait for some period of time and save up, or you could lend me money now and in so doing push my ability to command resources toward the present.' What the saver doesn't need until later, the borrower wants now. Ultimately they are trading time in the form of resources. Conceivably these intertemporal exchanges could take the form of specific capital goods, but the transaction costs would be prohibitive (for the same reasons as barter). Instead, time is traded in the form of perfectly liquid capital – money – which allows the conversion of the exchanged time into the specific capital good(s) or cash reserve desired by the borrower.[14]

This view of the relationship between money and capital is consistent with the classical loanable funds theory of the interest rate, itself consistent with the Austrian emphasis on 'time-preference' explanations of interest. Seeing banks as intermediaries in the time market is a way to reconcile the Austrian and classical accounts. Given that, all other things equal, humans prefer present goods to future goods, they will require some sort of compensation in return for delaying consumption to the future. Conversely, as implicit in our borrower's plea above, those who wish to speed up consumption will have to pay for the privilege since it can only be obtained by someone else's giving up a present good, which will require compensation. Time-preference is both necessary and sufficient to explain the emergence of interest.

Intertemporal exchanges cannot occur by directly trading time and are highly unlikely to occur using specific capital goods. They will take place through the form of money as those willing to part with resources will offer various amounts at various prices (interest rates), giving us the supply of loanable funds. Borrowers will be willing to acquire resources in the form of money to pursue production plans if they anticipate the return from the plans being higher than the price paid for the resources. They will demand various amounts of loanable funds at particular prices (interest rates). As with other simple supply and demand constructions, the market clearing rate of interest will be at the intersection of those two curves, with actual market rates of interest being (to one degree or another) related to these demands and supplies of borrowers and savers. The rate of interest on money loans derives from the loanable funds market, itself a product of time preferences.

Viewing the banking system as intermediating the market for time, but doing so in the form of money, enables us to re-examine the Wicksellian distinction between the natural and market rates of interest. The natural rate is defined as that rate which equilibrates the time preferences of savers and investors, while the market rate is the actual rate being charged by the banking system. If the banking system is accurately reflecting those underlying time preferences, then the two rates of interest should be equal. Some critics have questioned the usefulness of the Wicksellian framework, but our previous discussion points to its importance. Because banks translate preferences about time into exchanges of money, it is worthwhile having a way of differentiating between the 'before' and 'after' of that translation process. The natural rate of interest is determined by the time preferences that drive saving and investment. If saving and investment could take place by exchanging time as some physical entity, the distinction between the natural and market rate would disappear as there would be no translation of time into money. If saving and investment took place via the exchange of specific capital goods, the distinction would also disappear as the only relevant interest rate would be the one implicit in the market price at which the exchange takes place. This scenario is the one built into intertemporal general equilibrium models that lack money.[15] The natural rate–market rate distinction will be central to the view of macroeconomics we will develop in the following chapters.

Capital in the Hayek–Keynes debate

Confusion over issues in the theory of capital has permeated several important debates in the history of economic thought. This is particularly true of the defining debates in Austrian economics. The socialist calculation debate, for example, involved several capital-theoretic issues, especially those that surrounded the question of how the means of production were valued in the market and whether their value could be accurately calculated in the absence of private property.[16] Of more direct relevance for our task is capital's role in the debate between Hayek and Keynes during the 1930s. In order to illustrate the importance of some of the issues this chapter has brought to the fore, we can examine the ways in which Hayek and Keynes effectively talked past each other. I will argue that this was largely because Keynes did not understand Hayek's theory of capital (which was frequently implicit and admittedly incomplete) and its importance to his macroeconomic arguments. In addition, Keynes had no real theory of capital himself, leading to some of the fundamental differences between his view and that of the Austrians. The purpose here is neither to exhaustively treat this debate, nor to settle it, but simply to indicate how frequently the capital issue was front and center and document its role in the confusion that occurred.

The main texts for this exploration are Hayek's (1931–32) review of Keynes' *Treatise on Money*, Keynes' *The General Theory of Employment, Interest, and Money* (1936), and Hayek's brief remarks on that book in *The Pure Theory of Capital* (1941). In the *Treatise*, Keynes was concerned with the question that had been central to most of monetary and cycle theory throughout the early part of the twentieth century, namely the explanation of the various price changes that take place over the course of the cycle. Much of the argument there is built upon Wicksellian foundations, as was Hayek's work on business cycles which derived from Mises' extensions of Wicksell's work.[17] Keynes was concerned with the relationship between the natural and market rates of interest, and defines the former in terms of the equilibrium between savings and investment. As Caldwell (1995a: 26) puts it: 'In this sense, the barebones model of the *Treatise* is simply Marshall with a Wicksellian twist, a twist that allowed Keynes to focus on the role of the interest rate in an economy with a developed banking system.' This point is also made by Leijonhufvud (1981b: 160–73), who sees the Wicksellian themes of the *Treatise* and laments their passing by the time Keynes gets to *The General Theory*. Hayek was also concerned with these issues, and his own early work on the cycle had emphasized divergences between the natural and market rates and the effects that resulted.

The major difference between Hayek and Keynes on this point was the role of capital. The Mises–Hayek theory of the trade cycle attempted to trace out the systematic effects that a lowering of the market rate below the natural rate would have on the capital structure. The idea that the Austrian theory was a theory of malinvestment reflects this concern. Keynes, by contrast, was more concerned with the relations among, and movements by, various aggregates, especially the price level. This concern enabled Keynes to avoid presenting anything resembling a full-blown capital theory. This lack of a capital-theoretic microfoundation for his aggregates also made it possible for Keynes to overlook all of the important changes taking place within the capital structure. These are precisely the microeconomic effects of macroeconomic disturbances that we wish to address. Keynes' aggregation and consequent neglect of any microeconomic changes is the context for Hayek's (1995b [1931]: 128, emphasis in original) central critique of the *Treatise*:

> But, surely, an explanation of the causes which make investment more or less attractive should form the basis of any analysis of investment. *Such an explanation can, however, only be reached by a close analysis of the factors determining the relative prices of capital goods in the different successive stages of production* – for the difference between these prices is the only source of interest. But this is excluded from the outset if only *total* profits are made the aim of the investigation. Mr. Keynes' aggregates conceal the most fundamental mechanisms of change.

Those fundamental mechanisms of change are, of course, the processes that comprise the capital structure.

As Hayek (1995b [1931]: 130–1) said in his review, and as Caldwell (1995a: 26) notes in his introduction to the *Contra Keynes and Cambridge* collection, Keynes asked for this criticism by yanking Wicksell's theory of the interest rate off of its Bohm-Bawerkian capital-theoretic foundations. Keynes' only use for capital theory (in the form of his discussion of savings and investment, which is problematic in its own right) in the *Treatise* is to explain the level of the interest rate. The quote from Hayek above points to the problem that arises when one forgets that Wicksell's natural rate conception was derived from Bohm-Bawerk's work on capital. In that tradition, the interest rate has to be understood as the difference between the prices of factors of production at various stages in the production process (where those differences are a result of time-preference and the higher productivity of more roundabout methods of production).

Getting at these tricky intertemporal issues will involve disaggregating terms like 'capital' and 'investment', as Hayek implies above, to understand the specific production processes involved and the relationships among the goods at the various stages of production. To talk of the forces that lead to 'investment' as an aggregate, or enhance the capital stock as an aggregate, glosses over the crucial question of *where* investment will take place and in *what sorts* of capital goods. Already here we see an important trend in Keynes' treatment of capital – his tendency to treat both 'capital' and 'investment' as homogeneous globs. If one does so, it is much easier to speak of investment in the abstract and see interest rates as being determined by notions of savings and investment that have no reference to time-preferences and the time-structure of production. Hayek (1995b [1931]: 131) is very clear in saying of Keynes, 'Would not Mr. Keynes have made his task easier if he had . . . made himself acquainted with the substance of [the Bohm-Bawerk-Wicksell] theory itself?'[18]

The period between the *Treatise* and the *General Theory* saw no improvement along these lines. If anything, Keynes' problems with capital multiplied. The central problem faced in the latter book is that, in Leijonhufvud's (1981b: 163) words: 'the behavior of the banking system is edging out of the focus of Keynes' developing analytical scheme. By the time we get to the *General Theory*, it is out of the picture altogether.' What Keynes had done in order to solve the problems of the *Treatise* was to remove the one thing that, from Hayek's perspective, was right about it – its Wicksellian theory of interest. In the *General Theory*, of course, we get Keynes' famous monetary (or liquidity preference) theory of the interest rate in addition to more of the same treatment of capital and investment as homogeneous aggregates. The trouble with Keynes' views on capital in the *General Theory* (1936: 76), is clear in his reference to the Austrians in Chapter 7, 'capital consumption is said [by the Austrians] to occur in circumstances where there is quite clearly no net decrease in capital equipment as defined above'. Keynes appears to conceive of capital in physicalist rather than value terms and as linked to the quantity of capital equipment. He is puzzled by how capital can be consumed even though the amount of capital equipment has not diminished.

There are two Austrian responses to this claim. First, as Hayek clearly saw as far back as his review of the *Treatise*, Keynes wants to draw a sharp distinction between investment (or capital accumulation) that merely enables the reproduction of existing stock of capital (which Keynes does not count as investment) and 'new' investment which increases that stock. Hayek (1995b [1931]: 129) argues that this is an untenable distinction as it is linked to tightly to the production of physical capital goods:

> But this procedure involves him, as we shall see, in serious difficulties when he has to determine what is to be considered as additional capital – difficulties which he has clearly not solved. The question is whether any increase in the value of the existing capital is to be considered as such an addition – in this case, of course, such an addition could be brought about without any new production of such goods – or whether only additions to the physical quantities of capital goods are counted as such an addition – a method of computation which becomes clearly impossible when the old capital goods are not replaced by goods of exactly the same kind, but when a transition to more capitalistic methods brings it about that other goods are produced in place of those used up in production.

As the Austrian emphasis on heterogeneity has long implied, capital has to be understood in light of a subjectivist approach to economic phenomena that sees value (including that of capital) only in terms of its ability to produce goods or services that consumers desire, rather than its physical attributes. Investment, therefore, encompasses both the production of new physical goods and the expenditures constantly necessary to produce the existing quantity of consumer and producer goods from existing equipment. It is in this sense that the Austrian view of investment is a gross investment rather than a net investment conception. If entrepreneurs decide not to maintain their capital by not investing enough to enable it to maintain its past output production, then this, in Austrian terms, is capital consumption (or disinvestment), even though the physical quantity of capital equipment does not change.

The second Austrian response to Keynes' claim would be that he is forgetting that value can be created and lost not just by the addition or removal of specific pieces of capital equipment, but by their recombination. Lachmann's work on complementarity and substitutability are of relevance here. Capital is in some sense consumed if a given production plan turns out to be unprofitable and the existing capital equipment is reallocated to second-best uses. Here is a case where the quantity of capital equipment as not changed at all, but the value of particular capital goods, as socially appraised by the market, has clearly been reduced. When capital is understood as incomplete plans, then the value of capital goods must be assessed in light of their usefulness with respect to those plans. That usefulness will of necessity bring in the concept of complementarity. The value of a given capital good will depend on what complementary goods are available to produce particular outputs. The value of capital is often more dependent on the overall complementarity of the capital structure (or its composition) than on the sheer quantity of physical equipment.[19]

One can make similar arguments about the Keynesian treatment of investment. One central theme of Keynes' work that emerges most clearly in the *General Theory* is the argument that as the quantity of investment increases over time, there will be fewer opportunities for investment in the future and those that do exist will offer substantially lower rates of return. This is a kind of diminishing marginal returns to investment. Keynes' view clearly conceives of investment and capital as very homogeneous. What it seems to rule out is investment that does not merely add more of the same kinds of capital goods, but changes the composition of the capital structure by fitting into a 'hole in the pattern' through complementarity. This view also seems to ignore the possibility that current investment will create products that, in turn, will create new opportunities for investment. Lachmann (1978: 6) is worth quoting at some length here:

> As long as we cling to the view that all capital is homogeneous, we shall only see, as Keynes did, the unfavourable effects of investment on the earning capacity and value of existing capital goods, since all the elements of a homogeneous aggregate are necessarily perfect substitutes for each other. The new capital competes with the old and reduces the profitability of the latter. Once we allow for heterogeneity we must also allow for complementarity between old and new capital. The effect of investment on the profitability of old capital is now seen to depend on which of the various forms of old capital are complementary to, or substitutes for, the new capital.

One need only think of the growth in the personal computer industry to see this in action. The existence of the PC has created investment opportunities that were literally inconceivable before the original investments in PCs came to fruition. It is precisely this aspect of the capital structure that Lachmann refers to as 'increasing complexity'.

One of the most telling signs of Keynes' difficulties with capital theory is the sense one gets from reading the *General Theory* that he continually forgets that capital goods are scarce. This is a point distinct from, though not unrelated to, the much discussed claim he makes that 'proper' investment policy (i.e., socialization) could reduce the rate of interest to zero and make capital abundant.[20] As many critics of Keynes have pointed out, much of the book proceeds on the assumption of significant quantity of idle resources, without offering much of an explanation of why those resources are idle in the first place. In his brief discussion of the *General Theory*, Hayek (1941: 374) puts it bluntly:

> he has given us a system of economics which is based on the assumption that no real scarcity exists, and that the only scarcity with which we need concern ourselves is the artificial scarcity created by the determination of people not to sell their services and products below certain arbitrarily fixed prices.

Hayek goes on to complain about Keynes' neglect of the differences between the prices of factors of production and his treatment of the interest rate as a purely monetary phenomenon. Keynes' unwillingness to treat interest as related to the differential prices of factors of production through time reflects his previously noted lack of familiarity with the Bohm-Bawerkian tradition in capital theory.

One of Hayek's long-standing criticisms of Keynesian thinking is its misunderstanding of the relationship between the demand for consumer goods and the demand for production goods (capital).[21] Hayek's complaint is that those who believe that by stimulating the final demand for goods and services we can therefore stimulate the demand for the production goods needed to produce them ('derived demand') are guilty of the fallacy of composition. The doctrine of derived demand (i.e., that an increased demand for a particular good will increase the demand for its inputs) applies only at the level of individual goods. It cannot be applied in the aggregate.

The standard Keynesian textbook model of consumption and investment moving in the same direction, especially when consumption is increased, is not accepted by Austrians except perhaps under the most severe cases of idle resources. Instead, consumption and investment are more likely to move in opposite directions. As consumption increases, for example, it pulls resources away from saving and thus away from the higher orders of production. Although it is true that producers must continue to provide the final goods, they will do so in less roundabout ways, with fewer intermediate stages of production between their inputs and the final good. The reduction in the stages of production will show up as a decline in investment spending in response to the increase in consumption. Conversely, when the public chooses to reduce its consumption and save more, producers will respond with an increase in investment. Although the demand for final goods has slackened in the short run, there are now more resources available to add stages to the production process, increasing its productivity. This increase in investment spending (fueled by the hypothesized saving) lengthens the capital structure and provides employment for workers released by the falling off in the consumer goods market. Their income, plus the increases in overall income generated by the now more roundabout and productive production processes, will find their way into the consumer goods industries and cause a longer run increase in overall wealth. Both of these explanations are valid even in the presence of some idle resources.

Even if some capital is idle, the issue of complementarity arises. Is the idle capital able to be used in a cost-effective way to produce the consumer goods that are being demanded? Artificially stimulating consumer spending will not necessarily mean that it is profitable for producers to employ the specific capital goods that are lying idle. To say that there is 'idle capital' is to aggregate a heterogeneous collection of goods with specific uses that may not be relevant to the purposes for which they appear to be needed. If Keynesian theoretical arguments or policy conclusions rest on such conceptions, they are evidence of insufficient attention paid to capital-theoretic issues.

This was not intended to be an exhaustive treatment of the Hayek–Keynes debate. Rather, it was an attempt to show how central the Austrian conception of capital is to the other kinds of theoretical arguments that Austrians make. Ignoring the important differences between Austrian theories of capital and more conventional treatments can lead to serious intellectual confusion. Surely a large part of Hayek's reason for writing *The Pure Theory of Capital* was precisely his dissatisfaction at how his ideas had been understood through the late 1920s and early 1930s. To undertake a project as difficult as that book would seem to require that one believed there was something very definitely amiss in economic theory. Many of these same problems remain today and a healthy injection of Austrian ideas on capital can help us to clarify some important issues in macroeconomics.

Conclusion

Although the role of prices in coordinating market choices is central to any discussion of the microeconomic effects of macroeconomic disorder, the effects on capital are also of major importance. In fact, one way of interpreting the Austrian view is to say that discussions of price coordination ought to encompass capital-theoretic issues because, as has been the case since Bohm-Bawerk, the Austrian perspective on capital and interest is ultimately about the relationships among the prices of the different factors of production over time. The current structure of capital, and any reshuffling that occurs through time, reflect responses to actual and expected prices and price differentials. Capital begs to be treated separately because it is so complex, but at base it is but a subset of the general Austrian concern with the signaling function of disequilibrium prices.

It is precisely these price differentials and the capital goods that result that are an important path by which monetary disequilibria make themselves felt. As monetary disturbances work their way through the market, they affect the various prices of consumer and producer goods. In turn, these price effects lead to changes in the capital structure, many of which may be mistaken from the perspective of an economy maintaining monetary equilibrium. We will explore this process and the costs and consequences it generates in the chapters to follow.

Part II
The macroeconomics of monetary disequilibrium

3 Monetary equilibrium as an analytical framework

In as much as the Austrian approach is skeptical of general equilibrium theory, it might seem strange to build an entire chapter around an equilibrium construct, in this case the concept of 'monetary equilibrium'. The main theoretical use of the concept of monetary equilibrium will be as a foil for the parallel sets of consequences that follow when either of the two cases of monetary *dis*equilibrium occurs. The Austrian tradition is rich with examples of this foil use of equilibrium constructs.[1] The task in this chapter is to describe the concept of monetary equilibrium and explore the workings of an economy where that equilibrium is continually maintained. The following chapters use the monetary equilibrium benchmark as a foil for understanding the effects of inflation and deflation. Carrying out this task will also create the opportunity to compare the properties of the monetary equilibrium framework to those of Keynes, monetarism, and New Classical economics. We shall also discuss the relationship between monetary equilibrium and the Quantity Theory of Money and the various notions of money's 'neutrality' that one finds in the macroeconomic literature.

The monetary and the real economy

From the earliest investigations of monetary phenomena, economists have been careful to distinguish between the 'real' and the 'nominal'. The insight, of course, is fairly obvious: it is not the absolute numerical price attached to a good or service that matters, but its value *relative* to the other prices in the economy. For example, should the prices of all goods and services (including labor and the nominal quantity of money balances being held) instantaneously increase by 10 percent, the real effects would be nil. All values would be 10 percent higher, but no good would be more expensive relative to another, nor would incomes and wealth have changed relative to one another and the prices of goods and services. This simple insight is central to clarifying the different kinds of effects money might have on real variables in an economic system. If changes in prices result from changes in the money supply, and those changes in prices happen in the way described above, then changes in the money supply would have no real effects. These circumstances are often described as a situation where changes in the money supply are 'neutral' or where money is 'just a veil'.

There is another sense in which money is a veil over real economic activity. This second sense does not require the stringent and unrealistic assumptions from above. In a monetary economy, money's defining role is as a medium of exchange and as such, it is acquired primarily for the purpose of being exchanged at some point in the future.[2] This point can be seen in the various theoretical treatments of the evolution and function of money. Menger (1892) describes the transition from a barter to a money economy by reference to the differential marketability of commodities. As barterers find it difficult to exchange goods for goods due to the frequent absence of a double coincidence of wants, they discover that holding stocks of goods that are desired by a large number of other traders will make such trades more likely. As a result, they trade the products of their labor for such marketable goods, and then trade those goods for the goods they ultimately desire. At first, such indirect exchanges might take place using a variety of different intermediate goods. However, those goods whose marketability is strongest even among a group of very marketable goods will soon dominate and the process will eventually converge upon one (or perhaps two) generally accepted medium of exchange.[3]

What this implies is that the 'real' exchanges taking place in a market economy are *ultimately* goods and services for goods and services. Money's role is to facilitate the exchange process by making such exchanges easier. Note that this is not the same as saying money *merely* facilitates exchange, with the implication that in the absence of money, the economy would look more or less the same, aside from holdings of money and somewhat lower transactions costs. Rather, it is money's medium of exchange function that *makes possible* the complex division of labor and variety of consumption and production goods that characterize advanced market economies. The emergence and use of money fundamentally transform economic relationships, and the further monetized an economy is, the better it will perform, *ceteris paribus*. By reducing the barriers to exchange money enhances our ability to execute mutually beneficial exchanges with other producers.

This perspective on money also has implications for understanding the demand for money. If money is a medium of exchange, then the rationale for holding a stock of money is to have it available when exchange opportunities arise. Money is a placeholder between the sales of our assets or services and our purchase of the goods or services of others. This is particularly relevant when we recall that all of these exchanges are taking place in a world of uncertainty. Money is needed not just because there are temporal differences between receipts and expenditures (although this is important) but also because it is uncertain precisely when the need or opportunity to make certain exchanges will arise. Money helps us to overcome that uncertainty (as do other institutions) by providing a reservoir of purchasing power that is available when needed.[4] The demand for money, then, is a demand to *hold* balances of real purchasing power. Money is providing the service we demand of it when we hold stocks of it in waiting until purchasing opportunities arise.

Money can be accurately described as a 'veil' in the sense that the increasing production and consumption of goods and services, not increasing money balances, comprise economic growth. The transition from barter to monetary exchange facilitates growth, but more money is not equivalent to greater wealth. Money is fundamentally a claim to wealth, not wealth itself. In the same way that a ticket to a sporting event is a claim to a seat, and not the seat itself, money is just a claim. Just as printing more tickets than there are seats at such an event will not cause the number of seats to increase, so do changes in the quantity of money *by themselves* not cause a change in the amount of available wealth in the short run.

On the other hand, money is not a veil in the sense of it being unable to affect that structure of prices. Changes in the supply of money can affect that price structure in ways that undermine economic order. Although it is the underlying exchanges of goods and services that ultimately matter, inappropriate changes in the money supply can have real effects on those exchanges and the prices that emerge. Money might best be described as a 'fluttering veil'.[5] Ideally we want that veil not to flutter and we want changes coming from the money side to not systematically distort the pattern of exchanges (particularly intertemporal ones) in a market economy. Monetary equilibrium represents that ideal.

Monetary equilibrium defined

To understand monetary equilibrium, we can think of it in terms of the circular flow of consumption goods and services trading for labor and other factor services through the use of money. Each output and factor has a market and price of its own. We can also talk about a demand and supply for money. However, money, unlike other goods, has some unique circumstances of its own that make clearing its market a more complex task. The most important is that money has no market of its own and therefore has no price of its own.[6] If the quantity supplied of money exceeds the demand there is no one price that can adjust to remove the excess supply. The same is true of an excess demand for money.

In fact, excesses or deficiencies in the supply of money will make themselves felt across every market through changes in the prices of all goods and services that exchange against money. As Yeager (1968: 64) succinctly put it: 'Because money is traded on all markets and on none specifically its own, and because it has no single price of its own to come under specific pressure, an imbalance between its supply and demand has far-reaching consequences.' The explanation of this process is straightforward. Recalling that the demand for money is a demand to hold real balances, suppose the money supply is increased (see Figure 3.1) to an amount beyond that which the public desires to hold (from MS to MS', leading to a movement from O to A). As this excess supply of

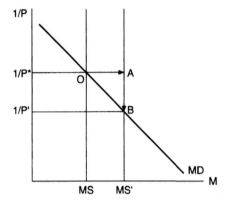

Figure 3.1   Inflationary monetary disequilibrium

money works its way through the economy, people find themselves with larger money balances than they wish to hold (by hypothesis, the excess money goes somewhere) and temporarily reside at point A. Assuming that there has been no change in their demand for money, these excesses will be spent on goods, services and/or financial assets driving up the prices of those items, and moving us from point A to a new equilibrium at point B. The increase in the price level ($P^* < P'$) normally associated with excess supplies of money is reflective of these individual increases.

It should be clear that there is no reason to expect that the percentage increase in each and every price should be precisely equal to the percentage increase in the money supply that triggered those price increases. The height of each individual price after the excesses are spent will depend upon a number of factors unique to each instance of excess money supply. Although it may be true that a broad enough price index would increase by a percentage more or less equal to the change in the money supply, that need not mean that each and every price does so. The changes in relative prices are the problem with excesses or deficiencies in the money supply. Keynesians might reply that the interest rate can perform the equilibrating function here. Some of the increased spending prompted by the excess supply of money may well go into interest-bearing financial assets, driving up their prices and driving down their interest rates. However, unlike orthodox Keynesian models where the portfolio choice is strictly between money and bonds, our discussion will assume that actors can allocate their wealth across a number of different assets and that crunching all non-money assets into the equivalent of interest-bearing bonds overlooks important real-world effects of excesses and deficiencies in the money supply.

Although the discussion has been framed in terms of an excess supply of money and rising prices, all of the same points about the relationship between individual prices and the price level, and the inability of 'the' price of money to adjust out disequilibria, apply with equal force to the case of an excess demand for money.

In the long run, any supply of money will be an equilibrium supply. Sticking with our example from above, consider the effect of the rising price level on the demand for money balances. Changes in a nominal variable like the price level will not affect the demand for real balances, but will affect the demand for *nominal* money balances. The rising price level is equivalent to a fall in the value of each dollar. In order to maintain the same real purchasing power in their money balances, actors will have to increase their nominal money holdings as prices begin to climb. This is reflected in the long-run movement from equilibrium O to equilibrium B in Figure 3.1. That movement along the nominal money demand curve is the long-run adjustment. As those nominal demands for money rise, the amount of excess in the real supply of money falls. More and more actors are now willingly holding portions of the higher nominal money supply, as doing so is necessary to keep their real money balances at the desired level. It is this process that brings the spending and price increase cycle to a stop. As the spending of the excess money balances continues, the price level continues to rise. Eventually it rises to a point (B) where the higher nominal supply of money is all being willingly held at the new higher price level ($1/P'$, where $P' > P^*$). When the price level reaches this point, the higher nominal money supply is no longer in excess, and the spending ceases and actors are once again satisfied with their holdings of real money balances.

Given enough time, any nominal supply of money can be an equilibrium real supply if we allow for intervening changes in the price level, understood as the inverse of the value of money. It is in this sense that it is true that the quantity of money does not matter – any supply of money is an optimal one. The problem with this view of the matter is that it is stuck in comparative statics and false aggregation. If movements from one supply of money to another were completely costless, then indeed it would not matter what the money supply was as any increase or decrease in that supply could be costlessly adjusted to by changes in the price level. But comparing two money supplies at distinct points in time, and assuming that there is a thing called 'the price level', distinct from the array of individual money prices, that bears the burden of adjustment, overlooks the whole reason why monetary disequilibria are to be avoided. In fact, adjustments to a new money supply are not costless and are not made only through changes in nominal variables. The fact that such money supply changes cause differential effects on individual prices is what makes it so necessary to study the path from one equilibrium position to another. To simply compare the beginning and end of that path is to ignore precisely the kind of problems that monetary theory and macroeconomics can analyze.

Monetary disequilibrium is a short-run phenomenon, as it contains within itself the process by which a new equilibrium can be reached, i.e., changes in the price level. Any definition of monetary equilibrium will have to be couched in terms that locate it in the short-run because long-run monetary equilibrium is a trivial phenomenon. For a first stab at such a definition, let us propose the following: monetary equilibrium holds when the supply of money is equal to the real demand to hold it at the prevailing price level. Another way to view this definition is to return to the real and nominal distinction. As with any real variable, there are two ways to change the real supply of money – one can change the nominal supply or change the price level. If the demand for real balances should change, either the nominal money supply or the price level can adjust to restore monetary equilibrium in the long run (see Figure 3.2). What our definition of monetary equilibrium proposes is that we are only in monetary equilibrium if such movements in the demand for money are responded to with changes in the real money supply through adjustments in the nominal money supply (a movement from point O to point A in Figure 3.2) and not the price level (a movement from point O to point A' in Figure 3.2).[7] As we shall argue in the following chapters, the primary task of a monetary system is to avoid money-induced changes in the price level precisely because they are not costless and they can wreak much havoc on economic performance and long-run growth. Unlike other goods and services, we do not want the price of money bearing the burden of adjustment in disequilibrium because that 'price' can only be changed by adjustments in the prices of (all) other goods and services, the effects of which dramatically undermine economic order.

Two other points should be made about this first attempt at defining monetary equilibrium. One is that there is no necessary relationship between monetary equilibrium and general equilibrium. Monetary equilibrium is perfectly compatible with disequilibria in the various markets for goods and services, as Myrdal (1965 [1939]: 36, emphasis in original) noted:[8]

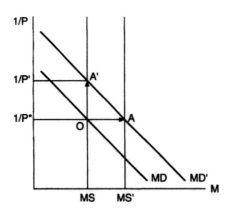

Figure 3.2   Responding to an increase in money demand

This monetary equilibrium has by no means the same character as the conditions for a perfect general equilibrium of prices in the static analysis of price formation . . . The monetary equilibrium condition fixes, furthermore, only *certain specific* relations of prices . . . and otherwise it permits any changes. Relative prices can change, and so can – as we will later find – the 'price level' and everything else, so long as those monetary equilibrium relations are satisfied.

It might be true that a monetary regime that is able to consistently stay in or near monetary equilibrium will be creating an environment where those individual markets work as well as they are capable. However, there is no reason to equate 'as well as they are capable' with 'in general equilibrium'.

The second point is that the argument so far should not be read as endorsing or criticizing any particular monetary regime. It is possible for any monetary regime to see maintaining monetary equilibrium as a desirable policy goal. A central bank might well be convinced by the argument so far, and the argument to follow, that monetary equilibrium is superior to alternative monetary goals and might well try to put that belief into practice. Recognizing the desirability of monetary equilibrium does not commit one to any particular monetary regime. Chapter 7 explores the operation of various monetary institutions and regimes and attempts to see whether certain regimes might be better at maintaining monetary equilibrium than others.

Monetary equilibrium, loanable funds, and interest rates

Our first stab at a definition of monetary equilibrium will require some clarification in order to trace out the macroeconomic implications of the concept. The most important addition we need to make is to bring the banking system and loanable funds market into the discussion more explicitly. It is the banking system that is responsible for supplying money to the economy, so we need to clarify its role in facilitating or preventing monetary equilibrium and loan market equilibrium more broadly. To simplify matters, this chapter's analysis will assume that the public's demand for money is satisfied only by bank-created money, rather than base money. This assumption is unrealistic of course, but will simplify the discussion by removing the possibility of changes in the composition of the demand for money between bank and base money. In the discussion of monetary regimes in Chapter 7, we will return to this assumption to see what happens if we drop it.

Such a banking system will be assumed to be not unlike modern commercial banks, in that banks hold stocks of reserves and issue demand deposit liabilities based on those holdings. The assumption of all money demand being in the form of bank liabilities can be understood in one of two ways: either there is a system with a fiat currency that serves as reserves and the public holds none of this cash, or there is a banking system where banks competitively issue both demand deposit and currency liabilities and where some commodity serves as outside money. In the latter case, assume that the public holds none of this base commodity. One further assumption is that banks are unconstrained by reserve requirements. They still wish to hold positive levels of reserves (so as to avoid liquidity crises during interbank clearings), but they will vary their holdings depending upon market conditions.

As banks also intermediate the market for time in the form of loanable funds, we must also consider the latter market and the role of the interest rate. The public has some set of time preferences that determine its willingness to supply loanable funds in the form of savings, including holdings of bank liabilities, as well as its willingness to demand loanable funds from the banking system and other lenders. In general, the quantity supplied of loanable funds (savings) will vary directly with the interest rate, which serves as a return to such supplies. The quantity demanded of loanable funds (investment) will vary inversely with the interest rate, as interest reflects the cost of acquiring loanable funds (see Figure 3.3). The monetary system's role as a supplier of money, and the public's role as a demander of money, are an important subset of the broader market for loanable funds. If monetary institutions are unable to maintain monetary equilibrium, they will create a disturbance in the loanable funds market. If monetary equilibrium is maintained, it makes it that much easier for the loanable funds market to smoothly translate time preferences into intertemporal exchanges.

It is important to stress that the savings and investment under consideration are *desired* amounts. One of the great contributions of the Swedish monetary theorists of the 1930s, especially Myrdal, was the important distinction between *ex ante* and *ex post* analyses. Looking at the *ex ante* level of saving and investment means seeing them in terms of what people desire, while an *ex post* view looks at what actually transpires in the market process. This might best be seen with reference to a simply supply and demand example. In standard

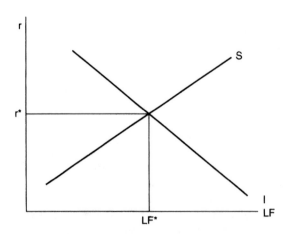

Figure 3.3   The loanable funds market

supply–demand presentations, the curves we draw are *ex ante*, reflecting what people wish to do. The intersection of the two curves represents a cleared market precisely because at that price and quantity combination, what suppliers wish to do is exactly equal to what demanders wish to do. Market clearing is understood as this *ex ante* equality, or a dovetailing of plans.[9] Figure 3.3 illustrates this in the market for loanable funds.

However, the existence of an *ex ante* equilibrium does not guarantee that the *ex post* result will match it, especially if entrepreneurs are somehow prevented from finding the price that will bring the equilibrium to pass. If the actual market price becomes equal to the equilibrium price, the *ex post* quantities supplied and demanded will be equal, and the fact that the *ex post* result corresponded to the *ex ante* equilibrium is the basis for standard arguments about the social welfare properties of unfettered markets. Suppose there is a price ceiling on this market. At that price, the quantity demanded will exceed the quantity supplied implying *ex ante* disequilibrium. Suppose further that the market process proceeds under that price ceiling. Comparing the actual quantities of goods bought and sold shows that they are equal. Whatever was sold, was bought. Of course that *ex post* equality will take place at the quantity corresponding to the controlled price on the supply curve (the short side of the market rules). The reduction in quantity exchanged, below the quantity exchanged at the unconstrained market-clearing price, is the source of the welfare loss normally associated with price ceilings.

Looked at from the *ex ante/ex post* perspective, there is something else going on here. Somehow a situation of *ex ante* inequality became a situation of *ex post* equality. The explanation is obvious: demanders are unable make their desires effective due to the price control. They are forced by that price control to miss an opportunity that, in its absence, they would be able to pursue. In order to move from an *ex ante* inequality to an *ex post* equality, actors on one or both sides of the market are going to have to lose out on an opportunity they either expected at the controlled price or could have grasped at the market-clearing price.

This analysis can be directly applied to the loanable funds market. In monetary equilibrium, the quantity of loanable funds supplied and demanded will be in *ex ante* equality at the current 'price', the interest rate. Of course, *ex post*, savings and investment are *always* equal; whatever was invested must have come from some savings somewhere, just as whatever got bought, must have been sold by someone else in our example above. The concepts of savings and investment we are using here are not those calculated *ex post* by looking at national income statistics, but those corresponding to the demand and supply of loanable funds. In loanable funds market equilibrium, the *ex ante* plans of savers and investors are precisely reflected in the *ex post* results of the market process: everyone's plans are executable.

Monetary equilibrium also has implications for the rate of interest, specifically the Wicksellian distinction between the market and natural rates of interest. The market rate of interest is defined as the rate that banks are actually charging in the loanable funds market. The natural rate, by contrast, corresponds to the time preferences of savers and borrowers as expressed in their underlying demand and supply schedules for loanable funds (r^* in Figure 3.3). As noted earlier, if it were possible to move goods through time *in natura*, there would be no difference between the market and natural rates of interest. If a borrower could simply acquire the capital good he or she desired directly from the ultimate saver, problems of intertemporal coordination would virtually disappear. However, uncertainty and a capital goods version of the double coincidence of wants problem prevent such a scenario. Instead, we must trade intertemporally through the financial system and the instruments it creates. The need to translate intertemporal preferences into monetary exchanges creates the possibility of intertemporal breakdowns. If the monetary system is unable to accurately reflect those underlying time preferences, then the actual outcomes in terms of banking system activity will be mismatched with the *ex ante* intertemporal preferences of savers and borrowers.

In monetary equilibrium, the monetary system is not a source of disturbance to the loanable funds market. In monetary disequilibrium, the monetary system becomes a source of disequilibrium in the loanable funds market by distorting the signals generated in the process of turning time-preferences into the supply and demand for loanable funds. The *ex ante* quantities of savings and investment are not equal, and someone has to lose out in order for them to be equal *ex post*.[10] In addition, the adjustment process from an *ex ante* disequilibrium to an *ex post* equilibrium will entail significant social costs. To discuss briefly an example to be explored more deeply in the next chapter, suppose there is an excess supply of money. Assuming the loanable funds market is otherwise in equilibrium, banks will be creating more loanable funds than are justified by people's real willingness to save, as determined by their underlying time-preferences. As a result, the market rate of interest will fall, as banks attempt to lure in new borrowers with their excess money supplies, but the

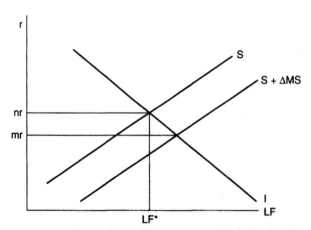

Figure 3.4   An excess supply of money in the loanable funds market

natural rate will not have moved, as no additional supplies of loanable funds have come forth voluntarily from the public (see Figure 3.4). Intertemporal coordination is dependent upon a myriad of other factors including the institutional framework of the markets in question and the entrepreneurial ability of the participants in them. The monetary system at its best does no harm to the intertemporal coordination process, and at its worst it undermines any possibility of intertemporal coordination.

The two key problems facing any capital-using economy are how to ensure (a) that the aggregate quantity of investment taking place is equal to that which savers are willing to provide; and (b) that the specific capital goods produced by the demanders of loanable funds are ones that will produce the quantity and kind of goods that will be demanded in the future. The banking system can prevent itself from being a source of harm with respect to the first issue, but the second can never be perfectly solved in a world of uncertainty and dispersed knowledge. However, by addressing the first, the banking system can remove one source of difficulty in addressing the second.

Monetary equilibrium and Austrian economics

The construct of monetary equilibrium is far from new. The concept has a long history in monetary thought and found much of its influence earlier in the twentieth century, only to be eclipsed, like much else, by the Keynesian revolution. The more recent work of Selgin (1988a and 1995a) and Yeager (1986) has done much to revive monetary equilibrium approaches to the problems of cycles and monetary regimes. Selgin's 1988 book, in particular, led many Austrian economists to explore the monetary equilibrium literature and to assess the relationship between that literature and the Austrian tradition. Given the task of establishing an Austrian perspective on macroeconomics, a brief discussion of that relationship is necessary.

The monetary equilibrium tradition is largely a European one. Much of the work on the doctrine prior to Keynes was in the hands of Swedish, British, and Austrian economists. Arguably, the whole approach begins in Sweden with the work of Wicksell, and in particular his development of the concepts of the natural and market rates of interest. In *Interest and Prices*, Wicksell (1965 [1898]: 102) defined the natural rate the following way:

> There is a certain rate of interest on loans which is neutral in respect to commodity prices, and tends neither to raise nor lower them. This is necessarily the same as the rate of interest which would be determined by supply and demand if no use were made of money and all lending were effected in the form of real capital goods. It comes to much the same thing to describe it as the current value of the natural rate of interest on capital.

The 'naturalness' of the natural rate refers to Wicksell's attempt to divorce the real forces determining interest rates and prices from the monetary ones.

Wicksell's basic insight was that if the two rates are equal, the price level will be constant and any differences between the two rates would manifest themselves as changes in the value of money.[11] Should the natural rate rise above the market rate, prices would rise as credit would be more easily available (via the lower market rate) than would be justified by the preferences of savers and borrowers (reflected by the natural rate). It is worth noting that Wicksell is here ignoring the possibility that the excess credit created in this process would return to the issuing bank in the form of redemptions, cutting off the upward pressure on the price level before it has any significant effects. Implicitly, he seems to be assuming some sort of non-redeemable monetary instrument.[12] Conversely, should the natural rate be below the market rate, prices would fall, as money in the form of credit would be in short supply in comparison to the preferences indicated by the natural rate (Wicksell 1965 [1898]: 100). If the two rates were equal, then the price level would be stabilized, for Wicksell the desired goal of monetary policy.[13] Wicksell saw himself as rescuing the Quantity Theory from what he saw as overly simplistic treatments that ignored the process by which monetary changes manifested themselves both in the price level and in real effects. In an important sense, Wicksell paved the way for further attempts to integrate monetary and real factors in this manner.

Wicksell's work had a clear Austrian connection in its reliance on Bohm-Bawerk's theory of capital in developing the concept of the natural rate of interest. Wicksell (1935: 205) said that the theory of interest 'has only in our own days been placed on secure foundations by the epoch-making work of Bohm-Bawerk'. The Austrian emphasis on time-preference and the temporal structure of production found its way into Wicksell's work on monetary theory. In Wicksell's further development of the natural rate concept, he defined it in terms of a purely technical 'profitability of waiting' or other measures of physical productivity.

Perhaps the best representative of the British development of the monetary equilibrium approach was in the work of Dennis Robertson. Although, in typical fashion, Robertson had his own idiosyncratic theoretical vocabulary for doing so, his work is squarely within the natural rate and monetary equilibrium tradition of Wicksell. In his extended discussion of the relationship between saving and the banking system in his 'Theories of Banking Policy' (1928: 42), Robertson is clear to say:

> The real value of a country's bank-money is the same thing as the amount of real savings which the public has put in the past at the disposal of industry through the medium of the banks, and its amount lies in the discretion of the public and not of the banks.

In addition, he later (ibid.: 43) adds that where the banking system is creating 'new' money, it can, for a period of time, 'extract from the public more savings than they public spontaneously decides to provide'. This corresponds to a market rate below the natural rate creating an divergence between *ex ante* savings and investment. Robertson (ibid.: 46) was also clear in arguing that it is more important for the banking system to maintain the savings/investment equality than to respond to supply-side driven changes in the price level. Should the banking system increase the supply of money in response to a productivity-engendered fall in prices (in order to maintain price-level stability), it will have the same consequences as expanding 'the supply of money in such a wise as to drive the price level upwards'.

In his excellent criticism of Keynes, Robertson (1940) is clearly working from a Wicksellian perspective and refers (ibid.: 33) explicitly to the need to maintain monetary equilibrium. Among the points he raises in that discussion are the need to distinguish *ex ante* from *ex post* when discussing savings and investment, the claim that Keynes does not sufficiently clarify the differences between the point of view of the individual borrower and the group of borrowers as a whole, and the problems of a purely monetary theory of the interest rate. In that essay Robertson also says:

> [I]f existing money is going to ground in this way [i.e., being held as money balances], it is prima facie the duty of the banking system to create more money, [and this] is quite consistent with the arguments of those who have expressed themselves in terms of 'neutral' money, or of a 'constant effective circulation', or of the maintenance of the equality between the market and 'natural' rates of interest.
>
> (ibid.: 19)

The references in the quoted terms are to Wicksell and Hayek, putting Robertson clearly in that tradition. Arguably, Robertson and Hayek were the foremost opponents of Keynes during the late 1920s and 1930s and the modern developments of Hayekian thought can learn much from Robertson's work.

The development of monetary equilibrium theory gave birth to two distinct lines of thought, each focused on one of the two cases where the natural and market rate equality did not hold. These two cases will be the subject matter of Chapters 4 and 5. Both lines of thought are clearly Wicksellian and in an important sense the task of this book is to reunite Wicksellian macroeconomics with Mengerian microeconomics. For the purpose of establishing the Austrian pedigree of monetary equilibrium theory, we can note that the inflationary disequilibrium theory that emerged from Wicksell's work was the Austrian theory of the business cycle in the hands of Mises and Hayek. What is of interest here is the degree to which these two thinkers made use of monetary equilibrium constructs.

Mises' relationship to monetary equilibrium theory is ambiguous. He surely made use of the natural and market rate concepts, developing Wicksell's analysis of the upward price spiral caused by a too low market rate into a theory of the business cycle. Developed further by Hayek, this theory was the dominant cycle explanation in Europe prior to the advent of Keynesianism. The major difference between Mises and Wicksell was over the mechanism by which the market rate was lowered below the natural rate. For Wicksell, coming out of the Currency School tradition, the problem was that banks overissue liabilities in response to an increase in the demand for loanable funds. For Mises, who despite his lip service to the Currency School was closer to those thinkers that White (1996: 63ff.) categorizes as the Free Banking School, the lower natural rate was caused by exogenous increases in the supply of loanable funds from the central bank. Mises' views on the relationship between the supply and demand for money were less clear. In Selgin's (1988a: 61–3) brief discussion of Mises' views, he points out that Mises generally thought that the issuance of fiduciary media (money not backed 100 percent by reserves) was the source of a falling market rate and loan market disequilibria. This would be the case even if there was a shift in the demand for money. Selgin's (ibid.: 62) strong implication is that Mises would have rejected monetary equilibrium theorizing because he mistakenly believed that 'commodity [i.e., non-fiduciary] credit is the only sort of credit consistent with loan market equilibrium'.

In Mises' later writings he held to views that were not consistent with monetary equilibrium theory. By suggesting that all increases in fiduciary media consist in what Selgin terms 'created' credit rather than 'transfer' credit, Mises appeared to deny that it was appropriate to increase the quantity of fiduciary media in response to an increased demand to hold it. At the same time, however, Mises did say in several places that banks would only create credit to the degree credit has been given to them by savers. He also appeared to link this line of thought to the supply and demand for money in a passage in *The Theory of Money and Credit* that attempted to define inflation:

> as an increase in the quantity of money (in the broader sense of the term, so as to include fiduciary media as well), that is not offset by a corresponding increase in the need for money (again in the broader sense of the term) so that a fall in the objective exchange value of money must occur.
>
> (1980 [1912]: 272)

If the 'need' for money is understood as the demand to hold money balances, then Mises can be interpreted as arguing that some increases in the supply of fiduciary media would be non-inflationary if they were in response to an increase in that need for money. Mises appears to define inflation as 'monetary expansions that cause the price level to increase'. This surely comes closer to a monetary equilibrium view than the outright condemnation of issuances of fiduciary media in his later writings. The crux of the issue remains whether the credit created by issuances of fiduciary media matched by an increase in the demand for such media reflect 'created' credit (and hence forced savings) or simply 'transfer' credit and voluntary savings.

Hayek's relationship with monetary equilibrium theory was also somewhat ambiguous.[14] In some of his early writings, he defended a constant supply of money and appeared to agree with Mises' claim that the creation of fiduciary media would disequilibrate the real capital market. On the other hand, as Selgin (1988a: 57) points out, there are numerous passages in Hayek where he recognizes that the nominal money supply should adjust to changes in the demand to hold money balances. Moreover, like Mises, his concern was with situations where the natural and market rates of interest diverged. In his summary of Wicksell's theory (Hayek 1967 [1935]: 24) he refers to the following as a 'correct statement': 'So long as the money rate of interest coincides with the equilibrium rate, the rate of interest remains "neutral" in its effects on the prices of goods, tending neither to raise nor to lower them.' Elsewhere in the second edition of *Prices and Production*, as we shall discuss later on, Hayek clearly calls for changes in the money supply that offset movements in velocity so as to stabilize the left side of the equation of exchange.[15] He was skeptical of the ability of any banking institution to actually accomplish this task, but he does indicate that this is desirable norm. Even as late as his 1978 book *The Denationalisation of Money*, he argued that:

> A stable price level . . . demands . . . that the quantity of money (or rather the aggregate value of all the most liquid assets) be kept such that people will not reduce or increase their outlay for the purpose of adapting their balances to their altered liquidity preferences.

> (1978c: 77)

In other words, Hayek is arguing that in response to changes in the demand for money (liquidity preferences), the monetary authority ought to adjust the supply of money so as to head off a scramble to obtain, or rush to get rid of, money balances.[16] Adjustments to changes in the demand for money should occur through the nominal supply of money, not via the price level. The problem is that adjusting the quantity of money in the way that Hayek recommends will only ensure a stable price level if we assume a static economy, in particular, one without productivity changes.[17]

Most of the modern Austrian work on cycle theory has been done by Murray Rothbard. Rothbard's relationship to the monetary equilibrium approach outlined above is far less ambiguous. Rothbard adhered firmly to the later Mises' perspective that any issuance of fiduciary media, regardless of changes in the demand for money, was inflationary (1962: 307n8 and 1994: 29ff., among others). Rothbard supported 100 percent reserve requirements as both a matter of sound economics and moral philosophy.[18] Like the later Mises, Rothbard believed that all creation of fiduciary media involved created and not transferred credit, and thus forced savings. As such, issuances of fiduciary media drove market rates below natural rates and caused upward effects on the price level. In addition, this view implied that changes in the demand for money would be followed by inversely related price level adjustment and the microeconomic effects they bring with them. Although we shall critically assess Rothbard's arguments in detail in later chapters, his perspective on the relationship between the supply and demand for money is one among several that can legitimately lay claim to an Austrian heritage.

The Austrian economists of the 1920s and 1930s were central players in the macroeconomic debates of the time. As such, the ideas of their contemporaries (such as the Swedes and D. H. Robertson) were influential on the ways in which they developed their ideas. With so much work being done on the concept of monetary equilibrium, it is not surprising that some of that work would find its way into the Austrian monetary theory of the period.

Capital-theoretic foundations of monetary equilibrium

From a modern Austrian perspective, perhaps the most troublesome aspect of traditional monetary equilibrium theory is the concept of the natural rate. The intuition behind the natural rate is a strong one: actors have intertemporal preferences and the actual structure of the economy, and capital in particular, should in some sense correspond to those preferences. To capture the possibility (or absence) of that correspondence, we need some theoretical constructions that stand in for both those intertemporal preferences and the opportunities available in the market. The latter is addressed fairly easily by some measure of current interest rates in the loan market, but finding a convenient shorthand for underlying time preferences is a bit more difficult. As noted earlier, Wicksell's natural rate attempted to do so by referring to the rate of interest that would obtain if all intertemporal exchanges took place *in natura*, rather than via money. Although this understanding of the natural rate is a way of getting at the underlying preferences of savers and borrowers, it is based on a thought experiment that is unacceptably unrealistic.

In a world where money was absent, the kinds of intertemporal exchanges we see in a monetary economy, not to mention the very capital goods that are the ultimate objects of those exchanges, would simply not exist. Conducting such a thought experiment seems to assume that the introduction of money would not change the (intertemporal) structure of the economic system. In other words, the system with money would look essentially like the system without it. This seems fundamentally at odds with an Austrian theoretical perspective that views the monetary economy as fundamentally different from a barter world. The existence of money enables the kind of calculative behavior that characterizes successful economic action and would be absent in any 'realistic' barter economy. Whatever validity there might be to the intuition behind the idea of the natural rate, from an Austrian perspective it should not be grounded in a money-barter comparison.

Additionally, as Myrdal (1965 [1939]: 49ff.) correctly argues, Wicksell's use of Bohm-Bawerk to define the natural rate more carefully cannot stand up to critical scrutiny. By viewing the natural rate in terms of physical productivity or, as Myrdal interprets it, 'the purely technical "profitability of waiting"', Wicksell's conception reflects an understanding of capital and interest that has been surpassed in the later literature. Myrdal (ibid.: 50) makes the telling point against Wicksell and it is one that leads naturally to a more subjectivist approach to capital and the natural rate:

> The idea of physical productivity presupposes, however, that there is only a single factor of production, besides waiting, and only a single product, and that, moreover, both are of the same physical quantity. This idea is therefore of no use in a realistic analysis, since such assumptions, if made at all, exclude the possibilities of a progressive adaptation of the analysis to reality.

Myrdal's interpretation also suggests that there is a link in Wicksell's mind between the natural rate of interest and the Bohm-Bawerkian notion of the 'average period of production'. The problem here is that measures of physical productivity or average periods of production break down in a world of heterogeneous capital goods where such goods may embody the mistaken expectations of entrepreneurs.

Myrdal points to a way out of this dilemma. The key is to recall that the interest rate is the time discount between present and future prices. The same forces that determine the structure of relative prices, determine intertemporal prices and therefore the relevant rate of interest. As Myrdal (1965 [1939]: 51) says of Wicksell's work, it shows how 'the determination of prices and price relations is tied up theoretically with the determination of the interest rate'. Myrdal concludes that to make sense of Wicksell, one has to replace any notion of physical productivity with 'exchange value productivity'. Myrdal's preferred way of doing so was to redefine the natural rate in terms of the 'yield of real capital'. Essentially, he tried to reformulate the natural rate/market rate relationship as 'the condition of equality between the capital value and the cost of reproduction of existing real capital', where 'capital value' reflected the natural rate and 'the cost of reproduction' reflected the market rate. In particular, Myrdal stressed that any notion of the yield of real capital had to be understood in *ex ante* terms, because it is the forward-looking behavior of capital owners that determined what actions would be taken in the market.

In an ever-changing world of heterogeneous capital goods traded though monetary exchange, it might be better to understand the correct intuition behind the natural rate in terms of a whole constellation of interest rates arising from the structure of relative prices existing at any point in time.[19] The natural rate of interest would then refer to the intertemporal exchange rates existing on the market when the price formation process is not distorted by fluctuations coming from the money side of the money–goods relationship. To the extent changes in the money supply are merely facilitating this relative price formation process, rather than distorting it, the market rate of interest will not be distorted by the monetary system. This definition runs a great danger of being circular, in that it defines monetary equilibrium as 'not monetary disequilibrium'. Answering the charge of circularity will take some more doing, particularly in the chapters to follow. For now, it is enough to argue that in situations of inflationary or deflationary monetary disequilibria, there are systematic distorting effects on the price formation process, as well as on the capital structure and intertemporal decision-making. When prices are not reflective of underlying intertemporal preferences, broadly predictable patterns of distortion will appear.

Put more positively, monetary equilibrium is that situation where relative price signals, particularly intertemporal ones, are accurate enough to allow entrepreneurs to create a potentially *sustainable* capital structure. The term 'potentially' recognizes that entrepreneurial error is likely to creep into the process and simply getting relative prices to be accurate signals is not enough. In addition, broader loanable funds markets may have their own difficulties, preventing the capital structure from being sustainable. The difference in monetary disequilibria is that in those cases, even perfect entrepreneurs could not create a sustainable capital structure because they would be acting on the basis of the faulty information embodied in the distorted price structure. Monetary equilibrium is necessary but not sufficient for natural-market rate equality and a sustainable capital structure. What the notion of a 'natural' rate of interest seems to capture is that there is some structure of relative prices that would permit at least the possibility of producing a capital structure that is sustainable into the long run.[20] Again, the realities of an uncertain world might preclude the possibility from becoming real, but unlike monetary disequilibria, that possibility exists in monetary equilibrium. Monetary equilibrium is a necessary, but not sufficient, condition for a sustainable capital structure.

The concept of sustainability is a useful one in this discussion. One of the primary effects of both inflation and deflation is to distort the price signals that lead to the integration of the intertemporal structure of production. These distortions render the structure unsustainable, in that once the distorting price signal disappears, decisions made under its influence will be found to be systematically mistaken. A systematic unsustainability in the capital structure suggests that the ruling market rate of interest is not equal to the natural rate. The concept of sustainability is also advantageous because it is compatible with the notion of building and maintaining a structure through time. This links sustainability up with the investment–savings relationship. If the savings financing the increasing depth, length, and complexity of the capital structure are coming from the genuine intertemporal preferences of market actors, then that structure will be, at least potentially, sustainable. What will be true in monetary equilibrium is that there will be no monetary source of *systematic unsustainability* in the intertemporal price formation process.

Monetary equilibrium, the Classics, and Keynes

In some ways, the monetary equilibrium framework is not all that different from the standard textbook model of the so-called Classical economists. At one level, this should be obvious in that the originators of the monetary equilibrium approach (e.g, Wicksell, Mises, Hayek, and Robertson, among others) were 'pre-Keynesian' economists. The problem with any comparison to the Classical economists is that the term in question was really invented by Keynes for the purpose of contrasting his own view with what he saw as a distillation of the then-current intellectual consensus. The label 'Classical', as used by Keynes and generations of textbooks since, refers to a number of different thinkers, many of whom held differing if not contradictory views. What did generally bind them together (at least in Keynes' view) was a broad belief in *laissez-faire*, normally linked up with some understanding of Say's Law, which precluded the possibility of general gluts or shortages.[21]

The Classical model

In the textbook model, the three central tenets of the Classical school are: Say's Law, the Quantity Theory, and the coordinative role of the interest rate. Say's Law is normally transformed into a claim about the relationship between an aggregate supply and an aggregate demand curve. More precisely, Say's Law ('supply creates its own demand') is said to imply that aggregate supply would always equal aggregate demand. The argument is that sales of goods supplied in the market produce the income necessary to buy up that supply. In other words, general gluts or general shortages are not possible, because the level of supply dictates the demand for those very goods. This view was part of the Classical belief in the powers of *laissez-faire*, in that no government intervention was needed to prevent general gluts and shortages.

The Quantity Theory of Money explained the price level, whereas various microeconomic factors explained the array of relative prices. Working from the tautology of the equation of exchange ($MV = PQ$), where the left side reflected expenditures (the money supply times the average velocity of money) and the right side receipts (nominal GDP), the Classical model offered an explanation of the price level. The move from tautology to theory was accomplished by three assumptions: (1) the exogeneity of the money supply; (2) the stability of the velocity of money; and (3) the level of real output depended upon tastes, technology and resources, i.e., real economic variables. Given those assumptions, one can hold V and Q as given and conclude that movements in P must correlate with movements in M. The mathematics of the equal sign compel such a relationship, although the theory as such offers no explanation of causality.

That explanation was provided by integrating the demand for money. If the demand for money (roughly the inverse of velocity) was understood as a demand to hold balances of real purchasing power, then one could explain why changes in the money supply *caused* changes in the price level. Given some demand for real balances, suppose that that demand is being met at the existing price level. Now suppose an increase in the money supply. Because that money must be in the possession of someone, some, perhaps all, agents find themselves with excess real balances. They shed those excesses by spending on goods, services, or financial assets, which drives up their prices. That rise in prices will continue until the price level is high enough to make the new higher level of nominal balances equal to the pre-existing demand for real balances. For the Classical economists, the price level was determined by the interaction between the money supply and the demand to hold money balances.

With relative prices explained by tastes, technology and resources, and the possibility of general gluts or shortages precluded by Say's Law, and the Quantity Theory explaining the price level, the only missing piece was intertemporal exchange. Here the Classical economists argued that the interest rate, understood as the outcome of the interaction of productivity (the demand for loanable funds) and thrift (the supply of loanable funds), would successfully coordinate those intertemporal preferences. In the simplest model, ignoring government and foreign trade, income (Y_i) is made up of either consumption (C) or savings (S), while expenditures (Y_e) were either on consumption goods (C) or investment goods (I) (see Equation 1). Suppose the preferences of income earners shift toward the future, causing a fall in C and an increase in S (see Equation 2). In the classical model, that increase in savings causes a fall in the interest rate, which induces additional investment expenditure. The increase in I implies a fall in C on the expenditure side (see Equation 3). Given that $C_i = C_e$, and that the increase in investment is precisely equal to the increase in savings, then the result of the shift in intertemporal preferences in simply a shift toward the future, but no disruption in the equality between income and expenditure and no change in total income (Equation 4). Central to this story is the assumption that both savers and investors base their decisions solely on the interest rate.

$$(1) \quad Y_i = C_i + S = Y_e = C_e + I$$
$$(2) \quad Y_i = C_i\downarrow + S\uparrow$$
$$(3) \quad Y_e = C_e\downarrow + I\uparrow$$
$$(4) \quad \text{If } S = I \text{ then } Y_i = Y_e$$

It should be clear that the monetary equilibrium approach shares much with the textbook Classical model. In fact, much of what Wicksell's contribution amounts to is more carefully clarifying how, and under what conditions, this textbook story holds. In particular, a monetary equilibrium approach allows us to bring the banking system and money into the Classical story in a more fully-fledged way.

Say's Law and monetary equilibrium

One standard objection to Say's Law is that, as usually stated, it ignores the role of money. This line of argument is that the income generated from supplying goods cannot be directly turned into demand for other goods because of money's role as a medium of exchange. As a result, changes in the demand for money can alter the relationship between aggregate supply and aggregate demand. If the demand for money rises, aggregate demand falls off and, apparently, Say's Law will not hold, given that aggregate demand will be less than aggregate supply. Conversely, a fall in the demand for money will force additional demand into the market, independently of the previous level of supply. More obviously, critics of Say's Law point to the numerous examples of real-world gluts and shortages. If Say's Law were literally true in the way that the Classical economists were sometimes seen as saying, then any example of an existing glut or shortage should disprove it. These objections can be countered by looking at Say's Law through the eyes of monetary equilibrium theory.[22]

One of the problems with discussions of Say's Law is that they tend to forget what Say himself had to say about his supposed law: 'it is production which opens a demand for products . . . Thus the mere circumstance of the creation of one product immediately opens a vent for other products' (Say 1971 [1880]: 133, 134–5). That is, production is the source of demand. One's ability to demand goods and services from others derives from the income produced by one's own acts of production. Wealth is created by production not by consumption. In its naïve version then, Say's insight could be construed to mean that the aggregate level of production always equals the aggregate level of expenditure. However, Say and others recognized that production is not instantaneously transformed into the ability to demand. This process takes place via the medium of exchange. In fact, the ability to demand is predicated on the possession of money. An actor might be potentially very productive, and thus able to demand a great deal of goods and services, but the ability to turn that potential demand into effective demand requires that the productivity be sold for money that can then purchase goods and services. The existence of money breaks any rigid link between production and demand. However, the non-existence of such a tight link does not mean the link between the two is completely broken, rather, it is simply a loose linkage.[23]

In fact, money's role is to provide the link between production and demand. It is only because of the existence of money that it is relatively easy to turn physical or human capital (potential demand) into goods or services for consumption (demand made effective through the use of money). That this link is a loose one simply captures the idea that the relationship between production and demand in a monetary economy will depend on how well money performs its intermediary role. For the translation of aggregate production into aggregate demand to be a one-to-one relationship, the supply of money must be precisely correct, that is, we are in monetary equilibrium. Because all goods markets are also money markets, the only way there can be a general excess supply or demand for goods is if there is an opposite excess supply or demand for money. Take the more obvious case of a glut of goods, such as one might find in a recession. What Say's Law properly understood suggests is that the explanation for an excess supply of goods is an excess demand for money.[24]

Goods are going unsold because buyers cannot get their hands on the money they need to buy them despite being potentially productive suppliers of labor. Conversely, a general shortage, or excess demand for goods, can only arise if there is an excess supply of the thing goods trade against, which can only be money.

Say's Law finds its most accurate expression when we are in monetary equilibrium (see Sechrest 1993: 49ff.). In monetary equilibrium, production truly is the source of demand. If there is an excess demand for money, production is not the source of demand because some potential productivity is not being translated into effective demand. If there is an excess supply of money, demand comes not only from previous acts of production, but also from being in possession of that excess supply, which may have little to do with productivity. What the textbook model of the Classical economists misses is how money and the banking system work to ensure the valid insight behind Say's Law. The money income spent on consumption corresponds to previously supplied productive services, while saving, including the holding of bank liabilities, reflects previous production that will be eventually transformed into effective demand by borrowers through the lending activities of the banking system. The loose linkage provided by money enables this process to take place, and widen and deepen the capital structure with its corresponding positive impact on economic growth. However, it is the very looseness of that linkage that allows the Say's Law process to break down if money is not properly supplied. It is not that Say's Law is invalidated by shortages or excesses in the money supply, rather the beneficence of its effects are lessened.

The Keynesian model from a monetary equilibrium perspective

A detailed critique of all of the problems with Keynesian economics is not one of the central tasks of this study. Previous, more in-depth discussions of the Keynesian approach by those sympathetic to Austrian approaches and monetary equilibrium theory are fairly numerous, and they should be read for more comprehensive critical assessments of Keynes.[25]

One of the difficulties in assessing Keynes, particularly in comparison to monetary equilibrium theory, is that Keynes was familiar with the work of its adherents and changed his mind about the value of monetary equilibrium theory over the course of his own intellectual evolution. For example, *A Treatise on Money* (1930) is, as was noted in the last chapter, very Wicksellian in places and appears to adopt a variant on the monetary equilibrium theme. Six years later, in *The General Theory* (1936), most of this approach has been jettisoned in favor of the income-expenditure model so familiar from textbooks. Because the discussion in Chapter 2 focused on capital and the differences between the two books, this discussion will stick to the Keynesian model as it has been developed through the macroeconomics textbooks.[26]

Many of the problems with the Keynesian model revolve around the monetary theory of the interest rate and the construction of the IS curve, both of which blur over important distinctions. The monetary theory of the interest rate neglects the Wicksellian distinction between the market and natural rate of interest and the IS curve overlooks Myrdal's *ex ante/ex post* distinction. In order to deny the Classical claim that interest rates are determined by the interaction of productivity and thrift, Keynes had to attack both sides of the argument. First, he had to show that the interest rate is determined by monetary factors and then he had to argue that investment and savings could not determine a rate of interest.

To accomplish the first, Keynes expanded on the Marshallian treatment of the demand for money by including the speculative component of that demand. Where previous work had recognized a subsidiary role for the interest rate in determining the demand for money, Keynes put rates front and center in his analysis. By portraying portfolio choice as being between a non-interest-bearing money and interest-bearing bonds, Keynes was able to effectively squeeze out any real relationship between money holdings and the price level. In Keynesian models, any excess supply of money that finds its way into the hands of consumers will be put into the bond market, driving up bond prices and driving down interest rates. The fall in interest rates eventually induces money holders to increase their real balances. An increase in the money supply reduces interest rates, rather than raising the price level, as in the Classical analysis. From this analysis, Keynesians are able to argue that the equilibrium interest rate is not the result of the interaction between productivity and thrift, but the supply and demand for money.

The claim that an unwarranted increase in the money supply will drive down real market rates of interest is consistent with the monetary equilibrium approach. However, when one goes deeper into that process, important differences arise, such as the different processes by which rates are driven down. In the Keynesian model it is money holders who, through their portfolio adjustments, cause the fall in rates. In the monetary equilibrium approach, it is the banking system that drives rates downward. The excess supply of money is presumed to enter the market through bank reserves. With excess reserves, banks lower their market rates of interest in order to attract in marginal borrowers. The loans now made filter their way through the economy, driving up aggregate spending and the price level. The assumption in most textbook Keynesian models of a fixed price level, or of a one-commodity world, is completely consistent with Keynesian treatments of the money–interest relationship. If the results of monetary excesses and deficiencies are all borne by the interest rate, where can one fit in the price level? Conversely, if one assumes the price level is fixed, then the adjustments to monetary disequilibria must take place through some other variable. By eliminating the banking system and by ruling out (almost by hypothesis) the possibility of price level effects tied with changes in market interest rates, these Keynesian models abandon the central concerns of monetary equilibrium approaches since Wicksell.

The abandonment is also clear from the absence of a distinction between the natural and market rate of interest in Keynesian models. The lack of a capital theory in Keynes implies no real concern with issues of intertemporal coordination, as does a one commodity model. The Austrian concern with the role of interest rates in matching up the time-preferences of savers with the time-preferences of borrowers is utterly absent. Keynes' assumptions that saving is a function of income and that investment is driven by animal spirits remove any linkage between future-oriented behavior and the rate of interest. The absence of any notion of the multi-period nature of capital goods also reduces the ways in which intertemporal coordination could take place in Keynesian models. As Garrison (1985: 321) summarizes it: 'there is no *conceivable* market mechanism in the Keynesian vision by which changes in intertemporal consumption preferences could be successfully translated into investment decisions.'[27]

Keynes' concerns were with the current volume of employment and output, not with intertemporal coordination and thus not with the *composition* of either quantity. Therefore, there is no reason for Keynes to be concerned with the natural rate/market rate distinction, as the set of issues that distinction is intended to address were not of concern to Keynes.[28] The Wicksellian analysis tells a story about how intertemporal coordination *might* occur (when the rates are equal) and when it will break down under particular institutional or historical circumstances (when the banking system allows them to diverge, either by commission or omission). By the time of *The General Theory*, the question of how markets might ever get intertemporal coordination right is not one which Keynes can see a possible answer too, thus Wicksell's contribution disappears from the scene.

It should be noted that the natural rate/market rate distinction is also absent from most textbook versions of the Classical model. There is simply 'the' interest rate that appears to perform the task of intertemporal coordination flawlessly. It is very easy to slide from that presentation of the Classical model into a tight linkage view of money and the interest rate, where the existence of money can never disrupt the intertemporal coordination process. In the textbook version of the Classical model, how can one explain the existence of real-world gluts and shortages? That presentation ignores the Wicksellian contribution of emphasizing the role of the banking system in driving a wedge between the natural and market rates. The likely explanation for leaving out the Wicksellian process is that most intermediate level textbooks do not introduce the banking system until much later in the book, well after all of the models have been fleshed out. In addition, it is hard to make much sense out of the Wicksellian concern with intertemporal coordination if one does not have an explicit theory of capital. Many of the Classical economists did not have such a theory, and a meaningful theory of capital is largely absent in both modern micro and macroeconomics.[29] The textbook approach puts monetary equilibrium theory at a disadvantage from the start, as an understanding of the banking system and capital is central to its approach.

The lack of an intertemporal coordination mechanism in Keynesian models is also evident in the IS curve of the neoclassical synthesis. The IS curve shows combinations of levels of income and interest rates (Y and r) at which the goods market (investment and savings) are in equilibrium. The basis for constructing the curve is the assumption that investment is equal to savings. If savings is a function of income (Y) and investment depends to some extent on the interest rate (a slight break from strict Keynesian animal spirits), then the rigid link assumed between investment and savings allows the theorist to relate Y and r. For example, suppose the interest rate rises. Investment will fall as a result, and given the assumption I=S, savings must also fall. The lower level of savings is functionally related to a lower level of income, thus along the IS curve, higher rates of interest are associated with lower levels of income. Movements along the IS curve are conditioned by the I=S equilibrium. Consider also movements in the whole curve. Suppose expectations become brighter, leading to an autonomous increase in investment. This will cause income to rise, via the multiplier. The increase in income will generate precisely enough savings to finance the original increase in investment, maintaining the IS equilibrium at a higher level of income. Once again, the story is constructed with the central assumption of an investment-savings equilibrium.

From a monetary equilibrium standpoint, that assumption obscures the crucial issues. In particular, it treats the definitionally true *ex post* equilibrium of savings and investment as if it implicitly held true *ex ante* as well. In other words, by assuming goods market equilibrium as a condition of the analysis, the IS curve does not allow for the possibility of discoordination, either at a point in time or intertemporally. As Myrdal's (1965 [1939]: 46) work established, the key issue from a monetary equilibrium standpoint is: 'How does [an *ex ante*] tendency to disparity in the saving–investment equation develop into an *ex post* balance?' Once again, the assumption of equilibrium obscures the Mengerian market process by which (1) *ex ante* expectations might be coordinated or (2) *ex ante* expectations that are discoordinated play themselves out to an *ex post* equilibrium. The extra savings or investment needed to turn *ex ante* inequalities into *ex post* equalities must come from somewhere, and that process presumably has important macroeconomic consequences, yet there is nothing in the IS curve construction that permits examination of those questions.

More generally, monetary explanations of the interest rate (to the exclusion of a natural rate concept or a productivity and thrift explanation) such as in both traditional Keynesian models and the neoclassical synthesis, invite a level of aggregation that obscures other fundamental market processes. The problems involved with aggregating additions to the capital structure under the term 'investment' are compounded with a monetary theory of the interest rate. In both traditional Keynesian and IS–LM models, treating the interest rate as a (nearly) pure monetary phenomenon eliminates its role in coordinating the various stages of production. Although the ruling rate of interest plays a central role in the total volume of investment taking place, its more important role is to ensure consistency among the various goods at the various stages in the production process. The uncertainty of the future, so eloquently emphasized by Keynes, requires some process by which producers can form expectations of consumer wants and the prospective value of their intermediate goods. In the Austrian approach, the microeconomics of the interest rate and capital structure are that process. However, if one disconnects the interest rate from both the aggregate supply and demand for capital and the structural composition of that capital, then one loses sight of those coordinative processes, and the way in which mistaken monetary or fiscal policy might undermine them. In the various versions of the Keynesian model, the lack of attention paid to the microeconomic role of the interest rate both allows for the theoretical blindness to how the market might provide coordination and the policy blindness as to why activist fiscal and monetary policy (by driving a wedge between the market and natural rates) might disrupt that coordinative market process.[30]

The Quantity Theory, monetarism, and New Classical economics

The relationship between monetary equilibrium theory and the Quantity Theory of Money has always been a complex one. Wicksell (1965 [1898]) explicitly sees himself as building from what is right in the Quantity Theory but correcting its mistakes and clarifying it where needed. Whatever its flaws, however, 'as an alternative to the Quantity Theory, there is no complete and coherent theory of money' (1965 [1898]: xxiii). Mises (1980 [1912]), although strongly endorsing the general quantity-theoretic proposition that changes in the supply of money will cause changes in the price level, was also careful to point out that aggregative, or 'naïve', versions of the theory could cause as many problems as they resolved. He saw his own contribution as putting the Quantity Theory framework on more solid theoretical ground by explaining its foundation in the subjective theory of value. Myrdal (1965 [1939]: 5–7) is more willing to see monetary equilibrium theory as 'another type of theory' or 'a different sort of monetary explanation'. For Myrdal, the key difference is that the 'new' approach 'no longer places the main emphasis on the amount of means of payment'. The emphasis in monetary equilibrium theory on the relationship between the means of payment and the demand for money (rather than the absolute quantity of money), as well as the implied relationship between the natural and market rates, constitute, in Myrdal's view, a distinct break with the Quantity Theory tradition.

Some of the differences of opinion noted above can be sorted out by distinguishing between the equation of exchange and the Quantity Theory of Money. The equation of exchange is simply the tautological statement that $MV = PQ$: the supply of money multiplied by the average number of times each monetary unit is used in a given period of time will be equal to the nominal value of the things purchased in that period. The equation of exchange simply says 'whatever gets bought, gets sold and both are done using money.' The

Quantity Theory of Money, by contrast, requires the assumptions we noted in the previous section: exogenous money supply, output determined by the real economy, and stable velocity. With those assumptions, the proposition that changes in M are associated with (and, with a transmission mechanism specified, cause) changes in P can be established.

Where the monetary equilibrium approach expands on the Quantity Theory is to offer a way of explaining the causal links between the terms of the theory in cases where the standard assumptions are altered. What monetary equilibrium theory suggests is that it is good policy to allow the nominal supply of money (rather than the price level) to respond to changes in money demand. If we take velocity to be roughly equal to the inverse of the demand for money, we can express this proposition in quantity-theoretic terms. The monetary equilibrium approach would argue that changes in V are the exogenous force, while M should move in response to those changes. An increase in the demand for money (equivalent to a fall in velocity, as money is turned over fewer times because it spends more time in people's real balances), should call forth an equal increase in the money supply. Understood in terms of the equation of exchange, monetary equilibrium is equivalent to holding the left side of the equation (MV) constant. The changes in the money supply in response to changes in velocity would have no effect on either the price level or real output, as long as they were precisely inverse to the velocity change. This is the sense in which Myrdal's claim about the lessened emphasis on the quantity of money is true: in this approach, not all changes in the money supply lead to changes in the price level. Of course, increases or decreases in the money supply that occur without a prior change in velocity will have the price level effects of the traditional Quantity Theory approach. The key to monetary equilibrium theory, however, is the refusal to make the assumption that velocity is stable and to specify what the response of the banking system should be to changes in velocity.

We should also briefly note the implications for the price level if monetary equilibrium results in a constant MV. Obviously, given the equation of exchange, the only way the price level can change if monetary equilibrium is being maintained is through an opposite change in real output, or more specifically, the productivity of the capital and labor that produce it. This topic will require a separate discussion to see its full implications, however, we can note here that monetary equilibrium will not lead to price stabilization. As the real economy becomes more productive, maintaining monetary equilibrium will imply a fall in the price level, while declining productivity (and real output) would lead to an increase in the price level. This conclusion puts monetary equilibrium theory at odds with most Quantity Theory approaches, which argue for some form of price level stabilization. This debate will be covered in more detail below.

The reason for monetary equilibrium theory's concern with the equality of the supply and demand for money (a constant MV) is the relationship between the monetary authority and the process of intertemporal coordination. It is because monetary disequilibria imply divergences between the natural and market rates of interest, which lead to intertemporal discoordination via distortions of the capital structure, that monetary equilibrium theory sees the constant MV as a desirable policy goal. These capital-theoretic microfoundations set the monetary equilibrium approach apart from the two most well-known modern quantity-theoretic approaches: traditional monetarism and New Classical economics.

As Roger Garrison (1989) has argued, all macroeconomic theories must have some account of the failure (and possible eventual self-reversal) of market coordination. In Keynesian models, the absence of a capital market and no apparent alternative market process of intertemporal coordination lead to the unemployment equilibria normally identified with that school of thought and imply aggregate demand management by an extra-market institution such as government as the solution. For monetarism, the story is different. Monetarists too have ignored the capital structure, and instead they have turned to the labor market. Rather than the intertemporal concerns of monetary equilibrium theory, monetarism is more concerned with the 'analysis of labor-leisure distortions spelled out . . . in terms of the short-run and long-run Phillips curve' (Garrison 1989: 17–18).

In the traditional monetarist story, agents are assumed to have adaptive expectations. In other words, they observe past values of a variable, in this case the money supply/price level, and form their expectations based on a weighted (more heavily to the more recent past) average of those past values. If the monetary system has held to zero inflation for a number of periods, then any positive value of inflation will catch workers off guard, leading them to accept greater employment at a lower real wage, bringing the actual rate of unemployment below the natural rate (defined as that rate determined by a real wage based on correct expectations). If the monetary system maintains a consistent policy for some period of time, agents' expectations will eventually catch up with it and perfectly anticipate the policy.[31] As agents' expectations catch up over time, they lessen the ability of the monetary authority to fool them with their current policy. When agents' expectations completely catch up, the economy returns to the natural rate of unemployment. This adjustment process parallels the capital distortion and correction that characterize inflationary monetary disequilibria, but posits the distortions in terms of changes in the level of unemployment in comparison to a natural rate of unemployment, rather than as capital distortions driven by deviations from a natural rate of interest.

The contrast between these two natural rate theories is central to the differences between the two approaches. Where monetary equilibrium theory is concerned with the intertemporal and capital structure effects of inflationary disequilibria, monetarism, because of its implicit Knightian theory of capital, does not possess a way to theorize about intertemporal discoordination and a structure of capital, thus the effects of monetary injections take place through the labor market. This difference is also consistent with the monetarist focus on aggregates such as the price level. In a monetary equilibrium approach with Austrian capital-theoretic foundations, the price level is not nearly as important as the interest rate, which itself derives from the constellation of individual relative prices. If one's theory is designed to explain intertemporal coordination failures, then interest rate problems and the temporal structure of production will be paramount. Where such problems cannot occur, and where labor markets are the focus, the concern will be different. This is even more obviously the case when one's labor market story is concerned with differences between nominal and real wage rates. If, as in the standard Phillips curve story, workers do not foresee a fall in their real wages, and employment rises at the expense of real wages, then the ability of workers to recognize and react to changes in the price level will be the key issue. By implication, preventing unexpected changes in the price level, which are presumably linked through the Quantity Theory to changes in the money supply, will be the primary goal of policy.

Contrast that perspective with monetary equilibrium theory's concern with intertemporal coordination. Here, the price level is of lesser importance than the relationship between existing market rates of interest and the natural rate reflecting the desired depth and width of the capital structure. What makes the price level even less important in monetary equilibrium theory is its level of aggregation. What matters to *producers* (as compared to *workers* in monetarism) is not the aggregate price level but the structure of relative prices, both at a point in time and intertemporally. Stabilizing the price level does not do much good here, and policy should aim at preserving the integrity of the relative price structure.

Some might object by asking why the monetary equilibrium focus on capital is to be prized above the monetarist concern with labor. One response is that while monetarism has no account of capital, monetary equilibrium theory can offer explanations of the idleness and misallocation of both capital and labor. Moreover, on a more inclusive conception of capital that includes human capital, one could subsume the good aspects of the monetarist story under the umbrella of monetary equilibrium theory.[32] However, there are two other responses that are even more powerful. One is that increases in the money supply usually make their way into the market via commercial loans, which suggests that a focus on producers and the effects on such increases on the capital structure makes the most sense. Finally, and most importantly, is the empirical phenomena the theory is trying to explain. The development of the Austrian theory of the business cycle as an explanation of the effects of inflationary monetary disequilibria grew out of the empirical observation that it was the production of higher order goods that was most affected by depressions. As Garrison (1989: 11, emphasis in original) summarizes it:

> it was largely the observed and widely acknowledged movements in capital-goods markets that initially motivated a theoretical explanation. Significantly, the various competing schools of thought – including the

Austrians – used the terms *business cycle* and *industrial fluctuation* synony-
mously. The idleness of producers' goods used in heavy industry was
perceived to be one of the most obvious and dramatic characteristics of
economic downturns.

Of course capital goods idleness would entail some unemployment, but it
was the intertemporal discoordination manifested by the idleness of those
goods particularly far from the final stages of production that was the empirical problem that demanded an explanation.

In the late 1970s and 1980s, the monetarist approach was attacked from
within by those who believed that Friedman's adaptive expectations models
were inconsistent with the utility-maximizing general equilibrium models of
contemporary microeconomics because they allowed agents to make systematic
errors by ignoring current information. What grew out of these concerns was the
New Classical macroeconomics, which is defined by its use of the assumptions
of both rational expectations and general equilibrium. There are numerous
criticisms that one can make of New Classicism from a monetary equilibrium
perspective.[33] Rather than provide a laundry list approach, I wish to focus on
New Classicism's failure (parallel to that of monetarism and Keynes) to integrate
the issues of time, money, and capital that are central to the monetary equilibrium
approach. At one level, those concerns are almost absurd in the world of New
Classicism. If one posits, as it does, a world of perfectly informed, rationally
expecting, agents who are in constant equilibrium, then the whole notion of
intertemporal discoordination makes no sense. By definition, any situation is
coordinated, since all agents are simply responding in utility- or profit-
maximizing ways to the available information, especially prices, and relevant
constraints. Even the concept of capital is hard to squeeze in, as instantaneous
market clearing appears to prevent the time-laden structure of production central
to Austrian capital theory, as well as eliminating any scope for the entrepreneur.
Monetary equilibrium theory's concern with the false signal generated by a
market interest rate not synchronized with the natural rate, leading to systematic
intertemporal errors, is irrelevant in the New Classical world.

As a number of observers have pointed out, many of the problems in the
New Classical approach derive from its failure to distinguish between knowledge *of* the economic system and knowledge *in* the economy. This distinction
seems parallel to Hayek's (1945) distinction between 'scientific' knowledge
and the knowledge of time and place. Denied knowledge of the system as a
whole, Hayekian actors rely on the knowledge imperfectly embedded in
market prices and other institutions to learn about the wants, opportunity
costs, and the failure of their own plans. The learning and feedback process
that characterizes these Mengerian microfoundations is ruled out by hypothesis with the New Classical assumption of instantaneous and continuous
market clearing deriving from its strong assumptions about knowledge.

The strong assumptions of rationality made by the New Classical
economists also enable them to make their case for the impotence of system-

atic monetary policy. As with the monetarists, it is assumed, due to the absence of capital, that labor markets will bear the burden of adjustment. However, in this model, agents are assumed to have rational expectations about the future; that is, their subjective expectations of possible future outcomes correspond to the objective probability distribution of such outcomes. That is not to say they will always get each expectation correct, but it is to say that they will not be systematically wrong – they will make the best guess possible at each point in time. Unlike the monetarist model where agents' expectations might be systematically wrong in the short run but correct in the long run, the New Classical model permits no systematic deviation from the natural rate in either run. The only way agents can be fooled into accepting a lower real wage is through random shocks to the money supply, and thus the price level, which by definition will not be expected.[34] Rational agents act as if they understand the Quantity Theory and are aware of the actions taken by the monetary authority, so they realize that a given increase in the money supply will lead to an equivalent increase in the price level. Workers immediately ask for higher nominal wages to compensate, and with instantaneous auction-market equilibria, they get it, preventing the actual rate of unemployment from deviating from the natural rate in any systematic way. The only deviations one should observe would be random from period to period, reflecting any random shocks to the money supply.

In order to explain empirically observed, serially correlated (i.e., non-random) movements in the unemployment rate, early New Classical models have been embellished to include various informational lags that give agents local information that might be ambiguous with respect to the global situation. The simplest of these models is the island-economy models of Lucas, where agents isolated on islands cannot determine whether a given change in the prices they face is temporary, due to monetary changes, or permanent, due to real factors. Their island isolation prevents them from accessing the global state of affairs, leading them to have to make the best guess they can about the price change. To the extent they guess wrong, their succeeding behavior might lead to changes in the level of employment that deviate from the natural rate. In more sophisticated versions, a weak notion of time enters the story, as decisions that agents make under a false price signal might have multi-period effects that can explain the observed serial correlation in output and unemployment. This brings the New Classical theory marginally closer to monetary equilibrium approaches, but it still fails to account for the possibility of an *ex ante* situation of disequilibrium, such as the market rate/natural rate divergence that interests monetary equilibrium theorists. In addition, the island economy models are but a pale reflection of the more complete time-ladenness of Austrian capital theory. Under the assumption of continual equilibrium, the notion of *ex ante* intertemporal discoordination is senseless.

More important, however, is the aggregation problem that New Classicism shares with monetarism. Without a meaningful presence for capital, the labor market is once again the focus of adjustment, with the price level doing all of the work. The emphasis on the price level once again obscures any changes in relative prices, particularly intertemporal relative prices, that might be taking place 'underneath' those price level changes. As we shall see in the next chapter, this aggregation has important effects on the ways in which New Classicism and monetary equilibrium theory understand the costs and consequences of inflation.

The neutrality of money and price level policy

There are few other concepts in macroeconomics that have as many alternative interpretations as the 'neutrality' of money.[35] There are several ways in which this term is used in the literature and other ways in which it has been used in the past. Despite all this confusion, the idea of neutral money remains useful when deployed with care and a recognition of the concept's limits.

The most common use of neutrality in modern macroeconomics concerns the effects of changes in the money supply on the structure of relative prices. More specifically, money is considered to be neutral if changes in the supply of money do not alter the structure of relative prices. In this view, changes in the supply of money are simply scalars that cause the upward (or downward, during deflation) adjustment of all nominal prices, wages, and money balances by the same factor as the change in the money supply, leaving the relative relationship among all of those prices and money balances untouched. We might refer to this as the 'equiproportionality' view of money's neutrality, in that it sees all relative prices as changing equiproportionately to the change in the money supply. This view is strongly associated with New Classical economics and, to a lesser degree, Friedmanite monetarism. For New Classicism, money is neutral in this sense in both the short and long run (ignoring random shocks), while only so in the long run for monetarism.

A different conception of neutrality is to define a neutral money as one that has no effect on the real economy. It is this latter notion of neutrality that was adopted by both Wicksell and Hayek in their contributions to the broadly defined monetary equilibrium theory tradition. As Hayek (1967 [1935]: 130) sees it, neutral money:

> refers to the set of conditions, under which it would be conceivable that events in a monetary economy would take place, and particularly under which, in such an economy, relative prices would be formed, as if they were influenced only by the 'real' factors which are taken into account in equilibrium economics.

Unlike barter, where the ultimate acts of purchase and sale occur simultaneously, the use of money allows for a temporal separation, creating the possibility of systematic mismatches between the two. If money were neutral, such mismatches would not occur, and the mere existence of money would not disrupt the underlying real economy. This view leads naturally to the monetary equilibrium recommendation that the supply of money be kept equal to the demand to hold it at the ruling price level. Money would be neutral if it simply reproduced the results of a perfectly flexible barter economy.[36]

It is worth noting one central difference between these two conceptions of neutrality. For the 'equiproportionality' view, neutrality is a description of a property a money might have in an economic model. If one can create the conditions under which equiproportionality would be true, then the quantity of money in use in that economy would be utterly irrelevant.[37] For these writers, neutrality is not about monetary policy, but a feature of a general equilibrium model that meets those conditions. For the Wicksell–Hayek view of neutrality, neutral money is understood as a criterion by which monetary policy can be assessed. It is desirable that money should be neutral and the question is how, and to what degree, can a monetary system ensure that neutrality. The desirability of the equiproportionality view of money in the real world is unclear, especially since its applications have all been to theoretical equilibrium models.

The Wicksell–Hayek view of neutrality can be enhanced by linking it back with our previous discussion of the sustainability of the capital structure in monetary equilibrium. Rather than grounding neutrality in some relationship between existing prices and hypothetical equilibrium prices, we can see neutrality as expressing some relationship between money and the capital structure. If the capital structure is understood as being comprised of the various intertemporal prices existing in the market, then money is neutral if the current monetary policy or regime is not a cause of any systematic distortion in those prices, leading to the potential unsustainability of that structure. Changes deriving from the money supply process are not providing too much or too little investment in comparison to voluntary savings, creating the possibility of a sustainable capital structure. In monetary disequilibrium, the mismatch of savings and investment implies a lack of synchrony between the signals facing entrepreneurs and the preferences of consumers, leading to the creation of a capital structure that is unsustainable and must eventually be reversed. It is in this sense that money is neutral in monetary equilibrium. This usage seems consistent with the meaning behind the Wicksell–Hayek conception, but without some of the baggage associated with its linkage to the barter prices of a Walrasian-type equilibrium.

A money that is neutral in the Wicksell–Hayek sense need not be neutral in the modern equiproportionality sense. In fact, as the discussion of inflation in the next chapter will argue, money can never be neutral in the way that New Classicism suggests. Here, too, a monetary equilibrium approach suggests the general reasons why. The New Classical approach is institutionless, particularly with respect to the banking system. Without a meaningful theory of capital, there is no need to include anything resembling a modern banking system and loanable funds market into the analysis. If the banking system is absent, there is no reason to be concerned with the precise ways in which changes in the money supply enter the market. In New Classicism, as in many monetarist models, it is just assumed that additions to the money supply magically appear in the bank balances and pocketbooks of money-users in proportion to their previous holdings. Of course this assumption is not true of the real-world money supply process, where particular banks and thus particular customers receive additions to the money supply first. In this more realistic story, it is easy to see why money is non-neutral in the New Classical sense, because the spending patterns of the first recipients will affect some prices and not others.

A further question is whether, if money is neutral in the Wicksell–Hayek sense, the price level will be stable. Part of the ongoing discussion of the neutrality of money has been the idea that a neutral money should minimize certain costs associated with writing and executing contracts and changing prices. The current debate is between those who believe that a neutral money requires stability in the price level and those who argue that it is better to allow the price level to move inversely to productivity changes. The argument for price-level stability has a long and storied history in macroeconomics, as does what George Selgin has termed the 'productivity norm'.[38]

The case for price-level stability has historically centered around issues of predictability. When writing contracts (whether for wages or debts) denominated in nominal terms, actors would like to know what the price level will be at various points in the future, so they can bring those price level expectations into the contract. If the monetary regime is credibly committed to maintaining a stable price level over time, contractors can safely ignore possible price level changes. Sticking to a price-level stability norm reduces the transactions costs associated with price level uncertainty.[39] Under the productivity norm, future price levels would be uncertain to the degree that productivity changes in the future are uncertain. Critics of the productivity norm, such as Dowd (1995), argue that the costs associated with price and contract adjustment under the productivity norm would be greater than the costs associated with maintaining a stable price level in the face of a productivity shock.[40]

The case for the productivity norm is fairly straightforward. If maintaining monetary equilibrium is desirable, then changes in productivity, which, if left to their own devices, will lead to changes in the price level, should not be offset with any action that undermines monetary equilibrium. For example, suppose an increase in productivity takes place. That shock will tend to drive prices downward. The productivity norm argues that such a fall in prices is perfectly appropriate and any attempt to forestall it will create greater problems. In terms of the equation of exchange, the productivity norm argues that changes in Q should be allowed to have offsetting effects on P (see Equation 5). This keeps the right side of the equation constant, implying that the norm can be achieved by a policy or regime that keeps the left side (MV) constant. Under price-level stability, the productivity-inspired fall in the price level should be offset by an increase in the money supply, which would tend to bring the price level back up. An upward movement in Q should be countered by an upward movement in M to prevent any change in P (see Equation 6).

Achieving this norm would require a policy or regime that used some measure of, or proxy for, the price level and was set up such that the money supply would change appropriately in response to any perceived movement in P.

$$(5) \quad MV = P{\downarrow}\, Q{\uparrow} \quad \text{(monetary equilibrium / productivity norm)}$$
$$(6) \quad M{\uparrow}\, V = P\, Q{\uparrow} \quad \text{(price level stability)}$$

Another way to look at this controversy is whether the price-adjustment costs will be greater if the output price level or the factor price level bears the burden of adjustment in the face of productivity changes. If productivity changes, no more than one of the two price levels can remain stable. The price-level norm implies that factor prices should bear the adjustment burden, while the productivity norm implies that output prices should (Selgin 1995b: 736). Dowd (1995: 726) argues that if productivity shocks are usually across a large number of factors (such as an increase in the productivity of labor generally), the productivity norm would require adjustments in a large number of output prices, while the price-level norm would require adjustments only in the prices of the factor(s) in question. Selgin (1995b: 736–7) responds by suggesting that the empirical evidence shows that perfectly uniform productivity shocks are quite exceptional and that most productivity changes happen in particular sectors, implying that the relative prices of outputs will change as a result, a possibility ruled out by Dowd. In the case of a non-uniform productivity shock, the productivity norm involves fewer prices changes, because both factor and output prices would have to change in order to maintain price level stability, while only output prices would have to change under the productivity norm.

As Selgin (1990: 276) points out, the fewer number of price adjustments necessary under the productivity norm makes it superior by the criterion frequently adopted by price-level stabilization proponents that a desirable norm for monetary policy should be one that recognizes the stickiness of prices and minimizes the number of such adjustments that would need to take place.[41] Stabilizing factor prices has one other advantage. Selgin (1990: 280) argues that other empirical evidence suggests that stickiness in product prices is a result of stickiness in factor prices combined with some sort of mark-up pricing behavior. If so, then under a price-level stability norm, the changes in aggregate demand that will be necessitated by productivity changes will, in turn, necessitate changes in factor prices, whose stickiness will lead to stickiness in output price adjustments. Under the productivity norm, factor prices can remain constant with output prices bearing the adjustment burden necessary to maintain profit margins when unit costs of production change due to productivity. If labor productivity increases, nominal wages need not be changed under the productivity norm, as output prices will fall and the resulting fall in the price level will provide the real wage increase corresponding to the increase in productivity.[42] Output prices can be changed more easily in this case because they are not dependent upon prior changes in (more sticky) factor prices. Moreover, to the extent productivity increases are deliberately aimed at by entrepreneurs, the consequent fall in output prices is both predictable and desirable, suggesting that productivity driven changes in output prices are more easily made than ones deriving from less predictable changes in aggregate demand (Selgin 1990: 280).

One more way to view this debate is the question of whether all changes in the price level are created equal. Dowd's (1995: 730, n13) position appears to be that any and all changes in the price level are highly problematic, regardless of their source. Selgin (1995b: 740, n7) responds by arguing that it is not price level changes in themselves that are problematic, but rather the problem is those changes that come from shifts in aggregate demand and not those associated with aggregate supply. This position is simply another way of saying that it is acceptable for movements in Q to cause inverse changes in P, but not for changes in M (or MV) to do so. Selgin does not expand upon this claim in his exchange with Dowd, but we can explore the logic of his position by linking it back to our discussion of monetary equilibrium and the capital structure.

Simply put, changes in the price level deriving from monetarily-induced movements in aggregate demand, must force the economy out of monetary equilibrium. These changes can be the result of either activist monetary policy unconcerned with price level stability, or changes in the money supply necessitated by the desire to keep the price level stable. In either case, if those changes in the money supply lead to a divergence between that supply and the demand to hold real money balances at the prevailing price level, we will not be maintaining monetary equilibrium. The ensuing monetary disequilibrium will also have capital structure implications. Suppose the monetary authority reacts to a positive productivity shock by increasing the money supply to maintain a stable price level in the face of the downward pressure coming from the productivity increase. From a monetary equilibrium perspective, this will mean that *ex ante* investment will exceed *ex ante* savings and that the market rate of interest will be at a level such that the ensuing capital structure will not be sustainable.

Supply side changes in prices will not be problematic because the increase in productivity will be reflected in a new constellation of relative prices, including intertemporal ones. The change in productivity will alter relative prices all the way through the various stages of production. On the assumption that those changes in productivity occur at specific places, it will be the owners of those factors that are now more productive who will be led to change their prices to correspond to those changes. This point is reinforced by Selgin's argument that because productivity changes are frequently a goal of entrepreneurs, the corresponding price changes can be made fairly easily. When changes in aggregate demand are causing price changes (even those that are designed to maintain a stable price level), those price changes will likely bear little relationship to underlying real factors and be more the result of the particular process by which the monetary disequilibrium is occurring. In the more easily seen case of an increase in the money supply intended to offset the price level effects of a productivity increase, some portion of the investment being driven by the excess supply of money will result from forced savings, and the resulting capital structure will not be consistent with the real underlying time-preferences of the public.[43]

Hayek's article 'Intertemporal Price Equilibrium and Movements in the Value of Money' sheds additional light on this point.[44] There Hayek argued that falling prices in response to an increase in productive efficiency is not only not detrimental, but vital, to maintaining what he called intertemporal price equilibrium (1928: 100). He linked this conclusion to the role that expected prices play in the plan formation processes of individual market actors. Consistent with his own theory of capital, Hayek argued that producers attempt to anticipate their time-paths of production on the basis of differences between current prices and expected prices. Presumably those prices include some consideration of the costs of production. Attempts to maintain price level stability by altering the quantity of money in response to productivity-gener-ated changes in prices will distort that intertemporal pattern of prices and cause time-laden errors in production. Excess supplies of money will lead to too little current production and excess demands for money will cause too much current production (ibid.: 94). Hayek's conclusion on this issue is worth quoting at length:

> Theory has hitherto scarcely progressed beyond this distinction between effects of changes in the price level originating on the one hand from the 'goods side' and on the other from the 'money side'. The view advanced here, that changes in the price level coming from the 'goods side' are not merely not detrimental but are even necessary if disturbances of equilibrium are to be avoided, may still appear to many to have something of the air of para-dox. This is especially so because the view that is dominant today, according to which only an invariable price level will ensure an undisturbed course of production . . . appears to be confirmed by general experience and the results of statistical investigations. Nevertheless the results of my analysis do not seem to me to be in any way in contradiction with the facts.
>
> (ibid.: 100)

Hayek's point can easily be translated into Selgin's terminology if we take 'the goods side' to be aggregate supply and 'the money side' to be aggregate demand. Permitting a productivity-generated (those due to shifts in aggregate supply) decrease (or increase) in the price level enables entrepreneurs to more accurately gauge production over time.[45]

This conception of the role of prices and entrepreneurial plans is rooted solidly in the Austrian theory of capital. The opening two sentences of Hayek's paper refer to the fact that all economic activity takes time and that 'all link-ages between economic processes necessarily involve longer or shorter periods of time' (ibid.: 71). He explicitly states that the only previous work examining the role of prices through time is Bohm-Bawerk (ibid.: 73) and also refers to Wicksell's and Mises' work on interest rates (ibid.: 74). Actors have plans that unfold over time and those plans are informed by prices that have the role of 'guide and regulator of all economic activity in the exchange economy' (ibid.: 71). How particular production processes and capital goods will be used, and when they will be used, are determined by this array of intertemporal prices. When excess or deficient supplies of money are present, as in attempts to offset changes in P coming from changes in Q, this array of prices will be distorted, providing faulty information to entrepreneurs that will be manifested as malinvested capital. Hayek argued that the appropriate monetary response to changes in Q is to allow various individual output prices to fall, so that the intertemporal pattern of prices can adjust to the new level of productivity, by *not* offsetting them with an increase in the money supply. Allowing this intertemporal adjustment process to take place is necessary to maintain money's neutrality (ibid.: 99): 'In describing the damaging effects which can arise from money, however, it is not changes in the value of money which should be at issue, but disturbances of the intertemporal price system which are without any economic function.'

If the case for price level stability is built on theoretical foundations that lack a real treatment of capital, as monetarist and New Classical ones do, it is easy to see why that policy looks superior. Without a theory of capital, one does not have to account for the effects that the necessary money supply changes would have on the capital structure. The price adjustments necessitated by the productivity norm are seen as costly, with no countervailing costs under a price level stability norm. However, on a more Austrian view, maintaining a stable price level will induce distortions in the capital structure that have costs of their own, even if those costs are less visible and more long term. The debate over whether it is more costly for the factor price level or the output price level to do the adjusting can be understood in terms of how either adjustment process affects the capital structure. From a monetary equilibrium perspective, enriched with an Austrian conception of capital, the intertemporal discoordination resulting from the monetary disequilibria necessary to maintain a stable price level in the face of productivity shocks is costly enough to outweigh any adjustment costs associated with the productivity norm.

A brief stocktaking

Before we turn to the detailed analyses of the next three chapters, it is worthwhile to pause to recapitulate the main argument thus far. We have stressed the notion that all macroeconomic analysis must ultimately be understood through the way in which macro-level movements in money and interest rates affect the microeconomic coordination process. In particular, our separate discussion of capital theory gave us a more thorough vision of the intertemporal price coordination process. Consistent with the Introduction's other claim that all macroeconomic analysis must account for the markets for time and money, we have used this chapter to construct an analytical framework that attempts to do just that. By providing a means for understanding how the money supply process is related to the intertemporal structure of production, monetary equilibrium theory enables us to see the important interactions between time and money. It also enables us to see the shortcomings in standard Keynesian models and the monetarist and New Classical models that arose in response to them.

Of central importance to our discussion of monetary equilibrium theory was our attempt to ground it in Austrian capital theory. This vantage point also gives us a way to explore the consequences of monetary disequilibrium. Because other approaches lack a true theory of capital, prior attempts to come to grips with the problems of inflation and deflation have overlooked some of their most harmful consequences. In the next two chapters, that capital-theoretic perspective will be deployed to understand the pernicious consequences of inflation and deflation.

4 Inflation, the market process, and social order

The framework provided by monetary equilibrium theory enables us to examine the economic and political consequences that emerge when the monetary system fails to maintain monetary equilibrium. Given our definition of monetary equilibrium as the equality of the quantity of money with the quantity demanded at the prevailing price level, there are two possible cases of disequilibrium that can occur. The first is when the supply of money is greater than the demand to hold it, and the second is when the supply of money is less than the demand to hold it. These disequilibria can come about because of demand side or supply side changes. In other words, it does not matter whether the inequality of the supply and demand for money occurs because of absolute changes in the money supply, or because of a failure to properly defend monetary equilibrium in the face of changes in the demand for money. Whether due to errors of commission or omission, many of the general effects will be the same, although not all of them. It is the relative relationship between the supply and demand for money that matters the most.

This chapter explores the consequences of the first of those two disequilibria, an excess supply of money. An Austrian perspective will show how the effects of an excess supply of money are far greater and far more pervasive than those presented in standard macroeconomic models. The disruptions caused by monetary disequilibria make themselves felt in each and every market because money trades in each and every market. These disruptions frequently manifest themselves as noisy money price signals, causing entrepreneurs to misallocate resources in a variety of different ways. These misallocations, including those associated with the Austrian theory of the business cycle, are the microeconomic effects of inflation. The pervasiveness of money and the centrality of price coordination imply very significant costs and consequences of inflation.[1] The waste engendered by inflation is analogous to the welfare costs of tariffs, monopolies, and theft identified by Gordon Tullock (1967). Existing literature on waste in alternative institutional arrangements helps us to understand the welfare costs of inflation.

The microeconomic havoc caused by inflation also has political consequences. To the extent that inflation undermines the communicative function of prices, it more generally undermines the efficacy of the market as a discovery process. At the margin, this will lead to increased calls for political intervention, with all of the problems such intervention brings with it. There is more truth than commonly recognized to the claim that there is no surer way to undermine capitalism than to debauch the currency.

Inflation and an excess supply of money

The standard use of the term 'inflation' is 'a rise in the general price level', or, what amounts to the same thing, 'a fall in the value of money'. Excesses in the supply of money are not the only factors that can cause movements in the price level; changes in productivity can also have across-the-board effects on prices. Although money-side changes and goods-side changes can both cause the price level to move, whether price level movements are benign will depend upon the side from which they emanate. Supply-side changes, such as productivity changes, are desirable, while demand-side changes, such as an excess supply of money, are not. The actual movement in the price level in any given period of time is likely to be a combination of both effects, rendering the job of historically separating the benign from the deleterious changes very difficult.[2]

Although the chapter's title makes use of the word 'inflation', it is not *all* upward movements in the price level that will be its concern. We will ignore negative productivity shocks and other possible non-monetary events that might cause the price level to rise, and focus on inflation caused by an excess supply of money. All upward movements in prices we discuss will be due to changes in aggregate demand via the money supply. Other cases do not concern us here, as the effects of monetary disequilibrium demand our attention. Monetary disequilibrium analysis offers a deeper understanding of the costs of inflation, especially when we examine inflation's effects on the capital structure.

The standard economics of inflation

Modern neoclassical monetary theory has spent significant energy attempting to come to grips with the effects of inflation. We can very generally group these attempts into two broad categories: the effects of neutral inflations and the effects of inflations that involve changes in the structure of relative prices.[3] Most neoclassical inflation stories begin by assuming that additions to the money supply enter the economy evenly across money holders. That is, *it is assumed that the nominal* (and, for the time being, real) *money balances of everyone are increased by the percentage increase in the money supply.* These excess real balances are then spent, either on goods and services, driving up the price level, or on financial assets, driving down interest rates. The rising price level and falling interest rates increase the quantity of nominal money balances demanded. The process ends when the price level has risen enough, and/or the interest rate has fallen enough, to restore money holders to their pre-inflation equilibrium real balances. It is frequently further assumed that the effects of the rising price level are evenly distributed across the prices of individual goods and services, so that those prices increase equiproportionately with the increase in the money supply. In the face of a 10 percent increase in the money supply, not only would the aggregate price level rise by 10 percent but so would the price of each and every good and service. This corresponds to the neoclassical use of the term 'neutrality' we identified in the previous chapter.

If inflations were neutral in this sense, then clearly they would not deserve to be feared as much as the public actually fears them. If they were to have no effect on relative prices, then they would have little or no effect on resource allocation. The allocation of resources depends upon relative prices. If we begin in equilibrium and then have an inflation that affects all prices equally, nominal values will change, but relative prices will not, since all prices have increased equally. Therefore resources would be allocated as they were prior to the inflation. If this is an accurate description of real-world inflations, then there indeed is reason to wonder why the public considers inflation to be so bad. Neoclassical economists have investigated what (if any) costs inflation would impose if it were neutral.

In the simplest case, assume that inflation is both neutral and *anticipated*. One effect of that inflation will be that by reducing the real rate of return from holding money (or alternately, raising the opportunity cost of holding non-interest-bearing money balances by raising the nominal interest rate on other assets), it acts as a tax on money balances.[4] Actors are induced to hold inefficiently small money balances.[5] The effort to hold smaller real balances consumes time and 'shoe leather' in additional transactions costs. In struggling to keep up with rising prices, money users will spend more money more frequently and will have to make additional trips to the bank to continually replenish their real money balances. These trips to the bank would not be necessary in the absence of the inflation, and thus represent a cost imposed by it. These costs occur even if the inflation is neutral and anticipated and will be magnified as the rate of inflation increases.

The welfare loss associated with inflation is 'fully analogous to the welfare cost (or "excess burden") of an excise tax on a commodity or productive service' (Bailey 1956: 93–4), and can be approximated by comparing the area under the demand curve for real balances before and after the inflation. The difference between them represents lost 'consumer' surplus. Later studies have extended the notion of this welfare loss to include the costs associated with using alternatives to money and the negative effects on the growth in the capital stock resulting from inflation-induced shifts away from both consumption and investment.

Various studies have attempted to quantify this inflation-generated welfare loss. Such estimates vary widely with the model used and the assumptions made. In general, the earlier estimates, using just the 'area under the demand curve' approach, were rather low, on the order of well under less than 1 percent of national income for inflation rates of around 4 percent. However, when one includes the costs of using alternatives to money and the capital stock effects, the estimates begin to climb into the neighborhood of 3 to 8 percent of national income for similar levels of inflation. Though just a small portion of the total costs of inflation, the problems identified by this approach are not completely trivial, although all involve assumptions and empirical techniques that could be biasing the results in either direction (Dowd 1996: 463–6).

Anticipated neutral inflations also force sellers to expend additional resources in order to more frequently change prices.[6] These so-called 'menu costs' will vary directly with changes in the rate of inflation. The more quickly prices are rising, the more often sellers will have to adjust them. The time spent in remarking inventory, or reprogramming computers, reflects a cost imposed by inflation. Note that these costs exist even if inflation is perfectly anticipated. Even if sellers instantly and correctly adjust prices from their pre-inflation equilibrium values to the post-inflation equilibrium, they must still expend time and resources in doing so.

If the inflation is neutral, yet not anticipated, an additional problem is the redistribution of wealth from creditors to debtors (Alchian and Kessel 1959). If the increase in the price level is unanticipated, and therefore not part of debt contracts, debtors will be paying back their nominally-denominated debts in real dollars that are worth progressively less. In real terms, they will have borrowed more than they are paying back. Unanticipated inflation reduces the burden on debtors and harms creditors. One might object that this is not really a 'cost' of inflation, because it amounts to a redistribution, not a net loss. However, if the inflation rate becomes more variable and less predictable as it rises, higher inflation will shift the supply curve for credit to the left as risk-averse lenders become less willing to lend at any real interest rate (they require an inflation-risk premium). The shrinkage of the credit market imposes a real loss in comparison with a world of zero inflation.

Even if inflations are believed to be neutral in the neoclassical sense, they still create welfare losses associated with sub-optimal money holdings (banking transactions costs), and menu costs, as well as the redistributive effects if the neutral inflation is unanticipated. Glossing over the debates over the empirical estimates of the costs of the tax on money balances, the sum of these effects does not seem to be mammoth. Surely shoe leather and menu costs are but a very small fraction of GDP. It would not be surprising if economists concluded that the costs associated with inflation, at least neutral inflations, were small enough to justify the potential gains in employment or output thought to be possible with slow, steady inflations. However, the other line of more recent research on the effects of inflation undermines this argument by focusing on the non-neutral effects of inflation. Here the concern is with the way inflation might affect relative prices.

The literature on inflation and relative prices (both the theory and empirics) is broad, deep, and complex. The present discussion can only scratch the surface and present the main lines of thought in a very general way. The critical overview in Dowd (1996: Chapter 15) is more detailed and thorough than what will follow. The literature can be, once again broadly, further divided into the relative price effects of anticipated and unanticipated inflations.

Even anticipated inflations can involve non-neutralities. This result can be derived from the menu cost approach mentioned previously. Because of the costs involved in making price changes and in recognizing the need to make such changes, prices will not move upward smoothly and instantaneously during inflations. Rather, they will be changed at discrete intervals. If the nature of those costs, plus other institutional factors in the marketplace, differ from firm to firm, which seems likely, each firm will have slightly different intervals at which it remarks prices. So even if the inflation is smooth and anticipated, at any given moment during the process some prices will have fully adjusted upward while others will have not (Caplin and Spulber 1987). As a result, at any moment, the vector of relative prices will not be the equilibrium one. The consequence of this variability in relative prices is resource misallocation, as not all existing market prices correspond to their equilibrium values. On this view, inflation causes diminished economic welfare by inducing resource misallocation through relative price effects even when that inflation is anticipated.

Most of the relative price effects literature has explored unanticipated inflations. The general proposition here is that agents have difficulty distinguishing between fluctuations in the real economy and inflation-induced changes when inflations are unanticipated. Agents face a signal extraction problem with respect to the price of the good or service they sell. When the prices of their goods begin to fluctuate they need to be able to distinguish the component of those price changes that is due to inflation from that which can be attributed to changes in underlying supply and demand conditions. If agents are perfectly able to extract the real signals from the noisy, inflation-ridden price changes, then no relative price effects will occur since they will then respond appropriately to the new prices. However, to the extent agents are unable to disentangle the two components of the change in price, they will mistake one kind of price change for another and therefore alter their behavior in ways that are in contradiction with the underlying fundamentals.

There are two ways in which such signal extraction problems might take place, both of which derive from the Lucas island economy models. In the first case, agents see the prices of their goods increase, and they must decide whether those price changes are specific to their products or reflective of a change in the overall price level resulting from inflation. If agents had perfect knowledge of their specific island and the general economy they could make such distinctions and adjust their production accordingly. However, lacking the knowledge of the general economy, they are forced to make their best guess at the source of the price change. To the extent their expectations are incorrect due to their incomplete knowledge, relative prices will be thrown out of equilibrium and resource misallocation will occur.[7] Presumably, one way to avoid these sorts of relative price effects is to try to make inflation information as global as possible so as to avoid or significantly reduce the signal extraction problem.

Another version of the same problem is found in Cukierman (1982). Here the confusion is not over the specificity or generality of the price change but its permanence. Agents are assumed to possess the same (perfect) past and present price and quantity information, but lack complete information about how permanent those prices and quantities will be. If a given price change is temporary, due to the effects of inflation, agents will want to react to it differently than if the change is believed to be permanent, due to underlying real factors. The key is that agents cannot know *a priori* whether a given price change is temporary or permanent. Rather they 'learn whether a change is permanent mostly by observing whether it persists over time or not' (Cukierman 1982: 132). As a result, agents have to make their best guess as to the permanence of the price change, and, again, to the extent they are wrong, relative prices will be altered. One consequence is that misperceptions of the permanence of a price change will persist through time until agents are able to learn enough to correct their earlier errors. Even though these models assume equilibria obtain in each period, such equilibria are partial-information equilibria, and the persistence of price misperceptions is manifested in prices and outputs that deviate from what would obtain in a full information equilibrium. As Cukierman (ibid.: 132) notes, one important difference between the 'permanence' confusion and the 'general-specific' confusion is that the former cannot be lessened by the publication of aggregate economic data. The degree of permanence of real changes will differ from industry to industry and will be difficult to know *a priori*, even if one were aware of the rate of inflation. In both versions of the signal extraction story, agents' misperceptions of the real meaning of price changes cause the relative price structure to deviate from where it 'should' be.[8]

Whatever the explanation for the phenomenon, there is ample evidence to indicate that such relative price dispersions occur during inflation.[9] For mainstream macroeconomics, these dispersions of relative prices reflect welfare losses because they involve deviations from the equilibria that are presumed to obtain in the absence of inflation. The discussion of the signaling role of prices in Chapter 1 emphasized that Austrian approaches to this issue emphasize the disequilibrium informational properties of prices rather than their equilibrium properties. Claims about losses arising from prices being out of equilibrium are not all that interesting to Austrians, as prices are thought to be always in disequilibrium. For Austrians, the question is what inflation does to prices that are already in disequilibrium and already involve interpretive problems for actors. To what degree, and how, does inflation make disequilibrium prices more troublesome as informational signals?

Moreover, Austrians are likely to ask whether this scrambling of the informational content of disequilibrium prices involves further economic and social costs, and, if so, what are they? These are questions that take us beyond the narrow confines of mainstream economics and into the broader world of the relationships between the economic, the political and the social. As Dowd (1996: 509) puts it:

Yet there are reasons to believe that much of the damage done by inflation arises precisely because it undermines certain features of the environment – features, moreover, on whose integrity the economic order, and more broadly the social order, depends if it is to function well. We can no longer assume that people's attitudes, exchange processes, contract forms, the legal system, or other social institutions remain substantially unaffected by inflation. Indeed, the very distinction between 'economic' and 'social' or other spheres on which we traditionally rely now breaks down, and we can no longer take the latter for granted while we play around with the former. We are no longer dealing with narrowly defined economic effects, but with much broader social repercussions of staggering complexity. These broader effects are perhaps the most important consequences of all, and we should not ignore them simply because we do not know how to model them.

The remainder of this chapter takes up Dowd's challenge.

Comparative institutional approaches

There are a number of ways to assess the welfare losses and broader consequences attributable to inflation other than by standard economic modeling. Economists try to make such welfare assessments in a variety of areas all of the time. For example, consider the textbook approach to competition and the welfare costs of monopoly. The monopolist is able to charge a price greater than marginal cost, make profits in the long run, and receive a larger amount of surplus than under perfect competition. Moreover, under monopoly, the total gains from exchange will be less than those available under perfect competition. These lost gains from exchange give economists reasons to condemn monopoly on welfare grounds. The divergence between price and marginal cost renders monopoly inefficient.

On this assessment strategy, existing market structures or practices can be compared to the welfare-maximizing efficiency of the perfect competition model and be found wanting. Because existing market outcomes do not look like the economist's model of efficiency, they are to be condemned and, presumably, altered by government policy to look more like the model of perfect competition. Leaving aside the question of whether the world described by perfect competition is a desirable one, there is a deeper question of whether comparisons with perfection are the best way to assess real-world outcomes, particularly if that perfection is beyond our ability to achieve. Many critics of what Harold Demsetz has termed the 'Nirvana' approach have tried to articulate alternative perspectives for assessing economic outcomes. The best alternative to these Nirvana approaches is a comparative institutions perspective.

Such a perspective requires that we ask what the institutional order of the market would look like with a given practice or policy and what it would look like otherwise, and attempt to compare the results. To pursue the microeconomic example for a moment, suppose we decide that advertising is monopolistic and ought to be outlawed. The Nirvana approach might support such an argument on the grounds that advertising expenditures would not be necessary if the world looked like perfect competition. A comparative institutions approach would ask, instead, what would be the likely effects on really-existing market processes if advertising were prohibited? The conditions of perfect competition are irrelevant to trying to trace out the likely consequences (especially the unintended ones) of such a policy change. The comparison is between an imperfect real world with advertising and an imperfect real world without it.[10]

The more difficult question is deciding on the criteria of comparison. What makes one institutional arrangement superior to another? Ultimately, one would hope, the answer is that people in a superior order can live better lives than those in an inferior one. A detailed discussion of what 'better' might mean in this context is beyond the bounds of this study, but given our earlier discussions we can make use of a proxy for 'better'. From an Austrian perspective, 'better' here will be taken to mean that there is a greater possibility of learning from one's mistakes and correcting them in ways that will enhance plan coordination. To the extent that a policy leads to an institutional order that is less reliable in enabling people to perform this epistemic task, that policy is making people worse off. If removing that policy enhances the epistemic task of social institutions, then its removal makes people better off. By judging alternative institutional arrangements by the degree to which they facilitate learning and error correction, we recognize the condition of radical ignorance faced by actors in any real-world situation and place the ability to deal with that ignorance as the fundamental task facing any set of social and economic institutions.[11] It is the ability of alternative institutions to cope with situations of disequilibrium that matters.

In addition, an Austrian perspective also emphasizes the role of subjectivism in the criteria of assessment. By making plan coordination and learning the crucial issues, Austrians recognize that it is the degree to which individual actors can achieve their purposes and execute their plans that matters for economic welfare. Non-Austrian approaches that focus on surplus or other more 'objectivist' measures of welfare (even when comparing institutions) miss what is fundamental about economic processes – their ability to enable individual actors to do the things those actors subjectively perceive as important.

How would we go about assessing the welfare effects of inflation in this manner? Given our understanding of how the price system and market process operate in the absence of inflation (as discussed in Chapter 1), we can then ask what the effects of inflation would be on that process and see how well an inflation-ridden market process facilitates plan coordination in comparison. More specifically, we can examine the degree to which inflation leads to wasted resources. One of the key arguments to be defended in this chapter is that inflation involves some significant welfare losses, understood both as a diminution in actors' ability to execute plans and learn from their mistakes, and as wasted expenditures induced by the inflation process. The first set of welfare losses results because inflation interferes with the price system's ability to serve as a communication process for economic actors. The second type of loss refers to the ways in which inflation diverts resources away from the direct satisfaction of human wants, toward activities that do not directly satisfy such wants and would not take place if the economy were in monetary equilibrium.

We can legitimately refer to these diverted resources as waste because in the absence of inflation, those resources could be used for direct want-satisfaction. As Richard Wagner (1980: 30) put it:

> Wastage of what could have been produced to satisfy human needs, had the monetary expansion not discoordinated individual plans, is also a cost of that expansion. . . . Different institutional orders will entail different degrees of waste, and an 'ideal' institutional order will entail the natural rate of waste.

For Wagner, the comparison is always among the degrees of waste produced by feasible orders. Even the ideal order is not waste-free, rather it simply produces the minimal level of waste feasible. We can then see the wastes associated with inflation as being those resource expenditures made to combat the effects of inflation that would not occur in its absence and could instead be devoted to other more productive uses. This conception of waste is the same one at work in the public choice literature on rent-seeking. Tullock (1967: 44) describes the wastefulness of rent-seeking the following way: 'These expenditures . . . are purely wasteful from the standpoint of society as a whole; they are spent not in increasing wealth, but in attempts to transfer or resist transfer of wealth.' In a later section, we will explore in much more detail the ways in which the wastes of inflation parallel the wastes of rent-seeking, in that both can be understood from a comparative institutions perspective.

The kind of waste that Wagner and Tullock point to will also not be captured by conventional GNP or GDP measures. The expenditures associated with rent-seeking or induced by inflation are counted as part of those statistical aggregates. Wagner (1980: 31) makes this point: 'The way that [national income] accounts are constructed, resources devoted to the correction of error are valued equivalently with resources devoted to other production.'[12] The payments for final goods and services associated with rent-seeking and coping with inflation are counted in GDP even though they represent a loss in want-satisfaction compared to an inflation-free economy. One important implication of this point is that the resource waste associated with inflation will probably be very understated if one looks primarily to GDP figures to measure it. Even in economies subject to significant levels of inflation, GDP numbers will tell only a small part of the whole story. Because they do not make the distinction pointed to by Wagner, GDP figures tend to understate the costs of inflation, which is to say that they overstate the health of inflation-ridden economies.[13]

Inflationary monetary disequilibria

We can begin by expressing some of the consequences of inflation in terms of our monetary equilibrium framework from the last chapter. As we have already seen, inflationary monetary disequilibria are those where the supply of money is greater than the demand to hold it at the prevailing price level. This excess supply of money has important consequences for the various other conditions of monetary equilibrium as well as for the way in which Say's Law operates.

The implications of an excess supply of money for the loanable funds market are straightforward (see Figure 4.1). To see these most simply, let us assume that the excess supply is created by a deliberate policy move by the monetary authority, rather than by not reducing the supply in response to a fall in demand. In line with the way inflation actually operates in contemporary central banking systems, let us also assume that the excess supply of money is created by an injection of bank reserves through an open market purchase, with the demand for real balances remaining constant. As a result, banks now have excess reserves to lend out, and this excess will cause banks to lower the rates of interest they are charging in order to induce in additional borrowers for those excess reserves, increasing the level of investment (shown by the S+ΔMS dotted line in Figure 4.1). In Wicksellian terms, *ex ante* investment (I') will exceed *ex ante* savings (S') and the market rate of interest (r') will fall below the natural rate (r^*).

At the lower market rate, investors will be more interested in borrowing and longer-term investment projects in particular will be more attractive at the new rate. However, because the time-preferences of consumers have not changed, there is no reason to expect that *ex ante* savings will have changed. If anything, the fall in the market rate of interest on loans might be linked to a fall in rates on deposits, discouraging some forms of saving. In either case, the additional borrowing that is taking place is not being financed by the

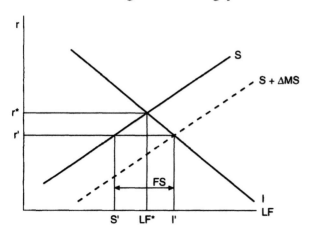

Figure 4.1   Forced savings in the loanable funds market

voluntary savings of the public. This mismatch between the time-preferences of the public and the cost of funds faced by investors will be dealt with in more detail in our discussion of the Austrian theory of the business cycle. For now, we can make the more general point that such intertemporal discoordination is created during inflation.

Our previous discussion of the Swedish distinction between *ex ante* and *ex post* values gives us a way to talk about the process by which the *ex ante* divergence in the loanable funds market is reconciled *ex post*. Banks are *in fact* making loans with the excess supply of money, so additional quantities of investment are *in fact* taking place, even if the public does not want that outcome, as reflected in their unchanging time preferences.[14] In Figure 4.1, I′ is the actual quantity of investment occurring after the increase in the money supply. Because *ex post* investment must equal *ex post* savings and *ex ante* investment is greater than *ex ante* savings during inflation, the missing savings to finance the investment that is occurring must come from somewhere. The total amount of *ex post* savings is greater than what the public voluntarily wishes, with the difference being referred to as 'forced savings' (FS).[15] The term forced savings indicates that some actors in the economy are seeing their purchasing power reduced against their will in order to finance the additional claims to resources provided to the recipients of the additional loanable funds.

The forced savers are the existing holders of money. Their ability to consume is impaired by the influx of new purchasing power represented by the excess supply of money. Those who receive the excess dollars get an increase in their proportional (to the total amount of dollars) claims over resources, while the proportional claims contained in previous holders' dollars are diluted by the increase in the total amount of dollars available for purchasing goods and services. Consider the following simple example. Suppose the total money supply is $1000, which is held by 10 persons in equal $100 balances. Now suppose the central bank increases the money supply by $500, but this $500 is all loaned to one of the 10 persons. Who gains and who loses from this increase in the money supply? The winner is obvious: the recipient of the excess supply of money now holds $600 of the $1500 total money supply. She previously had 1/10th of the total purchasing power but now has 6/15th, for a gain of 6/15 − 1/10 = 3/10. Her gain of 3/10ths of the purchasing power must be offset by some loss somewhere because the creation of an excess supply of money does not create additional goods, it only creates additional claims to the existing supply of goods. Who is losing here? The losers are the other nine money holders. Prior to the central bank injection, each held 1/10 of the total purchasing power, now each holds 1/15. That works out to a per person loss of 1/30 (1/10 − 1/15) of the purchasing power, or a collective loss of 9 × 1/30 = 9/30 or 3/10. The 3/10ths gain of the recipient of the excess money supply is matched by an equal aggregate loss of the non-recipients of that excess supply. An involuntary transfer of purchasing power has occurred, with non-recipients of the excess supply of money being forced to 'save' (understood as a fall in the ability to consume).

This provides a convenient way to define forced savings. Forced savings are the forced reduction in the purchasing power of non-recipients of excess supplies of money. The concept of forced savings explains the process by which *ex ante* divergences between investment and savings are turned into *ex post* equalities. The implications of forced savings are several. At one level, we might raise normative objections to a process that distributes wealth away from some market actors without their consent. A positive analysis can show how even though forced savings provide the resources necessary to undertake the inflation-driven investments, they cannot render the ensuing capital structure sustainable because the savings are not reflective of the actual time-preferences of the actors from whom the savings has been involuntarily extracted. Eventually some or many of the investments made during the inflation process generating the forced savings will be discovered to be in error, as the genuine time-preferences of consumers make themselves known and their inconsistency with the interest rate signal becomes clear.

An excess supply of money means that for the recipients of the forced savings, their effective demand is greater than their notional demand, i.e., their monetary purchasing power is greater than the real value of the productive services they have supplied. The receipt of the excess money does not reflect previous supplies, because the new recipients earn their purchasing power through either sheer luck or by being at the right place in the money supply process (Wagner 1977: 406). The whole chain of spending that the inflation generates, beginning with the original loan of excess reserves that starts it, is the result of the caprices of monetary policy, and is 'paid for' with purchasing power involuntarily relinquished by third parties. As such it does not represent a genuine market assessment, as sales of goods and services do in the absence of inflation. For those lucky enough to find themselves in this spending chain early enough so that they see an increase in their income before prices rise sufficiently to cancel it out, there is a gain in real purchasing power without a genuine act of production behind it. In addition, the victims of forced saving see their notional demand drained away as it is translated into effective demand. Their lost purchasing power drives a wedge between the value of the services or resources they have supplied and their resulting ability to demand through the use of money. In these ways, Say's Law (in the sense that the ability to demand derives from previous production) fails to hold for many, if not all, individuals during the inflation process, although it is still true in the aggregate that the total demand for goods and services derives from the total level of production.

Relative price effects and monetary calculation

In the standard view of inflation we discussed above, relative price effects involve costs because they throw the economy out of equilibrium. This argument is consistent with the now generally accepted proposition that prices provide information to market agents. On this view, inflation makes price signals informationally inefficient by injecting 'noise' into the otherwise fully-informative equilibrium price. This noise is what creates the signal extraction problem and the resulting relative price effects and resource misallocation. However, as we pointed out in our discussion of prices and knowledge, the standard argument is usually phrased in terms of the informational properties of equilibrium prices, whereas the Austrian focus is on the epistemic role of disequilibrium prices. Moreover, in exploring the effects of inflation on micro-economic equilibria, the standard accounts adopt a picture of the production process consistent with their use of equilibrium models. That is, the disequilibrium prices produced by the relative price effects of inflation are fed through production and utility functions and lead to less than Pareto-optimal results. The static nature of this vision of economic activity obscures the ways in which the relative price effects of inflation play havoc with the whole discovery process of the market.

In contrast to the standard picture where excess supplies of money enter the market through a helicopter-like process, an Austrian analysis begins with the recognition that such excesses enter at specific times and in specific places depending on the particular actions taken by the monetary and fiscal authorities. Empirically, if additions to the money supply are made through open market operations, new reserves arrive at those banks who either sell securities directly to the Fed, or to those banks who have the accounts of security dealers who participate in FOMC transactions. Specific banks receive the new money first, and their decisions about what loans they will then make, and the spending decisions of the recipients of those loans, will be the proximate causes of a first round of relative price effects. Because the first recipients of the excess money will spend it on specific goods, the prices of those specific goods will rise first. The sellers of those goods will see additions to their money holdings, which, assuming no change in velocity, will be spent on other specific goods, whose prices will rise. On this more institutionally-rich view of the inflation process, relative price effects are not simply the result of confusing a general price increase with a relative price increase, or of the costs involved in changing prices (though these do exist), rather they are inherent in the very institutional processes by which inflationary increases in the money supply take place.

The ways in which the recipients of the excess supplies of money decide to dispose of their excess real balances will begin the process of relative price disruption. The goods that see increases in their demands due to the inflation will see their prices rise, while other goods' prices will not. The sellers of the highly-demanded first-round goods will now have additions to their real balances and will spend them on other goods and services, whose prices will rise accordingly. As the excess supply of money diffuses through the market, prices will be affected in numerous (and unpredictable) ways. At the end of the process, the entire constellation of relative prices will differ from what it was prior to the inflation, and from where it would have been had the inflation not taken place. These kinds of relative price effects are inherent in all real-world inflationary episodes.

This point is even clearer when we examine the political motivations behind inflation. As has long been argued, governments that print money create seigniorage revenue for themselves, making inflation a politically preferred alternative to direct taxation. However, inflation can do more than just create general benefits for political actors. As Richard Wagner (1980: 11) argues, politicians gain very little through policies that affect all voters equally, rather:

> political action is concerned with achieving desired changes in the structure of prices. Any change in the level of prices that may happen to result because of a resort to money creation is an incidental by-product of the effort to change the structure of prices.

By altering relative prices, political actors can confer benefits on those voters whose support is most needed. Simply raising all prices equally would bring in the general benefit of seigniorage, but would forgo the potential benefits from inflation's differential effects on various groups. Wagner (1977: 401) makes this point the following way:

> Such a nondiscriminatory increase in aggregate spending as would result from a helicopter drop would confer benefits on such nonmarginal voters as strong supporters of both the incumbent party and the opposition. This type of policy would yield less political support than one that is designed to modify the structure of relative prices, for this latter type of policy would make it possible to concentrate the benefits on voters who are believed to be marginal in the forthcoming election.

Certainly, elected politicians cannot precisely control the paths that excess supplies of money take through the economy. However, they can influence whether the new money comes in through additions to bank reserves which, by lowering market rates of interest, might help those voters who have more indebtedness (agriculture or corporate borrowers, perhaps). Moreover, if inflation is being used to finance deficit spending, one can argue that the politicians can direct the additional spending toward specific interest groups or voters. Not only are relative price effects inherent in even politically-neutral money supply processes, the existence of political benefits from inflation create additional incentives to supply money in amounts and ways that affect relative prices.

One of the problems for a disequilibrium analysis of relative price effects is determining the nature of the distortion they create. From an equilibrium perspective, it is easy to talk about distortion by measuring the degree to which actual disequilibrium prices diverge from equilibrium values. However, if we wish to avoid either using equilibrium as a benchmark or assuming that in the absence of inflation prices would converge to their equilibrium values, we need some other way of talking about the distortions caused by relative price effects. The most obvious solution is to argue that inflation causes the induced variables of money prices to diverge from the underlying variables of tastes and preferences. A critic might respond by claiming we are still making an equilibrium argument here, by appearing to assume that in the absence of inflation the induced variables would line up with the underlying variables. Instead of arguing that way, we might ask what it is that inflation does to the relationship between the role of market prices as guides to production and the ability of entrepreneurs to get at the preferences that underlie them.

The key to a disequilibrium approach to relative price effects is to recall our discussion of monetary calculation from Chapter 1. What is important for our purposes is that the key aspect of this process is what Mises called the 'appraisement' of future conditions.[16] The process through which entrepreneurs formulate their expectations of the future constellation of prices begins with an examination of current relative prices, but adds to that a *verstehen*-like psychological understanding of the likely preferences and actions of others in the market. This knowledge is what Mises (1985 [1957]) would later call 'thymological' knowledge. Entrepreneurs combine the general information provided by current prices with their own particular understandings of human behavior to form their expectations of future prices. Profits thus reflect the accuracy of that thymological knowledge.

This entire process is taking place in disequilibrium. The current array of prices has embedded in it all sorts of producer and consumer errors and we are not making any assumptions about the 'rationality' of entrepreneurial expectations, other than that they draw upon their own general knowledge of other humans, and their unique histories and circumstances, in forming such expectations. The use of monetary calculation is the way in which actors attempt to overcome the immense epistemic problem they face in sorting out which production processes are economically rational in a world of heterogeneous capital goods. Equilibrium models assume such problems have already been solved, while the entrepreneurial discovery process view of the Austrians attempts to explain how we ever solve them.

The relative price effects associated with inflation affect monetary calculation in a number of related ways. All of these problems involve increased epistemological burdens on market actors. Because changes in the structure of relative prices now arise from both 'real' side changes in preferences and opportunity costs and 'money' side changes related to the inflation process, entrepreneurs who wish to form expectations of future prices must account for not only the market behavior they have always had to, but also the effects of the inflation. The standard literature on signal extraction problems recognizes this problem, but in a far more simplistic way than an Austrian perspective does. Where prices are seen only as inputs into a production function, it is natural to see the extent of the signal extraction problem as simply concerning the permanence or specificity of the price change. If all production is 'functional', the role of prices (and other forms of knowledge) in helping entrepreneurs to discover what to produce and how to produce it will be absent. Once the permanence or specificity of the price change is decided upon, the entrepreneur's task is complete in the neoclassical conception. For Austrians, the problem is much richer.

We can link these relative price effects back to our discussion of the three knowledge functions of prices from Chapter 1. The forward-looking (*ex ante*) informational role of prices is weakened by the influences coming from the monetary side. Prices become less reliable as informational guides as to future actions. They also lose their effectiveness as indicators of past actions. This problem is captured by long-standing arguments about the difficulty faced by accountants during inflation. If inputs are priced at historical cost, and outputs sold at current inflation-affected prices, then the profitability of the firm will be overstated, as will the profitability of particular production processes. To the extent entrepreneurs rely on accounting data as part of their decision-making processes in the next period, they will perpetuate the errors embedded in them. In addition, as prices become less tied to the underlying variables, they also perform their discovery function less desirably. Market actors will become more skeptical of the reliability of existing market prices, and they will find it more difficult to take advantage of the sorts of price differentials that would otherwise prompt market discoveries.

If entrepreneurs make use of current prices (possibly embedded with inflation-generated distortions) and their thymological knowledge to form their expectations of future prices and, therefore, their current production decisions, inflation has more serious consequences. First of all, it forces entrepreneurs to acquire and process a greater amount of knowledge than they would have to in the absence of inflation. Rather than just relying on their knowledge of market behavior, entrepreneurs would also have to make use of some sort of knowledge about the likely path and duration of the excess supply of money. Note also that the relevant knowledge here is not about the effects of inflation only on *existing* prices (as in the neoclassical story) but more its more important effects on *future* prices. In other words, knowing, for example, the Federal Reserve's current policy is not enough. Entrepreneurs would also have to form expectations about future policies, and their likely effects, to be able to form accurate expectations of the future constellation of prices. This additional epistemological burden reduces the reliability of monetary calculation as a guide for production decisions and undermines the ability of entrepreneurs in the market process to discover and correct market ignorance and mismatched plans.

Not only does inflation increase the quantity of knowledge entrepreneurs would need to process, it changes the kind of knowledge they must make use of. Assume that we have an economy that has historically been inflation-free. Entrepreneurs have built up years of contextual market experience that enables them to formulate their expectations of future prices. They have, perhaps, invested heavily in forms of human capital that facilitate that knowledge acquisition process. Now this economy experiences some inflation. Accurately envisioning the future constellation of prices now requires the kind of knowledge they already have, *plus* a new kind of knowledge about the likely behavior of the monetary authority *and* the possible effects of its policies. The latter may well require some knowledge of economic theory.[17] There is no reason to

expect that this kind of knowledge can be easily acquired by existing entrepreneurs who have invested in acquiring other kinds of knowledge. At the
onset of a period of inflation, monetary calculation will be undermined by this
shift in the kind of knowledge necessary for choosing profitable production
processes. The obvious effect of this shift is that actors will now begin to
invest in acquiring more of the new kind of knowledge. Of course, these additional investments are wasted resources in that they would be unnecessary in
an inflation-free economy.

However, even if such investments are undertaken, it is not unreasonable to
suppose that the new kind of knowledge is more ephemeral than the market
knowledge of the past. If it is true that the time horizons of political actors,
including monetary policy-makers, are notably shorter than those of market
actors, then knowledge about the inflation process will have a much shorter
shelf-life than knowledge of the market process. Because political actors face
re-election or re-appointment at regular, often short, intervals, and cannot
sell their stake in the political process at the conclusion of their participation,
they have little incentive to act in ways that provide long-run consistency.
Formulating long-run expectations about monetary policy is likely to be far
more difficult than forming expectations about the market for a similar time
period.[18] Because political actors themselves are not looking very far into the
future, while other market producers likely are, it would not be very easy for
market actors to form expectations about long-term monetary policy. Recall
also that the relevant expectations are not merely about changes in the average
price level, but about the very specific ways in which excess supplies of money
will affect relative prices. One has to form some guess about the particular path
those excesses will take through the marketplace.

It is in this sense that the most important effects of inflation are microeconomic ones. The distortion of relative prices induced by inflation, and the
consequent reduction in the reliability of monetary calculation, are the most
important 'costs' associated with excess supplies of money. Economic coordination is fundamentally about making use of the price system and inflation
scrambles the signals sent by prices to such a degree that market discovery is
less likely and market entrepreneurship is less reliable and market coordination
is therefore less frequent. It is not that specific prices deviate from equilibrium
but that the price system as a social institution is less reliable during inflation.
The economic waste, both in terms of the needless investment in outguessing
inflation and the entrepreneurial error generated by the less reliable price
system, that results from inflation can only be really understood when we take
relative price effects seriously and move away from a sole focus on aggregates
such as the total money supply and the overall price level. Inflation may be a
macroeconomic phenomenon, but its major effects are decidedly microeconomic in the way in which they undermine market coordination processes.
This scrambling of the price system can also help us see some of the other
microeconomic problems resulting from inflation.

The capital structure and Austrian business cycle theory

Consistent with our focus on the importance of intertemporal coordination, we can take our analysis of relative price effects one step further. Not only will such effects be of importance for the relative price structure at a point in time, but they will also matter for the intertemporal price structure. Some of the most significant welfare costs of inflation are those associated with the havoc it wreaks on the capital structure. Using Austrian microfoundations gives us the ability to understand, at least in general terms, the nature of these effects. This vantage point also enables us to look at the Austrian theory of the business cycle in a slightly different way. Rather than seeing the traditional Austrian story as a necessary consequence of inflation, or indeed the only sort of systematic set of consequences that will follow inflation, we can see it as one, perhaps the most likely, of a number of kinds of intertemporal discoordination that are induced by inflation.

Given that production processes take time, the onset of inflation during the course of such processes will create misleading profit and loss figures. If entrepreneurs calculate their profits using the revenues at the time of sale and match them against historical cost, inflation will tend to overstate their true profits. Suppose my inputs cost me $100 on January 1. Suppose further that over the course of the year which follows, inflation, as measured by some price index, is running at 10 percent. On December 31, I sell my output for $120. By standard accounting methods, I would subtract the $100 in historical cost from the $120 in revenue and record a $20 profit.[19] The most obvious problem with this process is that the $20 profit is overstating the real value I have added to the inputs. If the prices of everything have risen by 10 percent (on average), then some portion of my $120 and my $20 profit, reflects not real value added but the scaling up of nominal values attributable to the inflation. If entrepreneurs are unaware of the inflation, or choose to ignore its effects when interpreting their accounting data, they will be misled as to the profitability of their ventures.

One might respond by asking why entrepreneurs or accountants do not just use a price index to make some sort of correction in the revenue and profit figures to discount the effects of inflation. Why not, for example, just subtract 10 percent off of each figure to get the 'real' profitability of the production process? Isn't such a correction the equivalent of the cost of living allowances that workers receive? This proposed solution simply points out a further difficulty facing entrepreneurs during inflation: if we take our relative price effects story seriously then, although the price index figure (or even some accurate measure of the excess money supply) will give one the *average* increase in prices, it says little if anything about the relative price effects in the industry in question. Knowing that the money supply is 10 percent in excess says next to nothing about how much, if any, of that excess is affecting my corner of the market. Statistically one might be best off expecting the average, but it is no guarantee of being right, only minimizing the degree of error. Even

the sorts of accounting conventions one might adopt are likely to be insufficient in the face of the complexity of the paths that excess supplies of money
take through the market. Although it is, perhaps, better than nothing, to try
to discount revenues and profits by the use of some aggregate (and necessarily
unspecific) price index, doing so will not eliminate the erroneous information
conveyed by inflation-ridden accounting data.

This also raises the issue of the degree to which inflations can be anticipated. Because the standard literature is so focused on price level aggregates
as being the source of confusion both to producers and workers, anticipating
the movement of the price level becomes paramount. This is most obviously
seen in the signal extraction literature mention earlier, as well as the literature on the Phillips curve discussed in Chapter 3. However, for Austrians,
the price level is not all that crucial a variable when seen from the perspective of the discovery process of the microeconomy. What matters more to
producers are the individual prices they pay for inputs and imagine they will
receive for their products. Movements in the value of money as a whole say
nothing about the direction of the individual prices that matter to entrepreneurs. Taking relative price effects seriously should cast grave doubt on
whether the effects of inflation on prices can ever really be anticipated. Even
if one knew that the central bank was planning, say, a 10 percent increase in
the money supply, one would find it very difficult to anticipate the particular effects it would have on one's own specific industry. It is that kind of
microeconomic knowledge that matters in the market and that would make
an inflation truly anticipated. Without knowledge at that level of detail,
which is surely hard to come by, it is hard to treat any inflation as really
'anticipated'.

However, the problems do not stop with recognizing the real and monetary
content of current price signals. These relative price effects of inflation and the
capital gains and losses that they generate will lead entrepreneurs to reconsider
their production plans. In the face of the illusory profits of inflation, entrepreneurs may wish to expand particular lines of production by adding new
capital or labor. Alternately, as costs begin to feel the effects of inflation, losses
in later periods might lead entrepreneurs to abandon certain production
process and refit the capital involved to other uses. As Lachmann (1978) makes
clear, the importance of capital gains and losses is their role as signals in the
ongoing plan revision processes of entrepreneurs. Each entrepreneurial plan is
like a hypothesis to be tested by the events that follow in the marketplace.
Profits and losses are the way of determining the success of the plan. As profits or losses are realized, entrepreneurs must interpret that information (using
the sort of thymological knowledge referred to in our discussion of Mises in the
previous section) and, if they believe it necessary, revise their plan accordingly.
During periods of inflation, not only is plan revision likely to be considered
more frequently because prices are less stable, but the inaccuracy of price and
profit signals may mean that such revisions become more difficult and less
appropriate.

It is here where our earlier discussion of the roles of complementarity and substitution come in. In revising plans, entrepreneurs must take into account the capabilities of their own capital and labor, as well as what is available out on the market. If they wish to expand production, it will mean bringing in new labor or capital that is complementary to what they already have. Switching to a different production process, or producing a new output, will mean refitting what exists to work in new ways. If the entrepreneur has to go out on the market and purchase new capital or labor, it is likely that it will not be perfectly fitted to the new uses to which it will be put. Such a situation might necessitate reconfiguring machines and retraining labor from their previous uses to better fit into the apparently more profitable production plans. This process of making newly acquired capital and labor better complement existing inputs is costly. Refitting capital is a production process of its own, as is retraining labor. Those changes take time and resources.

The danger facing entrepreneurs is that they may be making such changes in response to erroneous price and profit signals. Continued inflation might well reverse those signals in the next period, leaving entrepreneurs with refitted capital and retrained labor that has again been rendered sub-optimal. More important, the process of retooling and retraining itself involves wasted resources. If inflation were absent, there would likely be fewer instances of mistaken plan revision, as the noise content of prices and profits would be less, and fewer resources would be devoted to retraining and retooling. To the extent inflation leads to more of these erroneous changes, it is creating waste. The resources devoted to refitting capital and retraining labor in ways that are later revealed to be mistaken are costs of inflation.

These irretrievable adjustment costs and misallocations of capital and labor are in addition to inflation's tendency to reduce the quantity of investment and the size of the capital stock (Dowd 1994). Inflation does more than reduce the total amount of capital available, it also leads to a capital structure that is not sustainable. This unsustainability appears in two ways. The first, as we have just discussed, is that the heightened instability in prices caused by inflation leads to a greater amount of (*ex post*) mistaken plan revision by entrepreneurs. Inflation embeds more errors into the capital structure at any one point in time precisely because entrepreneurs have more difficulty making use of monetary calculation and making wise decisions about capital and labor usage. With prices less reliable as production guides, any set of production plans (taken at a point in time) is less likely to be executable. This ongoing discoordination of plans is evidence of a capital structure that could not be sustained over time.

One implication of this argument is that inflation is not neutral even in the long run. That is, relative price effects will become embedded in the capital structure in the form of capital (and labor) that are being used in sub-optimal ways due to mistaken changes in production induced by the short-run relative price effects of inflation. A given bout of inflation changes the capital structure and the constellation of relative prices forever. The mainstream literature on relative price effects and neutrality discussed at the beginning of this chapter generally assumes that such effects are only short-run phenomena. In fact, the seminal contributions of Hercowitz (1981: 331–2) and Cukierman (1982: 132) explicitly treat money as neutral in the long run. Hercowitz's explanation for that assumption is revealing: in the long run relative prices are fixed 'because of perfect substitutability on the supply side' (1981: 332). This assumption of perfect substitutability is possible only in the absence of a meaningful theory of capital. The Austrian theory of capital is explicit in its claim that because capital is embodied in specific goods, individual production goods are not perfectly substitutable, even in the long run. Capital may be refit and labor may be retrained over time, reflecting their *imperfect* substitutability, but both processes consume resources and still frequently create sub-optimal (in comparison to building capital or 'creating' human capital from scratch) inputs. Even in the long run, inflation leaves its mark on the structure of economic activity precisely because of the specificity of capital goods and the necessity of adapting them imperfectly to changed economic circumstances. As Roger Garrison (in Snowdon, *et al.* 1994: 393) has phrased it, 'capital gives money time to cause trouble'. It can be added that more time will not reverse the trouble that excess supplies of money can cause.

Salerno (1995: 298ff.) offers two additional arguments for rejecting long-run neutrality from an Austrian perspective. In reconstructing Mises' analysis of the inflation process, he argues that:

> As long as individual value scales are differentiated from one another and either all goods are not available in infinitely divisible units or their marginal utilities with respect to money do not decline at uniform rates throughout each and every person's value scale, then a change in the quantity of money must effect a permanent alteration in the structure of market demands for commodities and services and, therefore, a permanent change in relative prices.
>
> (Salerno 1995: 300)

This argument from Mengerian microeconomics points to the way in which even short-run inflationary disequilibria can have long-run effects. The 'revolution', to use Mises' and Salerno's word, in prices that results will also have effects on the long-run structure of capital. A second source of non-neutrality arises from the distributional effects associated with the inflation process. As the excess supply of money works its way through the market, those who acquire the additional money before prices rise (i.e., the beneficiaries of forced savings) gain in real wealth at the expense of those who see higher prices before higher incomes. This redistribution of wealth will, in turn, affect market demands and relative prices and 'therefore result in a revolution and not a restoration of the relative positions of various groups of sellers in the new long-run equilibrium or "final state of rest"' (ibid.: 302). A process-oriented analysis of inflation that carefully traces out its effects on the market process will generally reject both the short-run and long-run neutrality of inflation.

The second form of capital structure unsustainability can be seen in the traditional Austrian business cycle theory story.[20] In that theory, the artificial lowering of the market rate that accompanies the excess supply of money leads to malinvestment by the owners of the means of production. When the market rate falls, investment in general looks more profitable, with longer-term projects looking even more so. As more of these long-term investments are undertaken, the structure of production lengthens out, as more stages are inserted in between the highest orders of goods and final consumer goods. The cost of the extra time involved in the (eventually) more productive production process appears to be justified by the lower rate of interest. In terms of intertemporal coordination, the lower market rate of interest appears to signal an increased willingness to wait on the part of the public, further justifying the increased time it will take to produce final goods. Indeed, in cases where the market rate of interest falls due to increased saving on the part of the public, that is, where the reduced market rate is moving *pari passu* with the 'natural' rate of interest, the decision to lengthen the structure of production is quite consistent with maintaining intertemporal coordination. The problem faced by producers is how to know whether a given reduction in market rates of interest reflects a genuine increase in saving on the part of the public or an artificial change resulting from inflationary monetary policy.[21]

The Austrian theory argues that the lengthened structure of production is unsustainable because the intertemporal decisions of producers are not coordinated with the intertemporal decisions of consumers. At the lower market rate, new capital projects are begun and additional labor is hired to help produce them. This is the upswing of the cycle. Wages rise as labor is bid away from existing uses into the new (apparently profitable) projects, and prices rise as the excess supply of money begins to work its way into the spending stream and any unemployed labor or capital is brought into use. The economy appears to be booming. The problem is that once the new money reaches the broad mass of consumers, they will continue the intertemporal allocation of wealth that they had prior to the fall in the market rate. The lower market rate appeared to signal to producers that consumers were more willing to wait for additions to output, making it sensible for producers to move labor and capital away from the production of final goods toward intermediate ones. However, consumers' time-preferences have not changed and as they continue their past demands for final goods, producers will eventually discover that they have misallocated their inputs. The prices of final goods get bid up as the smaller supply faces an unchanged demand and producers see that the longer-term projects they recently began do not look like they will pan out, as the longer-term demand they expected from the lower market rate will not be there.

The result of that realization (what Hayek called the 'snapback' effect) is the turning point of the cycle. Once producers realize that their longer-term investments were mistaken, the labor that was devoted to them will be released, the capital that was rented or purchased for those projects will be idled, and wages and producer goods prices will fall, signaling the onset of the bust phase of the cycle. In addition, if capital or labor that was refit or retrained for the now mistaken longer-term projects is not idled, it will have to be refit or retrained once more to move back to the shorter production processes. These expenditures are wastes of the business cycle. One of the signs of the bust phase of the cycle is the unfinished capital abandoned after the snapback. Attempts to refit those goods to uses other than those for which they were originally constructed will involve expenditures that would not have been necessary in the absence of inflation and the cycle. Eventually the mistakes are liquidated to the extent possible and, assuming no further monetary intervention, the economy will return to a market rate consistent with intertemporal preferences.

It is the unobservability of the natural rate that is central to understanding the Austrian theory of the business cycle. Because the natural rate of interest is a theoretical construct and not a phenomenon observable on any real market, we cannot know with certainty that any given market rate of interest is accurately reflecting the underlying natural rate. It is in this sense that the Austrian theory of the business cycle is ultimately a microeconomic process; the problem begins with a price that becomes severed from the preferences that are supposed to underlie it. The whole theory elaborates the microeconomic results of that mistaken price signal. Because the price in question is the price of time, and all economic production involves time, the effects of that erroneous price are much more pervasive than those of any other price. It is that pervasiveness that makes the Austrian cycle theory 'macroeconomic'. It is not, however, macroeconomic in the sense of explaining some relationship among aggregates. This confusion arises with some frequency, especially when the theory is referred to as an *overinvestment* theory. The problem is not that there is too much investment (*per se*), but that the wrong kind of investment is taking place. That distinction is not readily visible through the eyes of modern macroeconomics since Keynes, which has understood investment only in terms of some aggregate measure rather than as part of an interconnected capital structure where the composition of investment is just as important as its overall level.

Hayek's (1941, 1942, 1969) discussion of what he terms the 'Ricardo Effect' also sheds some light on the microeconomic nature of the Austrian cycle theory.[22] If bouts of inflation can send the economy into a boom (albeit artificial) and it is only when the additions to the money supply stop that the snapback will take place, critics of the theory asked why continuing the inflation could not forestall the snapback and the bust indefinitely. By providing borrowers with a continuous source of new funds for investment, what would prevent the boom process from never stopping? Hayek's response to that line of argument was decidedly microeconomic. He points out that the microeconomic insight we now call 'derived demand' is perfectly valid for *individual* final goods and their inputs, but cannot be true of all final goods and inputs collectively.[23] That is, it is surely true that the demand for the capital and labor necessary to make bread derives from the demand for that bread, and if the demand for bread rises, the demand for the inputs will rise and those inputs will be bid away from other uses. However, it is impossible to raise the demand for all capital goods simultaneously by increasing the aggregate level of expenditure on final goods. In the sort of continuous inflation envisioned in this example, the prices for final goods would be continually rising, apparently leading the critics to think that this increase in demand would lead to an increase in the capital and labor available to produce those final goods.

The problem, however, is that in the sound version of 'derived demand' the inputs are bid away from other uses. In the inflation story, *all* the lines of production are bidding after inputs, causing their prices to rise significantly and making the inflation-induced investments eventually unprofitable even if the additions to the money supply continue. Inflation-generated spending must eventually bump into the constraint created by the scarcity of capital goods. The critics of the Austrian theory seemed to suppose that capital could be created out of thin air (or at least was currently abundant enough) so that any increase in demand for final goods would somehow bring forth the capital necessary to produce it. Capital, however, is not abundant, and the bidding war that inflation would precipitate would drive input prices to heights that would make the production of the final goods involved unprofitable.[24] Moreover, given the imperfect substitutability of specific capital goods, the whole cost of bidding away capital includes not just the rental or selling price, but also the cost involved in any refitting that would have to take place to render the capital good complementary to the firm's existing capital goods. What the Austrian theory shows is that the entire business cycle can be understood as an ongoing microeconomic process of price discoordination and costly adjustment induced by the excess supply of money. It is this that Hayek was aiming for when he argued that any business cycle story must be consistent with the logic of choice.

Because the natural rate of interest is unobservable, the banking system comes to centerstage in all discussions of intertemporal coordination. We have to rely on the banking system to produce rates of interest that track the natural rate because we have no direct way of accessing the natural rate. This is why the neutrality criterion for monetary policy is so important and was introduced by Hayek around the same time as his work on cycle theory. If the divergence between the market and natural rates is the source of the problem, we need to be assured to the degree possible that the banking system can accurately translate consumer and producer time-preferences into the appropriate level of investment and money supply.

What is fundamental to the Austrian theory is the false intertemporal price signal generated by the market rate. The traditional Austrian story explains that bad signal as the result of inflation, but that need not be the only way an erroneous interest rate signal can happen. As Roger Garrison (1993) argues, one way to explain the recession of 1990–91 is to see it as resulting from an investment-driven boom during the 1980s. Instead of invoking inflation as the starting point for that boom, Garrison argues that various banking regulations and Treasury operations during the 1980s created a situation in which market rates of interest did not reflect underlying time-preferences of savers. In particular, implicit and explicit subsidies of risk allowed market rates to be lower than they otherwise should have been, leading to the boom of the 1980s. When some of those regulatory effects worked themselves out, or were removed, the mistakes of the 1980s were revealed, leading to the recession of the early 1990s. If Garrison's argument is correct, it suggests that the key feature of the Austrian story is the intertemporal discoordination, and not the mechanism that generates it. Given the changes in banking institutions and regulations since the theory was developed in the 1920s and 1930s, it is not far-fetched to suppose that new auxiliary assumptions will have to be imported into the logical structure of the theory, leading to new variations on the theoretical theme. Of course even in Garrison's version, the cycle story is still essentially microeconomic in that the bad price signal, and the resulting choices, are the central processes involved.

In a recent book, Tyler Cowen (1997) confronts the traditional Austrian theory of the cycle with recent theoretical and empirical work on cyclical behavior, especially work that examines cycles from a portfolio approach that looks at the riskiness of investment. Cowen is quite critical of the Austrian cycle theory on both theoretical and empirical grounds, but still holds that it may have some uses in explaining certain parts of some cycles. Specifically, he argues that:

> Inflation may lead to more errors, but it will lead to errors of various kinds, not of a single systematic kind . . . Rather than overcommitting business cycle theory to postulating a particular kind of mistake, I attempt to rebuild the traditional Austrian theory with an emphasis on the general likelihood of future mistakes.
>
> (1997: 11)

As the task of this study is largely theoretical, we can leave discussion of Cowen's empirical claims to others. At the level of theory, the sections that follow offer some ways in which, from an Austrian perspective, inflation leads to a variety of errors in addition to those normally associated with Austrian cycle theory. To that degree, Cowen's attempt to locate the particular sequence of errors associated with Austrian cycle theory in a larger context of inflation-induced errors is consistent with what follows. His portfolio-based approach leads him to focus on different sorts of errors than those illuminated by our emphasis on price coordination. Although I remain less skeptical of the applicability of Austrian cycle theory than is Cowen, our approaches may be more complementary than they first appear to be.

Coping costs and economic welfare

In addition to the relative price effects, capital distortion, and cyclical movements caused by inflation, one large set of costs it imposes, which are not well captured in standard models, are what might be termed 'coping costs'. The existence or expectation of inflation induces people to expend resources protecting themselves against the effects of inflation. These activities may be as simple and cheap as reading the newspaper to learn about Fed policy or the current price level, or as complex and expensive as finding and paying a financial expert to manage one's personal or business portfolio. All of the expenditures induced by inflation that are oriented toward coping with inflation are wasteful in comparison to a zero-inflation economy. In the latter, those same resources could be used to satisfy human wants directly.

The relationship between coping costs and economic waste can be seen as analogous to Tullock's (1967) work on the costs of rent-seeking.[25] In that paper, Tullock used three examples to make his point: tariffs, monopolies, and theft. The latter is the least noted of the three, but is the most relevant to this discussion here. In the same way that living in a crime-prone area will induce crime-protection measures by citizens, so does inflation induce inflation-protection measures by producers and consumers. Homeowners who buy additional dead-bolt locks or security systems are acting rationally given the level of crime in the area. Nonetheless, these resources are wasted from a comparative institutions perspective:

> The cost to society would be the investments of capital and labor in the activity of theft and in protection against theft. . . . Transfers themselves cost society nothing, but for the people engaging in them they are just like any other activity, and this means that large resources may be invested in attempting to make or prevent transfers. These largely offsetting commitments of resources are totally wasted from the standpoint of society as a whole.
>
> (Tullock 1967: 47)

In an alternative institutional arrangement where the crime rate is lower and where the resources spent on crime-protection and crime-commission could be used on other goods and services, people will be better off. Living in a small town that has an extremely low crime rate, one need not invest resources in home security systems, a car alarm, or even a dead-bolt lock. The resources saved by this state of affairs can be used for direct want-satisfaction. A person with the same real monetary income living in New York City will have less disposable income available because he will have to invest more resources in crime prevention and protection. Any policy changes that reduce the actual or expected crime rate will free some of all of these resources for want-satisfaction, which increases overall welfare.

These coping costs are difficult to capture in static models that focus on how inflation might disturb relative prices from their equilibrium values or on how inflation affects only money balances or menu costs. This is not unlike the way in which Tullock expenditures are invisible to those who are looking for the costs of monopoly in Harberger triangles. To get a sense for the pervasiveness of these important costs of inflation, a comparative institutions approach is very useful.

In addition to the two coping costs noted previously, there are numerous others we might include in a more comprehensive understanding of the costs of inflation. The standard shoe-leather and menu costs would fall in this category. The additional trips to the bank necessary to replenish one's nominal money balances are a way of protecting oneself against the damaging effects of inflation. Absent the inflation, these additional trips would be unnecessary and the associated costs would disappear. A similar story can be told for menu costs. Although price adjustments are always necessary in a dynamic market economy, the pushes and pulls of inflation, particularly when one takes relative price effects seriously, force entrepreneurs to make more price adjustments than they would otherwise. In an age of computers, such changes may not be all that costly, but they still require that labor and capital be devoted to purposes which would not exist in the absence of inflation. In addition, non-monetary factors might make this problem worse. For example, some areas, such as St Lawrence county, New York, have item-pricing laws for grocery stores. Almost every item in the store must have a price stamped on it, even though the shelf has a price tag and the store has optical scanners. With such a law on the books, the menu costs associated with even mild inflations might be very significant. Stores would have to invest a good deal of labor in remarking individual items in the face of a rising price level, in addition to changing the computer data base.[26] All of these menu costs reflect waste in comparison to an inflation-free regime.

Another set of coping costs would be all the costs associated with negotiating wage contracts in an inflationary regime. During even small inflations, labor and management will have to devote resources to figuring the inflation rate, in addition to the marginal increase in negotiation time and resources required to agree upon an appropriate cost-of-living adjustment. This activity is taken for granted after 30 years of continued inflation in the United States, but, in a regime where monetary equilibrium is (nearly) maintained, these costs associated with labor negotiations would not be necessary. It is important to stress that all of these coping costs are contingent only upon the *expectation* of inflation, not its actual amount. Even if actual inflation in the next year is zero, if actors expect some positive amount of inflation, they will be led to devote resources to protecting themselves, such as in labor negotiations. This point illustrates the importance of the monetary regime for determining the degree of damage caused by coping costs. Even a well-behaved central bank is more likely than a monetary rule or other alternative monetary institutions to generate the expectation of future inflation, as its behavior will fluctuate with whomever is in charge or which way the political winds are blowing. It is not just the current or past rate of inflation that matters for expectations of future inflation, but the reliability of the current monetary regime.

Accountants would be faced with similar problems. To the extent that accountants spend additional time trying to adjust their work to compensate for the effects of inflation, they are wasting resources. Resources devoted to computing price indexes, calculating replacement costs (rather than simply recording historical costs), or adjusting rates of return would all be devoted to direct want satisfaction in monetary equilibrium. During inflation, one area that accountants might particularly make use of, along with lawyers, is in writing contracts. If there is an expectation of inflation, contracts will have to be written in ways that take those expectations into account. This might require paying for additional financial or legal advice, not to mention the time involved with finding such advice and writing more complex contracts. Moreover, should such contracts become the cause of legal action (due to their inflation-related clauses), they will pose a burden on the judicial and/or political system. The time and resources either system spends on sorting out the contractual problems caused by inflation also represent waste in comparison to an inflation-free regime. These costs are analogous to rent-protection expenditures. The difference is that during inflation, it is not supra-normal rents that are often being protected, but normal (as would be the case absent inflation) rates of return that might be eaten away by inflation.

The two broadest forms of coping costs are producer and consumer portfolio adjustments. On the producer side, firms are more likely to spend resources hiring financial experts to better manage their portfolios in the face of inflation. The opportunity cost of hiring people in finance is the output that could have been produced by hiring people directly involved with the production process. As Leijonhufvud (1981c: 248) summarizes these problems: 'In short, being good at "real" productive activities – being competitive in the ordinary sense – no longer has the same priority. Playing the inflation right is vital.' In the absence of inflation, the firm could have both a well-performing asset portfolio and the output of those hired for direct production. In a report on Latin American inflations, *U.S. News and World Report* (March 5, 1990: 61) noted that 'Dow Chemical's São Paulo branch has three dozen employees who do nothing but monitor the financial market.' One measure of the cost of inflation is the forgone output that would have come from devoting those resources directly to production. In addition, these costs of inflation will not be picked up by GDP measurements. The wages used to pay financial experts rather than production line workers also count toward GDP. All that GDP measures is an aggregate of economic activity, it says nothing about the content of that activity, especially the degree to which it represents genuine want-satisfaction.

The waste associated with these shifts from production to inflation protection do not stop at the final payment level. Analogous to the capital structure effects that result from shifts in relative prices, we also might identify shifts in the structure of human capital that are likely to result from the inflation-induced shifts in the demand for certain kinds of labor. For example, the increased demand for financial market skills should feed back to cause shifts in the sorts of education and training demanded by young people and supplied by educational institutions. In the short run, supra-normal returns earned by those with the newly demanded skills will attract entry into those sectors of the labor market, putting a premium on the relevant sorts of training. Educational institutions, and their employees, will have to refit and retool themselves to provide the new kind of skills being demanded. The ability to forecast central bank activity, or political skills and connections that can be used in the face of the declining efficiency of markets will be highly prized and training will likely adjust accordingly. As with physical capital, any expenditures made to reconfigure the structure of human capital that later need to be undone can be considered wasted. In the absence of inflation, these pushes and pulls in the human capital structure would also be absent.

Consumers might also be more likely to hire financial consultants or simply devote more time and resources in trying to protect their portfolios against inflation. In an economy maintaining monetary equilibrium, those resources could have been used to purchase other goods or services while still maintaining a desired portfolio. The emergence of money market mutual funds in the early and mid-1970s is an example of this kind of response to inflation. With the limits on deposit rates enforced by Regulation Q, putting money in a standard savings or checking account meant a loss in real terms during the double digit inflation of that period. Savers began to devote resources to finding ways around those limits and entrepreneurial financial institutions came up with a solution by pooling small savings and buying larger denomination instruments that were not subject to the interest regulations. This second-best solution clearly made all parties better off, but the whole process would have been unnecessary had inflation not existed in the first place. In this comparative institutional sense, the resources devoted to discovering and maintaining these new instruments were wasted.

Calling these expenditures wasteful is not to say that they are irrational, given the existence of inflation. If inflation is taking place, then such decisions are quite rational. Recall that our definition of waste was a comparative institutions concept. The claim of waste rests on the existence of an alternative set of institutions where those resources would be used for directly satisfying wants. These expenditures are also wasted whether or not the financial experts are successful. Certainly if one hires a financial expert who gives bad advice, it is easy to make the *ex post* claim that the expenditures were wasted. However, in the case at hand, in a comparative institutions context, the resources are wasted *ex ante* even if the expert does a perfect job in adjusting the firm's portfolio. Had the inflation not taken place, no additional expenditures on financial advice would have been necessary. The waste might be compounded by mistaken financial expertise, but even perfect advice represents wasted resources. Again, returning to Tullock, the waste associated with rent-seeking has nothing to do with whether those activities succeed or fail for the individual rent-seeker, rather it is the whole process that involves waste in comparison to an institutional regime in which rent-seeking is less common or absent.

The political economy of inflation

Once the ways in which inflation undermines microeconomic market discovery processes are understood, one's perspective on the social costs of inflation immediately widens. Taking a comparative institutions approach allows us to explore these other consequences of inflation. Such an investigation cannot stop at the borders of economics narrowly defined. What happens in the market will have effects on the political process and its relationship to the market. Some of the most significant consequences of inflation are the ones that result from the increase in political intervention in the market that is likely to occur as inflation undermines the price system and monetary calculation as reliable guides for production decisions and promoters of economic and social order.

In his well-known article on the theory of the firm, Coase (1937) argued that the choice between markets and firms as coordination processes depends on the relative costs of each. If market costs (such as negotiating and monitoring contracts) are less than firm costs (administration and bureaucracy), then the market will be chosen, and vice versa. We can extend that framework to the choice between markets and politics as means for individuals to enhance their wealth. From the individual's perspective either process holds the promise of enhancing his wealth.[27] Which process any given individual will make use of will depend on the costs of using each. Because inflation disrupts the reliability of market prices in the ways discussed above, it raises the relative cost of using the market to acquire wealth, and will induce wealth-seekers on the margin to switch to the political process. This shift in resource allocation from markets to politics entails a number of costs that can be explored from a comparative institutions perspective.[28]

The most fundamental way this allocative shift takes place is when individuals are frustrated by inflation-induced market outcomes and perceive that the political process is the appropriate way to remedy the situation. The disruption of relative prices makes market entrepreneurship more difficult by undermining the monetary calculation process needed to allocate resources with any degree of rationality. The result is that people often turn to the political process for relief. However, as Leijonhufvud (1981c: 250, emphasis in original) argues, the public's response to inflation is different from other problems:

> If our political institutions allow unemployment to grow, the feedback will be in unmistakable clear text: You'd better do something about unemployment or else . . . ! If they err on the side of inflation, there will be widespread and general complaining about rising prices to be sure, but that diffuse message is quite drowned in the rising babble of *specific* demands and *concrete* proposals from identifiable interest groups – to compensate *me*, to regulate *him*, to control x's prices, and to tax y's 'excess profits,' etc., etc.

The 'babble' generated by inflation, resulting from the public's inability to connect the effects with the cause, creates opportunities for political actors to expand their influence.

If the demands being made of the political process are quite specific, as with unemployment, the scope for discriminating among possible programs and beneficiaries is very narrow; politicians must respond to the specific demand. However, the chaotic babble of responses during inflation allows legislators *selectively* to quiet the babbling by targeting programs and policies at those babblers who are the most valuable politically. Politicians want the freedom to confer benefits on marginal groups, and the varied demands made of them during inflations provide that freedom. The political benefits of inflation occur not just due to its discriminatory impact at its onset, but also from the induced increase in the quantity of future discriminatory programs being demanded.

The process does not stop here, however. Once these programs are created in response to the diverse effects of inflation, there is now a class of beneficiaries who will be unwilling to give up those benefits. Programs created in response to inflation will create further opportunities for rent-seeking and rent-protecting behavior as those programs come up for periodic renewal or review. Suppose that price controls are used to combat the effects of inflation. Although such controls damage the economy as a whole, they frequently benefit specific groups, particularly those with low opportunity costs of their time who can afford to wait in line for goods in short supply as a result of the price control. If moves are made to end the price control, these beneficiaries will put up a fight to keep them in place. The logic of concentrated benefits and dispersed costs suggests that they will likely be successful, as those bearing the costs of the control bear such a small proportion per capita that they are unlikely to see the net benefit of fighting for decontrol.

In addition, by satisfying the political demands of one group, two other problems arise. First, other groups will now have a greater expectation of their demands being satisfied and will likely increase their rent-seeking expenditures as a result. As Tullock (1967: 48–9) argued with respect to theft, monopolies and tariffs:

> As a successful theft will stimulate other thieves to greater industry and require greater investment in protective measures, so each successful establishment of a monopoly or creation of a tariff will stimulate greater diversion of resources in attempts to organize further transfers of income.

This will be particularly true the more that inflation undermines market price signals, rendering market processes more difficult as a way to enhance one's wealth. The willingness of the political process to acquiesce in meeting the demands of those groups that turn to it on the margin will send a signal to inframarginal users of the market that the relative cost of using the political process has further dropped in relationship to the market, causing some of them to turn to the political process. Because political actors gain by the exchanges inherent in the rent-seeking process, their acquiescence is very likely as is the gradual shift away from markets toward politics.

Furthermore, ~~the~~ existence of one set of government programs will likely cause further undesirable unintended consequences in the market process, leading to not only intensified demands on the part of pre-existing rent-seekers, but new sets of demands on the political process by the victims of the new programs. This is the dynamic of interventionism identified by Mises (1966 [1949]: 716ff.).[29] Mises argued that attempts to selectively intervene in market economies were unstable. The interveners would find that their actions created consequences that ran counter to their intentions, which would necessitate either abandoning the intervention or creating additional interventions that try to address the effects of the original intervention. This is particularly the case if the interveners can successfully convince the public that the undesired consequences are not attributable to the intervention but to the underlying market.[30] In the long run, either such interventions will be abandoned or they will be replaced by a more totalistic socialism. Of course, the latter is bound to fail eventually as well, so Mises argues that even to start down the interventionist path is to invite eventual failure. So not only does inflation itself lead to unintended consequences that lead to calls for remediation by government, but the programs intended to remedy the effects of inflation and/or satisfy the rent-seeking demands of the public will also create such undesirable unintended consequences. All of the rent-seeking activity involved in the inflation-driven version of the interventionist dynamic can be seen as comparative institutional waste generated by the inflation and the lack of constraints on the political process.

Even if the narrowly economic effects of inflation are largely in the short run, the political consequences, and their associated costs in terms of wasted resources, are likely to continue into the long run. If regulatory or spending programs are explicitly adopted as short-run responses, that does not guarantee that they will be short-lived. As public choice theory has long argued, any program that creates concentrated benefits and dispersed costs will be a political success, regardless of its stated goals or time-span. This process has been well documented in Robert Higgs' (1987) study of the growth of the US government in the twentieth century. Many current programs, policies, and whole agencies and departments arose as 'temporary' responses to specific short-run crises, but have lingered long after their original justification.

This general pattern of movement from markets to politics as the preferred process for seeking wealth is a large and fundamental cost of inflation. As inflation disrupts monetary calculation in the market and induces this shift toward rent-seeking activities, it generates economic waste and increases the politicization of resource allocation. If one accepts the general proposition that markets are superior to government in efficiently allocating resources, then this shift represents a pervasive cost of inflation. Laidler and Rowe (1980: 102) argue that: '[W]e would expect the consequences of [even] anticipated inflation to be not just an increase in the consumption of shoe-leather, but an adaptation of the social order away from money and markets toward a greater reliance on one form or another of command organization.' Not only are the rent-seeking activities waste compared to an alternative set of institutions, but the programs and regulations created in response to that activity fail to coordinate economic action as well as would market institutions in monetary equilibrium. It is precisely this consequence of inflation that is overlooked in standard approaches that fail to explore the epistemic role of prices suffi- ciently and more or less ignore the institutional framework within which economic activity occurs. Laidler and Rowe's (1980: 102) conclusion is worth quoting:

> In short, if monetary theory is best approached along Austrian lines, then we must conclude that mainstream monetary theory for all its considerable accomplishments, not only trivializes the social consequences of inflation in particular, as Axel Leijonhufvud has argued, but that it greatly under- estimates the destructiveness of monetary instability in general.

Contract, hegemony, and social order

In the previous section we looked at the way in which inflation feeds back to the political process and in this section we will explore inflation's effects on social order more broadly. The central concern is the role that exchange in gen- eral, and monetary exchange more particularly, plays in generating social cooperation. It is Mises (1966 [1949]: 143ff.) who gives us a framework for this discussion by pointing out that human society involves 'concerted action, cooperation'. Society is 'the total complex of the mutual relations created by such concerted actions' (ibid.). More specifically, those social relations emerge out of the division of labor and the combination of labor. As individuals spe- cialize in certain kinds of activities and then combine with other specialists to obtain the goods they desire, they have created a social order. Mises (ibid.), like Hayek, is careful to point out that:

> Society is the outcome of conscious and purposeful behavior. This does not mean that individuals have concluded contracts by virtue of which they have founded human society. The actions which have brought about social cooperation and daily bring it about anew do not aim at anything else than cooperation and coadjuvancy with others for the attainment of definite singular ends.

Social cooperation and society are the unintended outcome of the self-interested purposeful behavior made possible by the institutions of the market.[31] This 'socializing' aspect of the market is frequently overlooked. As Mises explores at some length, the concept of comparative advantage combined with market exchanges, enables us to cooperate with one another in unintentional ways. He refers to Ricardo's development of the law of comparative advantage as 'Ricardo's Law of Association' (Mises 1966 [1949]: 159ff.). Human beings learn that by dividing up labor and exchanging the products thereof, they can produce more and achieve a higher standard of living than by trying to survive utterly on their own. As this process of association widens and deepens, we become further embedded in intricate webs of cooperation and interdependence that are the unintended consequences of our attempts at improving our own well-being. As our own skills narrow, we are more and more reliant on the productivity of others to obtain the goods and services we need. In the modern market economy, each of us knows next to nothing about how to produce the large number of goods and services we rely upon every day. That network of interdependence makes us social beings in that our reliance on others creates reasons why we should treat them with consideration. Contrary to the commonly asserted claim that markets are all about selfishness and atomized individuals, Mises' argument forces us to recognize the deeply cooperative nature of the market. Of course social cooperation in the market is not intentional; individuals are not aiming for such cooperation as their goal. Rather, it is the by-product of their attempts to produce more efficiently and live better within the institutional framework of private property and exchange.

It is exchange that is central to this socialization process. Many early societies first stumbled across exchange as a form of interaction as a result of gift-giving rituals. This was particularly the case among social groups who had little or no previous contact. Mutual gift giving was a way to establish trust and peaceful intentions. Hayek (1977: 108) notes that the Greek word for 'exchange' also meant 'to admit into the community' and to 'change from an enemy to a friend'. From the earliest forms of human social interaction, gifts and exchange were associated with some process of socialization and interdependence. Again, the original motivation for such activity may well have been self-interest, e.g. to avoid the wrath of a powerful group, but if the exchange was genuinely mutually beneficial, then both parties had reason to gain by continued exchange activity.

For Mises (1966 [1949]: 195) there are only two kinds of social cooperation: 'cooperation by virtue of contract and coordination, and cooperation by virtue of command and subordination or hegemony'. Mises goes on to contrast the operation of contractual and hegemonic societies, focusing on the degree of freedom the individual has in either one. In hegemonic societies the individual is at the mercy of the individual or group who is in command, whereas in contractual societies, the individual has a relationship of mutuality with other actors. More specifically, Mises (ibid.: 196) points out that because individuals are pawns in the hands of those who command, it can be said that only the commanders 'act' in any meaningful sense. To the degree a contractual society evolves into a hegemonic one, it narrows the scope of who can undertake meaningful action from all of the members of society to only those who hold power. This links Mises' distinction between contract and hegemony into the literature on economic calculation under socialism. The hegemonic society is bound to produce a social order with a lower standard of living than the contractual one because the latter can take advantage of the knowledge of all actors, while the hegemonic society must settle for the knowledge possessed by those in charge.

Economic institutions can foster or hinder the development of social cooperation based on exchange and contract. Routines of behavior, social norms and practices, and the structure of markets are all important institutional aspects of market exchange. The most important of these institutions is the use of money and the calculation it makes possible. Given the existence of private property, it is money and monetary calculation that make possible the exchanges and contracts and calculation that are the bedrock of the contractual society. In order to make exchanges, particularly the intertemporal ones that require explicit contracts, individuals must be able to calculate the possible effects of their actions. This calculation is made possible by the use of money and the emergence of money prices. To that extent it is money that facilitates exchange and contract and is largely responsible for the interdependence and socialization that results from exchange and the division of labor. Money is in this way the symbol of the contractual society.[32]

This suggests the profound social chaos that inflation can create. As continued inflation undermines the ability of actors to cooperate through exchange and contract, it undermines these institutions as bases of social order.[33] Arthur Okun (1975: 359) makes this point nicely: 'Inflation fools people . . . not so much by disappointing their point-estimate expectations as by depriving them of a way of economic life in which they need not depend heavily on the formulation of costly and uncertain point-estimate expectations.' The institutions we associate with the market ease the epistemic burden on actors. If inflation causes those practices to fail, actors will be more likely to turn to the political process and that process is fundamentally based on power and hegemony. The increased politicization of economic activity that is likely to follow from inflation does more than simply retard economic efficiency and growth, it reflects a significant shift in the very foundations of the social order. Inflation has the potential to radically change the fundamental ways in which human beings interact and form anything resembling a society. By destroying the calculation needed for exchange to work, inflation causes the delicate network of social interdependence that exchange and the division of labor create to disintegrate with increasing rapidity. Being unable to interact and cooperate easily on the basis of exchange and contract, actors are more likely to turn to coercion and hegemony as the means to achieve their desired ends.

This can also explain why inflation is frequently associated with the rise of totalitarian regimes. The rise of National Socialism in inter-war Germany had much to do with both the inflationary finance of World War I and the hyper-inflation of the Weimar Republic in the 1920s. In both cases, the scrambling of market prices led to significant changes in wealth. In particular, financiers who understood the inflation process and had access to monetary information were able to reap large profits during the war and the later hyperinflation. One plank of the Nazi party platform in the early 1920s was the confiscation of profits made off the German war effort in World War I.[34] Of course this demand for economic retribution fit in nicely with pre-existing German anti-Semitism, as a disproportionate number of the suspected war profiteers were Jewish bankers and financiers. During the hyperinflation of the 1920s it once again became easy to target the supposed Jewish internationalist bankers for wrecking the German economy through hyperinflation. As inflation in both cases began to separate wealth from want-satisfying production and rewarded those with superior financial know-how, it is also not surprising that those on the losing end of the inflation would blame 'the market' for the perceived injustices in the distribution of wealth. Any political figure or party who can tap into that combination of anti-market and anti-internationalist sentiment can easily make it sound like contractual relationships are subversive of social cooperation (as they permit wide and not obviously explainable differences in wealth and allow 'national' wealth to move to other parts of the world) and that a more intentional form of 'cooperation' enforced by the state will better bring about social stability and cohesiveness.

With the economic chaos that inflation creates, along with the perceived injustices in the distribution of wealth, it is also understandable that societies suffering from significant levels of inflation would move away from contract and toward hegemony as the basis for social order. This is the ultimate danger inherent in the move from markets to politics as resource allocation processes. This danger is no less present in democratic societies than in non-democratic ones. The concept of the hegemonic society does not necessarily require totalitarianism. One can imagine a hegemony of ever-shifting coalitions of interest groups working their wills through a nominally democratic process. All the sorts of interventions we have seen, and might see, to combat the effects of inflation necessarily involve a substitution of command and control for contract and exchange. These interventions might well be passed by a democratically elected legislature, but they are still pushing the social order away from contractual cooperation and toward hegemonic relationships, though perhaps more polycentric ones than would be the case under a true dictatorship.

Undermining a market economy does not change the necessity of action in the face of scarcity and uncertainty, but it can surely alter the means by which individuals attempt to execute their various plans. The claim that market economies produce wealth and peaceful social interdependence is ultimately a claim about the means by which those outcomes are produced: the use of exchange and contract, presupposing the existence and protection of private property. Moreover, making efficient use of such practices requires a properly functioning money so that prices and calculation can emerge from exchange. When money becomes a distorting influence on this process, as it does during inflation, the beneficent results that are normally produced will soon disappear. Avoiding inflation is not just a matter of sound economics, but central to maintaining a peaceful social order based on cooperation and interdependence via the division of labor and exchange.

Conclusion

A monetary equilibrium perspective, supplemented by Austrian microfoundations and an appreciation for the interaction of the market and political processes, provides us with a much broader view of inflation and its consequences. Unlike standard neoclassical approaches that focus on the more narrow costs of inflation on money balances and nominal price adjustments, the approach developed in this chapter gives us a way to see the more numerous and destructive real resource costs of inflation and its larger effects on the market as a whole and social order more broadly. Because standard analyses overlook the institutional context in which inflation occurs, they miss the real significance of relative price effects and the role the banking system plays in passing the effects of inflation through to the capital structure. An Austrian understanding of the epistemic function of the price system and the important intertemporal coordination it provides in the form of interest rates and the capital structure enables us to broaden our conception of the costs of inflation and identify the shortcomings in the standard literature.

5 Monetary equilibrium theory and deflation

For reasons that are almost too obvious to mention, deflationary monetary disequilibria have received much less attention than inflationary ones, particularly by Austrian-oriented economists. Deflation is not anywhere near the real-world problem that inflation is, thus it has frequently been given short shrift in the literature. Deflation's relative absence from modern economies is a result of the near-universal phenomenon of government control over the production of money. Inflation happens far more frequently than deflation because it is in the interest of revenue-maximizing governments to use the banking system as a source of seigniorage, giving central banks that have political oversight every reason to err on the side of inflation.[1] In addition, the short-term effects of inflation are such that the economy appears to be doing better, enabling political actors to cash in on those benefits before the bill comes due down the road.

None of these political benefits are there when deflation occurs. To highlight some ideas that this chapter will raise, deflation's negative effects occur much more quickly and tend to be concentrated in the form of idled labor and capital. Rather than the 'babble' of inflation that Leijonhufvud noted, deflation consists in a much more clear message – people cannot find jobs and machines lie unused. Where inflation might lead to severe inefficiencies due to *misallocated* capital and labor, deflation is far more likely to manifest itself as 'unallocated' capital and labor as the relative dearth of money prevents the execution of mutually beneficial exchanges. In this way it is harder for political actors, including central bankers, to avoid or shift the blame for deflation-induced idleness and reduced output. As a result, central banks attempt to avoid deflation and it is not often a problem in modern economies.[2]

That having been said, understanding deflationary monetary disequilibria is important for at least two reasons. The first rationale is theoretical: such scenarios remain possible, if unlikely, and some notion of theoretical completeness should demand exploration of what would happen if an excess demand for money were to persist. The second rationale is an empirical one. Even if deflation is not likely in the near future, it has been a serious problem in the past. Friedman and Schwartz's (1963) account of the Great Depression places a great deal of emphasis on the 30 percent decline in the money supply during the early 1930s. Understanding the length and severity of that episode might require a systematic treatment of deflationary monetary disequilibria. Whether or not another episode of a significantly deficient supply of money will occur in the near future, understanding the past and being prepared to explain the future are reasons enough to explore the deflationary side of the coin.

As we saw in the previous chapter, despite this chapter's title containing the word 'deflation', we will only be concerned with price level decreases caused by monetary disequilibria. Again, we will ignore positive productivity shocks and other possible non-monetary causes of downward movements in prices. Later in the chapter, we will clarify some of the important differences between money-induced and productivity-induced declines in the price level. However, in the more general discussions that comprise most of the chapter, the effects of monetary disequilibrium will be our focus.

The primary sources for our theoretical story will be the largely complementary work of Yeager and Greenfield, on one hand, and Leijonhufvud and Clower, on the other. The differences between the two approaches demand distinct treatment, but the broad similarities will enable us to come to some general conclusions about the likely consequences of deflations. After sketching each approach, we will compare their stories to our monetary equilibrium framework to see whether the insights of Chapter 3 can add to what both groups of theorists have to say. We will pay some specific attention to the role of Say's Law and the capital structure and explore the welfare costs of deflation. All of this will be accomplished by returning to the market process microeconomic approach outlined in Chapter 1. The similarities between Yeager's approach and that of the New Keynesians will also be discussed, as both claim to be intellectual descendants of the early monetarists and both stress the role of sticky prices. The chapter finishes with a discussion of Murray Rothbard's perspective on changes in the purchasing power of money, with a focus on the role of the demand for money.

The Yeager–Greenfield approach

The key feature of both Yeager and Greenfield's approach to an excess demand for money is the centrality of money's role as a generally accepted medium of exchange. Again, because money has no market of its own and, therefore, every market is a money market, monetary disequilibria have no place to go but to spill over into the markets for the various goods and services (Yeager 1968: 51). In the case of inflation, we saw how individuals would shed their excess real balances, driving up the prices of goods and services either directly through spending or indirectly through increased holdings of financial assets, leading to lower interest rates and more investment spending. The price level would continue to rise until the excess supply of money was no longer in excess, that is, until the real money supply returned to its pre-inflation level (assuming no intervening change in the demand for real balances). Deflation entails the mirror opposite process.

If the money supply shrinks, or if the demand for real balances rises without being matched by an increase in supply, money holders will find themselves with holdings of real balances less than what they would wish to have (a movement from O to A in Figure 5.1). Increasing those real balances can occur in one of three ways. The first is that non-money financial assets such as bonds could be sold to acquire money and its attendant liquidity. If this occurs, bond prices will fall, interest rates will rise, investment will fall, and aggregate demand will be reduced. A second option is to sell off non-financial assets, perhaps at distressed prices, to acquire the desired real balances. This will tend to push prices down, as actors across the economy get into the act. A third possibility, and the most likely, is that individuals will simply cut back on their spending in order to allow their real balances to regain their desired level. As Yeager (1968: 51) points out, one of money's unique properties is that we acquire it through a 'routine' process of buying and selling and with the expectation that we can get rid of it if we do not want it. Most of us, in the short run, have more control over our spending than our income. Attempts to acquire additional money balances will likely come from spending reductions. These decisions will obviously reduce aggregate demand and put downward pressure on prices. In a parallel to the inflation process, the price level will continue to fall until the previously deficient nominal money supply becomes the appropriate real supply (the movement from A to B in Figure 5.1). The falling price level ($P' < P^*$) will reduce the demand for nominal money balances, enabling the previously insufficient money supply to be sufficient at the lower price level (the ultimate movement along the nominal money demand curve from O to B in Figure 5.1).

At first blush, as was also the case with inflation, this fall in the price level seems harmless. Is not the end result simply a lowering of nominal values with no real effects? A comparative statics of the two equilibria (pre- and post-monetary disequilibrium) would suggest that this is the case. The problem

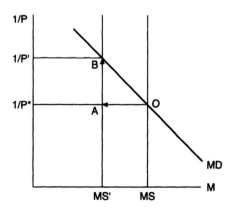

Figure 5.1 Deflationary monetary disequilibrium

again is that the path between the two equilibria is not smooth and costless. With inflation, we saw how injection effects and other factors would lead to changes in the structure of relative prices during the transition from one price level to another. That process of relative price distortion had real and negative effects on economic efficiency and growth. The same is true for deflation. Simply comparing the two equilibria assumes that the transition from one price level to a lower one is smooth and costless. Central to Yeager and Greenfield's approach is that this transition is highly problematic. In particular, they ask whether prices are able to fall smoothly, evenly, and quickly enough to prevent a slowing up of the spending stream and a consequent idling of labor and capital.

Their explanation for the problems of the transition path is that prices are not perfectly and smoothly flexible. The excess demand for money will make itself known as falling demand in all non-money markets (a movement from D to D′ in Figure 5.2). If prices (and wages) in those markets responded instantaneously and correctly to the decline in demand, the move from one equilibrium to another might well be costless. However, if such an instantaneous transition is not possible, that is, if prices and wages are less than perfectly flexible downward, then some of the effects of the excess demand for money will be on quantities rather than prices. The excess demand for money will be manifested as an excess supply of everything else, as sellers are unable to make sales at the market prices in place before the monetary disequilibrium (the difference between QS^* and QD′ in Figure 5.2). If prices remain stuck above their market-clearing values, then the resulting excess supply means a lower *ex post* quantity of goods exchanged, as the short side of the market will rule (the actual quantity of goods exchanged will be QD′). The analysis here is, of course, no different from the standard microeconomic treatment of a price floor.

The first round effects on quantities are not the end of the story. Because one person's expenditures are the source of another's income, the hesitation to purchase at existing market prices due to the desire to replenish money balances

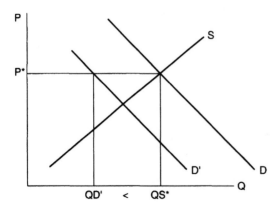

Figure 5.2   A representative market under deflation

means a reduction in the incomes of those who would normally have been the recipients of that withdrawn spending. A seller *would have* received a normal level of income if buyers *would have* spent rather than attempted to maintain their level of real balances in the face of a deficient money supply. The dual nature of the income-spending relationship, as emphasized by Clower (see below), implies that the buyer's unwillingness to buy translates into the seller's inability to buy further down the line, as his income is reduced. Of course, the persons who would have received that next round of spending see their income and their ability to purchase reduced as well. To the extent this process is not brought to a halt, either by prices finally starting to fall or an income-induced reduction in the demand for real balances, the results will be not only a significant amount of unsold goods, but a great deal of idled labor and capital. The key to deflationary monetary disequilibria is understanding that the exchanges that do not take place due to the lack of money are exchanges that would have taken place had monetary equilibrium been maintained. Like inflation, appraising of the costs of deflation must involve a comparison between what does happen during deflation and what would have happened in monetary equilibrium.

The question remains as to why Yeager and Greenfield believe prices are less than perfectly flexible. The broadest reason is a version of the Prisoners' Dilemma problem. In the classic Prisoners' Dilemma game, each of two players is presented with a pay-off matrix that makes it in each one's individual interest to choose a course of action that is collectively sub-optimal. The key is that the two players are unable to communicate with each other and thus coordinate their choices in a way to reach the optimal equilibrium. This lack of direct communication in the model makes it useful for describing some patterns of market behavior. In Yeager's and Greenfield's account, each individual seller would like to cut prices when faced with slackening sales, but none is willing to do so without some assurance that other sellers will do the same. Any seller who goes first in cutting the price of his output will face a price-cost squeeze if the sellers of his inputs do not also cut their prices. If each seller could be assured that every other seller would cut prices, then each would be willing to do so. However, without such an assurance, cutting prices is a bad move. No matter which strategy the other sellers choose, each individual seller sees it in his interest not to cut prices. The result is therefore suboptimal; no one cuts prices when everyone should.

Complicating this is the fact that individual buyers and sellers are normally unable to diagnose the source of the slackening demand. One line of response to the Prisoners' Dilemma argument is that monetary disequilibria are not single-play games, rather, they recur with some frequency. Game theoretical arguments show that in repeated Prisoners' Dilemma games, players can find ways to reach a Nash equilibrium.[3] So perhaps monetary disequilibria have those characteristics. Unfortunately, businesspeople normally do not concern themselves with the sort of global knowledge that might indicate the presence of monetary disturbances. In addition, monetary disequilibria are not quite like the typical Prisoners' Dilemma game in that the pay-offs begin to emerge only during the playing of the game.

In fact, the way businesspeople come to discover that there is an excess demand for money is through the price system. It is only when revenues begin to fall off, and prices no longer seem to be 'right', that sellers begin to ask whether something is afoot. As Yeager (1986: 375–6) nicely expresses it:

> One cannot consistently both suppose that the price system is a communication mechanism – a device for mobilizing and coordinating knowledge dispersed in millions of separate minds – and also suppose that people *already* have the knowledge that the system is working to convey. Businessmen do not have a quick and easy shortcut to the results of the market process.

It is through movements (or in this case the perceived need for movement) in relative prices that monetary disequilibria make themselves known. Even if sellers knew that money was in deficient supply, the Prisoners' Dilemma problem would still face them. Where money is in excess demand and knowledge is dispersed, price stickiness and quantity effects are sure to follow.

Once stuck in this deflationary rot, how does the economy get out? As with the Austrian theory of the cycle, there are endogenous long-run corrective processes. The most obvious is that, eventually, prices will begin to move downward.[4] As Shah (1997: 53) argues, the key to seeing why prices must eventually fall is to recognize that there is a monetary and a non-monetary component to prices. When aggregate demand begins to fall, firms will first adjust their non-monetary margins in a variety of different ways (as the survey evidence in Blinder (1991) bears out). In this entrepreneurial search for a better mix of components, buyers will face increasingly 'divergent offers because of the increased differences in full prices' (Shah 1997: 53). As a result, consumers begin to engage in additional amounts of search to find the best bargain and, as they do so, sellers begin to realize that they will have to lower money prices to attract the increasingly informed buyers. Thus, prices eventually begin to fall.

As prices fall, the real value of the insufficient nominal money supply will rise until it is back to a level consonant with the demand for real balances. Again, simply because the economy has endogenous corrective processes does not mean that the transition from one monetary equilibrium to a later one is costless. At the same time that prices are trying to fall, the decline in output and income associated with the transitional stickiness of prices will induce a decline in the demand for real balances, which also acts as a corrective to the excess demand for money. The combination of the eventual decline in prices and the falling demand for real balances will eventually restore monetary equilibrium, but only after a painful decline in output, employment, and income.

A different solution to the excess demand for money is to immediately increase the nominal money supply at the first sign of trouble. When deflationary monetary disequilibria occur, the banking system should ideally take immediate corrective measures by increasing the nominal money supply in order to facilitate the mutually beneficial exchanges that would be prevented by the insufficient money supply. Whether a central bank, or any other monetary regime, is able either to prevent monetary disequilibrium before the fact, or to respond quickly *ex post*, will be the subject matter of Chapter 7. For now, if whatever monetary regime is in place can appropriately adjust the nominal money supply, it can either prevent or remedy a deflationary monetary disequilibrium.

The Clower–Leijonhufvud version

Greenfield and Yeager's monetary disequilibrium story, which finds its roots in the early American monetarists, is paralleled by the work of Robert Clower and Axel Leijonhufvud that emerged in the 1960s in their attempts to come to grips with the Keynesian revolution. In many ways, the theoretical stories each group offers share some fundamental characteristics, including placing money as the medium of exchange at center-stage (and by implication the banking system as well) and emphasizing the stickiness of prices in response to excesses or deficiencies in the supply of money. One notable difference between Leijonhufvud's work and Yeager's is the former's more prominent emphasis on the Wicksellian natural rate/market rate mechanism. For Leijonhufvud, it is this 'Wicksell connection' (1981b) that links his perspective with Keynes' work, albeit Keynes of the *Treatise* rather than Keynes of the *General Theory*. In this section, I want to explore the Clower–Leijonhufvud version of the deflationary cumulative rot and the ways it builds off of the very Wicksellian monetary equilibrium framework developed in Chapter 3.

Clower's key contribution to this line of thought is the notion of the dual-decision hypothesis and its corollary dictum that 'money buys goods and goods buy money, but goods do not buy goods in an organized market' (1984b [1970]: 100). The dual-decision hypothesis simply recognizes the fact that decisions to buy are intimately linked with decisions to sell in both equilibrium and disequilibrium. In equilibrium, planned sales constrain planned purchases, as the former are the source for the latter. Given that equilibrium is defined in terms of complete compatibility of plans, this 'constraint' does not prevent anyone from executing their desired plans: we sell what we plan to and we buy what we plan to. However, in disequilibrium, this is no longer the case. Here, some, if not many, plans will not be completed and it is not necessarily true that one *is* able to do what one plans. In disequilibrium the constraint upon one's ability to actually *realize* particular purchases is one's *realized* sales. Once one excess demand appears somewhere in the system, there will be implications for the realization of all other planned purchases and sales. Some, if not many, people will be unable to realize their plans.

As Clower carefully points out, this point does not matter in the timeless and instantaneous world of equilibrium. However, when one takes a more process-oriented perspective, and sees that decisions to buy and sell are not made simultaneously but in sequences, then the fact that realized sales constrain planned consumption poses some interesting problems. To take Clower's (1984a [1963]: 48) example, suppose we have a person who is unable to realize sales of his labor services, that is, someone who is involuntarily unemployed in Keynes' sense. The problem is that he cannot consume without first selling his labor services. If sellers knew of his desires to buy, they would be willing to hire him and if he could get hired, he would, in turn, consume. Clower asks how this sort of signal gets sent through the marketplace. His answer is that it happens in a variety of ways, from lowering our reservation wage, to drawing on savings, to reducing our consumption substantially. Clower concludes from this that orthodox equilibrium analysis cannot explain the situation at hand:

> For if current receipts are considered to impose any kind of constraint on current consumption plans, planned consumption as expressed in effective market offers to buy will necessarily be less than desired consumption as given by the demand functions of orthodox analysis.
>
> (ibid.: 49)

Because we might choose to lower our consumption, or are forced to because we accept a wage lower than that which corresponds to our real productivity, our effective demands in the market are less than the demands we would have in equilibrium, where such demands would be driven by our being able to sell our labor services at their 'full' value. This condition is sometimes expressed as our effective demands being less than our 'notional' demands, where notional demand is based on the actual value of our labor's marginal product, rather than what the wages we are actually able to command at a particular instant in the market.[5]

The importance of this insight, according to Clower, is that these excess demands (the difference between our notional and effective demand) will not be registered anywhere in the market. Thus there is an informational breakdown between the sellers of labor services and the sellers of commodities. If those notional demands could be made effective, and therefore 'register' in the market, the buyers of labor services/sellers of commodities would be willing to hire the labor that was signaling its willingness to buy goods and services. This signaling process is further complicated by money's role as a medium of exchange. In barter, of course, all acts of demand are simultaneous acts of supply. The dual-decision hypothesis would still be relevant in a barter world, but in a money-using world, the ability to temporarily store the value of one's realized sales in the form of money may well weaken the ability of commodity buyers to signal their notional demands to commodity sellers.

Leijonhufvud's work, particularly the two essays 'Effective Demand Failures' (1981a) and 'The Wicksell Connection: Variations on a Theme' (1981b), takes Clower's analysis of the dual-decision hypothesis and places it in a Wicksellian framework. More specifically, in line with Keynes' analysis in the *Treatise*, Leijonhufvud is interested in describing the scenario where the market rate of interest is above the natural rate, what we have termed the deflationary monetary disequilibrium.[6] One fundamental concept in Leijonhufvud's work is the notion of the 'corridor'. He argues that within a certain corridor, market price signals generally work well and that deviations from monetary equilibrium will be self-corrected in a relatively short period of time, although not without some real effects. Outside of that corridor, when the exogenous changes impinging on the system are large enough, the Clower-like signaling failure comes into play and, in these scenarios, we cannot be confident at all that market mechanisms will be able to correct the problem. As a result, Keynesian-type unemployment equilibria may occur. Leijonhufvud argues that his analysis in 'The Wicksell Connection' is largely about what happens inside the corridor, while the 'Effective Demand Failures' paper explores what happens outside of the corridor.

Leijonhufvud's own theory, what he terms the 'Z-theory' interpolation between Keynes of the *Treatise* and Keynes of the *General Theory*, attempts to analyze the effects of a deflationary impulse. The focus of that theory is the Wicksellian insight that the central macroeconomic phenomenon is the relationship between the natural and market rates of interest. That relationship depends, in turn, on the relationship between savings and investment. As Leijonhufvud cogently argues, the Wicksellian tradition is defined by its concern about what conditions are necessary for the savings–investment equality to hold and what happens when it does not. This is in contrast to what he terms the Quantity Theory tradition, leading from Fisher up to Friedman, which ignores these interest rate questions because it 'assumes that the interest rate mechanism can be relied upon to coordinate the intertemporal decisions of households and firms' (1981b: 132).[7] Leijonhufvud also argues that this Wicksellian insight has been lost not only due to the rise of interest rate-free monetarism, but also because Keynes himself progressively eliminated the central role of the banking system in determining interest rates in his intellectual shift from the *Treatise* to the *General Theory*. Specifically, it is the liquidity preference theory of interest that drives the final nail in the Wicksellian coffin. As we have noted earlier, it is Keynes' assumption that saving and investment are continually equal that removes the banking system and leaves only liquidity preference as the interest rate determiner. As Leijonhufvud (1981b: 170–1) puts it:

> If saving and investment are continually equal, the rate of interest cannot possibly be governed by any difference between them. The possibility of a corresponding excess flow demand for loanable funds has then also been defined away. The loanable funds interest rate mechanism is gutted.

Hence, the flow part of the *Treatise*'s stock-flow analysis should be erased. The speculative element remaining from it now has to make do as a complete interest theory.

This is the result that Leijonhufvud wishes to avoid.

The Z-theory perspective begins with a hypothesized decline in the marginal efficiency of capital, that is, entrepreneurs turn pessimistic. The demand for loanable funds (investment) declines, while saving remains the same (a shift from I to I' in Figure 5.3). This corresponds to a decline in the natural rate of interest (from nr to nr'), as the pessimism of investors means that they will require lower interest rates in order to undertake projects they would have previously undertaken at higher rates. In the Z-theory model, this decline in the natural rate is not immediately transferred into a corresponding fall in the market rate, leaving the market rate above the natural rate. A fall in income and employment ensues, for either the kinds of reasons outlined in the previous section or a more Keynesian multiplier mechanism. In a truly Wicksellian framework, the fall in income and prices would eventually restore monetary equilibrium at the lower natural rate, but only after a painful adjustment process.

Where Leijonhufvud sees the Z-theory as breaking with Wicksell is over whether this endogenous adjustment need always occur. One central difference is that Leijonhufvud argues that the fall in income drags down savings with it (from S to S'), enabling the securities market to clear at a market interest (mr') rate still above the natural rate (nr'), i.e., the rate that would have held had market mechanisms fully adjusted. The problem here is that the securities market is now cleared, thanks to the income-induced decline in savings, and there is no 'excess flow supply of loanable funds whose accumulating time-integral progressively distorts the balance-sheets of banks and/or bearish speculators' (1981b: 166). Whereas in the truly Wicksellian model, the excess supply of savings at the too-high market rate generates pressure on banks to

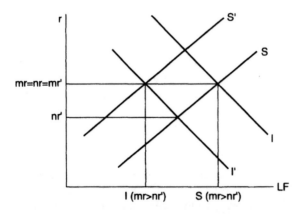

Figure 5.3   Leijonhufvud's Z-theory in the loanable funds market

lower those market rates in response, in the Z-theory model of Leijonhufvud, the income-induced decline in saving can cause the money/securities market to clear at a too-high market rate, with no consequent pressure on anyone to make the needed interest rate adjustments. The key to this result is that the original decline in investment is not immediately offset by price adjustments in the form of the banking system promptly reducing its market rate in response. Absent such price adjustments, output, employment, and income (and therefore saving) will bear the burden of adjustment.

Leijonhufvud does argue that it would take a sizeable shock to generate a reaction adverse enough to throw the economy that far out of whack. The problem faced when deflationary monetary disequilibria get underway is that quickly multiplying effective demand failures can take place. As Clower's work emphasized, realized sales are a constraint on purchases, the unemployment and general excess supply of goods that will accompany the scenario Leijonhufvud lays out may create further problems. To the extent that the current inability to sell labor services prevents workers from purchasing commodities, the sellers of those commodities see their own buying power constrained by the lack of output sales, further constraining other sellers. If income falls enough at the outset, the situation can rapidly turn into a cumulative rot, one which Leijonhufvud believes will require activist fiscal policy to remedy.

However, one cannot neglect the role of cash-balances here. Leijonhufvud (1981a: 117ff.) argues that stocks of liquid assets, such as cash, 'allow expenditures to be maintained when receipts fall off'. These asset stocks are referred to as 'buffers' and they prevent burgeoning effective demand failures from turning into a Wicksellian rot by providing a source of expenditures for the un- or underemployed. The key is that actors hold such buffer stocks based on their expectations of the system's stability. If the size or length of the disturbance is so large that the buffer stocks being held are insufficient, then the rot will set in and policy will be necessary, according to Leijonhufvud. It is these buffers that define what he calls the 'corridor'. As long as such stocks are sufficient, normal market processes will be sufficient to avoid massive excess demand failures, even in the face of exogenous events that cause monetary disequilibria. That is not to say that such disequilibria will be costless, only that eventually, and with some pain, they will be able to self-correct. Outside of the corridor defined by those buffer stocks, the self-correction mechanisms weaken and disappear and systemic breakdowns are possible. This implies 'a variable width of the corridor' as actors will hold buffer stocks based on their past experiences and expectations of the future (1981a: 123).

It is here where Leijonhufvud's perspective overlaps with Yeager's. Both are concerned about the cumulative downturn that can result from a monetary disequilibrium. For Yeager, the originating impulse is normally some error by the banking system that inappropriately reduces the supply of money. For Leijonhufvud, the problem seems to lie more in the banking system's inability to respond appropriately to changes in the factors underlying the natural rate. Despite this very important difference, and it is one that explains Yeager's focus on the role of money and Leijonhufvud's emphasis on the loanable funds market, their explanations of how a problem in the money/loanable funds sector can spill over into the real sector are quite similar.

There will be more to say about Leijonhufvud's theory in the next chapter's discussion of the labor market. For now, one important point is in order. On the surface, the Z-theory approach does not seem like a monetary theory of depression. Leijonhufvud assumes, as Keynes did, that the originating factor is a real disturbance in the form of entrepreneurial pessimism. This disturbs the natural rate, setting up the monetary disequilibrium. From the perspective of this study, however, this is indeed a monetary problem. It has been our contention that it is the responsibility of the banking system to maintain the market rate/natural rate equality. If the natural rate should move for any reason, a properly functioning banking system should respond with a corresponding adjustment in the market rate. Lying hidden in Leijonhufvud's theory is the question of why the banking system does not respond appropriately. Why, for example, does the banking system not, in response to balking borrowers, offer them lower interest rates to buy off their pessimism? This strategy would also reduce the quantity of loanable funds supplied, closing the gap between saving and investment. If the banking system could respond this way well before speculators began to worry about the direction of interest rate movements, or better yet, if speculators knew that a market rate response was quickly forthcoming, then the cumulative process could be choked off, perhaps with only a minimum of buffer stocks necessary. What Leijonhufvud does not point out sufficiently is that the size of the corridor might also depend upon the monetary regime and its perceived ability to make appropriate responses to changes in the natural rate, which could also affect the quantity of buffer stocks that the public holds.

Deflationary monetary disequilibria

Given the general similarities between the two approaches to deflation that we have looked at, we can try to sketch an overarching explanatory story that compares deflationary monetary disequilibria to our monetary equilibrium benchmark. During inflation, *ex ante* investment exceeds *ex ante* saving, and the market rate of interest is less than the natural rate. In deflation, all of those inequalities are reversed. Through precisely the kind of process that Yeager and Greenfield identify, the public's excess demands for money will make themselves known. Whereas during inflation, the excess supplies of real balances were spent on goods and services, driving up their prices, deflation occurs in reverse. Actors find themselves with smaller real balances than they would wish, either due to an absolute decline in the quantity of money or an increase in the intensity of their demands for it unmatched by a new supply, and need to find ways of replenishing them. All of the possibilities noted earlier put downward pressure on prices. In a parallel to the additional spending created during inflation, actors will most likely slacken off their purchases in their attempt to increase their real balances. This fall in aggregate demand puts downward pressure on prices as sellers see rapidly accumulating inventories. The downward pressure on output prices will also put downward pressure on input prices, as sellers get caught in a price-cost squeeze. Eventually, prices will give way and fall. They will continue to fall until the real value of money balances are restored to their pre-deflationary value. It may well happen that various wealth effects that occur during the decline in prices cause the demand for real balances to shift away from that pre-deflationary value. If so, then the price level will have to fall to the point where the (presumed) constant nominal supply of money is equal to the new demand for real balances. The key here is that, *in the long run*, the price level will bear the burden of adjustment and increase the real value of the existing nominal supply of money so as to restore monetary equilibrium.

However, for the reasons laid out in both stories explored in this chapter, this is not the ideal solution. If prices were to move freely and instantaneously to the new, lower level, then deflation would not concern us, but they do not do so, just as prices do not just move upward freely and instantaneously during inflation. The relative price effects we see during inflation, and their corresponding welfare losses, are mirrored by the stickiness of prices during deflations, which ensure that, there will be real welfare losses in the form of unemployed resources and decreased income. Even when prices do get moving, there is no reason to believe that the resulting relative prices, at the lower overall price level, will be the same as prior to the deflation. Much as the excess supplies of money during inflation make their way into market at specific times and places, there is no reason to believe that the excess demands for money will be evenly distributed across the marketplace. Given that estimates of marginal utility are subjective, even an economy-wide event that increased uncertainty and the decreased income velocity (e.g., a possible war) would not be reflected in absolutely equiproportional increases in individuals' demands for real balances. If the deflation is triggered by a decline in the money supply, once again, there is no reason to believe that such a decline will occur evenly. More likely, it will affect particular regions and persons first and the effects on particular prices would depend upon the buying habits and preferences of the persons in question. The structure of relative prices that emerges in the post-deflation monetary equilibrium will be significantly different from the structure that existed pre-deflation.

In general, however, the losses of deflation take the form of idled resources, where the losses of inflation are due to misallocated resources. Although deflations may involve these sorts of relative price effects, it is the idleness created by the process of price adjustment that is their biggest welfare cost. Deflations, therefore, tend to be prevented or headed off much more quickly than inflations because their social costs are so much more obvious. Inflations can be sustained for some period before the burden of the misallocations become obvious enough to be recognized and objected to.

The savings–investment relationship under deflation is also the mirror opposite of what happens during inflation. The excess demand for money implies an excess supply of loanable funds and a market rate above the natural rate. Because banks are not producing enough monetary liabilities to keep up with the demand for them, they find themselves with excess reserves either due to their own reluctance to match the increases in demand by creating more liabilities or due to an actual shrinking of their outstanding liabilities. Assuming equilibrium elsewhere in the loanable funds market, if banks are not intermediating the public's savings into investment funds, the market rate will be above the natural rate. The public genuinely desires to save more, but the banking system is not translating that desire into borrowing by those who want resources. This shrinkage in what we might term the 'effective supply of loanable funds' drives up market rates, or at least prevents them from falling appropriately.

Furthering the parallels between inflation and deflation, we can explore the way in which the *ex ante* inequality of saving and investment becomes an *ex post* equality. During inflation, it was the process of forced saving that provided the additional saving necessary to make possible the actual amount of investment taking place. What is particularly interesting about the loanable funds market during monetary disequilibria is that it is an exception to the usual price theory observation that the short side of the market rules in disequilibrium. With inflation, the long side is investment (which exceeds *ex ante* saving), while with deflation, saving is the long side (it exceeds *ex ante* investment). The reason that the long side rules here is because *in fact* either the banking system is producing the greater amount of investment during inflation, or because consumers are actually saving the *ex ante* larger amount during deflation. If banks are really making loans during inflation, the resources to fund those loans must be coming from some saving somewhere. If consumers are really saving a certain quantity of resources, then that saving must be showing up somewhere as investment.[8]

The answer to this last question, that is, the analog of forced saving during inflation, is that there is what we might term 'forced investment' during deflation. That forced investment takes the form of unplanned inventory accumulations and unintended excess productive capacity. The excess demand for money that defines deflationary monetary disequilibria implies a decline in aggregate demand. Presumably the deflation is unanticipated, and even were it anticipated in the aggregate, its individual microeconomic manifestations would vary from the average, so producers are expecting demand to be within some range of normality. The fall in aggregate demand will begin to manifest itself as falling sales. Producers will not yet have been able recognize the situation, nor to have reduced production or productive capacity in response. To the extent that effects on production lag behind effects on sales, inventories will accumulate beyond what producers wish during such deflationary episodes. For the same reasons that national income accounts consider such accumulations 'investment' so can we label them as such. Inventories are a particular kind of capital asset, one which is more liquid than traditional capital goods and machinery, but less so, of course, than financial assets. In that sense, increasing one's inventories is similar to purchasing a new capital asset. The excess demand for money is therefore matched by an excess supply of goods, specifically unplanned inventory accumulations. Because these inventory increases are unplanned, it seems legitimate to treat them as 'forced' in the same way that reductions in purchasing power are 'forced' on non-recipients of excess supplies of money during inflation. In the same way that the forced saving process turns an *ex ante* excess demand for loanable funds into an *ex post* equilibrium, so do unwanted inventory increases turn an excess supply of loanable funds into an *ex post* equilibrium in the loanable funds market.

Say's Law and the mediating role of money

A monetary equilibrium perspective on deflation can also help sort out the complex of issues surrounding Say's Law and underconsumption. It is easy to mistake deflationary monetary disequilibria as 'underconsumption' crises. After all, there are the classic signs of supposed underconsumption: rising inventories, slackened sales, and downward pressure on prices, including input prices. In addition, given that disposable income must either be devoted to saving or consumption, and that one defining characteristic of deflationary disequilibria is that *ex ante* saving exceeds *ex ante* investment, it seems reasonable to say that deflation involves 'oversavings' and, by extension, 'underconsumption'. Even more fundamentally, Walras' Law tells us that the sum of all excess demands must go to zero. Therefore an excess demand for money must be matched by a negative excess demand (an excess supply) somewhere else. That 'somewhere else' is the entire commodities (and perhaps securities) market. The excess demand for money implies an excess supply of goods. That excess supply of goods suggests that 'underconsumption' might be the problem – if goods are not being sold, it is because people are not buying enough.

The problem with this way of looking at deflation is that it shifts the blame onto consumers rather than the banking system. The reason consumers are not buying is not due to some fatal flaw in the price system, or some behavioral problem on their part, but because they literally cannot find the money they need to have in order to be willing and able to consume. This is where Say's Law comes in. Recalling the discussion from Chapter 3, it was argued that the proper understanding of Say's Law was the idea that production is the source of demand and that the process of translating productive power into effective demand requires the use of money. In a barter economy, Say's Law is trivially true – one buys with one's production. The stock of physical goods or services that one produces is the clear limit on one's ability to consume. Production here is literally the source of demand.

In a monetary economy, things are not so simple. We sell our productive assets and services for money, which in turn becomes the proximate source of demand. The earlier distinction between notional and effective demand comes into play here. Because money splits the sale of productive assets from the ultimate act of purchase, it creates the possibility of a wedge between our notional demand and effective demand. What matters in the market, of course, is effective demand, as that is what determines others' income and their subsequent ability to demand. Thus, in a monetary economy, there are two conceivable limitations on our ability to demand: we may be limited by the real productivity of our labor or capital or by our inability to turn those assets or services into money, which we require in order to effectively demand. Only one of these options, however, can be associated with apparent underconsumption. If we can only demand a little because we are not very productive, then there will not be much output on shelves to be bought in the first place. This is the truism of the colloquial version of Say's Law that 'supply creates its own demand'. If we do not supply much, we will not demand very much and there will be no mismatch between the two. Another way to put this is that our productivity limits our notional demand, so even if our notional demands are fully effective, they will be only as great as our productivity.

However, if money is insufficiently supplied in comparison to the demand to hold it, then our inability to effectively demand will be limited for a different reason – we are unable to translate our productivity (our notional demand) into effective demands. When there is an excess demand for money, the scramble to replenish those real balances implies that people are unable to both hold the real balances they wish and continue to spend on the goods and services they *would* like to have (and in some sense *should* be able to have, given their productivity). As effective demand slackens in one section and the resulting fall in income lowers effective demand elsewhere, producers find that they do not have the money they need to hire workers. A producer may firmly believe that a worker's marginal productivity will marginally exceed the wage both agree upon, but given what Leijonhufvud calls a 'cash constraint' deriving from the deficient supply of money, the producer cannot find the thing needed to effect payment. Deflationary monetary equilibria cause a leakage in the Say's Law transformation of productivity into demand. Labor and capital lie idle not because their productivity has suddenly fallen, nor because consumers do not want (at least notionally) their output, but because the excess demand for money prevents people from making purchases on both sides of the market. To blame consumers for not buying enough in this apparent underconsumption crisis misses the point. They cannot buy because they do not have what they need in order to effectively demand: money. The blame here rests with the banking system and its inability to get the money supply right.

The relationship between Say's Law and deflation depends heavily on money's fundamental role as a medium of exchange. Attempts to explain the problems associated with deflation, or to understand Say's Law more generally, that do not treat money first and foremost as a generally accepted medium of exchange are bound to obscure what is really going on. It is precisely because money is necessary in order to make notional demands effective that deflations cannot proceed costlessly. If money is only a store of value or an accounting device, it is not clear why the necessary price adjustments could not just take place quickly and smoothly. It is only because the lack of money prevents actors from engaging in desired exchanges that downward pressure is put on prices, and it is partially because the 'missing' money does not occur evenly across time and space in the market that the downward movement does not occur evenly and smoothly.

When money is added to a macro model as simply 'another good', these fundamental insights are overlooked. As Leijonhufvud (1968: 79) has said:

> Cash is the perfectly liquid asset. This suggests the 'essential and peculiar' role that money plays . . . Much of modern monetary theory deals with money as just one of the goods in a general equilibrium model. It is now clear that in general equilibrium all goods are perfectly liquid . . . Money has no special status, and in a model which deals only with situations characterized by exchange equilibrium, money is (at most) 'just another good.'

This suggests the importance of a Mengerian approach to microeconomics as the foundations for macroeconomics. General equilibrium theory is ill-suited to the task precisely because any introduction of a meaningful money into such models is quite *ad hoc*, whereas the notion of money as a medium of exchange grows naturally out of a process-oriented microeconomics like that of Menger. A view of the market process that contains a full-blown theory of money as a medium of exchange is necessary for understanding the macroeconomic havoc that monetary disequilibria can create.

Deflation, the productivity norm, and the price system

The preceding can also help us clarify Chapter 3's discussion of the productivity norm. An apparent objection to our line of thought might be that in our discussion of deflation we have been very concerned about the deleterious effects of falling prices necessitated by an excess demand for money, yet the productivity norm position argues that prices can and should fall when productivity increases, even if monetary equilibrium is maintained. More specifically, one might argue that our discussion of deflation cautions that we should avoid situations where increases in the demand for money are unmatched by increases in the nominal supply, due to the ensuing price level effects. By contrast, we seemed to say in Chapter 3 that if productivity increases, surely implying an increase in income and the demand for money, the proper policy is to let the price level fall, so as to increase the real supply of money to meet the now-higher demand for it. Are these two positions in contradiction with one another?[9]

The answer is no. The confusion creeps in because of the use of two different senses of the 'demand for money'. We can talk of money's 'income velocity', which refers to the demand to hold money relative to income, and we can talk of the 'demand for money' in the sense of the absolute amount of money people hold. This difference is important because the productivity norm and monetary equilibrium theory suggest that it is only changes in income velocity that require offsetting changes in the nominal money supply, while changes in the absolute demand for money, coming from productivity-induced changes in income, can be met by changes in the price level. Changes in either aspect of the demand for money require changes in the real money supply to maintain monetary equilibrium. However, changes in income velocity are best handled by changes in the nominal money supply and changes in the absolute demand for money are best handled by changes in relative prices, and by implication, the price level. Our discussion of money's pervasiveness and the sectoral nature of productivity changes provide the explanation for this difference. In quantity-theoretic terms, the proper response to a change in Q is an inverse change in P and the proper response to a change in V is an inverse change in M.

Whenever an excess demand for money appears (whether via changes in income velocity or the absolute demand), downward pressure on prices will be concurrent or follow shortly. We have argued that when income velocity, V in the equation of exchange, decreases, this downward pressure on prices will soon try to exert itself. The key here is that movements in the price level are always *unintended* consequences of innumerable microeconomic decisions. The problem during deflation is that no specific actor(s) in the market has any clear incentive to begin the necessary microeconomic process of lowering prices. The who-goes-first type problems come to the forefront. The falling price level is a public good of sorts and each actor wishes to reap the benefits of the needed decline, but no one is able to bear the cost of starting the process. With everyone trying to free ride off the desired result, it never occurs. No individual has an interest in doing what would, if done collectively, benefit all – a classic Prisoners' Dilemma.

This is but another way of emphasizing money's pervasiveness. A general decline in income velocity (perhaps resulting from increased uncertainty about the future) means that adjustments have to take place in all money-using markets, that is, almost all markets everywhere. These sort of changes in income velocity are money-side changes and are almost of necessity pervasive.

Changes in the absolute demand for money resulting from productivity-induced changes in income are different. Looking at the case of an increase in factor productivity that increases income and the absolute demand for money, this should be clear. The essential difference is that productivity increases are *intended* by individual producers, hence the decline in prices necessary to make the existing nominal quantity of money meet the higher demand for real balances, can be accomplished through the falling prices that are part and parcel of productivity increases (Selgin 1990: 280).[10] For example, suppose a particular firm develops a more efficient machine for producing its product. As a result, assuming some form of mark-up pricing, some of the productivity gains will be passed on as lower output prices. These lower prices mean increased income for those who purchase the product, as well as the producers who profit from the lower input costs despite the lower output price. These income increases will lead to a higher demand for real balances. But notice that this new demand gets met simultaneously through the falling output prices. If all other prices remain the same, the lower price for the good in question brings down the overall price level (albeit not by much, but then income has likely not risen by much either), rendering the existing nominal money supply sufficient to meet the higher demand for real balances. The more widespread or more frequent are such productivity gains, the larger will be the income increase and demand for money increase. Fortunately this would also mean that the fall in the price level would be greater, providing a built-in mechanism for meeting any increase in the demand for real balances.

In contrast to the decrease in income velocity case, where the necessary movement in the price level was a public good, the price level effects of productivity changes are private goods. The firms themselves have every incentive to lower output prices, both due to their lower input costs and their desire to attract additional business. Here too, the overall fall in the price level is an unintended result, but in this case the individual acts that comprise it are in the private interest of market actors. In the income velocity case, the price level decline that happens will be an unintended consequence, but only after painfully overcoming that fact that it is not in the private interest of actors to set the process in motion. Only after the wrenching effects of the deflation make themselves known do actors begin to react. With productivity changes, the requisite price level effects are simply an aspect of the productivity change, which is itself in the interest of various private actors to encourage.

It is important to recall that, although we can separate these two aspects of the demand for money for the sake of analysis, in the real world they will often go together. It is surely possible that a productivity increase might be such that the increase in income and the absolute demand for money move in such a way as to keep income velocity constant. It is also at least possible that separate income velocity effects might occur as well, implying that the productivity-induced movement in the price level will not be enough to satisfy the new demand for real balances. In such a situation, changes in the nominal money supply would be called for. Real world changes in productivity may lead to later-round effects on income velocity and the nominal money supply. To the extent that productivity changes only affect the absolute demand for money, however, they require no change in the nominal money supply as the productivity change brings with it the change in the price level necessary to adjust the real supply of money to the new demand for real balances.

The welfare costs of deflation

Unlike inflation, a discussion of the welfare losses associated with deflation is not overly complex. The reason is straightforward: to the extent that deflation *in combination with downward price stickiness* leads to quantity adjustments, the welfare losses are the forgone exchanges that would have taken place if the deflation had not happened. These forgone exchange are also obvious, in that unsold goods appear on store shelves and unsold labor shows up as increases in unemployment. The reductions in income that go with these forgone sales are also obvious to those they affect. Because real resources impose an upper limit on the kind and number of exchanges that can take place, during inflation the problem is that the wrong kinds of exchanges occur, rather than 'too many'. Diagnosing what makes an exchange 'wrong' in this sense is a more complex task than simply noting that exchanges have not occurred. Thus, as the last chapter's lengthy discussion illustrates, exploring the welfare costs of inflation takes a great deal of patience in searching out all the ways inflation redirects and wastes resources.

Nonetheless, there are some welfare losses associated with deflation that parallel those of inflation. One set of problems is the effects of the relative price changes that comprise the eventual fall in the price level. With all our discussion of the stickiness of prices, it is important to reiterate that prices will eventually fall, if they are not prevented from doing so by extra-market forces such as government intervention, and a new monetary equilibrium will be established. The losses due to forgone exchanges take place during the transition from one monetary equilibrium to another. But there are losses that remain even after the new equilibrium is attained.

For example, there is no reason to believe that relative price effects will be absent from deflation. In the same way that excess supplies of money enter the market in very specific places and take distinct paths through the market, so might excess demands for money arise in specific places and to varying degrees. One could surely imagine sectoral or regional changes in income velocity triggering this process. The unevenness of the original excess demand for money would suggest that the original downward pressure on prices will take a path that is dependent upon the buying habits of those trying to increase their money balances. If we assume that money balances are increased by slowing down one's spending, then the downward pressure will indeed be first felt by specific sellers. As the cash-constrained process spreads, the pressure will spread out in an uneven pattern, with unequal downward pressure on different prices. When the price level as a whole does eventually fall to the level consistent with monetary equilibrium, there is no reason to suppose that individual money prices stand in the same relationship to one another as they did prior to the deflation.

These downward relative price effects do not reflect changes in any real variables on the goods side of the market. Instead, they reflect distortions coming from the money side of the market, and as such, serve no efficiency-enhancing role in the larger view. Of course, general downward price movements are desirable given the excess demand for money because, if they do not occur, more significant quantity adjustments will have to take place. But money-induced declines in prices are not necessary if the banking system can maintain monetary equilibrium, and even if such declines should take place, they would be less harmful if they avoided relative price effects during the fall in the price level.

Such relative price effects create many of the same problems we discussed with respect to relative price effects during inflation. When relative prices are moving around for reasons both unconnected with the underlying variables of the goods side and avoidable through a proper monetary regime, their epistemic function is undermined and the monetary calculation process that is necessary for making rational economic choices is compromised. By divorcing prices from the underlying variables, deflation makes monetary calculation more difficult, which suggests that more errors will be made in the resource allocation process. To the extent that such mistakes involve irretrievable costs, then the relative price effects of deflation become an additional source of economic waste.

In particular, we might expect to see two specific kinds of relative price effects during deflation. One would be the understating of the profitability of firms. An unexpected fall in the price level will shrink the nominal revenues obtained in the future from the inputs priced at today's historical cost. As firms' balance sheets look more dismal, they may be led to make adjustments in their production processes (including, but not limited to, laying off workers) that will later be seen to be an erroneous reaction to a temporary phenomenon. Any irretrievable costs of adjustment are wasted. A second pattern of relative price effects would be those associated with the interest rate. During the initial excess demand for money, the market rate will be above the natural rate. This will encourage firms to shrink the length of their capital projects, that is, to squeeze together or eliminate stages of production. Firms that decide to make such decisions unaware that the deflation, and not any real factors, is causing the rise in rates may later regret the decision and will have wasted any irretrievable adjustment costs. As the market rate of interest becomes disconnected with underlying variables, due to the banking system's inability to maintain monetary equilibrium, it will induce precisely these kind of distortions into the capital structure. In the Yeager and Leijonhufvud literature on monetary disequilibria, there is little mention of capital structure effects, but to the extent such effects are expected to occur in inflationary monetary disequilibria, why would we not expect them during deflation?[11]

In our discussion of monetary equilibrium, and again in the exploration of inflation in Chapter 4, we argued that only in monetary equilibrium is the capital structure potentially sustainable. During inflation, the excess supply of funds for investment means that eventually the insufficiency of savings will make itself known when consumers' intertemporal preferences are found to be at odds with entrepreneurial expectations. During deflation, the unsustainability takes a different form. Here, producers believe that consumers want goods relatively more in the present (due to the erroneously high market rate) and must eventually discover that their production processes could have been profitably made more roundabout. The unsustainability lies in the fact that the too-short production processes will prove to be unprofitable. The excess supply of consumer goods resulting from the excess demand for money, and its consequent interest rate effects, is a signal that current production activities are not optimal. If we assume that firms will seek profits, then the shortening of the structure of production induced by the deflation will not be sustainable. And, again, all sunk costs incurred in the transition to the shorter production processes are economic waste.

These relative price effects, including those resulting from the erroneous market rate of interest, are one major reason why a policy of maintaining monetary equilibrium is so desirable. It is these relative price effects that are avoided by responding to a change in velocity with offsetting changes in the nominal supply of money. The attempt to move the general price level downward, resulting from uncompensated changes in velocity creates the kind of stickiness-induced problems we discussed at the outset of this chapter. The possibility of significant unemployment and reduced incomes resulting from excess demands for money is a significant reason to avoid such scenarios by encouraging monetary regimes that will produce offsetting increases in the nominal money supply. Even if the fall in the overall price level were to occur more quickly, we would still have the various relative price effects discussed above. The combination of price stickiness and the relative price effects that will occur when the stickiness is overcome is a powerful argument for attempting to avoid deflationary monetary disequilibria. Notice, however, that these arguments do not apply with equal force to productivity-induced downward pressure on prices. The explanation is that such price movements are supposed to be comprised of relative price changes – that is what non-uniform productivity increases are. Supply-side pressure on prices will never be market-wide because productivity changes are virtually never market-wide. Because such price changes are intended by producers, they both avoid the stickiness problem and pose no distortionary relative price effect problems. These relative price movements are desirable precisely because they reflect changes in underlying real variables, in this case factor productivity.

We can also briefly note that deflation will involve coping costs that are parallel to those created by inflation. Some of the costs of unanticipated deflation will be different for particular groups, as, for example, the fall in the price level will lead to increased wealth for lenders and people whose income is fixed in nominal terms. Of course, borrowers and providers of fixed incomes may find themselves having to incur various costs in adjusting portfolios to compensate for the losses deriving from unexpected deflations. So too would we expect to see employers push for more frequent wage negotiations (shorter contract periods) so as to avoid giving real wage increases as the price level falls against contractually fixed nominal wages. And, as during inflation, both sides would want to invest in finding a measure of the price level that works in their own interest. Individuals will have to consider portfolio adjustments, as cash holding might look marginally more profitable, while nominal interest rates may be falling. More generally, any movement in the price level (even if expected in some cases) will lead people to undertake the sorts of defensive measures we discussed in the last chapter. This is true whether the price level trend is upward or downward.

The relationship between monetary disequilibrium and the political process is different, but no less important, in deflation than it is in inflation. The similarity is that both monetary disequilibria will likely lead to calls for political intervention to clean up the mess that each makes. In both cases those interventions look like short-term cures but wind up exacerbating the problems created by each disequilibrium. In inflation, we saw that actors will want the government to intervene to keep prices down or to tax or support particular industries being affected by the inflation. During deflation, parallel demands for intervention will come from the public not in their capacity as consumers paying higher prices but as wage-earners who are being asked to accept nominal wage cuts as the price level falls. In the same way that political actors see votes in promising to keep prices down during inflation, they can benefit from promising to keep wages up during deflation. Pure political self-interest may be sufficient to explain why attempts to maintain nominal wages get through the political process, but they do not explain why the public would call for them in the first place, assuming politicians themselves do not stir up the issue (which is certainly a plausible scenario).

There are at least three possible explanations for the public resisting nominal wage cuts. The first is money illusion. It is possible that people do not understand that nominal wage cuts when output prices are falling will leave them more or less the same as they were. If people do not understand this, they will resist nominal wage cuts. A second explanation is that people hold false economic theories that argue that maintaining wage levels is necessary to maintain spending or purchasing power so that the economy can continue to grow. As Rothbard (1963) and Vedder and Gallaway (1993) document, this was a widely held view during the early 1930s and is a strong explanation for why various policies attempting to boost nominal wages were introduced under both Hoover and Roosevelt. This view sees wages only as income to workers and not as costs to firms. A third explanation is that the public *does* understand what they are doing and simply sees resisting nominal wage cuts as a way to increase their real wages. This explanation might fit the attitude of organized labor, for example. Whichever explanation or combination of explanations is at work, a deflation of any significance will likely engender calls for policies or jawboning designed to prop up falling nominal wages.

As with the price controls that frequently accompany inflation, wage supports treat only the symptom and not the disease. The disease is in the monetary sector, not prices *per se*. Wages are headed downward for monetary reasons, and those reasons are the place to look for 'cures'. Of course, trying to maintain nominal wages during a deflation will only exacerbate the ongoing problems. Even without government intervention, price and wage stickiness may be severe enough to create significant excess supplies of outputs and inputs. Bringing in more stickiness, if not outright rigidity, through government policy or jawboning further prevents the necessary price adjustments from taking place. As a result, unemployment and bankruptcies rise, leading to related problems, such as bank failures. Although the downward wage and price adjustments will be painful without government intervention, such intervention only rubs salt into the wound.

Like inflation again, the unintended undesirable consequences of this political intervention will themselves lead to additional calls for intervention. Widespread unemployment caused by exacerbating the downward stickiness of wages will lead to various forms of unemployment compensation or other assistance programs.[12] Price supports in areas such as agriculture will create excess supplies there, which will then lead to the sort of complex and arcane procedures for government purchase and payments not to grow that have characterized US farm policy in the twentieth century. Business failures will lead to calls for the nationalization of firms or the socialization of investment funds, and bank failures will lead to calls for deposit insurance and other regulations directed at the symptoms and not the disease. More generally, to the extent a mild deflation is exacerbated by price and wage minima, it will cause people to lose faith in the market as a system, not unlike the way inflation may also generate a shift from market-based resource allocation to the politicization of the resource allocation process. If the market economy is perceived as being the cause of the massive unemployment and failure of businesses and farms, support for the market principle will be slowly eroded.

Of course the previous paragraph blurs the line between theory and history as much of what it 'predicts' about the effects of a deflation exacerbated by price minima in fact occurred in the Great Depression in the US and much of the rest of the industrialized world. The evidence marshaled by Rothbard (1963) and Vedder and Gallaway (1993) shows that prior to the Great Depression, the US economy was able to avoid significant unemployment for any real length of time precisely because wages were relatively free to adjust downward when needed. The Great Depression brought an end to that policy, as bad economic ideas and the self-interest of labor and politicians led to calls for maintaining nominal wages in the face of a 30 percent decline in the money supply. It is of little surprise that the result was 25 percent unemployment, a failure of one-third of US banks, and widespread business bankruptcies. It is also no surprise that these consequences of government intervention led to calls for more intervention. The 1930s were a classic example of Robert Higgs' 'ratchet effect' and Mises' interventionist dynamic noted in Chapter 4. Bad policy leads to bad results, which lead to more bad policy, which leads to an ever-expanding role for government and an increase in the waste associated with the politicization of more of the economy.

All of those problems could have been avoided had the banking system been better able to maintain monetary equilibrium. Even in the face of the drastic decline in the money supply, allowing prices to fall to the extent possible would have minimized the effects of the excess demand for money on employment and output. By minimizing those effects, the further calls for intervention would have been less and many of the costly and inefficient policies adopted during the 1930s might have never been adopted. From this perspective, the welfare costs of deflation can potentially be enormous. Aside from the immediate output and employment effects, the misallocation coming from relative price effects, and the wastes associated with coping costs, we need to account for the longer-run effects on the relationship between the political sector and the market. The temptation to call for political intervention during a deflation of any real significance will be hard to resist for both the public at large and the political sector. The evidence from the US experience in the early 1930s suggests that giving in to that temptation will create significant welfare losses both in the short and long run. In many ways, the current US economy is still bearing some of the costs of the mistakes made during the deflation of the early 1930s.

This point just reiterates why maintaining monetary equilibrium is so important. Maintaining monetary equilibrium means avoiding price level pressures coming from aggregate demand, but not aggregate supply. The whole point of Chapter 1's discussion of the epistemic role of prices was that they *should* move when real supply factors change. To the extent the banking system can maintain monetary equilibrium, it will make the aggregate demand side of the quantity equation (MV) stable, and allow changes in productivity to have the appropriate effect on the price level.

The New Keynesians on price stickiness

The monetary equilibrium approach to deflation appears to share some central concerns with the body of work known as 'New Keynesian' economics. One of the core tenets of New Keynesianism is the stickiness of prices. We explored some of this literature (e.g., menu costs) in Chapter 4's discussion of the costs of inflation. For the New Keynesians, price stickiness is associated with the aforementioned menu costs, as well as the existence of various forms of imperfect competition, and game-theoretic coordination problems along the lines of the who-goes-first problem. In many ways the New Keynesian approach can be said to be a response to the New Classical models of the late 1970s and early 1980s, where the use of general equilibrium models, built on the dual assumption of perfect competition and perfect price flexibility, generated results demonstrating the impotence of systematic activist monetary and fiscal policy. New Keynesians, among others, found those microfoundations to be inappropriate for a real world economic system where perfect competition was absent, and where markets were characterized by price-making behavior and imperfect information. The New Keynesian approach can perhaps best be summarized by the following question: what are the theoretical and policy implications of building macroeconomics on the microfoundations of information asymmetries, imperfect competition, and imperfectly flexible prices?[13]

For New Keynesians, there is both a real and nominal component to the stickiness of prices, including wages. Nominal wage stickiness can be explained by the existence of long-term contracts that prevent instantaneous, auction market-like, changes in nominal wages in the face of changes in the price level. An early paper by Fischer (1977) first articulated this point in the context of responding to New Classical claims about the impotence of systematic monetary policy under the assumption of rational expectations. Subsequent work by New Keynesians has fleshed out the Fischer argument and its contract-market underpinnings. Nominal price stickiness can result from a variety of factors, including the menu costs problem discussed in Chapter 4 and the who-goes-first problem noted earlier in this chapter. In addition, the absence of perfect competition implies that changes in demand for a product need not lead to immediate changes in prices. If one assumes monopolistic competition, a decline in demand may not affect marginal revenue and marginal cost in a way that would necessitate a price cut to maintain profit maximization (Ball and Romer 1990). Monopolistic competitors may have sound incentives to wait before cutting price. Perfect competitors would have no such incentives.

There is a real component to price and wage stickiness as well. If, as Ball *et al.* (1988) and Romer (1993) argue, it is easier to sell outputs and purchase inputs when markets are active than when economic activity has slackened, then marginal cost and revenue curves will shift as the overall level of economic activity changes. Thus, during a recession, a rising marginal cost curve caused by these externalities associated with the 'thickness' or 'thinness' of markets will reduce a producer's incentive to lower the price. A belief in these externalities associated with the thickness of markets leads New Keynesians to posit a degree of real price stickiness. On the labor market side, the familiar New Keynesian notion of the efficiency wage can explain real wage stickiness, as can various insider–outsider and bargaining theories. If changes in wages cause changes in worker efficiency, then wages will be clearly sticky downward, as any cuts in wages will lead to reduced effort or the like, which will lead to increased average costs and lower profitability. The various costs associated with bargaining with existing workers or hiring new, and imperfectly substitutable, workers can also lead to firms being reluctant to change real wages during a recession.

All of these forms of price stickiness have consequences for real output and employment. The reason that New Keynesians are concerned about price stickiness is not all that different from those expressed by many monetary equilibrium theorists: if prices cannot appropriately adjust to changes in real underlying variables, then resource misallocation and waste will result, lowering the potential economic growth and prosperity a given economy can generate. In contrast to the New Classical economics, where the general equilibrium modeling strategy prevents theorists from even considering these questions, both a monetary equilibrium approach with Mengerian microfoundations, and a New Keynesian approach with (Stiglitzian?) microfoundations derived from models of imperfect competition, are both legitimately concerned with the ability of prices to do their job.

Despite these similarities, there are crucial differences to consider, especially as a way of looking forward to the policy implications to be discussed in Chapter 7. Perhaps the most fundamental difference between the monetary equilibrium and New Keynesian approaches concerns the *cause* of economy-wide fluctuations. For monetary equilibrium theorists, pervasive economic problems can only be caused by a good or service that is pervasive across markets. If disequilibrium occurs in the market for a particular good, there are strong incentives to prevent such a disequilibrium from persisting through time. Although individual markets, and markets in general, are never actually *in* equilibrium, monetary equilibrium theorists do tend to believe that the corrective powers of the market outweigh the discoordinating ones. Therefore, disequilibrium in any specific market is extremely unlikely to generate market-wide consequences. Disequilibrium in the market for a good with the pervasiveness of money, however, is another story. Thus for monetary equilibrium theory, as we have argued repeatedly, economic fluctuations must begin with disequilibrium in the money market. It is surely true that changes in specific markets might lead to pressure on the banking system, but it is the banking system's response that determines whether fluctuations will occur. Even changes in important markets such as the market for time must ultimately lead to monetary disequilibria if they are to have pervasive effects.[14]

New Keynesians, by contrast, offer a number of possible scenarios that can trigger economy-wide fluctuations: changes in expectations, changes in the marginal efficiency of capital, technological shocks, and even monetary factors can all begin the process. The various nominal and real rigidities just discussed become the process by which the original real or monetary impulse is propagated. An implication of this theoretical position is that macroeconomic disturbances are evidence of 'some sort of market failure on a grand scale' (Mankiw 1990: 1654, as cited in Shah 1997: 39). Mankiw and Romer (1993a: 3) put it this way: 'Because the theories developed in this book emphasize market imperfections, they usually imply that the unfettered market reaches inefficient equilibria.' Although they go on to say that it is an open question whether government policy can in fact improve on those outcomes, they clearly state that government intervention can 'potentially' do so. Thus, as Shah (1997: 39) puts it, the New Keynesian argument about wage and price stickiness 'is a normative proposition' (or an 'imperfection' of the market, as Mankiw and Romer note above) and not just a description of market reality. The market is to be condemned as imperfect for not achieving the perfect price flexibility associated with the perfectly competitive ideal, that is, not being perfectly competitive is deemed a 'failure'.

The irony of this point is that it suggests that the New Classicals and New Keynesians (frequently tacitly) share a fundamental perspective that sets them apart from a monetary equilibrium approach built on Mengerian microfoundations. Both schools of thought agree that the model of perfectly competitive general equilibrium can be used to render normative judgments about market reality. The New Classicals argue that government policy is pointless because it cannot improve upon the Pareto optimal outcomes generated by general equilibrium modeling strategies. New Keynesians appear to agree that if markets were the way New Classicism describes them, then there would be no macroeconomic problems and no scope for policy. Where they differ is by claiming that real markets do not behave the way the New Classical theory describes and, therefore, that the results such markets produce are inefficient or can be fruitfully described as market 'failures' or 'imperfections'. The notion of failure here is by comparison with the perfectly competitive ideal, an ideal shared by New Classicism.[15] The split is over whether it is useful and predictively accurate to treat real-world markets as if they were perfectly competitive. Neither school questions whether using perfectly competitive general equilibrium as a normative benchmark is a good theoretical strategy.

Questioning that benchmark is precisely what a monetary equilibrium macroeconomics based on an Austrian view of the price formation process can do. Historically, monetary equilibrium theorists have treated 'wage and price stickiness as a positive proposition' (Shah 1997: 39). Some in this tradition have argued that even perfect price flexibility might not be enough to remove the undesirable consequences of monetary disequilibria. If so, then the inflexibility of prices is not seen as an 'imperfection', rather as a fact of economic reality that has to be dealt with.[16]

There are numerous, quite rational, reasons why prices would be sticky even in an unhampered market. Just as one example, there are clear advantages to both parties from wage contracts that are renegotiated annually or even less frequently. Renegotiation has significant transaction costs that may dwarf any potential damage from changes in the value of money. If wages are subject to long-term contracts, a sudden decline in demand will put a squeeze on firms. If they drop their output prices immediately, they will either face diminished profits and/or have to lay off workers, being unable to lower their wages to match their lower output price. Even if no explicit contract exists, notions of what a 'normal' wage is in a particular industry may have a great deal of staying power, even after a somewhat lengthy decline in sales. Such inertia may be due to plain stubbornness or some goodwill toward employees that sees releasing them as being a choice of last resort. It might also be true that notions of 'normality' also apply to output prices, leading sellers to be reluctant to lower them during downturns. What seems clear is that both labor and goods markets are, in reality, not auction markets with standardized commodities where price is the only differentiating variable, making quick price changes more likely. Rather, they are customer markets where all sorts of non-monetary margins can be the focus of adjustment in the face of declines in aggregate demand.

With the market conceptualized as a process of entrepreneurial discovery in the face of genuine uncertainty, the fact that prices are less than perfectly flexible should come as no surprise. Lacking perfect knowledge, entrepreneurs are constantly in the business of interpreting market information rather than reacting to it in predictable, mechanistic ways. This is one explanation of the previously noted results Blinder (1991) found in his survey of how firms react to supply and demand shocks.[17] These non-price changes simply reflect firms searching for ways to find the optimal mix that consumers demand and to avoid constantly changing prices.[18] Thus, prices move in fits and starts, with no guarantee that they are headed toward market clearing at any particular point in time. Given the inherent uncertainty of market conditions, and that entrepreneurs cannot disentangle monetary from real impulses, a reluctance to change prices whenever some piece of market data changes or price changes that move in the wrong direction, is completely understandable. In addition, an Austrian approach to the market process will take seriously various institutional practices (such as long-term contracts) that may make price and wages less than perfectly flexible, but are nonetheless efficiency-enhancing, given an uncertain future. For Austrians, the less-than-perfect flexibility of prices is not to be lamented, but recognized as an inherent part of how the market is to be understood. Like all social institutions, prices must have some stability and continuity to help actors coordinate their plans in a world of uncertainty and dispersed knowledge.

Whatever the source, it is clear that there are good reasons to believe that input and output prices are less than perfectly flexible (even in an unhampered market), implying that any excess demand for money will not be immediately remedied by a downward adjustment in prices. Without such an adjustment, the effects of such a monetary disequilibrium will be on quantities purchased, both of outputs and of inputs, including labor. Given the imperfect flexibility of prices, excess demands for money will create excess supplies of goods and inputs. Rather than compare the outcome of real-world market processes to the unattainable ideal of an auction market in perfect competition, a Mengerian perspective forces us to ask whether there are removable barriers to the free flow of knowledge and action that are impeding the market discovery process. As Hayek (1978a: 185) argued, the proper standard of comparison for the market process is not the ideal of perfect competition, but the degree of economic coordination that would occur if competition were stifled or absent:

> We do injustice to the achievement of the market if we judge it, as it were, from above, by comparing it with an ideal standard which we have no known way of achieving . . . [W]e [should] judge it . . . from below, that is . . . against what would be produced if competition were prevented.

For monetary equilibrium theory, the stickiness of prices implies no claim about the performance of the market process.

The difference between the groups' approaches to sticky prices is also clear in their approaches to resolving the problems sticky prices create. According to monetary equilibrium theorists, policy-makers should avoid unnecessarily creating the need for price adjustments. In particular, they should avoid the need for the across-the-board price adjustments associated with monetary disequilibria. Although removing government impediments to increased price flexibility is desirable, it can only go so far. As long as prices are less than perfectly flexible, monetary disequilibria are to be avoided.[19] Because the source of the impulse that becomes an economy-wide breakdown is monetary, according to monetary equilibrium theory, the appropriate policy is to avoid those monetary mistakes.

For New Keynesians, by contrast, the appropriate policy solutions are either to make prices more flexible where possible or to use government intervention to overcome the problems created by unavoidably sticky prices. In particular, a role is seen for government in resolving the game-theoretic coordination problems involved with price adjustments. Where individual rationality leads to collective irrationality, the claim is that government can step in to impose a global solution (or broker a cooperative one) that could not be found through individual choices. Government could also increase nominal wage flexibility by limiting the length of labor contracts and it could increase real wage flexibility through the use of monetary policy.

It would be easy to conclude that the difference between the two groups boils down to a difference over the relative effectiveness of market and political processes. There is no doubt that this is part of the debate. However, more fundamental to explaining their differences is the use of the equilibrium benchmark. Both groups say prices are sticky, but as Shah (1997: 42) rightly asks 'sticky compared to what?' The normative power of the term 'sticky' derives from the acceptance of the perfectly flexible prices of the auction markets of general equilibrium theory as the welfare benchmark, and the implied preference for policies that better approximate that ideal. If that benchmark is dropped, then the normative connotation of 'sticky' prices disappears, and a different set of policy implications emerges. In addition, New Keynesian policy proposals of government activism are open to the usual sorts of Austrian criticisms, namely, do policy-makers have the knowledge and the incentives to do what models ask of them? In particular, activist proposals need to be scrutinized with the same critical eye as market institutions are, because it may well be the case that such policies are subject to government failures worse that the supposed market failures they are designed to correct.

Rothbard on changes in the purchasing power of money

The discussion of this chapter and the previous one would not be complete without addressing one of the foremost contributors to Austrian work on monetary issues. In his treatise on economics, *Man, Economy, and State* (1962), and elsewhere, Murray Rothbard put forward a distinct perspective on inflation and deflation. Rothbard's line of thought continues to be influential among some Austrian economists and is at odds with the approach taken in this study. It is, therefore, worth spending some time exploring Rothbard's views and determining where and why the monetary equilibrium approach differs. In doing so, we have to perform a bit of a high-wire act. Central to Rothbard's monetary theory is his preferred monetary regime. He was a strident defender of a gold standard and 100 percent reserve banking and a fierce opponent of fractional reserve banking of all sorts, calling it both fraudulent and inflationary. The discussion of that policy will wait for Chapter 7 and here we will simply address Rothbard's views on inflation and deflation. However, we will see that his definitions of inflation and deflation are so bound up with his views on fractional reserve banking that we will inevitably be drawn into some of those policy issues in this section.

Of necessity we will start with Rothbard's definition of inflation because he argues that inflation is the 'primary event' and that 'there can be no deflation without an inflation having occurred in some previous period of time' (1962: 851). The reason for this view is that he defines inflation as 'the process of issuing money beyond any increase in the stock of specie' or, alternately, 'any increase in the supply of money not matched by an increase in the gold or silver stock available' (1962: 851, 852). Immediately one can see the relationship between his definition of inflation and his argument for 100 percent reserves. This definition of inflation amounts to saying that any form of fractional reserve banking is inflationary. If a bank creates money in excess of its holdings of specie, then it is engaging in inflation. Conversely, deflation is defined (ibid.: 851) as a 'contraction in the money supply outstanding over any period (aside from a net decrease in specie).' By definition, therefore, Rothbard makes the claim noted above that deflation cannot occur without a prior inflation. Unlike inflation, where a bank can issue claims to money in excess of the bank's holdings of specie, it is in Rothbard's view impossible for a bank to issue claims for an amount *less than* its specie holdings. Presumably any depositor of specie will want a receipt for that amount and that receipt serves as money. In addition, a bank that acquired specie on its own and then decided not to monetize it by lending it out would be sacrificing the interest earnings necessary to compensate for the cost of obtaining the specie. By ruling out absolute losses in specie from the definition of deflation, Rothbard can only see deflation as occurring after an inflation.

In much of his discussion of the effects of inflation, Rothbard covers the standard Austrian ground of relative price effects, debtor–creditor redistributions, and the business cycle. He also recognizes that inflation is fundamentally a redistributive process. So much so that he is led to say that there is 'no social utility in an increased supply, nor any social disutility in a decreased supply, of money. This is true for the transition period [between monetary equilibria] as well' (1962: 711).[20] This is worded very carefully to leave open the possibility that inflation causes a decrease in utility and deflation an increase therein, but his emphasis is surely on the redistributive processes at work in both inflation and deflation. The nuances of that quote aside, in analyzing the effects of inflation, he is largely on target. What is interesting, but not surprising, is the dearth of attention paid to deflation. In the 30-page section where he discusses the effects of inflation (as an instance of 'the economics of violent intervention in the market'), his discussion of deflation is less than two full pages. It occurs in the sub-section on 'Secondary Developments of the Business Cycle' and is mostly laudatory concerning the ways in which deflation is necessary to undo the effects of the necessarily prior inflation. Even the redistributive aspect of deflation is praised because it 'takes away from the original coerced gainers [from inflation] and benefits the original coerced losers' (1962: 865). In addition, deflation can, by definition, never go farther than bringing the money supply down to equal the supply of specie, thereby doing the desirable deed of eradicating the inflation.[21]

What is missing from his discussion of inflation and deflation is any mention of the role of the demand for money. The monetary equilibrium perspective we have employed has emphasized that monetary disequilibria are to be understood in terms of the relationship between the supply and demand for money at the ruling price level. Rather than *any* increase in the money supply beyond an increase in outside money being seen as inflationary, we have argued that only such increases that are in excess of the demand to hold money balances at the current price level should be understood as creating the problems associated with inflation. Conversely, deflation occurs when the supply of money falls short of the demand to hold it at the prevailing price level. Both of Rothbard's definitions leave out any role for the demand for money. Presumably, then, with the money supply set equal to the stock of specie, a further increase in the demand for money relative to income would not be considered deflationary, nor would a fall in the demand for money (a rise in income velocity) be inflationary. From a monetary equilibrium perspective, if one were to hold the money supply effectively constant in the short run, changes in the demand for money would be disequilibrating and generate the same kinds of effects as would an opposite movement in the money supply.

One implication of Rothbard defining inflation and deflation without mentioning money demand is that changes in money demand with a fixed money supply would not be problematic. In his discussion of changes in the purchasing power of money, Rothbard more or less comes to precisely this conclusion. In his discussion of 'Changes in the Money Relation', Rothbard (1962: 668) describes changes in the demand for money with a fixed money stock in the following way:

> Thus, suppose that the . . . total-demand-for-money curve has shifted [to the right]. At the previous equilibrium PPM [purchasing power of money] . . . the demand for money now exceeds the stock available . . . The bids [for goods in exchange for money] push the PPM upward until it reaches the [new] equilibrium . . . The converse will be true for a shift of the total demand curve leftward – a decline in the total demand schedule. Then, the PPM will fall accordingly.   .

Rothbard then proceeds to a discussion of movements in the money stock with a given demand for money. He says there that, if the stock increases, 'the PPM will fall until it reaches a new equilibrium' and if the stock decreases 'the PPM will rise until the new equilibrium point is reached' (ibid.: 668–9).

There are several interesting aspects to this discussion. The most important is his treatment of movements in the purchasing power of money. In an earlier discussion (1962: 205), Rothbard defines the purchasing power of the monetary unit as consisting 'of an array of all the particular goods-prices in the society in terms of the unit'. In a note attached to that definition, Rothbard goes on to argue that the PPM is not a statistical average or 'measurable entity' (ibid.: 445, n. 2). This conception of the purchasing power of money is consistent with the line of argument we have developed in this study concerning the effects of changes in the relative supply of money on *individual prices*. As we have repeatedly emphasized, 'the' price level can only move if and when individual prices change.

In the brief discussion extracted above, Rothbard seems to assume that the PPM can 'just' adjust when necessitated by a change in the demand for money. He makes no mention of the fact that such adjustments can only occur through changes in the array of individual relative prices. For example, if the demand for money rises in his scenario, Rothbard implies that the fall in 'bids' for goods and services, with its implied increase in the desirability of holding money, will unproblematically lead to decreases in prices and the rise in the PPM. Note that there is no mention of any sort of non-coercive price stickiness such as the who-goes-first problem. There is also no discussion of changes in relative prices that might occur due to the unevenness of the increase in money demand and the differences in the discrete steps in each actor's demand schedule. Rothbard might have responded that such changes in relative prices are appropriate, given the higher value people are placing on money. Perhaps so, but if the process of adjusting to those new relative prices involves major quantity adjustments due to the stickiness of prices, then perhaps the adjustment process is not so unproblematic as Rothbard implies, making such price adjustments less desirable if it is possible to avoid them by maintaining monetary equilibrium.

What about the demand for money falling when the stock of money is fixed? This appears to be no different to a situation where the supply of money is expanded with demand fixed: individuals find themselves with more money than they wish to hold at the current price level and begin to shed the excesses by spending on goods and services, driving up the price level. Rothbard's response to the falling demand for money scenario is simply to say that the purchasing power of money will just 'fall'. If the fall in the PPM from a decline in money demand is unproblematic, why is the fall in the PPM from a rise in the supply of money not also unproblematic? Why all the talk of relative price effects, redistribution, waste, and business cycles? Why does the PPM not just 'fall' without any other consequences? One line of response might be that increases in the money supply have interest rate implications that declines in the demand for money do not. We shall address this shortly, but even if it were true, it says nothing about the redistribution or relative price effects that will occur.

Rothbard could have responded that the reason that the relative price effects of increases in the money stock are problematic is that the supply of money in excess of specie is by definition fraudulent and therefore coercive, so the resulting relative prices are distorted in the same way as any other result of coercive intervention in the market. By contrast, he might have continued, a decline in money demand involves no fraud or coercion, so the resulting array of relative prices, though different than what was the case at the previous PPM, is not 'distorted' because no coercion has occurred. The whole discussion would then boil down to the legal and moral status of fractional reserve banking. But notice that the logic of that argument would force one to recognize the similar economic effects that flow from both increases in the money stock beyond the stock of specie and declines in the demand for money with a given stock of specie. The question would be the *desirability* of those effects, depending on whether the originating action was considered to be coercive.

To understand the issues Rothbard raises, we need to take a closer look at the demand for money. As we argued in Chapter 3, holding a bank liability is an act of saving. More generally, to the extent the public chooses to invest its wealth in the form of money, it is abstaining from current consumption and postponing that consumption until some point in the future. Whether that 'saving' makes itself effectively known and can get translated into funds for borrowers who wish to consume now rather than later, will depend on the nature of the banking system and the particular form of money being held, e.g. bank liabilities versus base money. Regardless of whether the message is made effective, holding additional money balances rather than using them for consumption is an act of saving.[22] As such, if it goes unmatched by investment through the banking system, the natural rate would fall below the unchanged market rate and a deflationary monetary disequilibrium would follow. By contrast, if the demand for money falls, and those balances are put toward current consumption, then banks should respond by reducing the funds available for investment, which causes the market rate to rise in sync with the natural rate.

From this perspective, it does not matter which side of the money market initiates the process. When the supply of money is greater than the demand, regardless of whether it is due to an increase in supply or decrease in demand, the same results will follow. In the case under discussion, a fall in the demand for money will not mean that the purchasing power of money just 'falls'. That decline in money demand implies a decline in savings and an increase in the natural rate of interest, as people are consuming relatively more in the present. If the banking system does not respond with an equal increase in the money supply, the divergence between the market and natural rate will be no different than if it had been caused by an expansion of the money supply. Rothbard's neglect of the demand for money in formulating his view of inflation and deflation prevents him from seeing this. Some of the issues involved may come down to his claim that fractional reserve banking is fraudulent, but the economic effects are the same.

Conclusion

This discussion of Rothbard's work is a fitting way to end our discussion of the two forms of monetary disequilibrium. This chapter and the previous one have emphasized the way in which monetary disequilibria are both intertwined with the market for time and spill over into the markets for non-money goods and services. Our main argument has been that the relative price effects caused by injections or extractions of money, along with the imperfect flexibility of prices, especially downward, turn monetary disequilibria into economy-wide misallocations and/or idling of resources. Inflation and deflation are problematic because they undermine the microeconomic discovery process by diminishing the communicative power of money prices. Once some prices become separated from the underlying real variables, further misallocation or idling of resources will surely follow. Monetary disequilibria are a likely source of such distortions in the pricing process.

One of the advantages of a Mengerian approach to microeconomics is that it can illuminate these points more powerfully than can standard general equilibrium theory. By emphasizing the disequilibrium role of prices in the process of monetary calculation, both *ex ante* and *ex post*, and by reminding us of the importance of prices in prompting discovery in an uncertain and imperfectly informed world, Austrian microfoundations can make clearer the real costs of both inflation and deflation, namely their disruption of the entrepreneurial discovery process of the market. Because it focuses almost exclusively on the informational properties of equilibrium prices, general equilibrium theory, including the imperfect information variants thereof, misses the effects of monetary disequilibria on disequilibrium market processes. In the next chapter we will look a bit more at the role of prices, especially wages, in potentially generating economy-wide disturbances, even when monetary equilibrium is being maintained.

6 W. H. Hutt on price rigidities and macroeconomic disorder

So far, our investigation has focused on the ways in which monetary disequilibria create macroeconomic problems by disrupting the microeconomic coordination taking place through the pricing process. The contention has been that the effects of such disequilibria 'spill over' from money to the relative prices of individual goods and services, and in so doing, break the link between those prices and the underlying variables of preferences, knowledge, and scarcity. In this chapter, we shift this focus slightly to explore how the sort of pervasive idleness of labor and capital associated with macroeconomic disorder might originate from non-monetary sources. The line of inquiry here will not be real business cycle theory, but rather the apparently more mundane argument that unemployment results from labor being priced out of the market. If one group of workers is unemployed in such a fashion, it can lead to more pervasive unemployment through the reversal of Say's Law. We will also explore the relationship between this mispricing of labor perspective and the monetary disequilibrium explanations we have laid out in previous chapters.

The primary source for the mispriced labor argument is the work of the late William H. Hutt. One of the more prolific and neglected of twentieth-century economists, Hutt spent his life arguing against Keynesian interpretations of depression, particularly those based on the more hydraulic conceptions of aggregate demand and the paradox of saving, and attempted to resuscitate Say's Law and a broadly Wicksellian monetary theory in order to explain where both Keynes, and those before him, had gone wrong.[1] Hutt's work fits nicely with both the Austrians and the monetary disequilibrium theorists. Although these two groups both see macroeconomic disorder as being caused by pricing problems, they see those pricing problems as resulting from monetary disequilibria. Hutt also sees pricing problems as the source of disorder, but he sees those pricing problems resulting from policy-induced rigidities in the market that lead to overpriced labor. Although inflation might bring down the average real wage to make it in line with the expected value of marginal products (VMP), leading to a recovery in employment, Hutt argued, as do the Austrians, that the relative price effects of inflation are so pervasive that this apparent solution does more harm than good. Inflation might bring the *average* real wage down, but it can only do so by disrupting the array of individual relative prices and wages that comprise that average. Thus, while inflation might lead to what Hutt calls 'crude coordination' between wages and productivity, it is inferior to a policy that would remove the impediments causing the original idleness. In this way, Hutt's analysis dovetails nicely with the perspective we have laid out: the fundamental problem is always to be found in interference with the pricing process and a Mengerian perspective on the nature of price coordination elucidates this problem most fully.

Hutt on the labor market

Before we explore the monetary aspects of Hutt's work, we should carefully examine his understanding of the pricing process, especially in the labor market.[2] As is the case with macroeconomics generally, Hutt's major theoretical goal was to be able to explain the widespread idleness of labor and capital associated with events like the Great Depression. The cornerstone of Hutt's explanation for idleness was a rejection of the aggregative analysis that characterizes most of macroeconomics from Keynes onward. As noted above, the source of idleness is to be found in pricing errors in the microeconomic market process. Hutt (1979: 44) summarized his view:

> Pre-Keynesian anti-depression teachings are to the effect that unemployment (as a short-term phenomenon) and depression are due to a contraction of the flow of wages and other income through some discoordination of the pricing system. Discoordination is blamed on too many wage rates (and hence final prices) being fixed above market-clearing levels, that is, too high in relation to income or inconsistently with price expectations.

To explain this view, we need to unpack the two theoretical pillars it is built on. The first is Hutt's view of the nature of the labor market and the pricing process therein. The second is his understanding of Say's Law. Together, these two sets of ideas can explain why idleness occurs and why small amounts of idleness can quickly snowball into depression. The relationship between this non-monetary explanation for depression and the monetary theories held by the Austrians and monetary disequilibrium theorists will be taken up in later sections.

Hutt's theory of the labor market (and asset markets more generally) begins with an elementary insight: all value-producing assets are employable at some price. With respect to labor, Hutt argues that aside from the very young, the very old, and the infirm or insane, all human factors of production are capable of producing value. In more contemporary language, Hutt's point is that if the value of a worker's marginal product is greater than zero, that person is worth employing at any wage up to that VMP. The relevant wage calculation, of course, includes the costs of hiring and training the worker. Once all of those factors are taken into consideration, there is almost always some wage rate above zero at which it is worthwhile to employ any worker with a VMP above zero. Idleness, therefore, cannot be explained by some fundamental defect of freely operating labor markets.

Hutt makes one important addition to this rather standard factor market analysis. He is careful to clarify that it is always the *prospective* value of the marginal product that matters (1975: 93). Entrepreneurs cannot know with certainty what a worker's marginal product will be, so they must rely on their expectations of that productivity when making wage decisions. It may well be true that over time the worker's VMP will be discovered to be higher than originally expected, but entrepreneurs are in no position to know the future course of market events and can only set wages based on their expectations of that future in the present.

It is also interesting to note that Hutt's use of 'prospective' marginal product and his appreciation for the learning or 'groping' process by which VMPs are discovered in the market tie in nicely with the discussion of the Mengerian view of the pricing process described in Chapter 1. As Hutt (1975: 114, emphasis in original) points out, pre-Keynesians had 'a realistic recognition of the dynamic character of the economic process – *clearer in the Austrian tradition than in the Marshallian* – and in particular an awareness of the importance of the continual revision of entrepreneurial expectations in response to continuous changes in the data'.[3] For Hutt, the learning process that is stimulated by the progressive discovery of market data is central to the coordinative properties of the market. In his discussion of the relationship between Hutt's work and the Austrian view of economic coordination, Salerno (1991: 334) makes a similar point:

> The *ex post* discovery by some entrepreneurs that their courses of action have led to pecuniary losses therefore does not impede coordination. To the contrary, the experience of losses, if they are expected to continue to result from present resource combinations, stimulates a revision of entrepreneurial forecasts, production plans, and bids for productive inputs, leading to a restructuring of price relationships among higher-order goods.

Understanding the resource allocation decisions of entrepreneurs in terms of their expectations of marginal products and marginal revenue allows us to understand coordination in terms of the ongoing process of expectation revision and sharpening that takes place in response to feedback from the 'results' of the market at any one moment in time. In emphasizing the speculative nature of all input purchases, Hutt forces our attention away from equilibrium pictures of market order to ones that take full account of learning, expectation revision, and market discovery, such as the Austrian perspective informing the previous chapters.

Although Hutt (1977 [1939]) distinguishes among a number of different forms of idleness, in general they break down into three categories: (1) preferred idleness; (2) pseudo-idleness; and (3) price-driven idleness.[4] The first category is straightforward: some people simply have a strong preference for leisure and are willing to exercise it. This form of idleness is not necessarily a policy issue, unless such preferences are being indulged by generous unemployment benefits. Such policies will increase the amount of preferred idleness and have ripple effects across the whole economy. The second category refers to workers or assets that appear to be idle but are actually producing something. One example is an 'unemployed' worker who is actively engaged in a job search. Such searches are productive activity, 'prospecting' as Hutt calls it, and the worker is therefore not truly idle. Other examples are balances of money or stocks of inventory. Both are 'idle' in some physical sense, yet both produce the service of 'availability'. That is, both are there waiting to be used when needed.

The third category is the one of great theoretical and policy concern. This category lumps together a number of Hutt's own categories, but what all have in common is that the idleness is created when some or all of the factors of production are able to coercively maintain wages or prices above market-clearing levels. Hutt (1977 [1939]: 47) divides up these forms of idleness into: participating idleness, enforced idleness, withheld capacity, strike idleness, and aggressive idleness. If labor can force producers to pay all workers hired a wage greater than what would obtain in a competitive market, then it creates idleness both in those workers in the given industry who are not hired at the above-market wage and in those workers in other industries who are let go because of the contraction of the wages and income flow that results. Those workers who have some monopoly power, likely granted to a union as the agent of collective bargaining backed by state protection, are able to withhold capacity by forcing wages above market-clearing levels. Workers who are idled by such tactics and who remain associated with the industry in question, perhaps due to union membership or the like, are considered examples of enforced idleness. Strike idleness is fairly self-explanatory, as it arises when employers do not meet the conditions of workers and workers use strikes or other methods to force the employer to capitulate. Hutt (ibid.: 231) is clear to claim that lockouts by employers are the capital equivalent of strike idleness. Aggressive idleness is a category reserved for capital. When monopolists maintain excess capacity for the purpose of being able to undercut and crush new entrants ('interlopers' in Hutt's terms), it is an aggressive idleness of capital. In all of these cases falling under the third category, the key is some monopoly power possessed by capital or labor that enables either to keep its prices above market-clearing levels. This ability to misprice resources, and the idleness that results, are Hutt's main theoretical and policy concern.

Say's Law and the cumulative idling process

To understand why idleness can lead to a cumulative effect on income and employment, it is necessary to understand what Hutt (1975: 3) calls 'the most fundamental "economic law" in all economic theory,' namely Say's Law of Markets. As was argued in Chapter 3, one's ability to demand food, clothing and shelter derives from the productivity of one's labor or one's non-labor assets. The lower (higher) that productivity, the lower (higher) is one's power to demand. Hutt's (1975: 27) understanding of Say's Law is that: 'All power to demand is derived from production and supply . . . The process of supplying – i.e., the production and appropriate pricing of services or assets for replacement or growth – keeps the flow of demands flowing steadily or expanding.' Later, Hutt was to be somewhat more precise with his definition: 'the demand for any commodity is a function of the supply of noncompeting commodities' (1979: 160). The addition of the modifier 'noncompeting' is important. If I sell my services as a computer technician, it is presumed that my resulting demands will be for goods and services other than computer technician or similar services. The goods or services competing with those that I sell can always be obtained by applying my labor directly, so I am unlikely to demand them. The demand for my services as a computer technician is a result of the supplying activities of everyone but computer technicians.

Hutt uses Say's Law to get at the interconnections between the various sectors of the market. In particular, it makes sense of the claim that 'the employment of all is the employment of each'. As each worker finds employment, he or she is able to turn around and demand goods and services from all other non-competing suppliers, creating the opportunity for their employment. In Hutt's idiosyncratic language, the possession of productive assets enables market actors to demand those assets' 'money's worth' from other sellers. Because all movements between supplying and demanding have to take place through the medium of money, it is somewhat oversimplified to say without qualification that production is the source of demand. Actually demanding products requires the possession of money, which in turn requires a previous act of supply. Hutt is careful to point out that the exchange of money for goods and services isn't the 'spending' of money, unless one is permanently reducing one's stock of money. Money, for Hutt, is merely one asset in which we store wealth. It is a particularly convenient one because of its high liquidity, which enables it to be exchanged for more preferred assets. What enables us to purchase is not the possession of money *per se*, but the possession of productive assets that can fetch a 'money's worth' on the market.

For Hutt, therefore, production takes place not when money is exchanged for an input, but when the input first obtains its market value. For example, acquiring additional education in the hopes of raising one's productivity and one's wages, is an act of production. The exchange of money for services that will follow (if all goes well) is simply turning that productivity into its money's worth; it is not the production itself. What is ultimately happening in the market process are exchanges of production for production. The institution of money makes such exchanges easier and, by facilitating the process of price formation, provides a way for us to reckon the possible consequences of future actions and the success of past ones.

It should be reasonably clear that Hutt's conception of Say's Law is largely complementary to our discussion in Chapter 3. The key commonality is that production is the source of demand. Hutt, however, does not sufficiently emphasize the role that money plays in this process. Although he does recognize that some of the wealth generated by production might be used to demand the availability services of money held, Hutt minimizes the potential damaging effects of an insufficient supply of money. Hutt does recognize the dangers of inflation, but he is less concerned about deflation.

Hutt uses Say's Law to explain why a small amount of idleness can quickly multiply into widespread idleness even if monetary equilibrium is being maintained. Suppose one sector of the economy is able to force wage rates above their market-clearing level. Firms will offer fewer jobs at the higher wage. The wage flow lost by this withheld productive capacity means, via Say's Law, that the demand for non-competing commodities will shrink. The reduction in demand in those industries will put downward pressure on wages there. If wage reductions are resisted in those industries, the level of employment and the flow of wages will fall, implying an additional round of reduced demands in industries that do not compete with the ones in question. To the extent that wage rates inconsistent with the existing level of income and entrepreneurial expectations are maintained, potentially productive workers will go unhired and those workers will be unable to, in turn, demand goods and services from firms (and their workers) in non-competing industries. One original round of above-equilibrium wage setting can have multiplied consequences throughout the market. It is Say's Law that explains the multiplicative process by showing how frustrating the ability to acquire the money's worth of productive services in one sector spills over into reduced demand in noncompeting sectors.

The problem here is on the supply side and not the demand side. Where Keynesian approaches would see the difficulty as an inability to demand (a lack of 'aggregate demand'), Hutt's approach would argue that it is an unwillingness or inability to supply (at the market clearing price) that is starting the process. If, as Say's Law indicates, the ability to demand can only come from a prior act of supply, blaming insufficient aggregate demand begs the question. The power to demand can only be lacking if for some reason a productive asset has not been supplied. Given Hutt's starting point that all productive assets are hirable at some price, the most likely explanation for labor not being supplied is that something is preventing the market-clearing price from being reached. The depressive process must start with a barrier to price coordination somewhere in an input market. The more widespread such barriers are, the more quickly the depression will ensue when a need for a downward input price adjustment arises.

Faced with the widespread idleness associated with a depression, the cure is to undo the sickness. If barriers to price coordination created the problem, then those barriers need to be removed. If they are removed, the same Say's Law process that caused the cumulative reduction in output will now lead to an increase in the total flow of wages and a general recovery. When idle workers in one industry accept reduced wages and return to work, output will increase, prices will fall, and the newly employed workers' incomes become demands for noncompeting commodities. As the demand for those commodities rises, the demand for labor and wages will rise there, further increasing employment and output and leading to further increases in demands in other industries. The more pricing barriers that fall early on, the more quickly recovery will take place. In any case, true recovery will occur only when the barriers to labor price coordination fall and wages can be reduced to be in line with prospective marginal products.

In Hutt's view, the widespread idleness that macroeconomics attempts to explain is best understood as a pervasive, and multiplicative, failure of inputs, especially labor, to be priced in a way consistent with their optimal usage. Whether through inertia, strikes, the threat of strikes, minimum wage laws, or other psychological or institutional barriers to more flexible (especially downward) wage rates, unemployment is fundamentally a microeconomic problem. Casual empiricism also confirms this argument in very general terms by comparing the degree of labor market flexibility and unemployment rates found in Western European countries with those of the United States. The more powerful unions and more intrusive labor market regulations that typically characterize Western Europe prevent the price flexibility necessary to avoid idleness in the face of shifts in the composition of output demands. The shift from manufactured goods to a service and information economy requires that workers in declining industries be prepared to accept wage cuts as the value of their marginal products decline. If such workers are able to maintain coercively the existing wage structure, increases in unemployment will surely follow. Their unemployment, via Say's Law, will reduce the demand for noncompeting commodities, and drag down wages (and potentially create unemployment) in those sectors. The cause of widespread unemployment is to be found in the various barriers to wage flexibility.

Keynes and labor market coordination

To see Hutt's ideas in action, it is best to turn to his critiques of Keynesianism, found implicitly in *The Theory of Idle Resources*, but mostly in *Keynesianism* and *The Keynesian Episode*, as well as *A Rehabilitation of Say's Law*. Because *The Keynesian Episode* is an updated revision of *Keynesianism*, I shall be referring to it in elucidating Hutt's critique of Keynes. Hutt has numerous detailed criticisms of Keynes and the Keynesians, many of them surrounding the ways in which both have defined various concepts and the inaccurate portrait they have drawn of the classical economists. However, in the context of our argument so far, it is Hutt's critique of the central tenets of Keynes' theory of aggregate demand, the multiplier, and unemployment equilibrium that are most relevant. The discussion that follows will try to focus on those aspects of Hutt's work that emphasize the importance of price coordination and its relationship to monetary equilibrium.

According to Hutt, Keynes makes two central assumptions in arguing how deficient aggregate demand can lead to widespread idleness. The first of these is that Keynes assumes that wages are rigid downward (or perhaps *ought* to be) and the second is that the money supply is effectively fixed, that is, 'monetary flexibility' is absent. It is through this concept of monetary flexibility that the close relationship between Hutt and the monetary equilibrium tradition becomes clear. Hutt (1975: 22) defines monetary flexibility as a policy where the money supply

> can expand or contract sensitively, so as to be neither inflationary nor deflationary; and that means, in practice, when the market rate of interest is maintained at what is judged to be the non-inflationary, non-deflationary level (i.e., at the Wicksellian 'natural level').

This, in effect, is the same thing as maintaining monetary equilibrium. Recalling our earlier discussion in which we argued that in monetary equilibrium money is neutral in the Wicksell/Hayek sense, and that maintaining that equilibrium requires that the nominal money supply be adjusted to changes in the demand to hold real balances, it is clear that both conditions are contained in Hutt's concept of monetary flexibility. In *The Keynesian Episode* (1979), particularly in Chapter 8, Hutt is more clear to link this to the equation of exchange, by arguing that M should move inversely to V (or what Hutt calls M_r or the 'aggregate value of money in real terms'). If the monetary authority fails to respond appropriately to changes in V, inflation or deflation will develop and Hutt (1979: 197) places blame for those outcomes on the policymakers.

One point of contention among monetary equilibrium theorists is whether a neutral money is one that should stabilize the price level or allow for the price level to move inversely to changes in productivity. Hutt falls on the price level stabilization side, as shown by his claim that monetary flexibility will mean that 'an appropriate price index will oscillate within a narrow amplitude about a constant trend of zero' (1975: 22). Hutt also argues that the quantity MV should be adjusted to changes in the T or Q term of the quantity equation. Thus, Hutt would argue for increases in the nominal money supply in the face of increases in productivity that drove up real output. Most of Hutt's contributions, however, are valid independent of whether price stabilization or a productivity norm is better policy.

Where Hutt differs from the two groups of monetary equilibrium theorists we have explored is in his explicit discussion of the relationship between monetary equilibrium and real-side price rigidities. As Hutt (1975: 73) put it: '"Monetary flexibility" (in contrast to "price flexibility") alone is incapable of correcting the "automatic" process which throws men and assets into idleness.' In other words, although monetary equilibrium may be necessary to avoid widespread idleness, it is not sufficient. Monetary equilibrium theorists would surely not disagree, but Hutt has taken the additional step of explaining how real-side price rigidities can lead to widespread idleness, even in the presence of monetary equilibrium, and how the idleness resulting from such rigidities will not be reduced, and may well be exacerbated, if monetary equilibrium is not maintained. In his critique of Keynes, Hutt relies on both the monetary and real sides of that argument to dissect the problems with the Keynesian vision.

Hutt argues that Keynes' theoretical framework is constructed on the two assumptions of wage and monetary rigidity, without ever asking whether institutional changes that would make those assumptions inappropriate might better address the problems Keynes is trying to solve. For example, suppose entrepreneurs turn pessimistic. Because wage rates are based on prospective marginal products, these entrepreneurs will wish to reduce the wages they are paying existing employees. If wages are unable to fall, either for institutional reasons or psychological resistance by workers, idleness will result and will spread through the Say's Law process. Keynesianism would see this as a problem of deficient aggregate demand triggered by the original pessimism of the entrepreneurs and the resulting fall in the demand for inputs. The implied Keynesian solution is to boost aggregate demand back up through government spending or inflation. To the extent that such spending is not matched by taxation, and therefore requires debt, Hutt argues it is equivalent to inflation.

If the entrepreneurial pessimism is justified, then the proper result is a decline in wages. Resisting those wage reductions is ultimately a mistake for workers since idleness will result and the total wage flow will fall, reducing demand and wages and/or employment in noncompeting markets. If the pessimism was mistaken, markets contain a built-in correction mechanism that will kick in if workers accept the wage cuts. As some entrepreneurs discover that their pessimism was unwarranted, the larger than expected demand for their products will put upward pressure on prices and wages, driving wage rates back to the appropriate level. As workers in these industries receive higher wages, their demands for noncompeting commodities push up wages there, and correct the mistaken pessimism of those entrepreneurs. Once again, resisting the original wage cuts, even if entrepreneurs are mistaken, will only create more problems than will accepting them. Although entrepreneurs may be found to be in error, there is likely no one else in a better position to form accurate expectations of the future.[5] The ultimate source of idleness is not deficient aggregate demand, but barriers to coordination through market pricing.

In another Keynesian scenario, it is the desire to hold money balances (liquidity preference) that is the source of deficient aggregate demand.[6] As actors desire increased liquidity, perhaps because of pessimistic expectations, they will choose to hold additional money balances rather than spending on goods and services. In Keynes' eyes, this hoarding behavior would reduce the flow of income and the withdrawal of spending power would slow production and idle workers. Hutt's response to this scenario is to ask why assuming price and monetary flexibility, a change in the kinds of assets people wish to hold should lead to a drop in output and employment.

The key to this response is to recall Hutt's theory of the demand for money. Money is just like other assets, in that it provides services to its holder. In the Keynesian vision, holding money is anti-social because it diverts wealth into an unproductive activity. Money is assumed to be barren and have no yield of its own, therefore attempts at holding increased stocks of money are suspect. The problem with this view is that it appears to define 'yield' only in pecuniary terms. It is surely true that cash and some checking account balances provide no interest yield. That, however, does not mean holding balances of either is inexplicable. After all, we invest our wealth in numerous assets that have no pecuniary yield. Is the decision to hold a 'balance' of one compact disc player socially wasteful because one earns no financial return from it? Of course not, because the yield on a CD player is the music-playing services it provides. The same is true of money – it provides the service of 'availability'. Money's liquidity makes it desirable to hold stocks of it at hand so that the holder has flexibility in the face of an uncertain future. The fact that this yield is non-pecuniary and subjective makes it no less real. Investing in more 'availability services' is quite rational, and not socially wasteful, if individuals perceive the future to be more uncertain, or expect to have to make additional purchases in the near future. If the proper task of the monetary authority is to provide additional amounts of money when the demand to hold it rises, it is not clear why the reasonable decision to invest more of one's wealth in money rather than, say, clothing or food, should be an issue, assuming proper monetary policy.

It is money's pervasiveness as the medium of exchange that appears to allow for trouble when there are changes in the demand to hold it. As actors hold more of their wealth in the form of money, they do indeed hold less of their wealth as non-money goods and services. What happens next, however, depends upon the form in which they choose to hold their money. In modern central banking systems, where currency is issued monopolistically by the central bank and is used as a reserve medium by individual banks, the choice between holding money in the form of currency or bank deposits has important macroeconomic implications. What both have in common is that increased holdings of any form of money will require some downward price adjustments somewhere in the economy.

Suppose that the additional demand for liquidity takes the form of holding larger deposit balances at commercial banks, rather than purchasing goods and services. The increased deposits provide savings to the banking system that can be channeled into funds for investment. Higher deposit balances mean more reserves for banks, which increases their ability to make investment loans. The increase in investment spending would offset the loss in consumption spending deriving from the increased liquidity preference, thus maintaining the total level of demand throughout the economy. If savings and liquidity decisions are linked through the banking system, increased liquidity preference in the form of bank deposits will not mean that *all* prices and wages would have to fall, just those in the consumer goods industries, which are seeing slackening demand. The increased investment that results instead will drive up prices and wages in the producers' goods industries. Hutt's fundamental point remains, however: wages, at least in the consumer goods industries, have to be flexible downward to prevent increased liquidity preference from causing unemployment. The decision to hold more wealth in the form of bank deposits is not *by itself* a cause of diminished aggregate demand. In a world of wage rigidity, however, shifts in liquidity preference can cause trouble. Nominal wages may have to fall somewhere when the demand for bank liabilities rises, and if they do not, employment and output will have to fall instead. As Hutt (1979: 126, emphasis in original) puts it, 'Wise monetary policy *demands* nonmonetary coordination.'

If, on the other hand, the demand for liquidity takes the form of increased holdings of currency (outside money) the situation is somewhat different. The corresponding reduction in demand for non-money implies a fall in the prices of non-money goods and services. That fall in final goods prices will put downward pressure on input prices, including wages. If, for whatever reason, wages do not fall in step with the decline in output prices, then the shift to additional currency holdings will lead to trouble as firms will see costs remaining constant while revenues fall. Their likely recourse is to lay off workers, setting into motion the cumulative depressionary process explained by Say's Law. If input prices are free to fall with the falling output prices, then no change in overall wealth has taken place. Nominal wages are lower, but so are output prices, leaving workers' real incomes roughly the same, with no increase in unemployment. The Keynesian scenario misses the real problem, which is the downward rigidity of wages, and therefore misses the easiest cure, increased wage flexibility. Although the problem appears to be monetary, it is actually the inflexibility of input prices that is the source of trouble. As Hutt (1979: 107, emphasis in original) saw it:

> [W]hen the Keynesians . . . blame hoarding (liquidity preference), they are turning attention away from the failure of governments to tackle the problem of *unstable price rigidities*, that is, the unwillingness of governments to take the steps needed to permit prices continuously to reach a level at which further *general* price changes will be unexpected.

If one assumes irremovable downward price rigidities, then increases in the demand to hold either bank deposits or currency might well be a depressing influence. Putting that assumption up front, however, should make it part of the conversation, rather than a given.

One aspect of this argument that Hutt glosses over too lightly is the role that alternative banking institutions might play in aggravating or remedying increases in the demand for money. Hutt rightly notes that a properly working banking system should supply more money when the demand to hold it rises. However, under modern central banking systems, if the demand to hold additional currency balances rises, we have to rely upon the central bank to supply the desired liquidity. There is no reliable 'automatic' process by which increases in the demand to hold cash call forth additional supplies.[7] This is because increased currency holding draws reserves out of the banking system, leading to a cumulative decline in the overall supply of money that only the central bank can offset. Because currency is also outside money in modern central banking systems, increased currency holding will have multiplicative effects on the total money supply and possibly on employment and output. In a banking system where currency is a bank liability rather than a reserve medium, and banks are free to adjust their reserve ratios, increased liquidity preference in the form of a rising currency/deposit ratio or a higher absolute demand for currency would not require a change in the overall level of reserves to keep the total money supply sufficient. Increased demands for currency would be no different from increased demands for checking account money in that satisfying them would not imply reductions in the bank's holding of reserve media.[8] The key issue is that when money holding takes place through bank liabilities, that holding of money supplies loanable funds to the banking system.

Hutt also argued that Keynes' explicit and implicit solution to the idleness created by price rigidities was also problematic. With Keynes unwilling to attack those price rigidities directly, he had to find a way to restore the income flow other than by allowing prices and wages to fall. That other way was to use inflation, either explicitly, or implicitly through debt-financed government spending. The idleness created by nominal wages being held above their market-clearing values could be reduced by increasing the money supply. The keys to the inflation-driven recovery process were the imperfect flexibility of prices going upward and the very same Say's Law considerations that explained the cumulative depression.

Hutt assumed that the additional supply of money would make itself felt first in the demand for outputs and their prices. Workers would not see the rising output prices, or would be unable to react to them immediately, leaving nominal wages to lag behind output prices. The difference between those two sets of prices effectively reduced the real wage from its position above equilibrium enabling firms to offer increased employment opportunities to workers who were shut out when prices fell and wages did not. As these workers are induced out of idleness, by their lack of recognition of the effect of the inflation on their real wages, their increased incomes become the source of demand for non-competing commodities, driving up prices and leading to more employment there. The Say's Law process continues until the price level rises sufficiently to bring most or all of the formerly idle labor back into activity. In Hutt's (1979, p. 154, emphasis in original) words:[9]

> Keynesian policy seeks to restore coordination by making it possible for people to *afford to buy*, not by enabling them directly to increase their contribution to real income, but by increasing the money valuation of their income in the expectation that this will cause an increase in the contribution of others to real income . . . the increase in money income they recommend merely *circumvents* the discoordinating rigidities by inflating income to meet inflated prices.

Hutt's explanation for the recovery process is a version of the Phillips curve story. Of course, it is important to note that the increase in employment and output depends on the pre-existence of idle resources created by price coordination barriers.[10] At 'full' employment with price and wage flexibility, inflation cannot create sustainable additions to output and employment.

Inflation as crude coordination

Why, then, does Hutt think the Keynesian inflationary solution is inferior to his own call for increased price flexibility? There are a variety of reasons for that conclusion, all of them relating to what Hutt sees as the inefficiencies and injustices of inflation. In addition, workers will soon begin to adapt their expectations to the continuing inflation, frustrating the attempt to push output prices up ahead of wages. But perhaps most important to Hutt is the argument that inflation is 'a remedy which leaves the genesis of the disease [i.e., price rigidity] undisturbed' (Hutt 1979: 157). This is the sense in which the coordination generated by inflation is 'crude coordination':

> Such policies not only coordinate, they remove other pressures to coordination, and they create inducements to discoordinate. For instance, if organized labor knows that full employment of labor is guaranteed, demands for wage-rate increases will be relatively uninhibited. And if 'employers' know that inflation will follow in order to enable them to pay the higher rates, they will tend to lose sight of their social duty to resist the fixing of wage rates by the threat of private force. Indeed, for such reasons, when inflation is generally anticipated, its coordinative effects are completely destroyed.
>
> (ibid.: 158)

Again, inflation attacks the symptoms but not the disease.

Hutt goes on to explain more completely the 'crude coordination' caused by inflation. If the original depression is set in motion by selected wage rates being held above equilibrium, with others, as a result, being held below, what assurance is there that the pattern of spending resulting from a subsequent increase in the money supply will restore all the individual wages in question back to their appropriate market-clearing levels? The Keynesian remedy for wages struck too high was to lower them across the board by using unanticipated inflation to reduce their real value. Normally this solution has been couched in terms of a reduction in some aggregative measure of real wages. However, it is not some statistically constructed aggregate wage level that matters for achieving market coordination, rather it is the reliability of the market-generated individual real wages across the structure of production that matters to both work-seeking laborers and input-seeking employers. Once again, Hayek's admonition that Keynes' aggregates conceal the important market processes that underlie them comes into play. The question is not whether a given policy can bring down the average level of wages, but whether it can avoid influences that disrupt the communicative process of market competition. Such a policy will be more reliable in producing an array of market wages that facilitates coordination between firms and workers.

For example, suppose the wages in a small number of industries are coercively maintained above their market-clearing levels. Hutt's solution is to remove the coercive barrier and let wages drop to the appropriate level, with other input prices adjusting in turn. The advantage of this solution is that it lets the persons closest to the action be responsible for setting wages. That is, it simply turns over the wage-setting process to firms and workers in the industries in question, enabling them to bring their expectations and interests to bear on the process. The earlier discussion of tacit and contextual knowledge seems particularly appropriate here. By removing the barriers to wage coordination, we are giving freer play to the ultimate forces that matter in the market process.

The importance of freely adjusting wages is particularly clear when we recall the cumulative nature of the process generated by overpriced labor. If wages in several sectors are being held too high, this will induce a falling off of demands for noncompeting commodities, causing wages to fall in those sectors as well. It is plausible to assume that the degree to which wages are held too high in a small number of industries will be greater than the degree to which wages fall in the much larger number of noncompeting industries. In other words, the incremental decline in wages that occurs in the noncompeting industries will not be as noticeable as the artificially high wages in the sectors that started the process. As a result, the high wages will get focused upon but not the lowered wages elsewhere. Hutt's elucidation of Say's Law is necessary in order to see these secondary effects. The overall wage structure that results from a sectoral attempt at keeping wages up will differ radically from the wage structure that would have resulted had such barriers to price coordination not been adopted in the first place. If the goal of policy is to restore the wage–price relationships that would have held in the first place, i.e., those that are in line with entrepreneurial expectations and consumer preferences, then removing the barriers that created the problems seems the best answer.

Now suppose instead we resort to inflation to drive down real wages. At best, the resulting fall in real wages can only be understood in some aggregative sense. Additions to the money supply are not going to be targeted to particular areas or industries, rather, they will spread slowly outward from the financial centers in patterns that bear no relationship to the particular places where wages are being held too high. Moreover, the inherent broad-brush nature of attempts to drive up some aggregate measure of the price level paints over the complex set of discoordinated wage–price relationships created by the pricing barrier. What is required to restore the optimal use of resources is an undoing of the distortions created by that pricing barrier. Undoing those distortions involves myriad changes in relative prices and wages by individual producers and workers as the restored flow of income asserts itself. If inflation is used to accomplish this task, the excess supplies of money that find their way into consumers' hands will be spent according to their preferences, which cannot be assumed to be identical to the preferences of the workers who would have had income to spend had the barrier to wage coordination not existed in the first place.

Inflation may bring idle workers back into activity, but it does so driven by a pattern of consumption utterly different from what would have occurred with price flexibility. There is no reason to expect that the post-inflation array of market-clearing real wages across the affected industries will be identical to the one that would have been reached in the absence of pricing barriers. After all, wages are but one kind of price and we have already argued that one of the most disruptive effects of inflation is to distort the array of relative prices. That is no less true of input prices than output prices. The coordination created by inflation is in this way 'crude'; it cannot effect the various individual relative wage and price changes necessary to restore the price structure that would have existed without the original pricing barrier. In addition, the changes in the capital structure that result from the changes in relative prices will have lingering effects and inefficiencies because capital goods will not be perfectly substitutable as the relative prices of outputs continue to change.

As Hutt (1979: 111) rightly pointed out, one major problem with Keynes' theoretical apparatus, and most of Keynesian theory since then, was an over-reliance on aggregates, especially 'the' price of labor:

> When Keynes did think of this 'price' having a crucial task, he seemed to assume that the adjustment required to induce full employment is an equal percentage reduction in all wage rates and secondly to assume that rises or falls in the general level of wage rates correspond to rises or falls in the general flow of wage receipts. Neither assumption is acceptable.

The kind of coordination that inflation can induce is only of this aggregate sort. It can drive up the price level so that the *average* level of wages is back to its pre-depression level. However, that average will mask a whole 'wage revolution' that has created an economy very different to the one that existed previously. That wage revolution, and the price revolution that goes with it, entail significant irretrievable costs of transition, as labor is retrained and capital is refitted to meet the new, and false, structure of relative prices.

Although Hutt never goes very far with the relationship, this argument illustrates the need for microfoundations and also shows, by its emphasis on the epistemic role of relative prices, Hutt's affinity to the Austrians. What inflation does is to set the market off into a discovery process different, and less desirable, than the one that would be set in motion by the removal of pricing rigidities. Although both processes might wind up in full employment, the composition of that employment, and its relationship to underlying costs and preferences, will differ radically. There is a parallel here to Israel Kirzner's

(1985a) critique of regulation, which argues that much of the damage regulation does is by diverting the discovery process of the market onto a sub-optimal path by throwing up barriers along some paths on which it would like to go. The real costs of regulation are difficult to assess precisely because they are reflected in a future that was unknown at the time its discovery/creation was blocked. Who knows what phone service in the US would have been like if ATT had never been given its monopoly in the first place? The Austrian view that competition is a discovery procedure both tells us that we cannot know that future *a priori* and that the openness of the market process will ensure that the largest variety of possibilities gets explored in trying to discover it. Regulation, in Kirzner's view, is harmful because it prevents us from exploring particular possibilities in a circumstance of sheer ignorance. Closing off options when we don't know what it is we don't know cannot possibly enhance welfare.

Both price rigidities and inflation do the same thing. Coercively maintained price and wage barriers block off entrepreneurial discovery by preventing market actors from engaging in exchanges perceived to be mutually beneficial or by forcing them to engage in exchanges that at least one party does not see as mutually beneficial. The right to refuse an offered market transaction is as much a part of entrepreneurial discovery as is the right to use one's property as one best judges. The consequence of such barriers is that the discovery process of the market is hampered and the epistemic role of prices is diminished. Totaling the costs of these barriers is nearly impossible in that we cannot know what *would have* been discovered had those barriers been absent. We do know that we have blocked off avenues that some market actors thought were profitable and that those creating the barriers in question are in no better position to know *a priori* that those avenues were in error.

Wage rigidity, inflation, and sub-optimal full employment

Hutt's emphasis on the role of individual wage rates, and skepticism of aggregation in studying the labor market, led him to distinguish between 'optimal' and 'sub-optimal' situations of full employment. Optimal full employment occurs when wages are free to adjust and monetary equilibrium is being maintained. In those circumstances, workers will be able to find work, at some wage rate, in those areas where their skills lie. Capital assets will also be fully employed in the appropriate avenues of production. Of course, entrepreneurial error will still remain, as employers may misguess the expected marginal product of labor or capital resources. Workers too may make errors in accepting employment at wage rates that they later discover were lower than they could have obtained. Such errors are part and parcel of any conceivable economic system. What Hutt is emphasizing by 'optimal' full employment is that there are no additional barriers to assets finding their best employment, even though any particular market outcome may not reflect perfect optimality at a given moment in time. This is but another way of looking at our concept of a 'sustainable' capital structure from Chapter 3. Hutt's concept of optimal full employment is essentially the same idea applied to the labor market. In the absence of price rigidities, it is at least possible for all assets to be employed in their highest valued uses.

Hutt's concept of 'pseudo-idleness' covers him here too. For example, workers who are engaged in job searches are not considered unemployed to Hutt. They are 'self-employed' in the productive activity of 'prospecting' or searching. In a way that strongly anticipated modern search theory, Hutt (as early as 1939) argued that to the extent the probabilized return from search was greater than the cost of doing so, job-hunting should not be considered idleness. So we would expect that even in circumstances of optimal full employment, some laborers will not be employed in the conventional sense of the term, but they will not be idle, as they will be looking for new work. If they choose to not look for work, it is an example of 'preferred idleness' and to that extent it becomes optimal behavior for the worker in question. When employment becomes sub-optimal is when barriers to price coordination or subsidization of idleness enter the picture.

The concept of sub-optimal full employment is, as Hutt (1975: 55n) notes, related to Joan Robinson's notion of 'disguised unemployment'. In broad terms, all assets have found employment of some sort, but not in those areas that correspond to their highest valued uses. Various rigidities in the labor market have prevented workers from taking those jobs for which they are best suited, and they have instead ended up in employments that are sub-optimal. Conventional measures of unemployment would thus be quite low, but the aggregate potential productivity of the economy would be lower than would be the case if workers were able to be employed in the areas for which they were best suited. As a result, conventional unemployment figures may not accurately reflect the health of the economy.

Hutt sees two possible instances in which sub-optimal unemployment might be relevant. The first is when some workers are frustrated in their attempts to obtain employment at a wage related to the value of their marginal product because various sorts of labor market rigidities prevent such arrangements. Suppose workers in one industry are able to force wage rates above the market-clearing level. Some workers are retained at the higher wage, but some are laid off. The laid-off employees will begin to search for work in other (more wage-flexible) industries. The ease with which they will find work in other industries will be related to what Hutt (1975: 105) calls the 'versatility' of their skills.[11] The more versatile labor is, the more likely it is to find work at a wage close to what it would have received in its first-best use. Relatively unversatile labor will wind up in employments that offer substantially less pay, as that labor will likely not have the requisite skills. As long as not every sector of the economy is plagued by constraining wage floors, the workers laid off in one industry will find work, but second-best work, in other sectors. It is this sort of misallocation (but not idleness) of labor (and capital) that Hutt refers to as sub-optimal full employment.

An alternative to sub-optimal employment for workers who do not find employment after being closed out of one industry is what Hutt calls 'chronic idleness'. Unlike preferred idleness, where a worker chooses to forgo a contractual wage in order to consume leisure, chronic idleness occurs when idleness is subsidized by various income transfers (Hutt 1975: 104). Hutt (1975: 55–6) argues that such subsidies prevent the temporary idleness created by wage barriers from being eliminated through sub-optimal employment and turn it into chronic idleness:

> If it were not for various ways in which idleness is subsidized, unemployment could not long persist. 'Waste' would continue, and it could well be chronic waste, but productive resources would find other, less productive and less remunerative employment. The composition of the stock of assets would adapt itself, while displaced workers, and juveniles reaching working-age, would enter new or different occupations. When all resources . . . were employed in that manner, there would be 'full employment' – although 'sub-optimal employment'.

For workers idled by above-market wages in one sector, there are two factors to consider: what alternative employment is available to them (which is a function of their versatility and the existence of wage barriers in other sectors), and what is the incentive to find such employment (which is a function of the income transfers available to them if they are unemployed)? Hutt's argument is that although sub-optimal full employment may be sub-optimal, it is preferred to chronic idleness because the former, at least, involves additions to wealth, even if those additions do not represent first-best outcomes.

A second case where sub-optimal full employment becomes relevant is in the aftermath of attempts to use inflation to reduce coercively maintained above-market wages. As we noted above, the major problem with this solution is that the inflation process causes changes in relative prices and wages that reduce their signaling ability and undermine entrepreneurial discovery and market coordination. In Chapter 4 we discussed the ways in which these price changes affected the capital structure, via derived demand, and led to capital goods refitted for less than first-best uses. Hutt describes a similar phenomenon at work with labor. The new array of wages, distorted by the inflation process, attracts different workers with different skills than would have been the case without the inflation (and without the wage rigidities that led to the use of inflation). As a result, some significant amount of labor winds up in employments that are sub-optimal in comparison to their skills and, therefore, the employment they otherwise would have had. The reduction in average real wages enables previously idle workers to find employment, but the scrambling of individual wage signals means that a good portion of that employment will be in production that is sub-optimal in terms of the workers' best possibilities. As we saw with capital, inflation-induced sub-optimal use or refitting/retraining lowers economic well-being because of the irretrievable adjustment costs associated with such socially unnecessary refitting and retraining.

Part of Hutt's point is that wage barriers induce coping costs in the form of: job searches that would otherwise be unnecessary, accepting short-run reduced wages in sub-optimal employment, and investments in retraining or increased versatility to deal with the long-run shifts in the composition of output and employment. These adaptations are not costless, thus lowering overall wealth in comparison to an inflation-free economy with price flexibility. Inflation or waiting out the adjustments to price rigidities may both bring idle inputs into activity, but both involve economic waste in comparison to maintaining monetary equilibrium and ensuring price flexibility. Waste exists even though, in the aggregate, price flexibility, waiting for sub-optimal adjustments, and inflation all produce 'full' employment.[12] Once again, Hutt's focus on price coordination forces us to look beyond aggregates such as total employment to see the composition of those aggregates and their relationship to total wealth and consumer preferences. Although Hutt's primary focus is on labor, there is an obvious parallel between his discussion of distortions in the composition of the labor structure and Austrian arguments about the distorting effects inflation has on the capital structure. Some Austrians (Lewin 1999, for example) have suggested that Austrian capital theory can be fruitfully extended to the labor market by applying it to human capital, and Hutt's work can be seen as the obverse of that argument – everything he says about labor might be applied to capital. This point comes through quite clearly in Hutt's explanation for the short-run and long-run damage that can be done by sub-optimal full employment. That explanation is worth quoting at length:

> Chronic unemployment is conspicuous. Chronic misallocations are sometimes hardly recognizable and, in their most burdensome manifestations, often wholly unrecognizable. *Yet the wastes implied under 'sub-optimal employment' are, as I see things, normally the most virulent form which wastes can take, both in prolonged depression and in inflation-maintained 'prosperity'.* When duress-imposed costs are allowed to repress the source of demands for decades . . . *the composition of the whole stock of assets becomes adversely affected, just as does the composition of 'the stock of skills' acquired and the particular occupations to which workers 'become attached'.*
>
> (Hutt 1975: 107, emphasis in original)

This point also explains the political preference for inflation, or waiting it out, as a solution rather than removal of wage barriers: the costs associated with sub-optimal full employment are subtle, dispersed and long-run, while the benefits are obvious and immediate, in that people are able to find work.

Hutt's points about the 'versatility' of labor and the composition of its 'stock of skills' are also parallel to Austrian concerns about the effects of market interventions on capital goods. The issue of versatility echoes Austrian concerns with multiple specificity and the related concepts of substitution and complementarity. Workers face a trade-off similar to that faced by capital goods owners in that by sharpening a relatively narrow skill, they risk a lack of versatility should they become unemployed. Arguably, the facts that refitting capital may be easier than retraining workers and that labor involves choosing human beings who might have many reasons why they would wish to stay in a certain line of employment or not make adjustments when market signals suggest they are necessary, both indicate some limits to the analogy between physical and human capital. Nonetheless, Hutt's treatment of labor has much to offer the Austrian theory of capital, and vice versa. What they have in common is the recognition that both machines and people are not homogeneous and that a serious study of the workings of the market process has to include a prominent place for the multiple specificity of capital and the versatility of labor. When those concerns are included, the effects of wage barriers and inflation become simultaneously more subtle and more serious than those found in standard treatments.

Hutt on Yeager and Leijonhufvud

Having explored the affinity between Hutt and the Austrians, we can now take a look at the relationship between Hutt and the monetary disequilibrium theorists. This discussion is facilitated by Hutt's quite explicit treatment of two of the theorists who were prominent in the previous chapter, Leland Yeager and Axel Leijonhufvud. As Hutt acknowledges, the work of both Yeager and Leijonhufvud has significant similarities to his own approach, and his critical exploration of both thinkers is largely sympathetic. In the case of Yeager, his differences boil down to a dispute over just how flexible prices can be. Yeager, as we saw in the previous chapter, believes that there will always be some amount of irremediable stickiness in prices and wages, particularly downward, so that excess demands for money cannot be adjusted out completely through price movements, resulting in declines in employment and output. Hutt's critique of Leijonhufvud is more complicated, as he argues that Leijonhufvud's account of the inability of market economies to recover from deflationary disequilibria is implicitly focused on a general equilibrium endpoint and ignores the discovery process through which wages and prices recover.

Hutt (1975: 61) argues that both Yeager and Leijonhufvud put too much emphasis on money's uniqueness among goods, in that it has no price and no market of its own. Hutt's response to that claim is that money does have a 'value', if not a price, of its own, and that value is determined by the demand for monetary services, given the supply of money determined by the monetary authority or monetary regime. Therefore, changes in the demand for money, if there is both price and monetary flexibility, should not be of concern. As Hutt (1975: 62) summarizes it:

> I do not understand why Yeager thinks that these factors, which determine the size of the measuring rod [of money's value], induce income constraints in the form of the withholding of supplies and hence of demands, except in the sense that, in the presence of downward cost and price rigidities, deflation will aggravate the cumulative withholding process.

The crucial point here is the clause that begins with 'except'. The contention of the monetary disequilibrium theorists is that such rigidities are always at work, at the very least in the form of the game-theoretic 'who goes first' problem noted in Chapter 5. Because those rigidities are believed by Yeager to be irremovable, increases in the demand for monetary services not matched by increases in the money supply will begin a downward spiraling of wages and prices that cannot take place with sufficient speed and precision to avoid reductions in employment and output. In other words, given the existence of such rigidities, the monetary authority has an obligation to maintain monetary equilibrium.

Hutt (1975: 64) thinks he understands Yeager's argument here because he interprets Yeager's claim that the monetary authority must maintain 'an adequate money supply' as being an argument for the use of unanticipated inflation to restore the reduced income flow caused by price barriers or rigidities. But this is not the point Yeager is making. Rather, he is simply arguing that if such rigidities exist *and are not the consequence of mistaken policy but part and parcel of the market process*, the monetary system must be able to adjust the nominal money supply to changes, especially increases, in the demand for monetary services. If some degree of downward price stickiness cannot be eliminated by policy (which Hutt appears to deny), then an excess demand for money will initiate the depression process because there is no single price that can remove the monetary disequilibrium.

Hutt (1975: 66) also accuses Yeager (and Leijonhufvud) of being unable to shake off Keynesian ways of thinking about these issues. However, to the extent that Keynes was also concerned with wage and price rigidities, then Keynesian ways of thinking are appropriate. Nonetheless, our perspective (making use of both monetary equilibrium theory and Hutt's work) differs from Keynes' in two important ways. First, as Hutt rightly argues, Keynes assumed that wage and price rigidities were products of the political process that could not be undone, due to the political costs of doing so. As a result, he treated them as irremovable. Hutt, as well as Yeager and others, are willing to risk the political costs, particularly when the economic costs of the alternatives to price flexibility (e.g., inflation and the resulting sub-optimal employment) are so large. To the extent such rigidities can be removed, they should.

The second point of difference concerns the role of money. As Hutt (1975: 66, emphasis added) interprets Keynes, 'an excess demand for money . . . can be "choked off" *only* by depression and unemployment'. The key term is 'only'. What the monetary disequilibrium theorists have argued is that excess demands for money need not lead to depression and unemployment, *if* the monetary system responds quickly to such excesses by creating additional nominal supplies of money. Keynes' implicit assumption (Hutt 1975: 72) of a fixed money supply, and the institutional realities of monetary policy in the 1920s and 1930s, prevented him from seeing increases in the nominal money supply as a way out of the problems created by an excess demand for money.

Part of the disagreement between Hutt and Yeager is over the origin of depressions. Yeager wishes to argue that they are almost always monetary in origin, while Hutt's contention is that it is the price rigidities that are the originating factor. Settling this issue will depend upon whether one believes that some price rigidities are irremovable. Because Hutt thinks that virtually all such rigidities can be removed, it must be lingering ones that set off or magnify the cumulative decline. Hutt (1975: 73n) argues that 'When deflation is the initiating factor (under downward cost or price rigidity), the economy still runs down through the cumulative consequences of the withdrawal of supplies of nonmoney.' Yeager would probably not disagree with Hutt's description of the process here, but he would emphasize that it must be deflation that initiates it. In other words, with all removable price rigidities absent, depression can only occur if there is an excess demand for money. Of course, the monetary influence has real effects because it works its way through the price system and the capital structure and the rigidities therein. Again, however, it is ultimately a monetary cause, and it is the fact that monetary disequilibria must make themselves known through adjustments in individual prices rather than a 'price of money', that precipitates the decline in employment and output. And it is this monetary cause that makes the resulting cumulative idling process a concern of 'macroeconomics'.

Hutt's treatment of Leijonhufvud is similarly sympathetic and critical. His major disagreement with Leijonhufvud concerns the ability of the market to recover from a depression induced by wage rigidities. Specifically, Hutt believes, as we saw above, that once wage barriers start to fall in one sector, the increased employment and output there will stimulate the demand for noncompeting commodities and that this Say's Law process will ignite a general recovery. Leijonhufvud is skeptical of this argument and argues that the wage rates that will bring labor back into activity are far less than what is necessary to produce full employment and the general equilibrium level of output. As a result, the smaller-than-justified flow of income to newly rehired workers will not generate enough spending to get the economy moving again. In more Keynesian terms, wage reductions cannot lead to recovery because they do not create enough aggregate effective demand to get the job done.

Hutt's response to this argument is quite enlightening and very consistent with the Mengerian microeconomic perspective this study has utilized. He first acknowledges that: 'Market-clearing wage-rates may conceivably be well below the levels at which the idle labor would be profitably utilizable if other workers generally were not simultaneously holding out for wage-rates higher than the immediate market clearing levels' (Hutt 1975: 83). In other words, when recovery has fully taken place, labor will be 'profitably utilizable' at wage rates much higher than the present ones. What Leijonhufvud appears to believe is that the income-constraining process limits what firms can pay labor because the firms themselves cannot sell as much as they would like to at current prices, due to the reduced income of other workers/consumers. The firms do not realize that if they would simply start the process by either producing more or paying labor more, the recovery could ignite. But with no way of knowing this, we remain mired in a depression with no apparent endogenous market process that can create a recovery. More specifically, Leijonhufvud (1968: 35) argues that the employers will not hire more labor, 'even if no more than the money wage that the system would have in equilibrium is being asked for'. Because firms believe (wrongly) that reduced output prices will be necessary to sell additional output, they are reluctant to hire labor at the value of their marginal product in the eventual equilibrium; that is, where output prices are higher.

But, as Hutt argues, Leijonhufvud's argument is stuck in a general equilibrium perspective that overlooks the market process that causes a general recovery. Hutt (1975: 93) claims that

> When Leijonhufvud maintains that pessimistic entrepreneurs will not give employment to workers who merely ask their marginal product, he appears to be thinking of what their marginal product would eventually turn out to be if the workers generally were employed at market-clearing wage rates.

The problem, in Leijonhufvud's view is that employers are currently unwilling to pay workers what their marginal products would be if the system were in equilibrium. Of course, the observing economist can know this differential because the model is of his design. But how firms in an actual market process would ever know the relationship between the wages they were offering and equilibrium marginal products is a question left unanswered. The sorts of concerns that we raised in Chapter 1's discussion of Hayek's work reappear here. One has to be careful about the knowledge assumptions one is making about the actors in a model and the theorist constructing the model. Firms simply have no way of knowing what the equilibrium array of prices, wages, and marginal products would be and to deny the possibility of a 'market-driven' recovery because they lack this knowledge is to hold the market to an unattainable standard.

In fact, as Hutt (1975: 95) rightly points out, Leijonhufvud overlooks 'the path to that equilibrium'. The key is to return to Hutt's insistence that wages are based on the *prospective* marginal product of labor. Because firms in the real world cannot know with certainty what the exact selling price of their product will be, nor can they know precisely how productive labor will be, they make wage offers based upon their expectations about selling conditions and productivity. Thus, in a depression of the sort Leijonhufvud contemplates, pessimistic entrepreneurs may well believe that their output prices will stay low and will thus offer labor lower wage rates than would (or will eventually) hold in a recovered economy. The problem is that Leijonhufvud stops there and concludes that the unwillingness to pay the eventual market-clearing wage rate is enough to halt the recovery process because those wage rates cannot generate enough income to buy up the existing stock of goods at their equilibrium prices. But equilibrium prices are not the issue. The question is whether offering employment at those lower wage rates will lead to such wages being offered permanently, or whether they 'are the required mechanism – the first step in Walrasian "groping"'(Hutt 1975: 96).

Hutt's claim is that if workers accept jobs at those reduced wages, the spending that they then generate will begin to push up prices in noncompeting industries. As prices begin to rise, the value of labor's marginal product will rise, along with the demand for labor as output increases. The competition for labor will cause wages to rise to 'labor's *realized* marginal product' (Hutt 1975: 93). By offering wage rates equal to their initial expectation of the value of labor's marginal product, firms initiate what Hutt calls an 'exploratory' process through which they discover the price they can obtain for their product, the value of labor's marginal product, and the wage rates they can afford to pay their workers. From an Austrian perspective, this is an excellent example of the role competition plays as a discovery process. Firms and workers cannot know *ex ante* what the 'right' prices and wages are, but they can discover them through the competitive market process. By firms making the original offer and by labor being willing to accept employment at wage rates in line with their expected, rather than equilibrium, marginal products, that discovery process is set into motion. Leijonhufvud appears to argue that because the market cannot simply leap to the Walrasian solution when the problem is first recognized, that it therefore has no way of getting there. The differences between the Walrasian and Mengerian traditions could not be clearer.

In judging that equilibrium values are the 'right' values for prices and wages, and reproaching the market for not quickly arriving at them, Leijonhufvud nicely demonstrates the problems with general equilibrium approaches. From an Austrian perspective, the way to eliminate widespread idleness is to stop interfering with the epistemic role of prices. Such interferences might take the form of monetary disequilibria or price rigidities on the goods side. If those interventions are eradicated, the market contains processes for recovering from depressions induced by those interventions. As Hutt (1975: 100, emphasis in original) says of Leijonhufvud:

> [he] has not, as he thinks, shown that 'unemployment may persist even with the "right" level' of money wage-rates, unless *he* means by 'the right level' (in any employment) what *I* call 'the wrong level' because it is not adjusted to *current* entrepreneurial assessments of profitability, right or wrong, and although the *ultimate* level may be destined to be much higher.

The ultimate, general equilibrium, wage rate can only be called 'right' from the God's-eye view of the theorist. In real-world market discovery processes, the 'right' wage is the one, as Hutt argues, that is in line with entrepreneurial expectations of marginal productivity.

Even using the term 'right' is problematic here. Markets are perpetual processes of discovery so any snapshot of prices and wages at a point in time can be said to be 'right' in that wages paid will always be equal to the entrepreneur's expectation of marginal productivity (in the absence of the sorts of barriers we have discussed). Salerno (1991) uses this Huttian notion of prices and wages always matching expected values to argue that (unhampered) markets are always in full coordination. But this is a trivial notion of 'right'. Of course, firms will pay wages equal to the expected marginal product. The more interesting question is whether those expectations are correct and what happens if they are not. Salerno recognizes the existence of this learning process, but wishes to deny that expectations that are shown to be in error *ex post* can be called 'discoordinated' in the first place. It is surely true that we cannot know *ex ante* whether our expectations are correct, but the interesting activity in the market are the responses to the *ex post* realization that our expectations were wrong. The fact that expectations get revised in the light of market data should suggest that those original expectations were somehow 'wrong'. One need not argue that they are discoordinated in comparison to the relevant general equilibrium values, but simply incompatible with the preferences of others in the market.

The work of both Yeager and Leijonhufvud is clearly related to Hutt's contribution. Yeager rightly criticizes Hutt for not paying more attention to the monetary origin of cumulative declines in employment and output. The difference between Hutt and Yeager appears to be over whether all price rigidities in the market are removable. If they are not, as we argued in Chapter 5, then monetary disequilibria will trigger real side effects such as the sort of cumulative rot that Hutt discusses. If all such rigidities could be removed, and prices were perfectly flexible, then monetary disequilibria could be ironed out through the appropriate, and speedy, price adjustments. The historical evidence linking monetary disequilibria and depression, even when price rigidities were fewer than they are now, suggests that Yeager is correct here. Hutt's differences with Leijonhufvud are deeper and go to the core of the microeconomic perspective of this study. Both the cumulative decline and general recovery process, which are explained by Say's Law, will be best understood in terms of a Mengerian conception of the competitive process rather than a Walrasian conception of simultaneous equilibrium.

Price coordination and monetary equilibrium

In the end, how does Hutt's story of real-side discoordination fit in with the monetary explanations of idleness offered by the Austrians and the monetary disequilibrium theorists? The answer, I would contend, is that neither monetary equilibrium nor price flexibility alone is sufficient to prevent pervasive idleness and that both are necessary for truly full employment. The relevance of Hutt is that he persuasively argued that even if monetary equilibrium is maintained, macroeconomic disorder can still occur if prices and wages are inflexible, particularly downward. Because part of what it means for the monetary system to maintain monetary equilibrium through time is that it is facilitating changes in the intertemporal preferences of producers and consumers, monetary equilibrium must be accompanied by the highest degree of price flexibility possible, so that intertemporal prices can adjust appropriately. If consumers' time-preferences fall, and saving rises, it will necessitate a fall in the prices of consumer goods and the wages of those producing them, and a corresponding rise in the prices of producer goods and the wages of those producing them. If prices in either sector cannot adjust when needed, maintaining monetary equilibrium will not be sufficient to avoid widespread idleness and a decline in output and income.

It is important to point out that the price adjustments that are necessitated by the increase in saving are simply the manifestation of the hypothesized lowered time-preference, and corresponding lower interest rate, according to Austrian capital theory. As we noted in Chapter 2, interest rates in the Austrian view are nothing more than intertemporal price differentials. Thus, what it means for interest rates to fall is that the price differential between goods relatively closer to consumers and those relatively farther away will narrow. So one way of looking at downward price rigidities is that they are also barriers to intertemporal coordination, as they prevent changes in time-preferences from being adequately expressed in the market process. Therefore, if maintaining monetary equilibrium means ensuring that market rates of interest correspond to the underlying time-preferences of producers and consumers, price flexibility must work hand-in-hand with monetary flexibility in order to prevent widespread, and cumulative, idleness. If prices are inflexible, by implication so are interest rates. In that sense, Hutt is right to have argued that the core of the problem of idleness is the existence of barriers to price coordination. When 'price coordination' includes intertemporal prices, i.e., interest rates, then he is indeed correct. The question that can be posed to Hutt is whether perfect price flexibility is attainable, and, if not, what are the implications about the role of monetary equilibrium?

We should keep in mind the previous distinction we have made between the need for adjustments in individual prices due to changes in consumer preferences, including intertemporal ones, and the need for adjustments in *all* prices due to monetary disequilibria. Changes to individual prices are far more easy to make, especially in the absence of government interventions, when they derive from changes in the underlying variables in individual markets than when they are necessitated by a general excess supply or demand for money. The implication is that removing government interventions to price flexibility will go further in facilitating appropriate price changes deriving from the 'goods' side than they will for changes coming from the 'money' side. The issues raised in the last chapter point to why economy-wide changes in prices necessitated by monetary disequilibrium are problematic. There is nothing inconsistent in believing, with Hutt, that individual prices can be made more flexible so as to handle better changes from the goods side, and believing, with Yeager, that prices can never be so flexible as to completely iron out monetary disequilibria.

The problems in generating economy-wide price movements shows why either case of monetary disequilibrium can be the initiating factor in a cumulative decline. Hutt does seems to recognize that the degree of price flexibility that would be necessary to avoid idleness in the face of monetary disequilibria is probably beyond our ability to achieve. He (1979: 147) distinguishes between 'perfect' price flexibility and 'effective' price flexibility: 'it is important to accept as a realistic assumption the existence of unstable price rigidities . . . [this is] the sort of flexibility which is empirically observable under appropriate conditions; that is, under suitable economic policies.' Even if the monetary system is as flexible as possible, which also will be less than perfect, and even if coercive barriers to price flexibility are removed, there will still be some irremovable amount of price rigidity left in the system. This may be nothing more than psychological resistance to price cuts or a version of the Prisoner's Dilemma problem.

In broad terms, the implications for policy from this chapter and the three that preceded it are straightforward. The major goal of a monetary system should be to avoid monetary disequilibria. In making comparative judgments about the effectiveness of alternative monetary regimes, the question should be the degree to which any given regime contains the right knowledge signals and economic incentives for those in charge of the supply of money to maintain monetary equilibrium, or at least penalize deviations from that equilibrium. The relationship between the monetary regime and government's fiscal actors is also relevant here, as the state's fiscal interests may affect the degree to which alternative regimes are able to avoid inflationary monetary disequilibria. All candidates for desirable monetary regimes can be held up to this test, both in theory and in practice, to see how well they perform. On the real side, the goal of policy should be to reduce and eliminate all conceivable barriers to price flexibility. Even if the monetary regime is successful in maintaining monetary equilibrium, barriers to price coordination on the goods side can still trigger widespread unemployment through the Say's Law-driven cumulative decline that Hutt describes so well. Various labor regulations that encourage pricing barriers and inflexibility need to be understood in terms of Hutt's analysis. Whatever benefits such regulations might be supposed to provide, Hutt's work exposes their very serious costs. The next chapter explores these policy issues in more detail, particularly those concerning the comparative merits of alternative monetary regimes.

Part III

Policy implications and conclusions

7 Monetary policy, monetary regimes, and monetary disequilibria

We have argued in the previous chapters that monetary disequilibria are to be avoided because the effects of an excess supply or demand for money cannot be isolated to a specific 'money market'. Rather, disequilibria in the production of money spill over into every specific market in the economy, undermining the ability of prices to serve as knowledge surrogates. The conclusion we have drawn from this analysis is that inflation and deflation are to be avoided not so much because of their 'macroeconomic' effects, e.g., movements in aggregates such as 'the price level', but rather their microeconomic consequences, that is, the ways in which they undermine the epistemic function of money prices.

To this point, however, we have largely avoided the question of what monetary policy, or what monetary regime, is most likely to be successful at doing so. That is the task this chapter sets for itself. Much of the chapter's argument rests on the distinction between monetary *policy*, understood as what sorts of directions discretionary policy-makers should take, and monetary *regimes*, understood as the collection of institutions framing the production of money, e.g., central banking with discretion, central banking with a monetary rule, free banking, etc.[1] The argument to follow comes in two stages. First, we explore the options facing a central bank, specifically the comparison between providing central bankers with discretion or binding them to rules. We then ask how well either central banking regime performs in comparison to a regime without a central bank, in particular a free banking system along the lines described by White (1996), Selgin (1988a), Dowd (1989), Horwitz (1992b), and Sechrest (1993). We will attempt to show that free banking would avoid monetary disequilibria better than central banking, and that free banking is superior to other alternatives to central banking, such as the so-called BFH system discussed by Greenfield and Yeager (1983) and Woolsey (1992) as well as the 100 percent reserve gold standard. The case for free banking's comparative superiority will also make use of Austrian insights about the microeconomic discovery process by applying those insights to the banking system itself.

The discretion vs. rules dilemma under central banking

Most discussions of monetary policy in the economics literature take it for granted that some portion of the money supply is being produced monopolistically by a central bank. As a result, the debate tends to take place within a rather narrow range of options, none of which tend to question the whole framework in which policies are being developed. In particular, the time-honored debate between 'rules' and 'discretion' frequently takes center-stage. For the purposes of the discussion below, we need to clarify how the terms 'rules' and 'discretion' will be used. Discretionary monetary policy will refer to permitting the monetary authority to adjust the level of reserves or other targets within its proximal control in the way it sees fit based on whatever rationale it constructs. The monetary authority thus both defines the goals and the appropriate way of achieving them, and can change either at its convenience. A rule-based regime will refer to the monetary authority attempting to achieve some target determined by a rule or feedback process that binds current and future persons in the monetary authority and is set for some significant period of time. Either the ends or the means, or both, are outside of the control of the monetary authority.

The Federal Open Market Committee's (FOMC) procedure of setting annual targets for the money supply and total reserves would count as discretion, as which targets are of concern and what the values targeted should be, are determined by each new FOMC and are continually revised. A Friedman-like fixed growth rate for the money supply would, however, be an example of a monetary rule as the money growth rate is fixed for an indefinite period and binds current and future FOMCs. It is conceivable that a policy that fits somewhere in between could be developed, such as a rule that is revisited every number of years. To the extent that such innovative policies are examined, their costs and benefits would fit in between those of the 'purer' regimes of rules and discretion.

The case for discretion is that movements in income velocity and other macroeconomic variables are ongoing and that the supply of money should be adjusted in ways that offset those changes. This view has a long history, and it surely consistent with versions of Keynesianism that put the speculative demand for money at their forefront. In the broadest terms, when discretionary policy is operated with the best of intentions, it attempts to offset such changes to smooth out cyclical behavior or achieve other macroeconomic goals. In the discussion to follow, we are going focus on how well a central bank with discretionary power could offset changes in income velocity. In essence, we are going to use income velocity as a proxy for all the other variables that could conceivably be of importance to the central bank. Many of the problems faced in tracking velocity would also be faced in tracking other variables. Moreover, if we assume that the monetary authority genuinely wishes to use its discretionary power to maintain monetary equilibrium (which is doubtful given the pressure of seigniorage considerations), then examining the kinds of problems it would face in maintaining a constant MV would be of even more specific interest.

Without constant conscious adjustments to the money supply, movements in velocity will induce changes in nominal income, with any dramatic decline in velocity causing nominal income to fall with equal significance. If one firmly believes that velocity is unstable to any notable degree, then a decision not to engage in some form of discretionary policy (given a central bank) looks like intentional irresponsibility. The monetary authority would presumably know that velocity will be moving around, implying welfare-reducing movements in nominal income, so refusing to do anything about it seems reckless. By analogy, if one loses one's keys, one has to at least make the attempt to find them; they are not going to come back on their own.

The case for rules frequently rests on the claim that velocity is, in fact, not so unstable and that it will move in largely predictable ways over time. As a result, there is no need for discretionary policy, as some sort of fixed money growth rule, tied to the predictable changes (normally a decrease) in income velocity, will maintain monetary equilibrium or a stabilized price level. Advocates of discretion, however, might reply that even if this were true, how is it a case against discretion? If the monetary authority knows what velocity will be doing in the near future, why is it unable to simply use its discretion to take the appropriate money supply actions? If the demand for money did in fact grow at a constant rate over reasonably long periods of time, discretionary policy would be easy. The implication of this response is that the case for rules must also either incorporate some critique of discretion and/or have a more complex view of the demand for money.

Both of these possibilities may well be true. Defenders of a monetary rule have raised a number of criticisms of discretionary policy and have suggested that the velocity of money need not be completely stable nor predictable in order to make an argument for rules. Suppose that velocity did move around from period to period, but kept to some long-term downward trend. If so, the case for rules looks different. The critique of discretion begins by noting that all monetary policy processes are subject to long and variable lags. As a result, it may not be until sometime in the *future* when the results of monetary policy enacted in the *present*, based on information of the *past*, become effective. The consequence may well be that what would have been appropriate monetary policy at the point in time described by the data informing the policy shift is now either irrelevant at best, or pro-cyclical at worst. In Friedman's (1968: 16) classic statement of this problem, he says:

> The reason for the propensity to overreact seems clear: the failure of monetary authorities to allow for the delay between their actions and the subsequent effects on the economy. They tend to determine their actions by today's conditions – but their actions will affect the economy only six or nine or twelve or fifteen months later.

The same dark forces of time and ignorance that plague market processes and, for Keynes, implied the need for discretionary economic policy, also haunt the policy-implementation process.

These lags come in at several points in the process. The first is the *recognition* lag. If income velocity is moving around and needs to be responded to, it will take some time for the monetary authority to recognize this change. The data collection process is time-consuming, as is the process of entering and analyzing that data to spot any trends in velocity. By the time the analyzed data is available to the monetary authority, it may well be so out-of-date that it is useless. Even worse, one can argue that the primary pieces of data that central banks in fact rely on to tell them about shifts in important variables are the movements in macroeconomic aggregates that result from not offsetting those shifts when they occurred. For example, the monetary authority might only realize that velocity has fallen when it starts to see downturns in nominal income or other economic bellwethers. By the time this happens, of course, it is too late to make the necessary response, and the monetary authority must quickly extrapolate the likely trend embodied in those downturns. Even with advances in data collection and computational speed, discretionary policy will almost always be made from data directly relevant to the recent past and not necessarily the present.

The second lag is known as the *implementation* lag. Once the need for a policy shift has been recognized, the monetary authority must decide what to do about it. The time between recognition and actually implementing policy is the implementation lag. For example, there might be a significant time lag between the receipt of economic data and the next meeting of the Federal Open Market Committee.

The third lag is the *effectiveness* lag, which refers to the time it takes for any implemented policy to have the desired effect. The effect of expansionary open market operations undertaken today will not arrive until the new reserves have made their way into banks and those banks respond by making new loans. Even then, the loans need to be spent and the new money needs to make its way through the market before the increase in the money supply becomes fully effective. Even if velocity does move around in the short run, discretionary policy may not be desirable because the existence of these multiple lags might turn policy intended to be counter-cyclical into policy that is unintentionally pro-cyclical.

Proponents of a rules-based regime also argue that discretionary policy can be plagued by the influence of political preferences. Political actors see the monetary system as a source of revenue and, to the extent they can exercise leverage over it, they are likely to push the monetary authority to a higher rate of money growth than what might be justified by purely economic considerations. This is only possible where the authority has discretion as to what that growth rate will be. In a rules-based regime, the authority would have discretion only over how it chose to implement a growth-rate (or growth-rate formula) it takes as exogenous. In such a situation, political actors could not co-opt the process once the rate or formula had been determined.[2] Even where a discretionary regime is behaving well, the absence of any binding rules leaves open the possibility of political influence, to the detriment of maintaining monetary equilibrium, down the road. A regime of rules attempts to preclude such a possibility by binding the monetary authority to some pre-set growth rate or formula. Over time, argue the proponents of rules, discretionary regimes are less likely to be successful at maintaining monetary equilibrium given the ever-present possibility of the politicization of the money supply process.

When the lags and politics problems are put together, it suggests a somewhat different argument for a monetary rule. It is true that binding the monetary authority to such a rule prevents it from actively attempting to match changes in other variables, such as velocity. However, if the costs associated with activist monetary policy are significant, then the net benefits of abandoning an active attempt to offset velocity changes might be higher than the expected net benefits of a costly attempt. If in attempting to find a baseball lost in the woods, one continually trips over dead limbs, or steps in mud and so forth, one might well be better off by giving up the search. The same could be said of monetary policy; although attempting to use discretionary policy to maintain monetary equilibrium (or some other goal) is surely a noble idea, the costs of doing so may render it counterproductive, even accounting for the probability of getting the policy correct. A monetary rule might minimize the expected losses of monetary policy. If discretion cannot perfectly track velocity, then an alternative that incurs fewer net costs by refusing to even try is to be preferred.

A further argument for rules is that discretionary policy forces economic agents to spend significant resources in forming expectations about the monetary authority's intentions. Financial markets hang on every twitch of central bankers, trying to find some guidance about future policy in the metaphoric tea leaves. One advantage of having a publicly announced monetary rule is that there is no more guesswork as to what policy will be in the immediate or mid-range future. In the long run, of course, one could change the rule. But in the relevant run, policy is known and expectations can be formed using few resources. It is true that the ultimate impact of the rule on the price level will not be known with certainty, as information on the demand for money or changes in productivity will not be known so cheaply. Agents under a regime of rules would still have to invest some resources in forming price-level expectations (as they would under discretion), but under rules, the resources devoted to money supply growth rate expectations would be dramatically reduced.

Despite all of the advantages in comparison to discretion, a monetary growth rule does have one major drawback – it gives up on consciously attempting to match changes in velocity. Ideally, we would like to have a monetary regime that could track changes in velocity, but without both the lags and threat of political influence associated with discretion. Discretion and rules each provide one set of advantages, but bring another set of disadvantages. We are stuck on the horns of a dilemma.

The operation of a free banking system

The central argument of this chapter is that a free banking system can avoid this dilemma created by central banking. Such a system would enable banks to take advantages of the benefits of both rules and discretion while largely avoiding the pitfalls associated with each. Free banking would combine the flexibility provided by discretion with the boundaries (particularly the division of money production and the seignorage interests of the government) intended to be provided by a monetary rule. Unlike discretionary central banks, free banks would not adjust the money supply in *any* way they see fit, while waiting months until the effects of such changes appear in macroeconomic aggregates. Rather, the decisions individual banks would make about how much money to supply would be based on microeconomic considerations. The institutional structure of a free banking system would harmonize the profit-seeking interests of individual banks with the socially desirable result of maintaining monetary equilibrium. In addition, by taking advantage of the microeconomic knowledge-conveyance process of the market, free banks are quickly made aware when they produce too much or too little money, thereby avoiding an important component of the lag problem that faces central banks. What a free banking system allows for is that monetary disequilibria can be quickly remedied through changes in the nominal supply of money rather than through the changes in the price level, that is, rather than through changes in individual relative prices.

What is meant by free banking is a monetary system where banks are treated no differently than other corporate entities. That is, in the same way that restaurants or department stores have no limits on their geographic locations, nor on the sorts of products they can sell, so would banks under free banking be free to provide their customers with a range of products and services driven by market demands, rather than political intervention. The most important of these freedoms would be the ability to supply customers with currency for hand-to-hand use. In the same way that commercial banks currently produce money in the form of deposits, so would free banks offer the alternative of a bank-produced currency. Such a currency, along with demand deposits, would require something backing it as a reserve medium (or it would be unlikely to be accepted).[3] The reserve medium could be a commodity, such as gold, it could be some market basket of goods, or it could even be a frozen stock of Federal Reserve notes. The controversies among these options will not be a major concern here. What is important, however, is that currency under free banking takes on the same role on bank balance sheets as deposits; it is a liability of the individual bank and the bank needs to hold reserves against it.

In a free banking system of this sort, banks would be free to determine the level of reserve holdings they thought appropriate. Reserves for free banks would include their in-vault holdings of the redemption medium as well as deposits held at any one or more inter-bank clearing houses. Prior to the creation of the Federal Reserve System, such clearing houses were the way in which banks in a given geographic area exchanged the liabilities of other banks for reserves. In the absence of a clearing system in which membership is required, banks might well keep deposits at several different locations to facilitate the inter-bank clearing process.[4] If adjustments in these deposit balances are the way in which inter-bank liabilities are cleared, then such deposits serve as reserves. In the absence of statutory minimum reserve requirements, individual banks would be free to hold the level of reserves they believed were prudent. The basic trade-off in the reserve holding decision is the liquidity risk involved in holding fewer reserves versus the forgone interest from keeping resources tied up in reserves rather than having them loaned out to customers.[5] Free banks would try to jointly minimize these liquidity and forgone interest costs in order to find the most economical level of reserves.

Having chosen their desired reserve ratio, free banks could then expand their loans/deposits to a level that brings their reserve holdings in line with that desired ratio. Doing so implies that the bank is producing a quantity of deposits and currency just equal to the public's demand to hold those liabilities. Suppose, to take a simple example, a free bank desires to hold 5 percent of its outstanding liabilities in reserve. If the total supply of the bank's liabilities is $10,000,000 it will hold $500,000 as reserves. The market will quickly inform the free bank as to whether this ratio matches with the public's desire to hold balances of the bank's liabilities. If the supply of liabilities is too large, the public will disgorge them from their balances, sending them through the redemption process, which will begin to drain the issuing bank's reserves. That drain will bring the bank's reserve ratio below its preferred level, forcing it to rethink whether the previous ratio was sustainable. If the bank has insufficiently supplied liabilities, it will see its reserves grow, as it redeems the liabilities of other banks but sees relatively few redemptions of its own liabilities, as its customers attempt to acquire more of them. This piling up of its reserves will force the reserve ratio above the previously desired level, suggesting that the bank could loan out more than it previously thought. Only when it has produced a quantity of deposits and currency just equal to the public's willingness to hold them will the bank see no net gain or loss in reserves.

If the free bank over-issues, people who wish to shed their excess money balances have several options. The most obvious, but least likely, is to head directly to the issuing bank and redeem the liabilities for the base money. This clearly imposes direct liquidity costs on the issuing bank as it sees its stock of the redemption commodity depleted. A second option is to place that money on deposit at a bank other than the issuer. In this case, the bank receiving the deposit will acquire deposits at the clearing house while the issuing bank will see its deposits fall. This will also threaten the preferred liquidity position of the issuing bank. The money holder could also choose to spend their excess balances. In this case, the recipient of those expenditures would face the same options as the original money holder. Because most businesses operate through the banking system, it is highly probable that this expenditure will make its way into the seller's bank account, causing the same inter-bank clearing process as if it were deposited directly. Unlike central banking systems, where injections of currency have nowhere to go but into the supply of reserves if the public does not wish to hold them, excess supplies of currency in free banking systems will make their way back to the issuer as a *demand* for reserves. Of course, the deposit clearing process would work in much the same way as it does today.[6]

It is the adverse clearings facing over-expanding banks that keep the money supply equal to the demand to hold it under free banking. Banks that over-expand relative to their competition will see more of their liabilities returned to them than they return of other banks. This is the same process that ensures that banks under central banking cannot over-expand their deposits, given some amount of base money. One possible objection to this argument is to ask what happens if *all* the banks attempt to expand their money supplies in concert. If so, it would appear as if no bank would face adverse clearings, as each one's supply of liabilities relative to other banks will not have changed. However, as Selgin (1988a: 80ff.) has argued, this is not the whole story. Banks pick their level of reserve holdings based on both the average level of reserves they will need and the variation in daily clearings. Some portion of total reserves is 'precautionary' in that it guards against the fact that clearings on any given day may deviate significantly from the mean. Therefore, if all banks expand in concert, it may well be true that each bank's average daily net clearings may be no different, but the increase in gross clearings implies an increase in the variance around that mean, creating a need for additional precautionary reserves. If all of the banks were to attempt an 'in concert' expansion, they would soon find that they would need to devote additional reserves to the clearing process in order to maintain their desired reserve ratios and avoid a liquidity crisis. This problem would discourage the banks from attempting the joint expansion in the first place.[7]

In a free banking system, banks would be allowed to produce their own brands of currency. Despite fears about free banking being inflationary or deflationary, the incentive to remain sufficiently liquid created by the contractual obligation to redeem bank money in some base money ensures a determinate price level under free banking. As banks attempt to jointly minimize their liquidity and interest costs, their profit-maximizing decisions will unintentionally create a quantity of bank liabilities just equal to the public's willingness to hold them at the existing price level, that is, they will maintain monetary equilibrium. We explore some of the details of this process in the next section by comparing free banking to central banking.

Free banking, central banking, and monetary equilibrium

The sketch of a free banking system provided above demonstrates the congruity between the profit-seeking activities of free banks and their ability to maintain monetary equilibrium and avoid unnecessary movements in relative prices. Of course, a central bank might well adopt a policy goal of changing the nominal money supply in response to changes in the demand to hold real money balances. As Selgin (1990: 266) has argued, this is roughly equivalent to targeting per capita nominal income, as the changes in the nominal money supply keep MV constant, which implies that nominal income is constant as well. A central bank that embarked on any other policy goal (a stable growth rate in M, targeting interest rates, etc.) would be, by default, allowing the price level to bear some portion of the work in removing monetary disequilibria. This is precisely the result that we have argued should be avoided.[8]

Of particular interest is the rule proposed by Bennett McCallum (1987). He explicitly argues that the monetary authority should adopt a rule that targets a stable level of nominal income. Given the equation of exchange, such a rule amounts to maintaining monetary equilibrium by stabilizing MV. Unlike a Friedman-type rule, McCallum's proposal would allow the monetary authority to adjust the monetary base as needed to offset changes in payments technology and the like. McCallum's proposal also requires that the monetary authority make a guess at what the future growth rate in real GDP will be in order to know at what rate to change the base. This particular rule has several advantages, mainly that it does take complete discretion away from the monetary authority and it does bind it to the attempt to maintain monetary equilibrium. However, it faces the same sorts of problems that plague central banking in general: can it know with certainty what the growth rate in real GDP will be and can it know exactly how changes in the monetary base will translate into changes in the overall supply of money? Even though the central bank is being bound to a rule, it still must possess a great deal of information, centralized in one place, in order to be able to execute the rule effectively.

The question at hand is whether a free banking system would do a better job at maintaining monetary equilibrium than would a central bank targeting nominal income. It will be argued below that free banks are much more able to react, and to react quickly, to changes in the relevant economic data than are central banks. As a result, free banks are informed quickly and accurately when they deviate from maintaining monetary equilibrium, and that information comes with an incentive to make the appropriate correction, in the form of a threat to their profitability. Central banks, by contrast, even if they attempt to maintain monetary equilibrium, are unable to react as quickly or as accurately to changes in the underlying data of the market, in addition to lacking any incentive to do so.

Fundamentally, the advantage of free banking over central banking in maintaining monetary equilibrium is that free banking is not dependent on the centralization of information in order to generate the appropriate supply of money. In a free banking system, producing the right quantity of money is not a matter of intentional policy by individual banks, rather, it is the unintended consequence of those banks seeking to maximize their profits under the appropriate institutional framework. A free banking system relies upon 'invisible hand' processes to produce money, rather than the more visible hand of a central banker.[9] In that sense, it is an extension of the Austrian spontaneous order arguments of Chapter 1.[10] If the institutional 'rules of the game' are sound, the economic processes that play out within them will produce desirable and orderly results.

The attempt of discretionary policy to track the demand for money, or other variables, is laudable, but various informational problems (among others) prevent it from doing so with great success. Free banking solves this epistemic problem by applying the same logic as does the broader case for markets over central planning. Compare the way a discretionary central bank and a free bank acquire information about the demand for money. The central bank must go through the data collection processes discussed earlier. The free bank, on the other hand, does not need to collect data in this way at all. Rather, it observes movements in its reserve position and interprets those as reflective of changes in the demand to hold its liabilities. For example, suppose a free bank desires a reserve ratio of 3 percent. Assume further that it is not, on the day in question, adding to its liability issues. If it sees, at the end of the day, that its reserve ratio has dipped below the desired level, it knows that more of its liabilities are being returned to it than it is returning of other banks' liabilities. This suggests that the free bank has issued more liabilities than the public wishes to hold, as evidenced by the relative high rate of redemption it is seeing. Of course, it may also be true that the demand to hold the liabilities of all or many other banks has risen dramatically, thus making the bank's redemptions *relatively* high. For this reason, the bank will have to interpret the fall in its level of reserves in terms of past trends and the historical knowledge of its managers. Even so, the key piece of information the bank needs to make such determinations is present: the immediate effect of its liability issues on its reserve holdings.

This signal is also nearly immediate. Banks can monitor their own holdings of outside money quite easily and could access computer records of their current balances in any clearing house accounts. Careful scrutiny of reserve holdings has always been necessary to maintain liquidity in a fractional reserve banking system. Under free banking this would be even more important, given the absence of a lender of last resort that can provide liquidity through open market operations, discounting, or the printing of fiat currency. In a regime of central banking, this immediate feedback process to over-issuing is absent. The only way a central bank has to determine whether it has oversupplied currency (or reserves) is when the price level rises (or slows a secular fall) in response to the spending of the unwanted money. Because central bank currency is both irredeemable and monopolistically produced, any supply of it will find a willing holder, if the price level is allowed to rise. Should the central bank print more currency than the public wishes to hold, they will either spend it on goods and services, directly driving up the price level, or they will deposit it at their bank, in which case the bank now has additional reserves from which it can create new loans and deposits, which will eventually drive up the price level. Given that either process takes time and that data on the price level is only collected at discrete intervals, there will be a lag between the creation of new currency and the recognition, via the price level change, that too much has been created. Even then, the signal is not unambiguous, as the price level movement may be caused by productivity changes rather monetary factors.

These concerns go right to the heart of McCallum's proposal noted earlier. In order to consciously adjust the monetary base in order to stabilize nominal income, the central bank would have to obtain accurate information and have the incentive to use it correctly. Both are problems when the institution has monopoly powers and is shielded from the discipline of profit and loss. Free banking theorists might share McCallum's goal of targeting PY, but would disagree that a central bank is able to do that as effectively as a free banking system could. The concerns raised about knowledge and competition in this section form the basis for the free banking theorists' skepticism about the ability of central banking to do the job.

It is important to note that these informational problems are only lessened somewhat if the central bank currency is monopolized but redeemable into some commodity. In that case, the public would have the option of directly redeeming any unwanted currency for base money at branches of the central bank. To the extent they did so, the central bank would indeed get a fairly quick signal that it had over-produced currency. However, we need to ask whether such direct redemption is likely to be chosen by the public given their other alternatives. Once again, they could spend the unwanted currency, or they could deposit it at their bank. Even currency spent will eventually either be redeemed at the central bank or deposited at commercial banks. If the redeemable monopoly currency makes its way into the banking system, the feedback process will be short-circuited. The key here is that it is monopolistically produced. Because the individual banks will want to have stocks of that currency on hand for their customers' use, they will hold the deposited currency in their vaults and treat it as reserves even when it is redeemable. Simply making central bank currency redeemable in some base money is not enough to address the problem at hand because the currency will still 'stick' in the banking system due to its monopoly status.

The advantage of free banking is that currency is both redeemable and competitively supplied. Individual free banks will not treat either their own currency or that of other banks as a reserve item. Their own currency is a liability and that of other banks is an asset, but one which any given bank would prefer to return to the issuer to exchange for either base money or deposit credits at the clearing house. Free banks will accept on deposit but not hold in their vault the currency of their competition. The incentive to accept it is the same incentive they have to ship it back to the issuer – they can acquire a reserve asset in exchange. The credit to its clearing house balance that a bank receives from redeeming other banks' notes serves as the reserve for the deposit credit it gives the customer who deposited the notes of the other banks. Redeemability is necessary, but not sufficient, to ensure the quick flowback of excess supplies of currency to their issuer. Competition is the other necessary factor, as it ensures that no bank's currency will be used as a reserve medium and that all currency of other banks deposited at any given bank will be returned to the issuer for reserves. It is this latter process that provides the feedback to free banks that is missing in central banking.

This points to one of the distinctive characteristics of a free banking system. Allowing currency to be competitively produced shifts it from the asset side of an individual bank's balance sheet to the liability side. Under central banking, there is only one 'brand' of currency available for hand-to-hand use, so, assuming that actors wish to use currency, they will always want their banks to hold stocks of that currency. This is why central bank currencies are seen as assets – banks desire to keep stocks on hand to give to customers who prefer currency to deposits. Once monopolized currencies begin to play this role, it is but a small step to make them count 'officially' toward total reserves and include them in statutory reserve requirements.

One result of this switch in the balance-sheet status of currency is that free banking systems do a much better job at responding to shifts in the currency/deposit ratio than do centralized systems. In systems with a monopoly currency, increases in the public's currency/deposit ratio mean a drain in total reserves and a consequent reduction in the money supply, unless the central bank is able to see this change in the ratio and quickly inject reserves to offset it. To the extent central banks are unable to respond quickly and appropriately to such changes, movements in the currency/deposit ratio pose a threat to hitting money supply targets accurately. It is precisely because currency serves a dual role as both hand-to-hand money and bank reserves that this problem arises under central banking. In a free banking system, if customers wish to exchange deposits for currency, then the free bank simply makes the bookkeeping entry to debit the deposit account and then hands the customer currency. This is simply a switch in the form of bank liability that the customer wishes to hold and it has no effect on reserves whatsoever.[11] It does not matter to the bank in which form customers choose to hold liabilities, as either form must be backed by the redemption medium or deposits at a clearing house. Unlike central banking where movements in the currency/deposit ratio imply changes in the level of total reserves, such movements are unproblematic in free banking.[12]

If, under central banking, the public reduces its consumption and chooses to save by holding more currency (because it happens to be more convenient than deposits) then the banking system and investors get no signal that time-preferences have fallen. In fact, the signal is precisely the opposite, as the increased holdings of currency reduce bank reserves and lead them to increase market rates of interest and reduce their total lending activity when the wishes of the public may well be just the reverse. In a free banking system, currency's role as bank money means that increased holdings of currency (as a form of saving) do send the right signal to the banks and the banks, in turn, adjust interest rates and lending in the appropriate direction. Of course, should customers in a free banking system choose to hold more of the reserve commodity, then this would have the same effect as increased currency holdings under central banking. However, at the very least, free banking reduces the scope of the problems that arise when the demand for outside money rises because hand-to-hand currency, which is desired for its convenience by customers in any banking system, is no longer outside money, so the public's desire for outside money will be correspondingly less. In general, a free banking system takes the accepted understanding of the limits to deposit expansion and applies them to currency as well.

In the standard textbook treatment, the problem facing central bankers is seen to be that they cannot completely control the level of total reserves and they may guess wrong as to the exact value of the money multiplier. As a result, the best intentions of dynamic monetary policy may go awry and the bank will frequently find itself having to play defense to offset all of the outside changes. Add to that the knowledge problems facing their attempts to acquire the relevant data, and the task facing central banks is indeed difficult. This is further compounded by a lack of immediate feedback when they do make mistakes. Central banks frequently only know that they have made an error when they see the very thing happen they wished to avoid, e.g., an increase in the price level or unemployment. Even if data on money demand and so forth could arrive quickly and accurately, there still remains the question of what incentive a central bank would have to stick to a pre-announced policy of maintaining monetary equilibrium, when seignorage incentives suggest that inflation will be more profitable. This incentive problem suggests that central banks, in the face of the sort of data problems we might expect them to have, would have a bias in favor of inflation.

In these ways, free banking is superior precisely because it takes advantage of the knowledge signals generated by competition (specifically in the inflow and outflow of reserves through the competitive clearing process) so as to minimize the informational burden on bankers, and provides a profit incentive for using such information correctly. The managers of a free bank do not need to collect the equivalent data and face the recognition lag that plagues central banking. In addition, the implementation lag is not such a problem, as bank managers can make day-to-day or even hour-to-hour decisions about adjusting their lending based on the immediately accessible data on reserves. The effectiveness lag is likely to be shorter under free banking as free banks would get additions to the money supply directly into the hands of those who demand it, rather than going the more circuitous route that characterizes open market operations. Faced with the need to expand their supply of liabilities, free banks need only lower interest rates and offer loans to formerly supra-marginal borrowers. It would still take some time for that money to make its way into the spending stream, but it would be less so than under central banking.

In contrast to discretion, free banking would eliminate the possibility of political interference, at least in the short run. By completely separating the operation of the banking system from government intervention (other than any role government might have in setting up the legal framework in which the market process plays itself out), free banking takes politics out of money supply decisions. In doing so, it also takes away the ability of the government to use the banking system as a source of revenue. Without the ability to inflate and/or monetize the debt, governments in an economy with a free banking system will be more constrained in their ability to run deficits and accumulate debt. No longer will there be a central bank ready to buy up debt that the public does not want. Consequently, one would expect that free banking could be an effective component of any large-scale attempt to rein in the spending proclivities of democratic governments.[13] The elimination of political influence from the money supply process is a major advantage of free banking over a discretionary central bank.

So far, it looks like free banking shares the same advantages over discretion as does a regime of rules. The question now is, how well does free banking stack up against a monetary growth rule or formula? It does quite well because, unlike rules, free banking is not subject to the possibility of velocity-induced monetary disequilibria. The case for a monetary rule is normally built on the assumption, both theoretical and empirical, that the income velocity of money is stable over time.[14] To the extent that one can devise a monetary rule or formula that precisely tracks movements in velocity (or remains constant when velocity does), then such a regime can effectively maintain monetary equilibrium. The problem is that devising such a rule or formula and creating the incentives for a central bank to execute it may be impossible. One need not believe that the demand for money is highly unstable to accept the claim that it will, to some degree or another, oscillate around a long-term trend. If such oscillations are in any way significant, they will induce monetary disequilibria if the supply of money is fixed by a rigid growth rule.

The traditional response by defenders of a fixed growth rate rule is that these short-run movements in velocity are not as important as its general long-run trend. Friedman and others recognized that velocity might move around in the short run but argue that attempts to counteract those changes will largely be counter-productive due to lags. So, they argue, look at the long-run trend of velocity and fix a rule accordingly. Faced with the alternative of discretion, getting the growth rate rule right in the long run would be superior. The advantage of free banking is that it can actually respond to such short-run changes without suffering the adverse consequences associated with lags. The Friedman choice for targeting the long-run velocity trend is a second-best solution.

The largest challenge facing the attempt to institute a monetary rule is devising the growth rate or formula that will define the rule. Ideally, such a rule would take account of every possible influence on velocity and be able to respond instantaneously to every piece of incoming data. Of course both are impossible. Many of the factors that influence velocity are either inaccessible (for example, the tacit knowledge of market actors) or yet-to-be known (for example, a future financial innovation that we cannot now even imagine). Even the best humanly constructed rule would require periodic tinkering to take account of the latter kinds of problems and could never address the epistemic issues. To the extent one keeps changing the rule to deal with changing influences on the demand for money, one is losing the whole justification for rules in the first place: that they cannot be changed at the whim of central bankers. After all, it is central bankers who will presumably determine what goes into deciding on the rule, when changes in the rule are necessary, and what changes should be undertaken. If we propose to continually alter the rule in this way in order to keep up with changing knowledge and innovation, are we not back to discretion?

The advantage of free banking along these lines is that it does not require direct access to the demand for money either for conducting discretionary policy or for formulating some sort of monetary growth rule. The movements in reserves discussed above serve as a proxy for the underlying factors affecting the demand for money. Rather than having to gather and analyze data on the demand for money directly, free banks get all the requisite information packed into their observations of their reserve situation. Just as prices in general enable actors to make use of knowledge that they otherwise could not, so free bank reserve movements enable bankers to act 'as if' they had access to the underlying data.

The BFH system as a plausible alternative

Free banking and central banking do not exhaust the alternative monetary regimes we might consider. Two other possibilities have been proposed by monetary theorists interested in alternatives to central banking. In many cases these authors have also been influenced, to one degree or another, by ideas central to the main arguments of this book. In the next two sections we consider these two possibilities and see how they compare to free banking. In general, we will argue that while these two alternatives might perhaps be superior to central banking, they are not superior to free banking, despite sharing some important insights with the latter.

The first of these two alternatives is the so-called BFH (for Black–Fama–Hall) system discussed by Greenfield and Yeager (1983) and Woolsey (1992), among others. The core proposition of the BFH system is the attempt to divorce the medium of exchange from the unit of account. The idea behind this proposal is to eliminate the problem caused by money not having a market of its own. The BFH system tries to eliminate monetary disequilibria by artificially creating a separate 'money market' and 'price' for money.

In fact, in some sense 'money' disappears entirely in this system. Financial institutions could create whatever sorts of media of exchange that people find acceptable. The key is that prices are posted in a unit of account that is defined separately from the process of creating media of exchange. The unit might be defined as the value of a market basket of some wide variety of commodities with substantial non-monetary uses, particularly a bundle whose price would remain stable over time. The bundle 'as a whole, would, by definition, have the fixed price of one unit' (Greenfield and Yeager 1983: 305). It important to make clear that financial institutions do not need to hold stocks of the bundle, as media of exchange are *not* redeemable into the bundle. The bundle simply serves to define the unit of account, much as a 'meter' is defined by a specific number of wavelengths of the orange-red radiation of krypton 86. Payments are effected by transferring media of exchange worth however many units of account the good being purchased is priced at. In some sense, as Greenfield and Yeager readily admit, this is 'barter [but] not crude barter' (ibid.: 307).

Media of exchange might well take the form of shares of mutual funds not dramatically unlike those available today. The shares would be valued in terms of the defined unit of account and their value might well fluctuate on a daily basis. Since all of the securities held as fund assets are reckoned in terms of the defined unit of account, so could the shares be so priced. Check clearing would take place through the transfer of portfolio assets of the stated value mutually agreed upon by funds and their clearing houses.

Greenfield and Yeager (1983: 308–9) list several advantages for this system, many of which would be shared by free banking. However, their biggest argument, and the most interesting from the point of view of this book, is the claim that it would virtually eliminate monetary disequilibria. The key is that by separating the medium of exchange from the unit of account, changes in the supply or demand for the medium of exchange do not necessitate changes in the unit of account's general purchasing power, which is 'practically fixed by definition' (ibid.: 310). Because the price of media of exchange (fund shares) would fluctuate in terms of the unit of account (as the value of the fund's assets changed), it enables the specific prices of different funds to bear the burden of adjusting out the supply and demand for fund shares (i.e., media of exchange). This system manages, in theory, to give money 'a price of its own' to react to movements in money's supply and demand so as to avoid the sorts of economy-wide price adjustments that have been the central concern in the previous chapters. Funds that tried to 'over-issue' by buying up additional assets would find their shares being redeemed more frequently, forcing them to give up shares to other funds. Funds that 'under-issued' by not creating more shares would be sacrificing the potential profits of efficient intermediation. Much like the adverse clearings process of outside money in free banking, mutual funds in the BFH system would have profit incentives to produce the quantity of shares that their customers desire.

Under free banking, monetary disequilibria are 'equilibrated' by adjustments in the nominal money supply. For BFH, the adjustment variable is the 'price' of the medium of exchange in terms of the unit of account. The advantage of both these systems over central banking is that they avoid making the price level the adjustment variable that maintains long-run monetary equilibrium. Looked at this way, the BFH system shares with this study's perspective on free banking a recognition of the importance of maintaining monetary equilibrium and avoiding spillover effects on the relative prices of individual goods and services.

The question, however, is whether the BFH system can work in practice. In an incisive critique of BFH-type systems, White (1984) offers several reasons to believe such systems are unworkable: demand deposits are unlikely to disappear, outside money is unlikely to disappear, and it is also unlikely that the medium of exchange could ever be divorced from the unit of account. All three of White's criticisms are based on an evolutionary understanding of the emergence of money and various monetary institutions. In Menger's evolutionary theory of the origin of money, the crucial point is that money emerges as the most saleable of all commodities. Menger's theory shows how acts of self-interest by traders in a barter economy can unintentionally produce a generally acceptable medium of exchange by making use of indirect exchange using progressively more saleable commodities as intermediate objects of exchange. If Menger is correct, all usable moneys must have had a similar origin in some saleable commodity somewhere back in their historical evolution. As Mises (1980 [1912]: 131) put it: 'The earliest value of money links up with the commodity value of the monetary material.'

The importance of the Mengerian evolutionary story of self-reinforcing saleability comes into play in all three of White's responses. First, it is unlikely that demand deposits would disappear for a variety of reasons (White 1984: 182). One point is that customers may prefer a bank liability that pays a contractually assured nominal interest rate over time rather than one whose value can fluctuate with the value of the institution's assets. In addition, mutual fund shares of the sort the BFH system might involve currently rest on the foundation of the checking system. When fund shares clear, the drawn-upon fund presumably transfers a checking account balance to the bank of the customer drawing down the account. In the absence of such a possibility, funds would have to determine which assets were acceptable for clearing, and those assets would effectively be serving as an outside money in which the fund shares were effectively redeemable, making fund shares look more like current demand deposit accounts. The lower saleability of mutual fund shares is best illustrated by the fact that most funds today have a stiff minimum balance for check writing, indicating their unwillingness to either physically transfer ownership shares or to participate in the regular clearing process for smaller-sized checks.

Outside money is equally unlikely to disappear. In the Menger story, one good emerges as the most saleable, and its status as the most saleable must derive from its use-value as a commodity before it acquires the status of a money. The sort of market basket unit of account proposed by the BFH system (and other similar market basket-based proposals) is not something that could ever emerge as a unit of account through an actual historical process of exchange. Nor could a claim to such a basket emerge as a medium of exchange. As White (1984: 186) points out: 'A claim to a basket of commodities would not originally emerge as money, since in a barter setting it would be less saleable than the most saleable of its components.' Whatever the advantages of such systems in theory, getting them to actually emerge in practice appears to be a significant problem.

This last point is very clear in the case of the splitting of the medium of exchange from the unit of account. The unit of account under the BFH system represents a kind of sophisticated numeraire, not unlike those in general equilibrium models where trading takes place after prices are set by an auctioneer. In such a model, any good (or bundle of goods) can be chosen to serve as the numeraire because the process of price formation occurs separately from the actual process of exchange. In a more Mengerian conception of the market, it is real processes of exchange that simultaneously determine (non-equilibrium) prices and the medium of exchange. Therefore, the emergence of a unit of account occurs *during* the process that determines what the medium of exchange will be. It is hard to imagine, from that perspective, how such a separation could ever occur as part of an actual historical process, as opposed to a model in which price formation and exchange are treated separately.

Defenders of the BFH system might respond that the fact that something was unlikely to emerge historically is not necessarily a reason to prevent us from putting it into practice now if it appears feasible. The problem with this argument is that it ignores the fact that money is a social institution and, as such, its use and acceptability are conditioned by the actual preferences and experiences of those who make use of it. Simply defining some good or collection of goods as a new unit of account, independent of the trading activities of those who will make use of it, will not be sufficient to ensure its acceptability.[15] In order for social rules or institutions to function successfully, they must emerge from actual social practices. Otherwise, imposed social institutions will not 'stick' because they have no basis in actual practice (Boettke 1994: 281–2). Although BFH-type systems may look good in theory, whether they could ever be put into operation remains highly questionable as it is not clear there is any historical path to such a system, or that if it were to be imposed, that there would be enough of a social basis for it to be used effectively.

Austrian economics and 100 percent reserve banking

Another potential alternative to free banking as a way of avoiding the destructive effects of inflation, and possibly deflation, is a policy long-espoused by a significant number of self-described Austrian economists. This group, whose foremost member was the late Murray Rothbard, has argued that only a banking system based on a gold standard and 100 percent reserves can solve the problem of inflation and the business cycle, as understood by Austrians. For many years, particularly during the 1960s and 1970s when Rothbard was more or less the only Austrian writing on money and macroeconomic issues, the 100 percent reserve gold standard was generally agreed upon by Austrians as the desirable choice of regimes, at least by default. Arguably, it is only after the first edition of Hayek's *Denationalization of Money* was published in 1976 that younger Austrians began to rethink the Rothbardian position, and it was the publication of the first edition of Lawrence White's *Free Banking in Britain* in 1984 that led to a substantial shift away from the 100 percent reserve position among Austrians. The even more recent work by Selgin (1988a), Horwitz (1992b), and Sechrest (1993) has deepened the Austrian perspective on free banking.

This growing literature has not gone unnoticed by the defenders of 100 percent reserves, however. In the last few years the debate among members of the two groups has rekindled, with papers by Block (1988), Hoppe (1994), Rothbard (1995), de Soto (1995) and Hulsmann (1996) attempting to reaffirm the 100 percent reserve position by directly tackling the arguments of the free bankers. In turn, free banking theorists have responded, e.g., Selgin and White (1996) and Sechrest (1995).[16] This section reviews this debate with several questions in mind. First, how does a system of 100 percent reserves relate to the monetary equilibrium framework adopted in this study? Second, could 100 percent reserves avoid the problems associated with monetary disequilibria as effectively as free banking? And, third, is 100 percent reserves ultimately compatible with other portions of the Austrian approach to economics?

A banking system based on gold and requiring 100 percent reserves would differ dramatically from the systems that have historically emerged in most parts of the world. Money, in such a system, would consist in either full-bodied gold coins or in paper money or checkable deposits that represent fully-backed receipts to gold on deposit at a bank.[17] Currency and deposits in such a system would simply be more convenient forms in which to hold gold, which would be genuine money, rather than being the fiduciary media they have been at various times in history. For the 100 percent reserve theorists, the substitution of paper currency or checkable deposits for gold is not a matter of creating additions to the money supply through the fractional reserve process, but rather a substitution of different forms of receipts for the actual warehoused gold. This system would thereby separate money production and lending. Holdings of specie used to support the production of demand deposits or currency could not be lent out to others and would have to stay in vault to serve as 100 percent reserves against those money certificates. Banks could still perform their intermediary function, but only in the form of time deposits, where the depositor agreed to give up control over his resources for a contractually specified period, enabling the bank to lend for a similar period. A complaint of many 100 percent reserve theorists is that fractional reserve banking illegitimately confuses the lending and money production aspects of banking.

The idea of monetary 'policy' under such a system becomes non-sensical, even more so than under free banking. Free banks at least have the profit-seeking incentive to have to make conscious adjustments in the supply of their liabilities in response to changes in the demand to hold them. Banks in a 100 percent reserve system are far more passive. The only way the supply of money can change in such a system is through inflows of new specie. As more gold is mined and used for monetary purposes, the money supply will slowly grow. Those additions to the supply of gold enable banks to support additional currency or demand deposits as cost-saving substitutes for the actual gold. Any increase in currency or demand deposits beyond the amount of gold the bank holds in vault violates the rule of keeping 100 percent reserves.

The advocates of 100 percent reserves make two kinds of arguments against the practice of fractional reserve banking. The first is an ethical argument that fractional reserve banking is fraudulent in that such banks hold open the promise to pay off all of their liabilities in base money, yet, by definition, they could not do so on demand if all depositors presented such claims simultaneously. Only if fractional reserve currency or deposits came with an explicit statement of the conditions under which they are issued, especially the possibility of being unable to redeem, would they not be fraudulent. Leaving aside fractional reserve banking's undesirable economic effects, it is, argues this position, morally unacceptable.[18]

Defenders of fractional reserves have made numerous cogent responses to this argument (see especially Selgin and White [1996]). The first is that the nature of the demand liability contract is that it is payable *on demand* and not a bailment. Understood this way, 'fraud' can only occur if the bank in fact and not potentially fails to redeem a liability on demand. Such 'fraud' is really just breach of contract. Another line of response is that users of fractional reserve liabilities understand that they are not bailments and it is the 'commonly held' understanding of the product in question that matters in court.[19] Therefore, it is not fraudulent to create them, as their users do in fact understand the conditions under which they are issued.[20]

A twist on the fraud argument is that some, such as Hoppe (1994), have argued that the issuance of fiduciary media reduces the real value of others' holdings of money by driving up the price level. This, Hoppe argues, constitutes a coercive invasion in the form of a negative externality. As Selgin and White (1996) rightly respond, Hoppe confuses technological and pecuniary externalities. On his account, any activity of mine that affected the market value of another's assets should be prohibited. Of course, almost all market actions involve pecuniary externalities. It is only technological externalities, those that involve a physical violation of another's property, and not pecuniary ones that involve only value, that are problematic. Since the issuance of fractional reserve liabilities is itself a voluntary exchange, and the only externalities are pecuniary, third-party effects cannot be used as an argument against them.[21]

More important than the fraud argument is the belief that free banking based on fractional reserves is 'inherently' inflationary. Specifically, Hoppe and other defenders of 100 percent reserves argue that *any* increase in the supply of media of exchange beyond the amount of specie, that is, *any* issuance of fiduciary (fractional reserve) media of exchange, will cause the market rate of interest to fall below the natural rate and set into motion the business cycle described by Wicksell, Mises, and Hayek. From this perspective, the attempt by free banks to maintain monetary equilibrium in the face of any change in the demand to hold bank liabilities is disequilibrating. For example, if the demand for money should rise, and free banks respond by creating additional liabilities off their existing stock of reserves, they are triggering the cycle in Hoppe's view. As has been argued in earlier chapters, this is not how monetary equilibrium theory sees this process. The crux of the argument is whether the holding of fractional reserve bank liabilities constitutes a form of saving, with the appropriate implications about time preferences and interest rates.

Hoppe argues that the demand for money and time-preference are separate phenomena, and rightly so. A change in one need not imply a change in the other. As Selgin and White point out, an increase in money holdings might come from a reduction in 'holding other assets, and not a reduction in consumption; hence it may be part of a change in the manner of saving with no change in total savings' (1996: 103). If the public decides to move from holding bonds into holding bank liabilities, there is an increase in the demand for money but no increase in savings. What monetary equilibrium theory argues, and free banking makes possible, is that when such increases in the demand for money occur, they will be matched by an increased supply of bank liabilities, and the Wicksellian market rate/natural rate equilibrium will be undisturbed. Even this shift among forms of savings requires an expansion of bank liabilities to meet the new demand. As Selgin and White (1996: 104) argue:

> Assuming rising marginal costs of intermediation, the equilibrium rate of interest on bank deposits will have fallen, while the rate on bonds will have increased. The increased demand for intermediation raises the 'price of intermediation' represented by the spread between the deposit and bond rates. Banks are warranted in expanding their balance sheets to meet the increased demand for deposits, until the actual deposit rate falls to the new equilibrium deposit rate. (Meanwhile the market value of existing bonds falls *pari passu* with the increase in the bond interest rate.)

The ultimate effect of this portfolio shift is to leave the market rate of interest, understood as a composite of various financial market interest rates, unchanged, as the movements in bond and deposit interest rates effectively offset each other.

When the increased demand for bank liabilities comes from a reduction in the demand for goods and services the case is even clearer. Here, forgoing the purchase of those goods or services by holding money is, in fact, as form of saving. The money holder is postponing consumption to the indefinite future by choosing to hold money rather than the goods or services in question. This change does, in fact, push the natural rate of interest lower, as demand for future consumption increases at the expense of current consumption. Moreover, the decision to postpone consumption by holding additional quantities of bank liabilities supplies loanable funds to the banking system. As money demand increases, free banks that do not expand their liabilities to match it would see their reserves piling up as they experience positive clearings due to the decreased redemption of their liabilities. They could then afford to lend out the now excess reserves, and their failure to do so involves sacrificing potential interest earnings. To attract in new borrowers on the margin, they will have to reduce their market rates of interest. This reduction, however, is perfectly appropriate given that the increased holding of their liabilities constitutes a form of savings and, hence, reduced time-preferences. Issuing additional fiduciary media when those media are demanded for holding by the public does not cause the market rate to deviate from the natural rate and thus does not trigger inflation or the business cycle.

Hulsmann (1996) raises some further criticisms of the savings–investment argument made by monetary equilibrium theorists. He tries to rebut the claim that there can be differences between *ex ante* savings and investment by arguing that:

> Saving and investment are always identical. They are merely two aspects of the same action, just as buying and selling are two aspects of the same market exchange. One cannot save without investing, nor is it impossible to invest without saving at the same time.
>
> (1996: 26)

Thus it is impossible for the banking system to add to the quantity of investment due to some pre-existing excess of savings. He further argues free banking theorists are mistaken in believing that creating more funds for investment by creating more fiduciary media can increase economic growth: 'it is, even in the short run, impossible to generate output increases by printing money. Production capabilities for future and present goods are always limited' (ibid.: 28).

There are a number of problems with this argument, and I will address the two that seem to be the most directly relevant. The first is that Hulsmann's analogy to buying and selling in general proves too much. Of course it is true that sales and purchases are equal *ex post*; whatever gets sold by one person gets bought by another. But this need not be true *ex ante*. If existing market prices are above the market clearing level, *desired* purchases will fall short of *desired* sales. And if market prices are lower than the market clearing level, *desired* purchases will be greater than *desired* sales. The claim by free bankers that savings and investment can be unequal is a claim about *ex ante* quantities, as all such claims must be in economics. Hulsmann tries to get out of this criticism by saying that someone who increases his holdings of gold by selling an asset is simultaneously keeping his 'savings' in the form of gold and 'investing' in gold as well.[22] Hulsmann believes he has shown that increases in the demand for money (savings) do not require corresponding increases in the money supply (investment), because savings and investment must go together.

However, the example fails to prove the point Hulsmann thinks it does because it does not involve an increase in the demand for money. Rather, the gold has simply moved from one person's money balances to another's, i.e., there is no increase in the total amount of saving here as Hulsmann seems to believe. Free bankers are concerned about *overall* movements in money demand. This mistake seems to be a perfect example of confusing what Yeager called the 'individual' and 'overall' viewpoints in monetary theory.[23] Individuals can always increase their money holdings with no adverse macroeconomic consequences by selling an asset to someone who wishes to *reduce* their money holdings. Examples such as these, including Hulsmann's, are irrelevant to the case of an excess demand for money across the entire economy. Instead, suppose everyone wished to 'invest' in gold this way by attempting to sell off their assets or reduce their expenditures. This would reflect a true increase in the aggregate demand for money. The monetary equilibrium argument is that it is impossible for everyone to do this successfully without a decline in the price level (or an offsetting increase in the nominal money supply). During the time it takes the price level to fall, firms will find themselves with unintended inventory accumulations, implying that *desired* saving (holding of gold) is not equal to *desired* investment. This further implies that increases in the money supply would be warranted in order to bring desired saving and investment back together.[24]

More important, though, is the point that free banking theorists claim that maintaining monetary equilibrium is always a matter of marginal adjustments. The issue is simply this: given the current money supply, how should money producers react if the public wishes to hold larger balances of bank liabilities? Hulsmann argues there is nothing to worry about under 100 percent reserves since the higher saving (the reduction in spending) is matched by 'investment' in gold. However, from a monetary equilibrium perspective, if this new saving is not matched by an increase in the supply of bank liabilities (investment by commercial borrowers), there will be downward pressure on prices and, barring perfect price flexibility, a drop in output and employment. Free banking theorists argue that free banks will respond to this increase in demand by producing more bank liabilities, thus preventing the fall in output and employment that would otherwise result.

Hulsmann (1996: 28) appears to interpret free bankers as saying that *any* increase in the money supply can create wealth and that they appear to have no reason not to encourage politicians from continually increasing the money supply. He concludes, as noted earlier, that one cannot generate output increases by increasing the money supply. This claim misinterprets the free banking claim, however. The point is not necessarily that a higher total money supply under free banking would be better than a lower one under 100 percent reserve. The claim, instead, is that, *on the margin*, when the demand for money increases, banks should respond by creating more liabilities. Creating those new liabilities does *not* create new wealth, rather it simply prevents existing wealth from going to waste when the ensuing excess demand for money begins to reduce employment and output. Free bankers agree wholeheartedly with the belief that creating bank liabilities beyond the demand to hold them cannot create wealth, any more than creating more tickets than there are seats on an airplane can create additional seats. But they also believe that *not* creating bank liabilities that are demanded will reduce wealth, just as not printing as many airline tickets as there are seats will waste pre-existing seating capacity (and lower overall utility) by frustrating the attempts of individuals to make mutually beneficial exchanges.

This last point leads to what remains the fundamental issue between free banking theorists and 100 percent reserve advocates, namely whether there are harmful effects associated with the downward pressure on prices that results from excess demands for money. Hulsmann (1996: 14–17) attempts to tackle this issue head on. His first claim is that the fears of a money shortage are misplaced as we do not fear shortages of other goods like shoes, bread, and milk. However, this misses two crucial points. First, the free banking argument is not primarily that 100 percent reserve banking will lead people to *think* money will be in short supply (although it may), but that regardless of what people think, it will *in fact* allow for excess demands for money. Second, money is different from the other goods Hulsmann mentions. As we have argued from the beginning, the nature of money as a generally accepted medium of exchange means that accepting it in payment is routine and that it has no price of its own to equilibrate discrepancies between the actual and desired amounts people are holding. None of that is true of shoes, milk, or bread, which is why shortages of those items do not cause the prolonged, economy-wide difficulties caused by shortages of money.

Hulsmann (1996: 15) further argues that the monetary equilibrium theory explanation of price stickiness during excess demands for money has no way of explaining how prices 'can ever fall. Yet this is what free bankers consider as the long-run outcome of a growing economy.' This criticism was addressed in Chapter 5, which distinguished between falling prices necessitated by declines in income velocity unmatched by increases in the nominal money supply and falling prices caused by increases in factor productivity in specific areas of the economy. The latter are perfectly easy to explain precisely because they occur in specific times and places and are consistent with the profit-seeking interests of the entrepreneurs in question. Downward movements in the general price level due to excess demands for money present Prisoners' Dilemma problems that changes in factor productivity do not. In addition, prices, even in the case of an excess demand for money, will eventually become unstuck and fall, although not without major unemployment and output declines in the meantime.

Hulsmann then goes on to say that falling prices should not be a problem because entrepreneurs will simply lower the nominal wages they pay, enabling them to stay in business with lower prices. He says (1996: 16): 'Wage earners will have lower nominal incomes. Yet, all other prices are lower, too. Thus their real incomes have not declined.' Hulsmann begs the question, however. He simply states that 'all other prices are lower' without explaining how such a lowering of prices is to occur. He assumes that wages can be lowered by employers instantaneously, ignoring any long-term contracts that might be in force as well as any other considerations that might delay the wage reduction. He ignores the fact that, given wage stickiness, it is in no producer's interest to be the first to lower his prices. He seems to overlook the fact that finding the newly appropriate level of prices is a Mengerian discovery process and not an instantaneous shift. As he later states:

> The quantity of money is irrelevant for the benefits derived from its use, in the long run and in the short run. There is no need and no possibility to adjust it according to its changing employment. There is no need because the adjustment can be achieved by a change of prices and particularly a change in wages.
>
> (Hulsmann 1996: 16)

Again, the necessary lowering of prices and wages is asserted but no explanation of how that will take place is offered, nor is there recognition of a costly transition process. This is precisely the step in the argument that free banking theorists argue must be included in order to show that excess demands for money are not matters of concern. The major advantage of free banking, as detailed above, is precisely that it does adjust the nominal quantity of money to equilibrate potentially devastating monetary disequilibria rather than leaving that burden to the price level. One central shortcoming of 100 percent reserve banking is that it is unable to do this and relies on the price level to bear the burden of adjustment.

Selgin and White (1996: 101) rightly point to the inconsistency of the 100 percent reserve Austrians on this issue:

> Some economists deny the importance or even the conceptual coherence of short-run monetary disequilibrium as sketched above. New Classical theorists do so, with a certain internal consistency, because they subscribe to a Walrasian model implying instantaneous and complete price adjustment. Some Austrians do so, with a regrettable *in*consistency, when they recognize the destructive consequences of price inflation driven by monetary expansion, but nonetheless try to argue that price *deflation* is always okay, in any amount. It is inconsistent to apply short-run, Wicksellian, disequilibrium analysis when talking about increases in the stock of money and price inflation, and then switch exclusively to a long-run, Humean, equilibrium-always analysis when talking about increases in money demand and deflation.

If the price level can simply adjust downward in the face of an excess demand for money, why cannot it costlessly just adjust *upward* in the face of an excess supply of money? If money's purchasing power can simply bear the adjustment when prices fall, why do we get all of the short-run effects associated with the Austrian theory of the cycle when prices rise? This can be seen in the following example: a fall in the demand for money under 100 percent reserves would not call for a change in the supply of money, but an adjustment in the price level. The money supply is determined by the quantity of specie, which is not presumed to move *pari passu* with changes in money demand. One central difference between free banking based on fractional reserves and 100 percent reserve banking is that the latter, like central banking in practice, is willing to let the price level bear the burden of adjustment rather than a quick and accurate response via the nominal quantity of money.

The example of the falling demand for money poses an interesting dilemma for 100 percent reserve Austrians: if the demand for money falls and that spending power is let loose on the market place, why will this not cause the same disequilibrating effects as an absolute increase in the supply with money demand constant? The key issue is recognizing that choosing to hold wealth as money implies that one is refraining from current consumption and deferring that consumption to the future. If so, when the demand for money falls, it suggests an increase in the natural rate of interest, as consumption is shifted relatively more to the present, reflected in the increased consumption of current goods. Since the banks cannot reduce their supply of money in response, the market rate of interest will not change, implying a natural rate above the market rate. The 100 percent reserve theorists argue that the increased prices of those consumption goods will raise the price level enough to reduce the real quantity of money downward to the now reduced demand to hold it. But that is no less true of the case where the money supply is increased in absolute terms.

A monetary equilibrium approach, in contrast, would point out that the reduction in savings involved in the decreased demand for money should be matched by a rise in the market interest rate (and a corresponding reduction in bank lending) to keep it equal to the now higher natural rate. If not, a reduced demand for money with a constant supply (recall that under 100 percent reserves loan production and money production are completely separate) will send no market signal to producers that consumers' time-preferences have shifted. The advantage of free banking is that when changes in time-preferences take the form of changes in the demand to hold bank liabilities, banks receive a signal that they can pass on to producer/investors, signaling them to make the appropriate adjustments in intertemporal production. A 100 percent reserve system has no comparable signal.

It is this set of issues that suggests a tension between the Austrian approach to the microeconomic price formation process and the preference for a 100 percent reserve banking system. A Mengerian perspective on the pricing process suggests that prices cannot move costlessly and perfectly when confronted with monetary disequilibria. The disequilibrium process by which prices move is necessarily less than smooth and costless, unlike the idealized auctioneer process of general equilibrium theory. Monetary disequilibria introduce unnecessary and counterproductive economy-wide pressure on individual prices, making the imperfect discovery process of the market that much more imperfect. If one fully recognizes that all market discovery processes, including those by which prices are formed, involve fits and starts and also include various institutional devices such as long-term contracts, then shielding those processes from unnecessary disequilibrating influences would seem to be a priority. From a monetary equilibrium perspective, a 100 percent reserve gold standard fails in exactly this way by forcing individual prices (i.e., the price level) to bear the burden of adjustment in most cases of monetary disequilibria. Free banking's advantage is that it does a better job in protecting the price formation process from the disequilibrating effects of monetary disturbances.

The question remains: if a fall in the demand for money under a 100 percent reserve system comes from a rise in time-preferences and thus an increase in the natural rate of interest, what incentive would banks have to respond by raising their market rates? If they have none, which appears to be the case for 100 percent reserve banks, then why does the resulting divergence between the market and natural rates of interest not trigger the business cycle in exactly the same way as would such a divergence caused by an increase in the nominal quantity of money with money demand unchanged? From a monetary equilibrium perspective, the problem with 100 percent reserve banking is an error compounded by a contradiction. It permits the price level to bear the burden of adjustment in the case of monetary disequilibria (an error from the perspective we have developed), with the exception of the case where the money supply is absolutely expanded beyond the demand to hold it (a contradiction in that this case is formally no different from any other possible example and cause of monetary disequilibrium). From the perspective we have developed here, all divergences between the supply of money and the demand to hold it should be equilibrated out through adjustments in the nominal supply of money rather than the price level because 'price level adjustments' require and cause unwarranted changes in relative prices that induce significant economic discoordination. A 100 percent reserve banking system only applies that logic in one case of disequilibrium. In all others, the system is incapable of making the appropriate adjustments in the nominal supply of money and, unlike free banking, will therefore be highly vulnerable to the damaging consequences of monetary disequilibria, both deflationary and inflationary ones.

Free banking and the microeconomic discovery process

The central Austrian theme of the epistemic function of prices comes back in the argument for free banking. At one level, the advantage of free banking is that it lets the producers of money take advantage of the competitively determined prices and other signals of the marketplace in determining how much money to supply. If we believe price signals in the non-money sectors are so important that we do not want the spillover effects of monetary disequilibria to undermine them, then it would seem equally important to give those signals full play in the industry that produces money itself. This is precisely what a free banking system proposes to do. The appropriate quantity of money to produce is not known prior to the market process unfolding and must, like the appropriate supply of any other good, be discovered through the competitive process. As Selgin (1988a: 96) has put the question: 'Is the price system, which is supposed to be superior to central planning as a means for administering resources, itself dependent upon the centralized administration of money?' The three other monetary regimes we have looked at (central banking, the BFH system, and 100 percent reserves) in one way or another do not give full play to that competitive process.

Before exploring this last point in a bit more detail, there is one criticism of the preceding argument that should be addressed. Some might object that the argument is circular in that the claim is that one needs a properly functioning money sector for market prices to do their job elsewhere, yet a properly functioning money sector requires that market prices in *that* sector already do a good job in conveying knowledge. Which comes first, the properly functioning money or the properly functioning prices? The apparent paradox is illusory. Like so much else in the market, the monetary sector and the money price system it supports co-evolve through the discovery process of the market.[25] Functioning market prices can emerge from simple exchange without the presence of complex financial intermediaries like banks. As even commodity money makes possible a price formation process, it also makes possible the somewhat more complex structure of a banking firm. Even relatively 'primitive' market prices are enough to generate equally primitive financial organizations. As these firms begin to produce new media of exchange and new financial instruments more generally, the markets for goods and services expand and become increasingly complex, making a more complex financial system both more necessary and possible. This upward spiral of increasing creativity, complexity, and coordination has been outlined in more detail elsewhere, but this simple example can go to show why the charge of circularity in the relationship between free banking and market prices is a false one.[26]

The ways in which a central banking system prevents market prices from fully performing their epistemic function in the money sector seem obvious enough. The most glaring example is that the production of currency is monopolized by the central bank. To even talk of currency being produced in response to price-informed profit-seeking behavior is misguided here, as the monopoly privilege eliminates any such behavior as well as the prices that might inform such behavior. The quantity of currency being produced is solely at the whim of the central bank, subject to any political pressure it might feel one way or the other. By definition, this sort of monopoly is intended to prevent market signals from having a role. More broadly, the power to adjust the level of bank reserves through open market operations gives central banks a way to over-ride market signals and incentives. Even though a non-zero reserve ratio puts an upper limit on the degree to which the total money supply can expand in response to a change in reserves, open market operations can still cause banks to produce demand deposits that they otherwise would not. If bond traders sell to the Fed and deposit the proceeds at a commercial bank, the bank will have every incentive to lend out the newly created reserves they get as credit for that deposit. Although it is true that their decision to lend out such reserves will be dictated by market forces, the fact that reserves were increased in the first place is a result of an extra-market decision by the central bank. As we have discussed above, in doing so it is not responding to current market signals. The resulting frequency of monetary disequilibria should not be surprising, as central banks lack the market signals and incentives provided by the pricing process that could aid in producing the right quantity of money.

This point is no less true if our central bank is bound by a Friedman-like monetary rule. In this case, the bank will not be moving reserves around period by period, but increases in reserves, and the money supply, will be determined by a rule or formula whose link to the underlying market data will be fairly tenuous. We have noted the problems involved in formulating a rule that takes account of all of the factors that go into decisions about how much money to demand, particularly when one recalls the inaccessibility of some or much of the knowledge underlying those decisions. In addition, a regime of rules still implies a monopolized currency and the ability to adjust the level of reserves by the central bank creating liabilities of itself. In both cases, the quantity of high-powered money is not subject to market forces, and neither is the supply of hand-to-hand currency, as well as (indirectly) demand deposits. Although a monetary rule may prevent some of the more egregious distortions created by discretion, it still over-rides market forces that could be brought into play.

The BFH system also attempts to override the price signals of the marketplace by artificially splitting the medium of exchange and the unit of account, which is an outcome that is unlikely to be produced by a competitive market process. The very evolutionary process that enables money prices to emerge simultaneously with the monetary institutions that produce the money necessary for the emergence of those prices, will also produce a medium of exchange and unit of account that are wedded to each other. The emergence of money prices, monetary institutions, and a medium of exchange/unit of account are all part of the same Mengerian process of competitive evolution.

A 100 percent reserve gold standard system prevents market signals from providing feedback to money producer for the reasons outlined in the previous section. A free banking system allows changes in the demand for bank liabilities to 'announce' themselves through changes in bank reserve flows and, therefore, bank profitability, whereas 100 percent reserve banking precludes any such signaling process from taking place. The net clearings a free bank faces during any given period is analogous to the relative price of its currency, as those clearings reflect the demand to hold it relative to the supply and to the desirability of substitutes. Continued positive clearings suggest the bank's liabilities are in high demand (their relative price is 'high') and that the bank can profit further by issuing more of them. Conversely, continued adverse clearings indicate that a bank's liabilities are not highly valued (their relative price is 'low') and that the bank can increase their value by reducing the supply of them. Clearing balances, whether at a clearing house or in terms of specie-in-vault, send a market signal to free banks that indicate the need for more or less currency and/or deposits.

By definition, 100 percent reserve banks lack these market signals about the demand for the money they produce. As we noted above, the implication of this is that 100 percent reserve banks will have to rely on the price level to bear the burden of adjustment in the face of movements in the demand for money. The costs of such a policy are potentially enormous, as our discussions in Chapters 4 and 5 indicated. The irony of the 100 percent reserve position is that by cutting off access to these market signals in the money market, there is a large possibility that price signals in all other markets will be eventually disrupted as a result. Or, putting it more positively, free banking prevents the disruption of the signaling function of prices in non-money markets by making sure such signals are taken advantage of in the production of money. By rigidly tying the quantity of money in use to the costs of producing specie, rather than the demand to hold money, 100 percent reserve banking uses signals from *another market* to guide the production of money, rather than relying on signals that could be provided about the demand for what they are producing in *their own* market. The supply of money should be, like the supply of any other good, linked with the demand for the services that money provides, that is, the demand to hold balances of real purchasing power. In a free banking system this link is established through the market signals of the clearing process. Under 100 percent reserves no such signal exists and under central banking, the signals that are present are too little and too late.

Conclusion

In this chapter's assessment of alternative monetary regimes, we have continued our stress on the importance of relative prices as guides to efficient production by arguing that only free banking, among the systems we have examined, allows money suppliers to fully utilize market signals in determining the quantity of money they should produce. In so doing, free banking is able to minimize deviations from monetary equilibrium and quickly correct the ones that do occur. There is, then, an interesting internal consistency to the argument of this study: if one takes price signals seriously, and wishes to prevent them from being undermined by monetary disequilibria, then one should find ways to make use of price signals in the production of money. The conclusion that those monetary regimes that do not allow price signals full play are less likely to maintain monetary equilibrium should not be surprising. If price signals in non-money markets are worth protecting, then they are worth making use of in the production of money.

8 Conclusion
Microfoundations and macroeconomics

The last chapter's discussion of monetary regimes and its argument for the superiority of free banking bring us full circle. We began this study with a discussion of the importance of prices as knowledge surrogates and their indispensable role in the generation of economic coordination. We argued that this perspective on prices could serve as a starting point for examining the consequences of monetary disequilibria once we recognized that such disequilibria would make themselves known through movements in the prices of individual non-money goods and services. The price level effects of monetary disequilibria had to be understood in terms of the numerous individual price changes that comprise the price level; the effects of monetary disequilibria are ultimately microeconomic in nature. Our later discussion of the role of capital served to amplify this point by stressing the coordinative role of capital and the importance of intertemporal coordination through a reliable interest rate signal.

The chapters on monetary equilibrium, inflation, deflation, and the work of Hutt explored the desirability of monetary equilibrium and the adverse consequences of failing to maintain it. Throughout those chapters, we stressed the point that the waste associated with monetary disequilibria resulted from the scrambling of the price system that would occur as a result of excesses or deficiencies in the money supply. There are certainly effects beyond those associated with movements or stickiness in relative prices, but those price effects remained front and center in our discussion.

In this sense then, both our analysis of monetary disequilibria and our assessment of monetary regimes rests on Austrian microfoundations. If one of the defining insights of modern Austrian economics is the epistemic function of prices and their role in making possible the entrepreneurial discovery process of the market, then we have made use of that insight in both describing the effects of monetary disequilibria and determining what monetary system will be most likely to preserve the communicative function of those prices. Rather than building our microfoundations on general equilibrium theory, or even imperfect information economics, and letting that guide our understanding of monetary phenomena and monetary regimes, we have chosen the Austrian path. Whatever its comparative merits, the Austrian approach to these issues asks different questions and offers different answers and hopefully, at the very least, illuminates some issues that would go overlooked in alternative approaches.

As noted in the introduction, macroeconomics has been less well developed in the Austrian tradition than has microeconomics. Rather than look at this fact as a problem, we might view it as an opportunity. Austrian analyses of the competitive market process have become more sophisticated and complex in the post-revival years, as even a cursory look at the literature would reveal. In addition, Austrian work on microeconomic issues has made inroads in the profession at large. Austrian analyses of competition as a discovery process, the Hayekian emphasis on prices and knowledge, and the focus on the central role played by institutions, have all affected the way economists outside the Austrian tradition are doing their work. However, with the exception of work on the theory and history of free banking, the same cannot be said of the limited work in Austrian macroeconomics. Perhaps the aforementioned microeconomic influences present an opportunity for Austrians to begin such a process with macroeconomics.

If they continue to be developed, macroeconomic analyses that take seriously competition as a discovery process, the epistemic function of prices, and the importance of institutions as coordination process under uncertainty will also begin to have an effect on mainstream thinking. Movements in this direction have taken place in the last decade or two, as New Keynesians have grabbed the limelight by attempting to show the contractual nature of the labor market and the ways in which standard general equilibrium models need to be supplemented to reflect more realistically various aspects of that market. The unreality of New Classical models, especially in both their lack of appreciation for the ways in which knowledge must be discovered under uncertainty and their lack of institutional detail, was, and continues to be, a major problem. The New Keynesian responses have been helpful in reminding macroeconomists to put some real world content back in their analyses.

However, as was suggested in Chapter 5, the New Keynesian models have problems of their own, particularly their inability to break more completely away from seeing general equilibrium as a norm to be aspired to. This is where a macroeconomics resting on broadly Austrian foundations could find its market niche. The growing interest in microeconomic analyses that take knowledge, uncertainty, and institutions seriously, and the recognition that many macro models fail to grapple seriously with such concerns, create a void that could be filled by a macroeconomics built from microfoundations that *do* grapple seriously with these concerns. It is my hope that this book is a contribution to just such a project.

To be successful, such a macroeconomics will probably have to move beyond the relatively narrow label of 'Austrian'. In a recent paper, Richard Wagner (1999) has suggested the term 'coordinationist macroeconomics' for an approach largely parallel to what I have sketched out above. His suggestion is in many ways a good one, as taking knowledge, uncertainty, and institutions seriously poses the question of how actors are able to, or fail to, coordinate their actions. Under the 'coordinationist' umbrella might fit contributions from a variety schools of thought in both microeconomics as well as macroeconomics, not to mention political economy. Although I have not used Wagner's terminology, it does seem to capture the spirit of what a sound macroeconomics might look like.

As I hope has been clear in the preceding chapters, my understanding of the 'Austrianness' of my analysis is a very broad one. There are many economists who would not consider themselves Austrians whose work is highly relevant both to the microfoundations (e.g., those working in New Institutional Economics or Constitutional Political Economy) and the macroeconomics (e.g., the work of Yeager, Leijonhufvud, Clower and others whom we have made use of in this study) that inform my perspective. I have chosen to focus on the Austrian tradition because that is the one I am most familiar with and the one, I believe, that has developed the microfoundations most clearly. But that tradition can be, and should be, integrated with other work that is exploring the same issues.

By whatever name it is known, however, a sound macroeconomics will be one that builds on microfoundations that take issues of knowledge, uncertainty, and institutions seriously, and also takes account of the ways in which the political process interacts with the macroeconomy. Integrating political economy, particularly in its public choice and constitutional varieties, into a macroeconomics built on market process microfoundations would provide a framework for analysis that is both solidly rooted in human choices and cognizant of the broader contexts in which choice takes place. It will also be one that takes time and money and capital seriously. It is my hope that this book, through its emphasis on the Austrian contribution to such a project, is a step in the right direction.

Notes

Introduction

1 For a representative sampling of these works and their strong, although not exclusive, emphasis on microeconomics and methodology see Kirzner (1973, 1979, 1989, 1992a and 1997), O'Driscoll and Rizzo (1996), Thomsen (1992), Cordato (1992), Caldwell and Boehm (1992), Vaughn (1994) and Ikeda (1997). For my own perspective on the uniqueness of the Austrian tradition, with its own emphasis on microeconomics and methodology, see Boettke, Horwitz, and Prychitko (1986) and Horwitz (1992b, Chapter 2). As will be noted in the discussion to follow, Austrian macroeconomics is alive and well, but not usually part of works making a claim to identifying themselves as articulating a school of thought that is distinctly Austrian.

2 See Leijonhufvud (1981a, 1981b), Yeager (1973, 1986, and 1997), and Greenfield (1994).

3 Garrison's paper is foundational for any discussion of macroeconomics from an Austrian perspective and this study is, in many ways, an attempt to spin out the implications of the core ideas he articulates there.

4 See the larger discussion in Horwitz (1992b, Chapter 1).

5 Throughout this book, my use of the term 'goods' should be understood to include services and information as well as material goods.

6 See Yeager (1968) and Clower (1984b [1970]).

7 Although this phrase is sometimes used in the popular press and economic journalism to describe financial markets, it really is a serious misnomer. In fact, most of the activities colloquially referred to as occurring on the 'money market' are savings and investment activities, and really should be termed the 'time market'. See the discussion that follows.

8 See Mises (1966 [1949]: 113): 'The necessity to adjust his actions to other people's actions makes [man] a speculator for whom success and failure depend on his greater or lesser ability to understand the future. Every action is speculation.'

9 See Lewin (1997a) for more on the relationship between time preference and uncertainty.

10 This was Bohm-Bawerk's path-breaking insight into the existence of interest: why should the price of the final good be greater than the sum of the price of the inputs? His answer was time-preference and the increased productivity of roundabout methods of production.

11 Note also the distinction between profit and interest implicit here. Interest simply compensates the producer for the passage of time. Profits occur when revenue is in excess of all costs, including interest.

12 Austrians define the interest rate as the price of *time* rather than the price of *money*, as in more Keynesian approaches. The reasons for this difference will be explored later.

13 Although as Bruce Caldwell (1995a: 15–16, n. 35) observes, Hayek, at least, believed that there were several other factors that could trigger the cycle besides excess supplies of money.
14 Boettke (1997) provides an overview of twentieth-century economics focusing on the problems with various mainstream approaches as seen from the perspective of Austrian economics.
15 A number of these issues are addressed in Axel Leijonhufvud's (1981b) excellent overview of then-contemporary macroeconomics entitled 'The Wicksell Connection'. I shall return to these themes later.
16 It is interesting to note that the equilibrium orientation of the IS–LM model leads to explanations that involve what 'must' happen to maintain equilibrium and leaves out intuitive explanations of *why* such changes take place. As Meir Kohn (1997: 200–1) points out in his intermediate level textbook, one needs to add a loanable funds market story to make any intuitive sense of IS–LM.
17 It also forced the theory to seek adjustment to broader disequilibria in inventories, employment or income.
18 See Horwitz (1990b) for more on an Austrian approach to the demand for money. Also see Maclachlan (1993) on the relationship between Keynesian and Austrian approaches to the interest rate and liquidity preference.
19 Again, I do not wish to diminish the importance of Friedman's recovery of the essential quantity theory insight that changes in the money supply will have on price level effects. Had the Keynesian revolution and neoclassical synthesis continued unabated, even more damaging levels of inflation would have surely followed in their wake. It was clearly better that macroeconomics rediscovered the quantity-theoretic insights of the monetarists than not, but they simply did not go far enough.
20 The likely explanation for the absence of capital theory in monetarism is its roots in the Chicago School. Since Knight, and his treatment of capital as a homogeneous aggregate, Chicago School economists have paid little attention to the issues of capital structure and intertemporal relative prices that interest Austrians. See Chapter 2 for more on this issue.
21 One piece of evidence for this is that most of modern macroeconomics is what Roger Garrison (2000) calls 'labor-based macro' as opposed to the 'capital-based macro' of the Austrians and some others. This difference reflects the more complete treatment of capital in the Austrian tradition, descending from Menger's own discussion of capital in his theoretical work, as discussed in Chapter 2.
22 Hayek (1995a [1931], p. 113) made this point early in his career in the context of his critique of Foster and Catchings' inflationist scheme for combating business cycles:

> What they entirely lack is any understanding of the function of capital and interest . . . many writers on this subject still labour under the sway of the dogma of the necessity for a stable price level and this makes recognition of these interconnections [i.e., capital theory] extraordinarily difficult.

23 This point is explored at length in an excellent paper by Shah (1997). We shall return to his analysis in Chapter 5.
24 See Rizzo (1992) and Boettke (1995) for more on the relationship between Austrian economics and ideology. The various divisions among Austrians over the correct monetary regime (and policy within that regime), as well as the evolution of the policy recommendations of individual thinkers (e.g. Hayek's move from a defender to a critic of central banking) within the Austrian tradition should quell some of the complaints about policy-driven theories.
25 See Horwitz (1988a and 1997), Egger (1994) and Salerno (1991) for more on Hutt and the Austrians.

1 Prices, knowledge, and economic order

1 Kirzner (1997) provides an excellent overview of the literature.
2 To be fair, the other two distinguishing characteristics Colander lays out are in clearer opposition to Walras: bounded rationality and the recognition of institutions and non-price coordinating mechanisms. He also mentions Hayek as someone whose work might well fit into the Post Walrasian framework.
3 This project is best captured in the *Investigations*, where Menger poses what is sometimes called the 'Mengerian question': 'How can it be that institutions which serve the common welfare and are extremely significant for its development come into being without a common will directed toward establishing them?' (1985: 146). This same theme pervades the *Principles*. His discussion of price formation is an exemplary spontaneous order story, as is his more famous discussion of the origin of money. See also Menger (1892).
4 See Arrow and Hahn (1971: vi–vii), where they enlist Adam Smith in defense of the general equilibrium project.
5 See Endres (1995) for a critical overview of Menger's theory of price formation.
6 See O'Driscoll's (1981) paper on Austrian monopoly theory for more on Menger's views.
7 The broad themes of this section owe much to Israel Kirzner's (1994b) brilliant introduction to the inter-war period volume of his edited collection *Classics in Austrian Economics*.
8 See the essays in Mises (1976 [1933]. In addition, the German book that would later become *Human Action*, was published in 1940 and written during the 1930s. Lachmann (1977b [1950]: 110, n. 7) recognized the role of the Mayer essay by citing it in support of Mises' approach to economics in his review of *Human Action*.
9 Most of these Hayek articles are collected in Hayek (1948), and the page citations refer to the versions in that collection.
10 Compare this to Ludwig Lachmann's (1971) later claim that 'the plan' should be the central concept of economics and his discussion of the relationship between human plans and changes in knowledge.
11 This point was central to Hayek's (1940) critique of the Lange-Lerner type market socialist schemes. Hayek (p. 196) argued that:

> In the discussion of this sort of problem . . . the question is frequently treated as if the cost curves were objectively given facts. What is forgotten is that the method which under given conditions is the cheapest is a thing which has to be discovered, and to be discovered anew . . . by the entrepreneur.

Also see the discussion in Caldwell (1997b).
12 This interpretation of Hayek's thinking is supported by the papers on wartime restrictions and economic planning recently published as part of Hayek's collected works. See Caldwell (1997a) for an overview.
13 Many of these Austrian concerns with perfect competition theory are covered by Machovec (1995), who provides an excellent overview of the history of the doctrine.
14 Kirzner (1973: Chapters 3–5) argues that the various models of imperfect competition (such as Robinson's or Chamberlin's) are guilty of the same equilibrium orientation, despite their claims to be more 'realistic' than perfect competition.
15 See Vaughn (1994) for more on this period. The list of attendees at South Royalton (most of whom were then either young faculty or graduate students) now reads like a 'Who's Who' of contemporary Austrian economics.
16 Of course, Kirzner did not probably see himself as setting out an Austrian research agenda. His explicit intention, based on the book itself, was to reinject the entrepreneur into then-contemporary discussions of competition. He spends much time pointing out that the perfectly competitive model is flawed precisely because

it cannot comprehend the activities of the entrepreneur. Over twenty-five years later we might well see the significance of a text in a way dramatically different from the author's original intentions.

17 Expanding on one of Kirzner's favorite examples can illustrate the difference. Intentional, maximizing search would be when one has forgotten a friend's phone number and one uses a phone book to look it up. We are aware of what we do not know and know how to go about removing that ignorance. Suppose while searching for that number one discovered that a different old friend had moved into town (seeing the name in the phone book) and saw his phone number. In that case, deliberate search would not have been possible, as one was unaware of one's own ignorance concerning the new phone number, not having known the friend had moved.

18 The discussion that follows in this section owes a large debt to Esteban Thomsen's (1992) careful and thorough discussion of these issues. I claim no great originality for much of what follows, although I do hope that its application in this particular context pushes the argument beyond Thomsen's own work.

19 Arguments for this claim can be found in the literature dealing with the socialist calculation debate. In particular, see Lavoie (1985a, 1985b), Steele (1992), and Boettke (1993). Ikeda (1997) provides an argument for the market's superiority to the mixed economy on similar grounds, and Horwitz (1996a and 1998a) links these arguments about the relationship between prices and calculation to the role of money.

20 See Lavoie (1986) and Horwitz (1992a) for more on these issues.

21 The two basic positions are best represented in Kirzner (1985b) and Lachmann (1985). Boettke, Horwitz, and Prychitko (1986) provide an overview of the issues and an attempt at a resolution, as does Vaughn (1994). The more recent and refined position of Kirzner can be found in Kirzner (1992c), while one of Lachmann's (1994) last articles lays out his view a few years later.

22 An exception to this neglect is a recent series of papers by Salerno (1990a, 1990b, 1993, 1994). Although I find his discussion of monetary calculation to be generally on target, I would reject his attempt to both distinguish Mises and Hayek in this regard and portray Mises' contribution as the superior one. See my discussion of Salerno's work in Horwitz (1998a). See also Boettke (1998).

23 These issues are covered in more detail in Horwitz (1992b: chapter 1).

24 See the discussion in Horwitz (1998a) for specific examples.

25 The following two paragraphs draw heavily from Horwitz (1998a).

26 Compare the similar, if somewhat more abstract, point in Hayek (1977: 107, 116).

27 This argument also shows the fundamental congruity between Mises' emphasis on the importance of monetary calculation and Hayek's focus on the link between prices and knowledge. Both of them are exploring the same issue and making the same fundamental point. Mises is working from the perspective of the individual calculator, while Hayek is looking at the economy-wide processes at work. In addition, the way in which each thinker phrased his argument was highly related to the particular intellectual context each was in at the time of writing (Boettke 1998).

2 The missing link

1 The phrase 'missing link' to describe capital theory's role in the relationship between microeconomics and macroeconomics is also used by Skousen (1990: 208).

2 It is also true that there may well be some aspects of the labor market effects that do not require a distinctly Austrian approach. Some fundamental insights of neoclassical economics will suffice for our purposes here and pursuing a distinct Austrian spin on those insights would take us too far from our main task.

3 See Caldwell (1995a) and the discussion later in this chapter on the Hayek-Keynes

debate. On the socialist calculation debate, see Hayek's (1945) remarks on Schumpeter's views on the imputation process. This lack of understanding was not limited to the Austrians' opponents. Austrian capital theory was in need of repair during the 1930s, as it was still largely stuck with the weaknesses of Bohm-Bawerk's presentation. It is not mere coincidence that Hayek writes *The Pure Theory of Capital* as he sees himself losing both of the aforementioned debates in the eyes of the profession at large. Even so, Hayek's book did not fully escape the objectivism of Bohm-Bawerk's approach. It is in Mises, Lachmann and Kirzner that a more fully subjectivist approach to capital is outlined. An excellent treatment of these issues can be found in Boettke and Vaughn (1999).

4 In addition, as our discussions of inflation and deflation will explicate, GDP figures do not distinguish between expenditures that produce net additions to output and those that simply 'clean up after a mess'. For example, the economic activity involved in rebuilding after an earthquake adds to GDP but does not reflect net additions to human welfare over the long run. It simply gets us back to where we were.

5 A fine overview of the history of capital theory, with particular attention paid to the Austrian contribution, can be found in Skousen (1990: Chapters 2–4).

6 Peter Lewin (1994: 241) says of capital:

> The importance of understanding capital in terms of the plans from which it derives can be seen by noting that the plans provide the reference points for interpreting any given capital structure. We understand the role of capital goods only in terms of the plans that they help to fulfill and it is only to the extent that we understand these plans that we see meaning in the structure of capital.

See also Lewin (1997b).

7 Note the relationship to Hayek's distinction between individual and social equilibrium. Equilibrium makes sense for the individual because one mind can integrate everything into an *ex ante* plan. This is not possible for society as a whole, except to the degree that the market can tend toward it. In addition, individual and firms can make such plans because the society as a whole is not planned and informative money prices exist to help construct such plans. As Lewin (1998: 3–4) argues:

> Planning within firms proceeds against the necessary backdrop of the market. Planning within firms can occur precisely because 'the market' furnishes it with the necessary prices for the factor inputs that would be absent in a full blown state ownership situation.

8 The perfect substitutes view is clear in Knight's Crusionia plant example. This plant, which Knight uses as a metaphor for capital, grows at some constant rate, 'except as new tissue is cut away for consumption' (as cited in Kirzner [1966: 63]). It matters neither which portions of the plant are cut away for consumption nor what is used to cultivate the plant. Pieces of the plant are perfectly fungible. As Kirzner's critique suggests, there is probably no view of capital more opposite to the Austrian than Knight's. Even Hayek (1941: 93), who was not known for harsh critical language, was led to refer to these 'abstract fund' views of capital as 'pure mysticism'.

9 This corresponds to the discovery function of prices discussed in Chapter 1.

10 See O'Driscoll (1986) and Horwitz (1992a, 1993) as well as the extension of Menger's theory by Selgin and White (1987).

11 A more thorough development of this argument can be found in Horwitz (1990b). Prior versions of the argument are Hutt (1956) and Selgin (1987).

12 Another example of this relationship between liquidity and capital is the role of inventories of the consumer goods one is producing. Keeping stocks of the final product on hand, but not right out 'on the shelf', is a kind of investment in a very

liquid form of capital. Such stocks can be turned into money quite quickly, though perhaps at distressed prices. They are surely far more liquid than the higher order goods that went into their production. The role of inventories as a kind of capital investment will reappear in Chapter 5.

13 The same could be said of spare parts – not all spare parts will be second-line assets. We might expect some parts to wear out on a regular schedule, but others may do so unexpectedly. Buying an extra set of automobile tires to store in the garage knowing you will need new ones in the next few months is different from carrying a spare in the car.

14 There is nothing uniquely modern nor uniquely Austrian about this point. It was recognized, perhaps more crudely, by classical and pre-Keynesian neoclassical econ-omists. See Say (1967 [1821]: 16–17): 'The value of capital at the moment in which it is borrowed may have the form of money: but it has it only transitorily . . . when we desire to use [it] as capital, we exchange [it] again for products necessary for production'; and D. H. Robertson (1957: 8): 'People tend to confuse the pieces of money, which are mere certificates of a right to draw goods . . . with the goods themselves.'

15 These issues were central in the Hayek–Sraffa exchange in the 1930s (see the essays collected in Caldwell (1995b)). Both Hayek and Sraffa appeared to agree that in a moneyless economy, where loans were made in the form of commodities, there would exist 'as many "natural" rates of interest as there are commodities' (Hayek 1995c [1932]: 218). With no money, there would be nothing corresponding to the market rate as defined by Wicksell. In such a world there could be no divergence between the market and natural rate since the former would not exist and the latter would be would be unique to each commodity. The difference between Hayek and Sraffa on this issue was whether it would be correct to refer to each of those commodity rates of interest as 'equilibrium rates'.

16 On these issues see Boettke and Vaughn (1999).

17 See Mises (1980 [1912], Chapter 19).

18 One possible explanation for Keynes' apparent lack of familiarity with Bohm-Bawerk's theory is his well-known difficulties in reading German, admitted to in his brief and cursory review of Mises' *The Theory of Money and Credit*. That book itself relied on many of Bohm-Bawerk's ideas on capital and Keynes' inability to grasp its central theme should have been a signal about his likely reaction to Hayek's later extensions of Mises.

19 Leijonhufvud (1981b: 173, n. 62) echoes this point with respect to Keynes' decision to abandon the use of Wicksell's natural rate terminology: 'The reasons for getting rid of the Wicksellian terminology [is] that he had given very little thought to problems of capital and growth theory.' In a note to this sentence, Leijonhufvud elaborates:

> Keynes' reaction to the overinvestment theory of Hayek . . . was . . . that over-investment in the past . . . should [not] cause any problems in the present; the only result would be to leave us with more capital in the present – and so much the better off for it . . . His argument reveals, of course, an aggregative concept of capital on his part.

20 See Meltzer (1988) and Garrison (1992).

21 See Hayek (1941: 433–9; and 1978b) for example. See also Moss and Vaughn (1986) for a treatment of some of these issues.

3 Monetary equilibrium as an analytical framework

1 In his discussion of the evenly rotating economy, which he uses as a static foil for real, dynamic markets, Mises (1966 [1949]: 248) says:

This so-called static method is precisely the proper mental tool for the examination of change ... In order to grasp the function of entrepreneurship and the meaning of profit and loss, we construct a system from which they are absent. This image is merely a tool for our thinking. It is not the description of a possible and realizable state of affairs.

He later (1966 [1949]: 250) refers to this process as 'argumentum a contrario'. Hayek (1941: 22–3) also subscribed to this use of equilibrium constructs in *The Pure Theory of Capital*:

It seems natural to begin by constructing, as an intellectual tool, a fictitious state under which these plans are in complete correspondence without, however, asking whether this state will ever, or can ever, come about. For it is only by contrast with this imaginary state, which serves as a kind of foil, that we are able to predict what will happen if entrepreneurs attempt to carry out any given set of plans.

The Swedish economist Myrdal (1965 [1939]: 41) also specifically argues for this foil use of the monetary equilibrium construct: 'The equilibrium relations, therefore, are studied at first only as important auxiliary instruments for the analysis of actual or hypothetical monetary and price situations, situations which themselves need by no means fulfil the equilibrium conditions.'

2 It is important to distinguish between money and other financial assets. Money refers, both here and later, to the kinds of money that are used in most day-to-day transactions, roughly an M1 concept including cash, coin and demand deposits. As one moves away from M1 toward M2 and M3, one is moving away from money as a medium of exchange and more toward money substitutes that look more like interest-bearing financial assets.

3 For more on Menger's theory see O'Driscoll (1986) and Horwitz (1992a). For a critical perspective see Hodgson (1992). Neoclassical treatments of the origin and function of money from a broadly Mengerian perspective can be found in Jones (1976) and Oh (1989).

4 Money's role is analogous to that of fire engines standing ready in firehouses. What may look like wasteful waiting is in fact necessary given that we cannot predict the outbreak of fires. Fire engines (and fire fighters) also provide the service of being available.

5 The phrase is taken from the title of a collection of Leland Yeager's (1997) essays.

6 Yeager (1968) provides an excellent discussion of the role of money from this perspective.

7 If we conceive of the real money supply as the fraction M/P, maintaining monetary equilibrium requires that we change M and not P when the demand for real money balances changes.

8 In the quote that follows, Myrdal allows for movement in the price level, which would appear to violate our definition of monetary equilibrium. However, we will see later in this chapter that there are non-monetary factors that can affect the price level while monetary equilibrium is still maintained.

9 Recall our Hayekian interpretation of the equilibrium concept from Chapter 1.

10 As noted in the Introduction, this discussion will be of particular importance in contrasting our argument with textbook Keynesianism, which treats savings and investment as *ex post* quantities along the IS curve.

11 As we shall see later, other monetary equilibrium theorists did not believe that the equality of the market and natural rates implied price level stability.

12 I thank Larry White for this observation.

13 Wicksell (1965 [1898]: 4) argues: '[T]he ideal position ... would undoubtedly be

one in which, without interfering with the inevitable variations in the relative prices of commodities, the general average level of money prices . . . would be perfectly invariable and stable.' We shall explore some problems with this position below. What is particularly notable about Wicksell's phrasing is that he is squarely within the framework we have developed earlier in seeing the importance of monetary changes not interfering with the relative price structure. However, he is also assuming a static world with no changes in productivity, if he thinks that monetary equilibrium would assure price level stability.

14 White (1999a and 1999b) provides an excellent historical overview of the development of Hayek's monetary economics, tracing his ongoing flirtation with monetary equilibrium-oriented ideas. See also Selgin (1999).

15 Selgin (1999) notes that there were important differences between the first and second editions of *Prices and Production* that reflect Hayek's movement toward a more solidly monetary equilibrium view. Selgin suggests that Robertson's influence may have played a crucial role in that evolution.

16 In a draft chapter of *The Fatal Conceit* which did not appear in the final version, Hayek (n.d.) had a brief discussion of inflation. He argues there that '[money's] value does not depend simply on the total quantity of it being available but also on the variable demand for it'. He also refers to the 'harmful effects of an *excessive* supply of money' and claims that inflation is 'caused solely by an *undue* increase of the quantity of money' (both emphases mine). These passages were probably written not long after the 1978 book, so they appear to reflect Hayek's thinking late in his career.

17 In fact, when push comes to shove, Hayek (1978c) argues for price level stability over a monetary equilibrium policy of maintaining the equality of *ex ante* savings and investment, claiming that the gains from price level stability are greater than the costs of the minor deviations from loanable funds market equilibrium that it would entail.

18 His view was that any form of fractional reserve banking was fraudulent in that liability holders could not simultaneous and instantaneously redeem their claims for base money. See Rothbard (1994: 27–53), and the discussion of this argument in Chapter 7.

19 Compare Rothbard (1962: 317): 'It is important to realize that the interest rate is equal to the rate of price spread in the various stages [of production]. Too many writers consider the rate of interest as only the price of loans on the loan market. In reality . . . the rate of interest pervades all time markets.'

20 This concept seems parallel to Selgin's (1995b: 734) argument that the macroeconomy is doing its best when outcomes correspond to what would happen if actors had full information.

21 It is interesting to note that the label 'classical' is quite well understood in *micro*economics. It refers to thinkers prior to the marginalist revolution of the early 1870s, particularly those who held to labor or cost-of-production theories of value. As such, writers who came after that revolution, and accepted its broad conclusions, are generally termed neoclassical. This produces the rather strange situation that in the microeconomic sense of the term Alfred Marshall and A. C. Pigou are the antithesis of the Classical economists, yet in Keynes' mind, Marshall and Pigou reflect the very essence of what he calls the Classical approach. It is also worth pointing out that the microeconomic label of 'classical' comprises folks with widely differing ideological perspectives – everyone from Marx, to the Mills, to Ricardo, to Smith, to Bastiat, might correctly be labeled as 'classical'. In Keynes' dichotomy, the ideological similarities of the 'classicals' are much greater.

22 The following material draws on Horwitz (1996b) and the excellent discussion in Sechrest (1993, Chapter 3).

23 The image of a tight, broken, and loose linkage between production and demand

derives from Hayek's use of a tight, broken, and loose joint to describe the role of money. See Hayek (1941: 408–10).

24 Microeconomic miscoordination, such as might result from price floors or ceilings across a number of different goods might look like a general glut or shortage, but is not. True *general* gluts and shortages must find their origin on the money side. See the discussion of Hutt's work in Chapter 6 for more on this issue.

25 See, among others, Hazlitt (1959), Hutt (1979), Garrison (1985, 1987, 1989, 1992), Horwitz (1989, 1996c and 1998b), Selgin (1989) and various comments in Hayek (1941, *passim*) and Mises (1966 [1949], *passim*).

26 See Selgin's (1999) discussion of the evolving views of Hayek and Keynes on the question of price level behavior.

27 This perspective also, as Garrison (1985: 317ff.) expertly discusses, explains Keynes' concern with expectations. Given the uncertainty of the future, expectations will drive economic behavior. However, without any process of intertemporal coordination, there is no assurance that the expectations of parties on all sides of the market will be led into consistency. Thus the solution is to reduce or eliminate the possibility of expectations affecting outcomes, as in Keynes' proposals to make capital ownership permanent like marriage (a quaint analogy from the modern perspective), or by tying savings decisions tightly to decisions to consume specific goods in the future. The idea that expectations could be *ex ante* coordinated is utterly absent in Keynes.

28 And to the extent Keynes concerned himself with the issue of intertemporal coordination, it was mostly to deny that it was possible in a market economy without the help of government intervention. See the enlightening exchange between Garrison (1985, 1987) and Snippe (1987).

29 Again, the blame here may rest with Knightian theories of capital. As modern microeconomics largely views the question of intertemporal coordination as being within its purview, and then addressed by fairly straightforward models involving trade-offs through time, it is not surprising that such issues are absent from macroeconomics textbooks. In addition, with microeconomics focused on variations on perfect competition models, there is no scope for the entrepreneur, who is the key maker of capital-relevant decisions. Knight might also be unintentionally responsible for the rise of the perfect competition model and the corresponding absence of the entrepreneur.

30 The absence of capital in the Keynesian model has had long-run repercussions. In particular, it has artificially divided capital theory and macroeconomics, to the detriment of both, especially the latter. As Garrison (1989: 373) puts it: 'Macroeconomic theory is implicitly defined as all those relationships that can be identified among macroeconomic magnitudes on the assumption of a fixed capital stock. Theory involving a changing capital stock is, by definition, growth theory.' Such an approach defines Austrian concerns, along with much of the Wicksell-inspired work of the twentieth century, out of macroeconomics. Perhaps no other aspect of the Keynesian revolution has retarded our understanding of macroeconomics and monetary theory more than this one.

31 How quickly they will catch up depends upon how heavily their expectation formation formula is weighted toward the more recent past. As the consistent policy dominates the recent past values, its weight will eventually comprise 100 percent of the formula. One way of seeing the concept of rational expectations is that it is 100 percent weighted to information of the absolutely most recent past possible.

32 Peter Lewin's (1999) recent work attempting to extend Austrian capital theory into a theory of human capital holds a great deal of promise in helping accomplish just this task. The parallels should be clear, but one is most obvious: human beings must make intertemporal plans just as capital owners do and various changes in the

economy might upset those plans and discoordinate labor markets in a fashion similar to monetary disequilibria.

33 Some New Classical economists claim their theory has roots in the Austrian business cycle theory of the early 1930s. See Lucas (1981: 215–17) and Laidler (1982: 18). There is quite a literature dissecting this claim. See, among others, Arena (1994), Garretsen (1994), Ruhl (1994), and Van Zijp and Visser (1994).

34 If the shocks to the money supply are mathematically random, their expected value would be zero, and they would have no effect on rational expectations. Any non-zero value of that random variable would therefore cause expectations to be incorrect in a way that could not have been foreseen, even by fully rational agents.

35 The following discussion owes much to the marvelous little essay by Lutz (1969).

36 As Lutz (1969: 107) points out, the comparison being made here is not really between a money economy and a barter economy, but between an imperfectly working money economy and a perfectly working money economy. After all, a true barter economy would be incapable of developing to a point where sophisticated intertemporal exchanges were even possible.

37 Those four conditions are: perfect flexibility of prices and wages, the absence of money illusion, static price expectations, and the absence of uncompensated distribution effects.

38 Selgin (1997) offers greater technical detail on the productivity norm, while Selgin (1995a) traces its place in the history of economic thought.

39 In a well-known analogy, Buchanan (1962) compared this to the economic benefits of accurate weather forecasts. If we can rely on weather forecasts, one source of uncertainty facing economic behavior is reduced or eliminated.

40 The exchange between Dowd and Selgin in the Fall 1995 issue of *The Journal of Macroeconomics* gets to the heart of many of the issues in dispute.

41 This is particularly important in response to a negative productivity shock, which, under a stable prices norm, would require a decrease in the aggregate demand (presumably via the money supply) and therefore necessitate a fall in factor prices, including labor. If workers are highly resistant to renegotiating wages, or institutional factors such as multi-period contracts are present, the stable prices norm will require some very painful adjustments. If those adjustments do not come reasonably quickly, the stable prices norm could lead to significant unemployment in the case of a negative productivity shock.

42 We may well be seeing precisely this process in the US economy over the last few years. Productivity increases associated with technological progress have caused the prices of many goods to fall, as measured by the labor hours required to purchase them, while nominal wages (and real wages, with respect to the price level rather than labor hours) have not risen all that much, although non-wage forms of compensation have. The result is that the consumption levels of US citizens have climbed steadily and significantly, despite the relative flatness of monetary wages. This seems consistent with what should happen under a productivity norm regime, although there is no evidence that such a policy is guiding the behavior of the Federal Reserve System. For an excellent overview of these issues, and the current US economy in general, see Cox and Alm (1999).

43 See Selgin (1990: 281):

> Only under the productivity norm will aggregate (effective) demand continue to be just adequate to buy the fruits of industry at prices covering their (money) cost of production, without causing that cost to alter over time except in response to growth in capital and population. In Wicksellian terms, the productivity norm manages, where stability of the price level fails, to keep interest rates at their natural levels.

44 The following is excerpted from Horwitz (1996b).

45 A problem with Hayek's argument in this article is that he is only concerned with the effects of productivity changes on the path of the price level, and ignores the role of changes in velocity. Thus he ended up supporting a policy of a constant M, arguing that M should not change in response to changes in productivity. As White (1999b) points out, given Hayek's assumptions of perfect foresight, this conclusion does not necessarily follow, particularly under regimes other than a fixed gold standard. In addition, once one takes into account movements in velocity, then there are reasons to prefer a policy of stabilizing MV, rather than just M. Hayek's reference to the 'money side' seems to refer only to the *supply* of money, when in fact he should have also referred to the *demand* for money, in the form of movements in velocity.

4 Inflation, the market process, and social order

1 The phrase 'costs and consequences of inflation' is taken from the title of Leijonhufvud's (1981c) excellent essay on the subject, which has been very influential in the development of the ideas in this chapter. Interested readers might also wish to see Wagner (1977, 1980), Horwitz (1991), and Dowd (1996) for more.

2 Moreover, expectations can also play a role. If actors are expecting some increase or decrease in the price level due to real or monetary factors, and pricing accordingly, but the expected change does not occur, the price level will move nonetheless, as a result of the expectations. This is a third possible source of price level movements.

3 Of course these broad categories and the summary nature of this section gloss over many interesting and subtle distinctions in the mainstream literature. An excellent critical overview of many of the issues in the inflation literature can be found in Dowd (1996).

4 The pioneering study here is Bailey (1956). See also Kessel and Alchian (1962) as well as later work by Howitt (1990), Laidler (1990), Cooley and Hansen (1989, 1991), Benabou (1991) and Imrohoroglu (1992).

5 It should be noted that this analysis assumes that the money in question is non-interest-bearing. If the money bears interest, then we would expect nominal rates to rise to compensate for the price level effects of inflation, offsetting the implicit tax.

6 See, for example, Mussa (1977), Parkin (1986), and Caplin and Spulber (1987).

7 Hercowitz (1981) and Cukierman and Wachtel (1982) are among the earliest attempts at building such models.

8 As indicated earlier, the relative price effect literature is large and complex and there are other approaches to explaining the relationship between inflation and relative price movements. For example, Paroush (1986) uses a search theory model to argue that inflation's tax on real balances causes individuals to shorten their searches for the best price available. As a result, during inflation, relative prices are less likely to lie at the equilibrium values as a lower amount of search effort has been put forth to find the best prices.

9 On the empirical evidence see Vining and Elwertowski (1976), Parks (1978), Hercowitz (1981), and Blejer (1983) among others. See also the summary of this literature in Cowen (1997: 131–4). Alternate interpretations of those empirical relationships exist. For example, Hartmann (1991) argues that one can show that the empirical relationship exists without a model that includes the sorts of misperceptions or menu costs discussed in the text. In addition, there is the question of whether the causality runs from inflation to relative price movements or vice versa. If the relative price of some important commodity were to shift for non-monetary reasons, it might be countered by expansionary monetary policy, leading to inflation.

10 Public choice economics is one example of a comparative institutions perspective in

that it refuses to accept a Nirvana view of the political process as the standard of comparison. This de-romanticizing of politics enables the analyst to compare the effects of resource allocation through messy real-world market processes and messy real-world political processes.

11 For an elaboration of an Austrian perspective on these issues, see Ikeda (1995).

12 Another example of this phenomenon is the cleaning up process after a natural or social disaster, such as an earthquake or riot. The resources hired to clean up the mess get paid and those expenditures are counted equivalently to the expenditures that would have been made hiring those resources had the disaster never occurred. Of course the cleaning up process produces nothing new (seen over the longer run), as those expenditures just return society to where it was prior to the disaster. GDP may be the same in both cases, but the amount of goods available to satisfy human wants will be less after the disaster than what there would have been had it not taken place.

13 The fact that the empirical literature appears to show that inflation is nonetheless associated with lower growth rates in GDP simply illustrates the degree to which inflation really does undermine economic growth. For two such studies see Fischer (1991) and Barro (1995).

14 It should be noted that this is an exception to the general rule of prices held below equilibrium: the short side does not rule here. The reason is that the good being priced (bank reserves) is provided costlessly to the banks via the open market operations process. Thus when the 'selling price' of the good falls, there is no reason to reduce the quantity supplied. In fact, the whole reason the price falls is because the supply curve has shifted out due to an increase in the supply of a zero price input.

15 On the concept of forced savings, see the similar discussions in Hayek (1975 [1939]: 183ff.), Robertson (1928: 43 and 1957: 70ff.), Cassel (1927–28: 332) and Selgin (1988a: 60ff.).

16 See Mises (1966 [1949]: 331–5) as well as Salerno's (1990b) excellent extension of these themes.

17 In Mises' (1976 [1933]: 130–45) terms, their knowledge must involve both 'conception' (theoretical knowledge) and 'understanding' (thymological knowledge). I thank Joe Salerno for calling my attention to this point.

18 For more on this point, see the recent work by Koppl and several co-authors on the problems associated with 'Big Players'. Koppl argues that Big Players, such as central banks, pose much more serious problems for accurate expectation formation than do anonymous, and much less powerful, market actors. See, for example, Koppl and Yeager (1996).

19 This ignores any notions of opportunity cost, including the time involved in the production process, as is standard when reckoning accounting profits.

20 See Hayek (1966 [1933], 1967 [1935], 1975[1939]), Mises (1966[1949]), Rothbard (1963: Chapter 1) and Mises *et al.* (1983).

21 Cowen (1997) provides a detailed critical assessment of this theory, including a discussion of its implicit assumptions and some relevant empirical evidence.

22 See also Moss and Vaughn (1986).

23 Perhaps Hayek's clearest statement of this point is in the third appendix of *The Pure Theory of Capital* (1941: 433–9), where he discusses Mill's fourth postulate that 'demand for commodities is not demand for labor'.

24 Hayek (1941: 395–6) argues that Keynes' theory requires the assumption that capital goods are 'freely reproducible in practically unlimited quantities'. He also points out that Mill's fourth postulate (see previous note) is only strictly valid in the absence of idle resources and that this was well understood by the classical economists. The problem remains explaining why resources are idled in the first place, rather than assuming they are idle and moving on from there.

25 Let me be clear to state that these coping costs are *analogous* to rent-seeking

expenditures, not an example thereof. The next section will discussion the relationship between inflation and rent-seeking.

26 It makes sense that the optical scanners were first introduced in the early 1980s in the aftermath of significant inflation. Changing a computer data base is far less costly than remarking each and every good in the store. St. Lawrence county's item-pricing law was passed in the early 1990s despite the objections of stores. One would expect that the objections would have been much greater had the inflation rate been much higher at the time. It will be interesting to see whether any renewal of inflation would lead to attempts to repeal the law.

27 Even if it is true that the political process can only redistribute, not create, wealth, it does not matter to the individual. The source of wealth (i.e., whether it is 'created' or redistributed) is not the issue. As long as the individual perceives each process as a net gain to *his* wealth, he will treat them as equivalent, independent of the social consequences of using each.

28 The discussion that follows elaborates on some of the themes of the excellent analyses of these issues by Laidler and Rowe (1980) and Leijonhufvud (1981c).

29 For a book-length treatment of the interventionist dynamic, see Ikeda (1997).

30 As Mises (1966 [1949]: 855) described it:

> The interventionist doctrinaires and their followers explain all these undesired consequences as the unavoidable features of capitalism. As they see it, it is precisely these disasters that clearly demonstrate the necessity of intensifying interventionism. The failures of the interventionist policies do not in the least impair the popularity of the implied doctrine. They are so interpreted as to strengthen, not to lessen, the prestige of these teachings.

31 The second sentence in the prior quote from Mises should be enough to reject Salerno's (1990b) attempt to view Mises as a 'social rationalist' in contrast to the supposed 'irrationalism' of Hayek. That sentence clearly shows that Mises believes society is a spontaneous order, that is, the product of human action, but not human design, just as Hayek does. It might well be true that Hayek underemphasizes the calculative behavior that all spontaneous order processes involve, but he has surely not ignored it. By the same token, Mises understood that no matter how calculative individual action is, the social order that emerges is the result of no one person's intentions.

32 In much more colorful language, the novelist Ayn Rand (1957: 415) made the same point: 'When money ceases to be the tool by which men deal with one another, then men become the tools of men. Blood, whips, guns – or dollars. Take your choice – there is no other.'

33 Robert Clower (1984c [1976]) raises some similar points in his discussion of the weaknesses of competitive models of inflation that assume an auctioneer-driven pricing process. In fact, real world economies rely on a variety of institutional arrangements and practices to set prices, all of which can be undermined by inflation.

34 See Remak (1969: 28–30).

5 Monetary equilibrium theory and deflation

1 Deflation has recently moved a bit closer to the front of the economic news. Inflation rates as officially measured in the United States are in the 1 to 2 percent range, and some observers (Jude Wanniski, for one) see falling gold prices as evidence of ongoing deflation that is being masked by problems in the measurement of the price level. Others see the recent problems in the Japanese economy as evidence of an excess demand for money there, caused by poor monetary policy and misguided bank regulation. Innovations in monetary institutions and the increasing globalization of the economy have made it more difficult for central banks to engage in prolonged or significant inflations.

2 Of course, the obvious example of deflation in the twentieth century is the Great Depression. For a number of reasons, it would seem clear that the reduction in the money supply in the USA was not an intentional policy of the Fed's, but rather due to an erroneous understanding of both the situation in the economy and the tools at its disposal. It is worth noting that the Fed, and other central banks, have not made the same mistake twice, having paid the price one time. We will have more to say about the Great Depression below.

3 This result is found in the early work of Axelrod (1984). A good discussion of these issues is Kreps (1990: 503–15).

4 Even so, downward price movements may not be enough to get the economy out of a deflationary monetary disequilibrium. Fisher's (1934) debt-deflation theory argues that falling prices may generate an expectation of a further price decrease. If so, then buyers may hold off spending until prices fall even further. This aggravates the existing deficiency of aggregate demand. In addition, the falling prices increase the real burden of debtors, limiting their ability to contribute to reigniting aggregate demand.

5 Suppose I know that the value of my marginal product is $10 per hour. Suppose further that I am currently unemployed, perhaps as a result of a Yeager-type deflationary depression. In this case, my notional demand is $10 per hour (that is, what I am capable of purchasing based on my underlying productivity), while my effective demand would likely be far less, unless I draw on savings or asset sales to finance my current consumption. See the discussion in the next section for more.

6 In looking at Leijonhufvud's work, I am going to sidestep the question of whether his work is what Keynes 'really' meant. Whatever way one comes down on that question, what matters for the purpose at hand is the degree to which Leijonhufvud's argument (regardless of its pedigree) fits into our monetary equilibrium framework and sheds light on real world monetary disequilibria.

7 Note that Leijonhufvud is making a point similar to the one discussed in Chapter 3. The monetarist tradition is not concerned with interest rates and the saving–investment relationship because it assumes the job will get done. I would argue that such an assumption is a natural outgrowth of a Knightian view of capital, where issues of capital heterogeneity and the intertemporal coherence of the capital structure never develop.

8 One could see this as just another case of the short side ruling if one views the good being exchanged as debt rather than credit.

9 This discussion builds off of a response to this criticism raised elsewhere. See Horwitz (1996b) and the comments by Cottrell (1996) and my rejoinder.

10 See also the more extended discussion in Selgin (1997).

11 Leijonhufvud (1981b: 197), however, does make a brief mention of capital theory, declaring himself more or less an Austrian on the matter, but does not tell any story of systematic structural effects on capital during the kind of crisis described by the Z-theory.

12 In the world of the second-best, one might argue that such programs are desirable in that they could temporarily restore the flow of spending to those who have been thrown out of work, even though the first-best solution would still be to restore monetary equilibrium. Even the second best solution faces two problems. First, would such programs remain temporary? Would they not outlive their intended period of use? Second, the resources to support such programs would have to be taken from elsewhere in the economy, restricting the flow of spending there. Unless the spending is created by additions to the money supply (the appropriate solution), or we are to assume that those taxed to support the unemployment programs will not reduce their own spending or saving in response, such transfers may not solve the problem on net.

13 The collection edited by Mankiw and Romer (1993b) is organized around a similar

understanding of the New Keynesian research program.

14 Thus changes in time-preferences by themselves cannot cause cyclical processes. It is only when the banking system does not react appropriately to such real changes that monetary disequilibrium and recession or inflation will occur. Money must be the original impulse. See the discussion in Garrison (1996: 180–1).

15 The very fact that 'stickiness' has a negative connotation to it suggests the degree to which the perfect price flexibility associated with the general equilibrium model has penetrated the thinking of most modern economists. There is a difference between upholding 'open competition' as a benchmark for making welfare judgments and upholding 'price flexibility' as such a benchmark. The gradual displacement of an older, more process-oriented, understanding of 'competition' by the perfectly competitive model is the cause of the widely held negative connotation of price stickiness. See the excellent study by Machovec (1995). For these older theorists, as for modern day Menger-inspired market process theorists, the lack of barriers to entry and exit was far more important to a market being 'competitive' than the degree of flexibility in prices, *per se*.

16 These issues are covered in much more depth in Shah (1997).

17 As Shah (1997: 44) notes, very little empirical work has been done on the stickiness of prices. Two attempts at such work are Cecchetti (1986) and Kashyap (1990). Blinder's (1991) study referred to in the text is flawed because he was much more interested in why firms do not change prices than asking them what they do instead of adjusting on that margin (Shah 1997: 46).

18 Shah (1997: 50–4) offers a more thorough statement of this view and brings in insights from information economics to flesh out the argument.

19 See the discussion of Hutt's work in Chapter 6.

20 Two interesting sidelights of this quote involve his choice of words. In his discussion of utility earlier in the book, Rothbard rightly emphasizes that utility is (1) an individual phenomenon; and (2) a ranking not a hedonic. If that is true, then the concept of 'social utility' seems problematic, and, more important, the phrase 'social disutility' is doubly non-sensical. If utility is individual, it cannot be social, and if it is a ranking, the concept of 'disutility' is meaningless, as is, perhaps, the notion of an economic 'bad'. See White (1995).

21 Rothbard (1962: 866) notes that this process will not cause unemployment unless prices are coercively maintained above their market-clearing values. This parallels the view of Hutt to be discussed in Chapter 6.

22 These issues are explored more thoroughly in Chapter 7.

6 W. H. Hutt on macroeconomic disorder

1 Hutt's major contributions to macroeconomic issues include (1977 [1939]), (1975), and (1979). A good overview of Hutt's work can be found in the various papers collected in the symposium on Hutt in the *Journal of Labor Research* in the spring of 1997, including Horwitz (1997). Papers by Horwitz (1994a [1988]), Salerno (1991), and Egger (1994), as well as Yeager (1973), also offer perspectives on Hutt's work congenial to that taken in this chapter.

2 Portions of the rest of this chapter are revised versions of Horwitz (1997).

3 This point becomes important when examining the differences between Hutt's work and the similar themes that pervade Leijonhufvud's interpretation of Keynes. See the discussion later in this chapter.

4 This condensation of Hutt's (1977 [1939]: 47) total of nine categories of idleness leaves out two: the 'idleness of valueless resources' and the idleness associated with 'diverted resources' or 'sub-optimal full employment'. The former is not of much importance when talking about labor. The latter will be the focus of a separate discussion later in this chapter.

5 Of course, Keynes did not accept this last claim: 'I expect to see the State, which is in a position to calculate the marginal efficiency of capital on long views and on the basis of the general social advantage, taking an ever greater responsibility for directly organizing investment' (1936: 164). Keynes, however, overlooked the problems governments face in acquiring the relevant knowledge. Some of that knowledge may be very costly to obtain and some may be in a form that is not even obtainable. In addition, public choice considerations suggest that even well-meaning and well-informed political actors may face institutional incentives that favor their own interests over any long-run public interest.
6 See Horwitz (1996c and 1998b) for a more detailed discussion of the Keynesian claim that saving, in the form of holding money balances, is a cause of reduced aggregate demand and depression.
7 In fact, since the monetary authorities normally rely on macroeconomic data such as employment and the price level to tell them *ex post* how they have affected the macroeconomy, by the time they realize the need for such adjustments it is probably too late.
8 These issues will reappear in the next chapter's discussion of the merits of alternative monetary regimes. With respect to the relationship between monetary regimes and Keynes, see Horwitz (1989).
9 Elsewhere (1979: 129), Hutt refers to inflation as 'the buying off of antisocial pricing'.
10 Vedder and Gallaway (1993: 39) put the shift to Keynesian methods of driving down real wages in historical terms:

   [E]arly in the century, private decision-making in the private sector in response to market conditions seemed to initiate downward real-wage adjustments in several years; in modern times, downward real wage adjustments seem to have resulted from price increases that may be largely initiated by macroeconomic policy.

11 It should be clear that the 'versatility' of labor is the analog of the 'multiple specificity' of capital emerging out of the Austrian tradition, as stressed in Chapter 3.
12 The possibility that decreases in the unemployment rate might reflect 'sub-optimal' movements toward full employment is not discussed in Vedder and Gallaway's (1993) otherwise excellent treatment of unemployment. Although they explicitly deny that price inflation is irrelevant to the time path of real economic growth (ibid.: 219), they do not, which is understandable given how much they do cover, attempt to investigate the effects of inflation on the optimality of the composition of employment.

7 Monetary policy and monetary disequilibria

1 This distinction is from Brennan and Buchanan (1981) and Buchanan (1983).
2 Of course, political actors would have a great interest in the process by which the rate or formula was determined, just as they would (and did) have a great interest in establishing central banks in the first place. These are, in Buchanan's terms, 'preconstitutional' questions.
3 Hayek's (1978c) proposal to have competing fiat currencies is different from the free banking system under discussion here. As many critics have pointed out, Hayek's system would face problems in generating acceptance for such currencies and the mechanisms guarding against depreciation would be far weaker in Hayek's system than one in which privately produced currency was redeemable in some base money.
4 A growing trend in the US banking system is the continued expansion of competition in the check clearing business. A number of firms offer this service to banks, and they have successfully undermined the Fed's former virtual monopoly over this

process. The result has been a lowering of bank costs and more rapid check clearing.
5 One likely difference between a free banking system and the Federal Reserve System in the USA would be that private clearing houses would be under competitive pressure to pay interest on bank deposits. Deposits at the Fed currently earn no interest and effectively serve as a tax on banks, encouraging them to keep their deposits there as low as possible. Paying interest on deposits would reduce the earnings spread between keeping resources at the clearing house and lending them out to borrowers.
6 This brings up the interesting point that the USA and most of the world is actually quite a long way toward truly 'private' money, in that the majority of the money supply is comprised by deposits, which are created privately and are the liabilities of the creating banks. They are certainly built off of a monopolized base money, but the deposits themselves are indeed private money in some significant sense. The advent of electronic moneys will only hasten this process.
7 This argument provides a response to de Soto (1995: 33), who argues that free banks could inflate by over-expanding in concert with one another. He specifically claims that this would be an example of the tragedy of the commons as he believes that during an in-concert expansion, all of the costs of expansion are externalized. However, he completely overlooks the fact that an in-concert expansion does impose costs on the expanding banks through the increased need for precautionary reserves described in the text.
8 Such policies also create problems other than monetary disequilibria.
9 Selgin and White's (1994) *Journal of Economic Literature* survey article on the free banking literature was thus appropriately titled 'How Would the Invisible Hand Handle Money?'
10 Friedman and Schwartz (1986) explicitly credit the resurgence of interest in Austrian economics, specifically its emphasis on spontaneous ordering processes, as one factor behind the recent work on free banking systems.
11 Changes in the currency/deposit ratio under free banking might have other effects if the deposit account pays interest and the currency does not. In this case other balance sheet changes will be necessitated, but none that affect reserves.
12 For more on this point, see Selgin (1988b). Another way in which government intervention can undermine the attempts of banks to facilitate the conversion of deposits into currency is to force banks to hold specific assets to back currency, as was the case during the National Banking System in the USA (1863–1914). See Horwitz (1990a) for an exploration of the role played by the bond-collateral requirements of that system in turning shifts in the currency/deposit ratio into crisis-inducing demands for base money.
13 For example, some combination of free banking, a flat tax, and some constitutional limitation on spending might be quite powerful in reducing the size and scope of government.
14 This, of course, is the link between Milton Friedman's empirical-historical work, his theoretical framework, and his favored monetary regime. He has argued that velocity is stable historically, thus changes in the money supply will equiproportionately affect nominal income, which in turn leads to a monetary rule created in such a way to lead to a stable price level.
15 Selgin (1994) makes the same kind of point about the introduction of new fiat moneys in the reforming countries of Eastern Europe. Governments there cannot introduce new fiat money out of nowhere. Such currencies must be linked with existing moneys to have any value whatsoever.
16 My earlier, and brief, contribution to this debate can be found in Horwitz (1988b).
17 In Mises' (1980 [1912]) typology, these would be 'money certificates'.
18 The congruence of these positions is not surprising given Rothbard's (1956) work on welfare economics. There he argues, in essence, that all voluntary exchanges are

utility-enhancing and all coerced exchanges are utility-diminishing, thus it is not coincidental that fractional reserve banking is both coercive and harmful. Those two conditions are inseparable. See also Rothbard (1973: 40): 'Fortunately . . . the utilitarian and the moral, natural rights and general prosperity, go hand in hand.' The use of the word 'fortunately' is because Rothbard earlier in the same paragraph comments that even if a despotic society lead to greater productivity, a libertarian like himself would still support the free, but less productive, system. His view on these matters is helpful in understanding why he would support 100 percent reserves even if the economic consequences of doing so were disastrous. In his eyes, it is the moral issue (that fractional reserve banking is fraudulent) that trumps all other arguments. I would add that not all self-described libertarians would agree with his preference for the free but less productive society. Many libertarians like freedom because it leads to a better world (normally defined in terms of well-being or happiness), rather than because of any intrinsic value freedom might have. Such libertarians would presumably support various state interventions if they could be convinced that such interventions would truly make society better off. See J. Friedman (1994).
19 As Selgin and White (1996: 86ff.) point out, this is what Rothbard's own legal theory says should be the case.
20 Some anecdotal evidence for this point can be taken from twelve years of teaching money and banking courses to undergraduates. Every year, I ask them how much of the money they deposit at the bank remains inside the bank's vault. I give them an original range of 0 to 100 percent broken up into quintiles. Rarely does even one student out of 25 pick the 80 to 100 percent range. Most are down in the bottom two quintiles. This provides some slim evidence that, contrary to Hoppe's (1994) assertion, the public does in fact understand how banks work and that it does not seem to bother people very much.
21 It is also worth noting that once fractional reserve liabilities have been created, further issuances of them, as long as they are warranted to maintain monetary equilibrium, serve to prevent a deflationary drop in prices and output. Such a deflationary depression might dramatically reduce the value of the assets of many money holders and throw a number of them out of work. If Hoppe is really so concerned with such third-party effects, then he might do well to consider the third-party effects of a 100 percent reserve policy when the demand for money rises.
22 Incidentally, Hulsmann's example (1996: 26) of the man who sells his car for 50 ounces of gold that he 'intends to hold until his retirement age' would appear to contradict his earlier claim that 'money is demanded to be spent' (ibid.: 23). Is the man in question investing in gold for his lifetime or is he holding money? Apparently one cannot do both at the same time, if gold is money and money is demanded to be spent.
23 See (Yeager 1981), which was his contribution to a volume celebrating the centennial of Mises' birth.
24 Some confusion here might be avoided by substituting 'the supply of loanable funds' for saving and 'the demand for loanable funds' for investment. By doing so, it should be clearer that the *ex ante* quantity supplied and demanded need not be equal, contrary to the implication of Hulsmann's argument. All monetary equilibrium theory argues is that if money is over- or under-supplied, the market rate and natural rate will be out of line with each other and there will be an *ex ante* divergence between the demand and supply of loanable funds, i.e. investment and savings.
25 Selgin and White (1987) offer an explanation of how a sophisticated banking system might emerge out of a simple exchange economy with commodity money.
26 The creativity, complexity, and coordination story is told in more detail in High (1986) and Horwitz (1992b, Chapter 2).

Bibliography

Alchian, A. A. and Kessel, R. A. (1959) 'Redistribution of Wealth Through Inflation', reprinted in A. Alchian, *Economic Forces at Work*, Indianapolis: Liberty Press, 1977.

Arena, R. (1994) 'Hayek and Modern Business Cycle Theory', in M. Colonna and H. Hagemann (eds), *Money and Business Cycles: The Economics of F. A. Hayek*, vol. 1, Aldershot: Edward Elgar.

Arrow, K. and Hahn, F. H. (1971) *General Competitive Analysis*, San Francisco: Holden and Day.

Axelrod, R. (1984) *The Evolution of Cooperation*, New York: Basic Books.

Bailey, M. J. (1956) 'The Welfare Cost of Inflationary Finance', *Journal of Political Economy* 64: 93–110.

Ball, L., and Romer, D. (1990) 'Real Rigidities and the Nonneutrality of Money', reprinted in N. G. Mankiw and D. Romer (eds), *New Keynesian Economics*, Cambridge, MA: MIT Press.

Ball, L. Mankiw, N. G. and Romer, D. (1988) 'The New Keynesian Economics and the Output-Inflation Trade-off', reprinted in N. G. Mankiw and D. Romer (eds), *New Keynesian Economics*, Cambridge, MA: MIT Press.

Barro, R. (1995) 'Inflation and Economic Growth', *Bank of England Quarterly Bulletin* 35, May: 166–76.

Benabou, R. (1991) 'Comment on "The Welfare Cost of Moderate Inflations"', *Journal of Money, Credit, and Banking* 23: 504–13.

Blejer, M. I. (1983) 'On the Anatomy of Inflation', *Journal of Money, Credit, and Banking* 15: 469–82.

Blinder, A. (1991) 'Why are Prices Sticky? Preliminary Results from an Interview Study', *American Economic Review* 81, May: 89–96.

Block, W. (1988) 'Fractional Reserve Banking: An Interdisciplinary Perspective', in W. Block and L. H. Rockwell, Jr. (eds), *Man, Economy, and Liberty: Essays in Honor of Murray N. Rothbard*, Auburn, AL: Ludwig von Mises Institute.

Boettke, P. J. (1990) *The Political Economy of Soviet Socialism: The Formative Years, 1918–1928*, Boston: Kluwer Academic Press.

—— (1993) *Why Perestroika Failed*, New York: Routledge.

—— (1994) 'The Reform Trap in Economics and Politics in the Former Communist Economies', *Journal des Economistes et des Etudes Humaines* 5, 2/3, June/September: 267–93.

—— (1995) 'Why Are There No Austrian Socialists? Ideology, Science and the Austrian School', *Journal of the History of Economic Thought* 17: 35–56.

—— (1997) 'Where did Economics Go Wrong? Modern Economics as a Flight from

Reality', *Critical Review* 11, 1, Winter: 11–64.

—— (1998) 'Economic Calculation: *The* Austrian Contribution to Political Economy', *Advances in Austrian Economics* 5, Greenwich, CT: JAI Press.

Boettke, P., Horwitz, S. and Prychitko, D. L. (1986) 'Beyond Equilibrium Economics: Reflections on the Uniqueness of the Austrian Tradition', reprinted in P. Boettke and D. L. Prychitko (eds.) *The Market Process*, Aldershot: Edward Elgar.

Boettke, P. and Prychitko, D. L. (eds.) (1994) *The Market Process: Essays in Contemporary Austrian Economics*, Aldershot: Edward Elgar.

Boettke, P. and Vaughn, K. I. (1999) 'Knight and Hayek on Capital and the Problem of Socialism', Working Paper, Department of Economics, George Mason University.

Bohm-Bawerk, E. (1922) *Capital and Interest*, New York: Brentano's.

Brennan, H. G. and Buchanan, J. M. (1981) *Monopoly in Money and Inflation*, Hobart Paper #88, London: Institute for Economic Affairs.

Buchanan, J. M. (1962) 'Predictability: The Criterion of Monetary Constitutions', in L. B. Yeager (ed.), *In Search of a Monetary Constitution*, Cambridge, MA: Harvard University Press.

—— (1969) *Cost and Choice*, Chicago: The University of Chicago Press.

—— (1983) 'Monetary Research, Monetary Rules, and Monetary Regimes', *Cato Journal* 3, 1, Spring, 143–6.

Butos, W. N. (1993) 'The Recession and Austrian Business Cycle Theory: An Empirical Perspective', *Critical Review* 7, 2/3, Spring/Summer: 277–306.

Caldwell, B. (1988) 'Hayek's Transformation', *History of Political Economy* 20, 4, Winter, 513–41.

—— (1995a) 'Introduction', in B. Caldwell (ed.) *The Collected Works of F. A. Hayek, vol. 9: Contra Keynes and Cambridge*, Chicago: University of Chicago Press.

—— (ed.) (1995b) *The Collected Works of F. A. Hayek, vol. 9: Contra Keynes and Cambridge*, Chicago: University of Chicago Press.

—— (1997a) 'Introduction', in F. A. Hayek, *the Collected Works of F. A. Hayek, vol. 10: Socialism and War*, Chicago: University of Chicago Press.

—— (1997b) 'Hayek and Socialism', *Journal of Economic Literature* 35, December: 1856–90.

Caldwell, B. J. and Boehm, S. (eds.) (1992) *Austrian Economics: Tensions and New Directions*, Boston: Kluwer Academic.

Caplin, A. S. and Spulber, D. (1987) 'Menu Costs and the Neutrality of Money', *Quarterly Journal of Economics* 102, 4, November: 703–25.

Cassel, G. (1927–28) 'The Rate of Interest, the Bank Rate, and the Stabilization of Prices', reprinted in *AEA Readings in Monetary Theory*, New York: The Blakiston Company, 1951.

Cecchetti, S. (1986) 'The Frequency of Price Adjustment: A Study of Newstand Prices of Magazines', *Journal of Econometrics*, August: 255–74.

Clower, R. W (1984a [1963]) 'The Keynesian Counter-Revolution: A Theoretical Appraisal', in D. Walker (ed.), *Money and Markets: Essays by Robert W. Clower*, Cambridge: Cambridge University Press, 1984.

—— (1984b) 'Foundations of Monetary Theory', reprinted in D. Walker (ed.), *Money and Markets*, Cambridge: Cambridge University Press, 1984.

—— (1984c [1976]) 'A Reconsideration of the Theory of Inflation', in D. Walker (ed.), *Money and Markets: Essays by Robert W. Clower*, New York: Cambridge University Press.

Coase, R. H. (1937) 'The Nature of the Firm', *Economica* 4: November: 386–405.

Colander, D. (1996) 'Introduction', *Beyond Microfoundations: Post Walrasian Macroeconomics*, Cambridge: Cambridge University Press.

Cooley, T. F. and Hansen, G. D. (1989) 'The Inflation Tax in a Real Business Cycle Model', *American Economic Review* 79: 733–48.

—— (1991) 'The Welfare Costs of Moderate Inflations', *Journal of Money, Credit, and Banking* 23: 483–503.

Cordato, R. (1992) *Welfare Economics and Externalities in an Open Ended Universe: A Modern Austrian Perspective*. Boston: Kluwer.

Cottrell, A. (1996) 'Comment on Horwitz's Article', *Journal of the History of Economic Thought* 18, 2, Fall: 308–13.

Cowen, T. (1997) *Risk and Business Cycles: New and Old Austrian Perspectives*, New York: Routledge.

Cox, W. M. and Alm, R. (1999) *Myths of Rich and Poor: Why We're Better Off Than We Think*, New York: Basic Books.

Cukierman, A. (1982) 'Relative Price Variability, Inflation, and the Allocative Efficiency of the Price System', *Journal of Monetary Economics* 90: 131–62.

Cukierman, A. and Wachtel, P. (1982) 'Relative Price Variability and Nonuniform Inflationary Expectations', *Journal of Political Economy* 90: 146–57.

de Soto, J. H. (1995) 'A Critical Analysis of Central Banks and Fractional-Reserve Free Banking from the Austrian Perspective', *Review of Austrian Economics* 8, 2: 25–38.

Dolan, E. G. (ed.) (1976) *The Foundations of Modern Austrian Economics*, Kansas City: Sheed and Ward.

Dowd, K. (1989) *The State and the Monetary System*, Oxford: Philip Alan.

—— (1994) 'The Costs of Inflation and Disinflation', *Cato Journal* 14, 2, Fall: 305–31.

—— (1995) 'Deflating the Productivity Norm', *Journal of Macroeconomics* 17,4, Fall: 717–32.

—— (1996) *Competition and Finance: A New Interpretation of Financial and Monetary Economics*, London: Macmillan.

Egger, J. (1994) 'The Contributions of W. H. Hutt', *Review of Austrian Economics* 7, 1: 107–38.

Endres, A. M. (1995) 'Carl Menger's Theory of Price Formation Reconsidered', *History of Political Economy* 27, 2, Summer: 261–87.

Fischer, S. (1977) 'Long-Term Contracts, Rational Expectations, and the Optimal Money Supply Rule', *Journal of Political Economy* 85, 1: 191–205.

—— (1991) 'Growth, Macroeconomics, and Development', *NBER Macroeconomics Annual 1991*, vol. 6, O. J. Blanchard and S. Fischer (eds), Cambridge, MA: MIT Press/NBER.

Fisher I. (1934) 'The Debt-Deflation Theory of Great Depressions', *Econometrica* 2: 337–57

Foss, N. (1995) 'More on 'Hayek's Transformation', *History of Political Economy* 27,2, Summer: 345–64.

Friedman, J. (1994) 'Economic Consequentialism and Beyond', *Critical Review* 8, 4, Fall: 493–502.

Friedman, M. (1953) *Essays in Positive Economics*, Chicago: University of Chicago Press.

—— (1968) 'The Role of Monetary Policy', *American Economic Review* 58, 1, March, 1–17.

—— (1969) *The Optimum Quantity of Money and Other Essays*, Chicago: Aldine.

Friedman, M. and Schwartz, A. J. (1963) *A Monetary History of the United States, 1867–1960*, Princeton, NJ: Princeton University Press.

—— (1986) 'Has Government Any Role in Money?', *Journal of Monetary Economics* 17, 37–62.

Garretsen, H. (1994) 'The Relevance of Hayek for Mainstream Economics', in J. Birner and R. Van Zijp (eds), *Hayek, Coordination, and Evolution*, New York: Routledge.

Garrison, R. (1984) 'Time and Money: The Universals of Macroeconomic Theorizing', *Journal of Macroeconomics* 6, 2, Spring: 197–213.

—— (1985) 'Intertemporal Coordination and the Invisible Hand: An Austrian Perspective on the Keynesian Vision', *History of Political Economy* 17, 2: Summer: 309–19.

—— (1987) 'Full Employment and Intertemporal Coordination: A Rejoinder', *History of Political Economy* 19, 2, Summer, 335–41.

—— (1989) 'The Austrian Theory of the Business Cycle in the Light of Modern Macroeconomics', *Review of Austrian Economics* 3:3–29.

—— (1992) 'Keynesian Splenetics: From Social Philosophy to Macroeconomics', *Critical Review* 6, 4, Fall: 471–92.

—— (1993) 'The Roaring Twenties and the Bullish Eighties: The Role of Government in Boom and Bust', *Critical Review* 7, 2/3, Spring/Summer: 259–76.

—— (1996) 'A Subjectivist Theory of a Capital-using Economy', in G. P. O'Driscoll and M. J. Rizzo *The Economics of Time and Ignorance*, 2nd edn, New York: Routledge.

—— (2000) *Time and Money: The Macroeconomics of Capital Structure*, New York: Routledge.

Greenfield, R. (1994) *Monetary Policy and the Depressed Economy*, Belmont, CA: Wadsworth.

Greenfield, R. L. and Yeager, L. B. (1983) 'A Laissez-Faire Approach to Monetary Stability', *Journal of Money, Credit, and Banking* 15, 3, August, 302–15.

Hahn, F. (1970) 'Some Abstract Problems', *Econometrica*, 38.

Hartmann, R. (1991) 'Relative Price Variability and Inflation', *Journal of Money, Credit, and Banking* 23: 185–205.

Hayek, F. A. (1928) 'Intertemporal Price Equilibrium and Movements in the Value of Money', in *Money, Capital and Fluctuations: Early Essays*, R. McCloughry (ed.), Chicago: University of Chicago Press, 1984.

—— (1933) 'Price Expectations, Monetary Disturbances and Malinvestments', reprinted in *Profits, Interest, and Investment*, Clifton, NJ: Augustus M. Kelley, 1975.

—— (1937) 'Economics and Knowledge', in F. A. Hayek, *Individualism and Economic Order*, Chicago: University of Chicago Press.

—— (1940) 'The Competitive Solution' in F. A. Hayek, *Individualism and Economic Order*, Chicago: University of Chicago Press.

—— (1941) *The Pure Theory of Capital*, Chicago: University of Chicago Press.

—— (1942) 'The Ricardo Effect', reprinted in F. A. Hayek, *Individualism and Economic Order*, Chicago: University of Chicago Press, 1948.

—— (1945) 'The Use of Knowledge in Society', in F. A. Hayek, *Individualism and Economic Order*, Chicago: University of Chicago Press.

—— (1946) 'The Meaning of Competition', in F. A. Hayek, *Individualism and Economic Order*, Chicago: University of Chicago Press.

—— (1948) *Individualism and Economic Order*, Chicago: University of Chicago Press.

—— (1966 [1933]) *Monetary Theory and the Trade Cycle*, New York: Augustus M. Kelley.

—— (1967 [1935]) *Prices and Production*, second revised edition, New York: Augustus M. Kelley.

—— (1969) 'Three Elucidations of the Ricardo Effect', reprinted in *New Studies in Philosophy, Politics, Economics, and the History of Ideas*, Chicago: University of Chicago Press, 1978.

—— (1975 [1939]) *Profits, Interest, and Investment*, Clifton, NJ: Augustus M. Kelley.

—— (1977) *Law, Legislation, and Liberty, vol. 2*, Chicago: University of Chicago Press.

—— (1978a) 'Competition as a Discovery Procedure', in *New Studies in Politics, Philosophy, Economics and the History of Ideas*, Chicago: University of Chicago Press.

—— (1978b) 'The Pretence of Knowledge', in *New Studies in Politics, Philosophy, Economics and the History of Ideas*, Chicago: University of Chicago Press.

—— (1978c) *The Denationalisation of Money*, second edition, London: Institute for Economic Affairs.

—— (1988) *The Fatal Conceit: The Errors of Socialism*, W. W. Bartley III (ed.), Chicago: University of Chicago Press.

—— (1995a [1931]) 'The "Paradox" of Saving', reprinted in B. Caldwell (ed.) *The Collected Works of F. A. Hayek, vol. 9: Contra Keynes and Cambridge*. Chicago: University of Chicago Press.

—— (1995b [1931]) 'Reflections on the Pure Theory of Money of Mr. J. M. Keynes', reprinted in B. Caldwell (ed.) *The Collected Works of F. A. Hayek, vol. 9: Contra Keynes and Cambridge*. Chicago: University of Chicago Press.

—— (1995c [1932]) 'Money and Capital: A Reply', reprinted in B. Caldwell, *The Collected Works of F. A. Hayek, vol. 9: Contra Keynes and Cambridge*. Chicago: University of Chicago Press.

—— (n.d.) 'The Muddle of the Middle', unpublished ms, part of an early draft of *The Fatal Conceit*, Chicago: University of Chicago Press, 1988.

Hazlitt, H. (1959) *The Failure of the 'New Economics': An Analysis of the Keynesian Fallacies*, New Rochelle, NY: Arlington House.

Hercowitz, Z. (1981) 'Money and the Dispersion of Relative Prices', *Journal of Political Economy* 89, 2: 328–56.

Hicks, J. (1935) 'A Suggestion for Simplifying the Theory of Money', reprinted in *AEA Readings in Monetary Theory*, New York: The Blakiston Company, 1951.

—— 1939. *Value and Capital*, Oxford: Oxford University Press.

Higgs, R. (1987) *Crisis and Leviathan: Critical Episodes in the Growth of American Government*, New York: Oxford University Press.

High, J. (1986) 'Equilibration and Disequilibration in the Market Process', in I. Kirzner (ed.), *Subjectivism, Intelligibility, and Economic Understanding*, New York: New York University Press.

Hodgson, G. M. (1992) 'Carl Menger's Theory of the Origin of Money: Some Problems', *Review of Political Economy* 4, 4: 396–412.

Hoppe, H.-H. (1994) 'How is Fiat Money Possible? – or, the Devolution of Money and Credit', *Review of Austrian Economics* 7, 2: 49–74.

Horwitz, S. (1988a) 'Prices, the Price Level, and Macroeconomic Coordination: Hutt on Keynesian Economics', reprinted in P. Boettke and D. Prychitko (eds) (1994) *The Market Process*, Aldershot: Edward Elgar.

—— (1988b) 'Misreading the "Myth": Rothbard on the Theory and History of Free Banking', reprinted in P. Boettke and D. Prychitko (eds) (1994) *The Market Process*, Aldershot: Edward Elgar.

—— (1989) 'Keynes' Special Theory', *Critical Review* 3, 3/4, Summer/Fall, 411–34.

—— (1990a) 'Competitive Currencies, Legal Restrictions and the Origins of the Fed:

Some Evidence from the Panic of 1907', *Southern Economic Journal*, 56: 4, January, 639–49.

—— (1990b) 'A Subjectivist Approach to the Demand for Money', *Journal des Economistes et des Etudes Humaines* 1, 4, December: 459–71.

—— (1991) 'The Political Economy of Inflation: Public and Private Choices', *Durell Journal of Money and Banking* 3, 4, November, 26–37.

—— (1992a) 'Monetary Exchange as an Extra-Linguistic Social Communication Process', *Review of Social Economy* 50, 2, Summer, 193–214.

—— (1992b) *Monetary Evolution, Free Banking, and Economic Order*, Boulder, CO: Westview Press.

—— (1993) 'Spontaneity and Design in the Evolution of Institutions: The Similarities of Money and Law', *Journal des Economistes et des Etudes Humaines* 4, 4: 571–87.

—— (1996a) 'Money, Money Prices, and the Socialist Calculation Debate', *Advances in Austrian Economics* 3: 59–77.

—— (1996b) 'Capital Theory, Inflation, and Deflation: The Austrians and Monetary Disequilibrium Theory Compared' and 'Reply', *Journal of the History of Economic Thought* 18, 2, Fall: 287–308.

—— (1996c) 'Keynes on Capitalism: Reply to Hill', *Critical Review* 10, 3, Summer, 353–72.

—— (1997) 'Labor Market Coordination and Monetary Equilibrium: W. H. Hutt's Place in "Pre-Keynesian" Macro', *Journal of Labor Research* 18, 2, Spring, 205–260.

—— (1998a) 'Monetary Calculation and Mises's Critique of Planning', *History of Political Economy* 30, 3, Fall: 427–50.

—— (1998b) 'Keynes and Capitalism One More Time: A Further Reply to Hill', *Critical Review* 12, 1–2, Winter/Spring: 95–111.

Howitt, P. (1990) 'Zero Inflation as a Long-term Target for Monetary Policy', in R. G. Lipsey (ed.), *Zero Inflation: The Goal of Price Stability*, Toronto: C. D. Howe Institute.

Hulsmann, J. G. (1996) 'Free Banking and the Free Bankers', *Review of Austrian Economics* 9, 1:3–53.

Hutt, W. H. (1956) 'The Yield From Money Held', in M. Sennholz (ed.), *On Freedom and Free Enterprise: Essays in Honor of Ludwig von Mises*, Princeton, NJ: Van Nostrand.

—— (1975) *A Rehabilitation of Say's Law*, Athens, OH: Ohio University Press.

—— (1977 [1939]) *The Theory of Idle Resources*, Indianapolis: Liberty Press.

—— (1979) *The Keynesian Episode*, Indianapolis: Liberty Press.

Ikeda, S. (1995) 'The Use of Knowledge in Government and Market', *Advances in Austrian Economics*, 2A, Greenwich, CT: JAI Press: 211–40.

—— (1997) *The Dynamics of the Mixed Economy*, New York: Routledge.

Imrohoroglu, A. (1992) 'The Welfare Cost of Inflation under Imperfect Insurance', *Journal of Economic Dynamics and Control* 16: 79–91.

Jones, R. A. (1976) 'The Origin and Development of Media of Exchange', *Journal of Political Economy* 84, 4, August, 757–75.

Kashyap, A. (1990) 'Sticky Prices: New Evidence from Retail Catalogs', Board of Governors of the Federal Reserve System, Finance and Economics Discussion Series 112, March.

Kessel, R. A. and Alchian, A. A. (1962). 'Effects of Inflation', reprinted in A. Alchian, *Economic Forces at Work*, Indianapolis: Liberty Press, 1977.

Keynes, J. M. (1930) *A Treatise on Money, vols. 1 and 2*, London: Macmillan and Company.

—— (1936) *The General Theory of Employment, Interest, and Money*, New York: Harcourt, Brace and Company.

—— (1937) 'The General Theory of Employment', reprinted in *Collected Works*, London: Macmillan.

Kirzner, I. M. (1966) *An Essay on Capital*, New York: Augustus M. Kelley.

—— (1973) *Competition and Entrepreneurship*, Chicago: University of Chicago Press.

—— (1979) 'Hayek, Knowledge, and the Market Process', in *Perception, Opportunity, and Profit*, Chicago: University of Chicago Press.

—— (1985a) 'The Perils of Regulation: A Market-Process Approach', in *Discovery and the Capitalist Process*, Chicago: University of Chicago Press.

—— (1985b) 'Review of *The Economics of Time and Ignorance*', reprinted in P. Boettke and D. Prychitko (eds) (1994) *The Market Process*, Aldershot: Edward Elgar.

—— (1989) *Discovery, Capitalism, and Distributive Justice*, New York: Basil Blackwell.

—— (1992a) 'The Meaning of Market Process', in *The Meaning of Market Process*, New York: Routledge.

—— (1992b) 'Prices, the Communication of Knowledge, and the Discovery Process', in *The Meaning of Market Process*, New York: Routledge.

—— (1992c) 'Market Process Theory: In Defence of the Austrian Middle Ground', in *The Meaning of Market Process*, New York: Routledge.

—— (1994a) 'Introduction', in I. M. Kirzner (ed.), *Classics in Austrian Economics Vol. I*, London: Pickering and Chatto.

—— (1994b) 'Introduction', in I. M. Kirzner (ed.), *Classics in Austrian Economics Vol. II*, London: Pickering and Chatto.

—— (1994c) 'Introduction', in I. M. Kirzner (ed.), *Classics in Austrian Economics Vol. III*, London: Pickering and Chatto.

—— (1997) 'Entrepreneurial Discovery and the Competitive Market Process: An Austrian Approach', *Journal of Economic Literature* 35, March: 60–85.

Kohn, M. (1997) *Macroeconomics*. Cincinnati: South-Western Publishing.

Koppl, R. and Yeager, L. B. (1996) 'Big Players and Herding in Asset Markets: The Case of the Russian Ruble', *Explorations in Economic History* 33: 367–83.

Kreps, D. (1990) *A Course in Microeconomic Theory*, Princeton, NJ: Princeton University Press.

Lachmann, L. M. (1971) *The Legacy of Max Weber*, Berkeley, CA: The Glendessary Press.

—— (1977a [1947]) 'Complementarity and Substitution in the Theory of Capital', reprinted in W. Grinder (ed.) *Capital, Expectations and the Market Process*, Kansas City: Sheed Andrews and McMeel.

—— (1977b [1950]) 'The Science of Human Action', reprinted in W. Grinder (ed.), *Capital, Expectations, and the Market Process*, Kansas City: Sheed Andrews and McMeel.

—— (1977c [1959]) 'Professor Shackle on the Economic Significance of Time', reprinted in W. Grinder (ed.), *Capital, Expectations, and the Market Process*, Kansas City: Sheed Andrews and McMeel.

—— (1978) *Capital and Its Structure*, Kansas City: Sheed Andrews and McMeel.

—— (1985) 'Review of *The Economics of Time and Ignorance*', reprinted in P. Boettke and D. Prychitko (eds) (1994) *The Market Process*, Aldershot: Edward Elgar.

—— (1994) 'Austrian Economics: A Hermeneutic Approach', in D. Lavoie (ed.), *Expectations and the Meaning of Institutions*, New York: Routledge.

Laidler, D. (1982) *Monetarist Perspectives*, Cambridge, MA: Harvard University Press.

—— (1990) *Taking Money Seriously*, Hemel Hempstead: Philip Allan.

Laidler, D. and Rowe, N. (1980) 'Georg Simmel's *Philosophy of Money*: A Review Article for Economists', *Journal of Economic Literature* 18, March: 97–105

Lavoie, D. (1985a) *National Economic Planning: What is Left?*, Cambridge, MA: Ballinger Publishing Company.

—— (1985b) *Rivalry and Central Planning: The Socialist Calculation Debate Reconsidered*, Cambridge: Cambridge University Press.

—— (1986) 'The Market as a Procedure for the Discovery and Conveyance of Inarticulate Knowledge', *Comparative Economic Studies* 28, 1, Spring, 1–29.

Leijonhufvud, A. (1968) *On Keynesian Economics and the Economics of Keynes*, New York: Oxford University Press.

—— (1981a) 'Effective Demand Failures', in *Information and Coordination*, Oxford: Oxford University Press.

—— (1981b) 'The Wicksell Connection: Variations on a Theme', in *Information and Coordination*, Oxford: Oxford University Press.

—— (1981c) 'The Costs and Consequences of Inflation', in *Information and Coordination*, New York: Oxford University Press.

Lewin, P. (1994) 'Knowledge, Expectations, and Capital – The Economics of Ludwig M. Lachmann: Attempting a New Perspective', *Advances in Austrian Economics* 1: 233–56.

—— (1997a) 'Rothbard and Mises on Interest: An Exercise in Theoretical Purity', *Journal of the History of Economic Thought* 19, Spring: 141–59.

—— (1997b) 'Capital in Disequilibrium: A Re-examination of the Capital Theory of Ludwig M. Lachmann', *History of Political Economy* 29, 3, Fall: 523–48.

—— (1998) 'The Firm, Money, and Economic Calculation: Considering the Institutional Nexus of Market Production', *American Journal of Economics and Sociology* 57, 4, October: 499–512.

—— (1999) *Capital in Disequilibrium*, New York: Routledge.

Liebowitz, S. J. and Margolis, S. E. (1995) 'Path Dependence, Lock-In, and History', *Journal of Law, Economics, and Organizations* 11, 1, April: 205–26.

Lucas, R. E. (1981) 'Understanding Business Cycles', reprinted in *Studies in Business Cycle Theory*, Cambridge, MA: MIT Press.

Lutz, F. A. (1969) 'On Neutral Money', in E. Streissler (ed.) *Roads to Freedom: Essays in Honor of F. A. Hayek*, London: Routledge and Kegan Paul.

McCallum, B. (1987) 'The Case for Rules in the Conduct of Monetary Policy: A Concrete Example, Federal Reserve Bank of Richmond', *Economic Review* 73, September/October: 10–18.

Machovec, F. (1995) *Perfect Competition and the Transformation of Economics*, New York: Routledge.

Maclachlan, F. C. (1993) *Keynes' General Theory of Interest*, New York: Routledge.

Mankiw, N. G. (1990) 'A Quick Refresher Course in Macroeconomics', *Journal of Economic Literature* 28, 4, December: 1645–60.

Mankiw, N. G. and Romer, D. (1993a) 'Introduction', in N. G. Mankiw and D. Romer (eds), *New Keynesian Economics Vol. 1: Imperfect Competition and Sticky Prices*, Cambridge, MA: MIT Press.

—— (eds) (1993b) *New Keynesian Economics Volume 1: Imperfect Competition and Sticky Prices*, Cambridge, MA: MIT Press.

Mayer, H. (1994 [1932]) 'The Cognitive Value of Functional Theories of Price', reprinted in *Classics in Austrian Economics Vol. II*, London: Pickering and Chatto.

Meltzer, A. H. (1988) *Keynes's Monetary Theory: A Different Interpretation*, Cambridge: Cambridge University Press.

Menger, C. (1892) 'On the Origin of Money', *Economic Journal*, 2, 239–55.

—— (1981 [1871]) *Principles of Economics*, New York: New York University Press.

—— (1985 [1883]) *Investigations into the Method of the Social Sciences with Special Reference to Economics*, New York: New York University Press.

Mises, L. von. (1920) 'Economic Calculation in the Socialist Commonwealth', in F. A. Hayek (ed.), *Collectivist Economic Planning*, Clifton, NJ: Augustus M. Kelley, 1935.

—— (1966 [1949]) *Human Action: A Treatise on Economics*, Chicago: Henry Regnery.

—— (1976 [1933]) *Epistemological Problems of Economics*, New York: New York University Press.

—— (1980 [1912]) *The Theory of Money and Credit*, Indianapolis: Liberty Press.

—— (1981 [1922]) *Socialism: An Economic and Sociological Analysis*, Indianapolis: Liberty Press.

—— (1985 [1957]) *Theory and History*, Auburn, AL: The Ludwig von Mises Institute.

Mises, L. von, *et al.* 1983. *The Austrian Theory of the Trade Cycle and Other Essays*, Auburn, AL: The Ludwig von Mises Institute.

Moss, L. S. and Vaughn, K. I. (1986) 'Hayek's Ricardo Effect: A Second Look', *History of Political Economy* 18, 4, Winter: 545–65.

Mussa, M. (1977) 'The Welfare Cost of Inflation and the Role of Money as a Unit of Account', *Journal of Money, Credit, and Banking* 9, May: 276–86.

Myrdal, G.(1965 [1939]) *Monetary Equilibrium*, New York: Augustus M. Kelley.

O'Driscoll, G. P. (1981) 'Monopoly in Theory and Practice', in I. M. Kirzner (ed.) *Method, Process, and Austrian Economics*, Lexington, MA: Lexington Books.

—— (1986) 'Money: Menger's Evolutionary Theory', *History of Political Economy* 18, 4, Winter, 601–16.

O'Driscoll, G. P. and Rizzo, M. J. (1996) *The Economics of Time and Ignorance*, 2nd edn, New York: Routledge.

Oh, S. (1989) 'A Theory of a Generally Acceptable Medium of Exchange and Barter', *Journal of Monetary Economics* 23, 101–19.

Okun, A. (1975) 'Inflation: Its Mechanics and Welfare Costs', *Brookings Papers on Economic Activity* 2: 485–98.

Parkin, M. (1986) 'The Output-Inflation Trade-off When Prices Are Costly to Change', *Journal of Political Economy* 94, 1: 200–24.

Parks, R. W. (1978) 'Inflation and Relative Price Variability', *Journal of Political Economy* 86, 1: 79–95.

Paroush, J. (1986) 'Inflation, Search Costs, and Price Dispersion', *Journal of Macroeconomics* 8: 329–36.

Rand, A. (1957) *Atlas Shrugged*, New York: Random House.

Remak, J. (ed.) (1969) *The Nazi Years: A Documentary History*, New York: Simon and Schuster.

Rizzo, M. J. (1992) 'Afterword: Austrian Economics for the Twenty-First Century', in B. J. Caldwell and S. Boehm (eds), *Austrian Economics: Tensions and New Directions*, Boston: Kluwer Academic.

Robbins, L. (1932) *The Nature and Significance of Economic Science*, London: Macmillan.

Robertson, D. H. (1928) 'Theories of Banking Policy', reprinted in *Essays in Monetary Theory*, London: Staples Press, 1940.

—— (1940) 'Mr. Keynes and the Rate of Interest', in *Essays in Monetary Theory*, London: Staples Press, 1940.

—— (1957) *Money*, Chicago: University of Chicago Press.

Romer, D. (1993) 'The New Keynesian Synthesis', *Journal of Economic Perspectives*, Winter: 5–22.

Rothbard, M. N. (1956) 'Toward a Reconstruction of Utility and Welfare Economics', in M. Sennholz (ed.), *On Freedom and Free Enterprise*, Los Angeles: Van Nostrand and Co., 1956.

—— (1962) *Man, Economy, and State*, Los Angeles: Nash Publishing.

—— (1963) *America's Great Depression*, New York: Richardson and Snyder.

—— (1973) *For a New Liberty*, New York: Collier.

—— (1994) *The Case Against the Fed*, Auburn, AL: The Ludwig von Mises Institute.

—— (1995) 'The Present State of Austrian Economics', *Journal des Economistes et des Etudes Humaines* 6, 1, March: 43–89.

Ruhl, C. (1994) 'The Transformation of Business Cycle Theory: Hayek, Lucas and a Change in the Notion of Equilibrium', in M. Colonna and H. Hagemann (eds), *Money and Business Cycles: The Economics of F. A. Hayek, vol. 1*, Aldershot: Edward Elgar.

Salerno, J. (1990a) 'Postscript: Why a Socialist Economy is "Impossible"', in *Economic Calculation in the Socialist Commonwealth*, Auburn, AL: The Ludwig von Mises Institute.

—— (1990b) 'Ludwig von Mises as Social Rationalist', *The Review of Austrian Economics* 4: 26–54.

—— (1991) 'Commentary: The Concept of Coordination in Austrian Macroeconomics', in Richard M. Ebeling (ed.), *Austrian Economics: Perspectives on the Past and Prospects for the Future*, Hillsdale, MI: Hillsdale College Press.

—— (1993) 'Mises and Hayek Dehomogenized', *The Review of Austrian Economics* 6, 2: 113–46.

—— (1994) 'Reply to Leland Yeager on "Mises and Hayek on Calculation and Knowledge"', *The Review of Austrian Economics* 7, 2: 111–25.

—— (1995) 'Ludwig von Mises on Inflationary Expectations', *Advances in Austrian Economics* 2A, Greenwich, CT: JAI Press.

Say, J. B. (1967 [1821]) 'A Catechism of Political Economy', reprinted in *Letters to Mr. Malthus and a Catechism of Political Economy*, New York: Augustus M. Kelley.

—— (1971 [1880]). *A Treatise on Political Economy*, New York: Augustus M. Kelley.

Sechrest, L. J. (1993) *Free Banking: Theory, History, and a Laissez-faire Model*, Westport, CT: Quorum.

—— (1995) 'Rothbard on Money and Banking: 100% Gold Reserves', paper presented at the annual meetings of the Southern Economic Association, New Orleans, LA.

Selgin, G. A. (1987) 'The Yield on Money Held Revisited: Lessons for Today', reprinted in P. Boettke and D. Prychitko (eds) (1994) *The Market Process*, Aldershot: Edward Elgar.

—— (1988a) *The Theory of Free Banking: Money Supply Under Competitive Note Issue*, Totowa, NJ: Rowman and Littlefield.

—— (1988b) 'Accommodating Changes in the Relative Demand for Currency: Free Banking vs. Central Banking', *Cato Journal*, 7 (3), Winter.

—— (1990) 'Monetary Equilibrium and the Productivity Norm of Price-Level Policy', *Cato Journal* 10, 1, Spring/Summer: 265–87.

—— (1994) 'On Ensuring the Acceptability of a New Fiat Money', *Journal of Money, Credit, and Banking* 26, 4, November: 808–26.

—— (1995a) 'The "Productivity Norm" versus Zero Inflation in the History of Economic Thought', *History of Political Economy* 27, 4, Winter: 705–35.

—— (1995b) 'The Case for a "Productivity Norm": Comment on Dowd', *Journal of Macroeconomics* 17, 4, Fall: 733–40.

—— (1997) *Less than Zero: The Case for a Falling Price Level in a Growing Economy*, Hobart Paper 132, London: Institute of Economic Affairs.

—— (1999) 'Hayek versus Keynes on How the Price Level Ought to Behave', *History of Political Economy* 31, 4, Winter: 699–721.

Selgin, G. A. and White, L. H. (1987) 'The Evolution of a Free Banking System', *Economic Inquiry* 25, July.

—— (1994) 'How Would the Invisible Hand Handle Money?', *Journal of Economic Literature* 32: 1718–49.

—— (1996) 'In Defense of Fiduciary Media – or, We are *Not* Devo(lutionists), We are Misesians!', *Review of Austrian Economics* 9: 83–107.

Shah, P. (1997) 'The Theory of Business Fluctuations: New Keynesians, Old Monetarists, and Austrians', *Advances in Austrian Economics* 4, Greenwich, CT: JAI Press: 33–62.

Skousen, M. (1990) *The Structure of Production*, New York: New York University Press.

Snippe, J. (1987) 'Intertemporal Coordination and the Economics of Keynes: Comment on Garrison', *History of Political Economy* 19, 2, Summer: 329–34.

Snowdon, B., Vane, H. and Wynarczyk, P. (eds) (1994) *A Modern Guide to Macroeconomics*, Aldershot: Edward Elgar.

Steele, D. R. (1992) *From Marx to Mises: Post-Capitalist Society and the Challenge of Economic Calculation*, LaSalle, IL: Open Court.

Thomsen, E. (1992) *Prices and Knowledge: A Market-Process Perspective*, New York: Routledge.

Tullock, G. (1967) 'The Welfare Costs of Tariffs, Monopolies, and Theft', reprinted in J. Buchanan, R. Tollison, and G. Tullock (eds), *Toward a Theory of the Rent-Seeking Society*, College Station, TX: Texas A&M University Press, 1980.

Van Zijp, R. and Visser, H. (1994) 'Mathematical Formalization and the Domain of Economics: The Case of Hayek and New Classical Economics', in J. Birner and R. Van Zijp (eds), *Hayek, Coordination, and Evolution*, New York: Routledge.

Vaughn, K. (1990) 'The Mengerian Roots of the Austrian Revival', in B. Caldwell (ed.), *Carl Menger and His Legacy in Economics*, annual supplement to *History of Political Economy* 22, Durham, NC: Duke University Press.

—— (1994) *Austrian Economics in America*, New York: Cambridge University Press.

Vedder, R. K. and Gallaway, L. E. (1993) *Out of Work: Unemployment and Government in Twentieth-Century America*, New York: Holmes and Meier.

Vining, D. R. and Elwertowski, T. C. (1976) 'The Relationship between Relative Prices and the General Price Level', *American Economic Review* 66, 4, September: 699–708.

Wagner, R. E. (1977) 'Economic Manipulation for Political Profit: Macroeconomic Consequences and Constitutional Implications', *Kyklos* 30: 395–410.

—— (1980) 'Boom and Bust: The Political Economy of Economic Disorder', *Journal of Libertarian Studies* 4, 1, Winter: 1–37.

—— (1999) 'Austrian Cycle Theory: Saving the Wheat while Discarding the Chaff', *Review of Austrian Economics* 12, 1: 65–80.

Wallace, N. (1983) 'A Legal Restrictions Theory of the Demand for "Money" and the Role of Monetary Policy', *Quarterly Review*, Federal Reserve Bank of Minneapolis, Winter.

White, L. H. (1984) 'Competitive Payments Systems and the Unit of Account', reprinted in *Competition and Currency: Essays on Free Banking and Money*, New York: NYU Press, 1989.

—— (1995) 'Is There an Economics of Interpersonal Comparisons?', *Advances in Austrian Economics* 2A, Greenwich, CT: JAI Press.

—— (1996) *Free Banking in Britain*, 2nd edn, New York: Routledge.

—— (1999a) 'Why Didn't Hayek Favor Laissez-Faire in Banking?', *History of Political Economy* 31, 4: Winter: 753–69.

—— (1999b) 'Hayek's Monetary Theory and Policy: A Critical Reconstruction', *Journal of Money, Credit, and Banking* 31, 1, February: 109–20.

Wicksell, K. (1935) *Lectures in Political Economy, v. 2: Money*, London: Routledge and Kegan Paul.

—— (1965 [1898]) *Interest and Prices*, New York: Augustus M. Kelley.

Woolsey, W. W. (1992) 'A Model of the BFH Payments System', *Southern Economic Journal*, 59 (2), October.

Yeager, L. B. (1968) 'Essential Properties of the Medium of Exchange', *Kyklos*, January/March.

—— (1973) 'The Keynesian Diversion', *Western Economic Journal* 16, 150-63.

—— (1981) 'Individual and Overall Viewpoints in Monetary Theory', in I. M. Kirzner (ed.), *Method, Process, and Austrian Economics*, Lexington, MA: Lexington Books.

—— (1986) 'The Significance of Monetary Disequilibrium', *Cato Journal* 6, 2, Fall, 369–99.

—— (1997) *The Fluttering Veil: Essays in Monetary Disequilibrium*, G. Selgin (ed.), Indianapolis: Liberty Press.

Index

CPSIA information can be obtained at www.ICGtesting.com
Printed in the USA
LVOW07s1337240814

400499LV00003B/38/P

9 780415 569576